A HUNDRED YEARS
OF PSYCHOLOGY

THE 'HUNDRED YEARS' SERIES

A Hundred Years
of Psychology

1833-1933

by J. C. FLUGEL

Late Assistant Professor of Psychology
University College, London

Part V: 1933–1963
revised by
DONALD J. WEST
M.A., M.D., D.P.M.

GERALD DUCKWORTH & Co. LTD.
3 HENRIETTA STREET, LONDON, W.C.2

First Edition Published in 1933
Reprinted 1934, 1935, 1941, 1945 and 1948
Second Edition 1951
Reprinted 1953, 1959
Third Edition 1964

PRINTED IN GREAT BRITAIN BY
WESTERN PRINTING SERVICES, LTD., BRISTOL

CONTENTS

5

6 CONTENTS

PAGE

PREFACE

SUCH a book as this is almost inevitably bad; in the sense at least that what the reader will find will not correspond to what he hopes for or expects. Things in which he is little interested will be treated at apparently unnecessary length and with unreasonable emphasis; while other aspects of the subject, on which he would willingly linger, are summarily dismissed or omitted altogether. No doubt this happens to some extent in any historical treatment of a branch of knowledge. In the case of psychology itself, one of the most balanced and comprehensive of the several excellent histories that have been written in recent years speaks of its own "strange silences and vast lacunæ." I fear that in the present volume, which is deliberately constructed on more impressionistic and less systematic lines, such faults will appear even more glaring and outrageous.

Nevertheless something can often be learnt even from a bad book—if only through the arousal of a critical attitude which will help the reader to seek out the author's omissions, discount his prejudices and correct the shortness of his vision; and I hope that the following pages will at least have this much salutary influence. I believe moreover that any student of a science (even the beginner) will do well to supplement his textbook by a treatment of his subject from the developmental point of view; since the value to be obtained from the study of a science lies, not merely in an understanding of the relevant facts and principles, but also in a contemplation of the struggle of the human mind with the peculiar problems of the science; and in a realization of how our present knowledge has resulted from the overcoming of obstacles, the devising of methods, the flashes of insight, the correction of errors, the clashes of opinion, and above all from the patient, plodding routine of daily observation and experiment carried out by a multitude of workers. If this present inadequate and somewhat sketchy story of how psychology has become an independent discipline—albeit still a humble one—will lead the reader to consult in turn one of the ampler and more detailed histories, I shall be more than satisfied.

7

It remains for me only to acknowledge my indebtedness to the writers of these histories. I am grateful to them all; and more especially to Professor Gardner Murphy and Professor Edwin Boring, who—in their *Historical Introduction to Modern Psychology* and *History of Experimental Psychology* respectively—have produced scholarly, accurate, and eminently readable books, of which our young science may very well be proud.

I am much indebted also to Mrs. E. C. Fowler for the preparation of the indices.

PREFACE TO THE THIRD EDITION

IN his first revision of this book the late Professor Flugel wisely allowed his original text to remain intact as a statement of the development and contemporary position of psychology as it appeared in 1933. That statement, admirable in itself, has now acquired an additional historical interest, and any attempt to modify it would be an unnecessary impertinence. On the other hand, the supplementary review of developments from 1933 to 1947, which was added in the second edition, has been substantially rewritten so as to give some account of more recent trends.

D. J. WEST

London, 1963

I

PSYCHOLOGY IN 1833

I. HERBART AND THE CONCEPTION OF PSYCHOLOGY AS SCIENCE

To compare the psychology of today with that of a hundred years ago is like comparing a lusty one-year infant to an embryo. The infant has some solid achievements to its credit. It engages in a multitude of vigorous, though often ill-directed, activities; it has attained some preliminary degree of understanding and co-ordination and shows signs of embarking upon the great and momentous undertakings of speech and locomotion. Considered in the light of what has already happened to its elder brothers and sisters, it is full of promise; or at least of hope, for in its case suggestions of a Messianic mission are not wanting—and, although our infant is no prodigy, there is as yet nothing to show that these suggestions are entirely false. At the very least it is impossible to ignore the existence of the child; its behaviour, crude and unsophisticated as it is, is sufficiently striking constantly to force itself on our attention.

With the embryo, however, things were very different. It was quite an easy matter to overlook it altogether. Looking back a hundred years, it is now possible to discern the first beginnings of this organ and of that, corresponding to the various branches and methods of psychology as we know it today. But at the time, even if the beholder had been acute enough to perceive it as an independent entity within the matrix of existing scientific knowledge, he would have found it wellnigh impossible to foretell the lines of its development. For the most part it was neither named nor noticed, but grew in silence and obscurity. Even its birth, which we can fix at about the middle of the last century, failed to attract much attention, and it is only in the last thirty years or so that its presence and its possibilities (beneficent or otherwise) have

9

been at all widely recognized by the educated portion of humanity.

A student of the present day has but little difficulty in embarking on a course of psychology. He must, it is true, be careful to avoid a limited number of venerable institutions (I only know of one from personal experience, but others perhaps exist) where philosophers will prove to him that such a science is impossible and therefore non-existent. Elsewhere he will find that he can take it as an ordinary subject of a University curriculum—either for an "Honours" or a "Pass" degree; or, at the very least, it will appear in some of its aspects as an integral portion of the prescribed course in Philosophy, Medicine or Education. He may even be able to take a Diploma purporting to show that he is qualified in the "practical" aspects of the subject. Textbooks are abundant, though baffling in their variety of presentation, and specialist journals are so numerous that even the best-equipped libraries fail to extend their hospitality to all.

A century ago none of this existed. True, the word "psychology" was to be met with, having been employed in something approaching its present sense by Wolff, whose *Rational Psychology* had appeared a hundred years earlier still, in 1734. A good deal of the subject-matter of our present-day psychology was, of course, also matter for discussion then, as it had been since Plato and Aristotle (and, no doubt, before). But there was no question of a separate branch of study with teachers, University departments and journals of its own. A student interested in the problem of the human mind or curious concerning the behaviour of his fellow-men had two main avenues of approach—Philosophy and Medicine. The former was the more obvious and the better trodden. From the beginning of philosophic thought it had been clear that our knowledge of the Universe was dependent upon some understanding of the mind as the vehicle of knowledge. The Schoolmen had debated the psychological problems of knowing with endless patience and much subtlety and skill. And philosophy itself had become in a sense psychological through the labours of that sturdy trio of English empiricists, Locke, Berkeley and Hume. From the field of philosophy had come the two main lines of explanation in psychology—in terms of "association" and of "faculties" respectively; lines of explanation which have retained their importance throughout our "hundred years."

Philosophy was, then, the straight and natural pathway to psychology. But medicine had from time to time made contributions in the same direction. Galen was responsible for the classic doctrine of the four temperaments, which, through the ages, had done duty for a better understanding of the emotional nature of man. Locke himself had been a physician, and, at the opening of our period, the realization of the intimate dependence of mind upon the brain and nervous system, together with the rapid progress of the science of physiology, might have made it seem that the field of medicine was now becoming a more favourable line of approach than ever before.

There were also two other ways in which our hypothetical student might perhaps have entered upon the study of mind. One was education. Rousseau, and following him Pestalozzi and Froebel, had endeavoured with some success to supersede the idea of education as a mechanical implanting of information by the very different conception of eliciting the *natural* responses of the child. And this inevitably led to a more empirical and psychological attitude towards the mind. A little later, Herbart definitely combined psychology and education, and endeavoured to bring pedagogical practice into clear harmony with his own system of psychological principles; so that education seemed in a promising way to become the first field of applied psychology.

Still another, though perhaps an even remoter, method of approach, was through the physical sciences, and especially through that branch where the three empires of physics, physiology and psychology most closely meet—the study of sensation. Such an approach was most likely to be made through the sense of vision. In 1807 Sir Thomas Young challenged Newton's corpuscular theory of light, and went on to formulate his own three-colour theory of vision, which was later to be supported by Helmholtz. Three years later came Goethe's *Farbenlehre*. Knowledge of the physiological mechanisms involved in seeing continued to increase rapidly during the first decades of the century, and in 1833—the year in which our period begins—the complications brought about by the fact that we possess a double visual organ were brought into prominence by Wheatstone's invention of the stereoscope. The physical study of optics was, therefore, beginning to offer a bridge whereon to cross to psychology for those who were willing to essay the passage.

Let us imagine that our student, by one or other of the channels indicated, has reached the domain of psychology itself. He is obviously an original and enterprising, perhaps somewhat daring, individual, not afraid of doing his own thinking. Naturally, however, he will want to survey the territory that he has entered. Having realized that the study of the mind is one which may be worth pursuing for its own sake, he will want to see how this study stands at the moment when he is himself embarking on it. Let us examine the situation as it presents itself to him, with particular reference to the events of the immediately preceding years.

It is not our task here to review the growth and changes of psychological doctrine from Aristotle onwards. Throughout its history this doctrine had been intimately connected with each of the main inquiries of philosophy—logical, metaphysical, epistemological and even ethical—and there was scarcely a single philosopher of note who had not made his contribution to psychology. Suffice it to say that, as a result of all these labours, our student would find himself confronted with a number of fairly definite (though to some extent interconnected) problems. There was the problem of the relation of mind and body, with the alternative solutions of interactionism and parallelism (traceable in their modern form to Descartes and Leibnitz respectively), the problem of explanation in terms of faculties or of association of ideas, the further closely related problem of the part played by innate tendencies and experience respectively, the problems of Activity and Structure, of Free-will and Determinism. Of these problems and their attempted solutions, that concerning "faculties" and "associations" as explanatory principles was the one that was most directly in the psychological tradition, and, of these two principles themselves, "association" was perhaps the most favoured by progressive thinkers at the moment.

A brilliant line of empiricists had taken up the principles of association as originally enunciated by Aristotle, and had dealt with them in such a way as to make it seem that they afforded the essential and only key to an understanding of the development of mind. The gradually increasing knowledge of the nervous system and of its connection with mental phenomena seemed to fit in well with this conception, according to which the mind was an elaborate piece of machinery, which responded in a complicated but causally determined way to the influence of the environment. Such a view would be most likely to appeal to our student, who would doubtless be attracted by the prospect thereby afforded of applying to the mind some of the methods and concepts that were proving so successful in physical science.

However, there were not wanting those who had dealt severely with the over-simplifications to which associationism often led. And of these there was one outstanding figure, that of Immanuel Kant, most famous of all modern philosophers, who, although he had died some thirty years before our period begins, still cast his gigantic shadow over the whole of philosophy and its attendant disciplines. Although Kant's influence on psychology was much smaller than that on most other branches of philosophical study, he has nevertheless exercised an immense effect on the whole outlook and treatment of mental science—an effect that was strong a hundred years ago and is still perceptible today. It was Kant's adoption of the major faculties of knowing, feeling, willing (Cognition, Affection and Conation, as they are commonly called today in scientific jargon), that has perpetuated this division through the textbooks and curricula of the whole century. It was Kant who, by his insistence on the unity of perception and the notion of an active self which organizes experience with the help of the categories of space and time, was the forerunner of the modern schools of Function and Gestalt. Kant's "transcendental unity of apperception" is a complex and somewhat awe-inspiring doctrine to the novice in philosophy, but it led to a whole series of elaborate treatments of the psychological process of apperception, from Herbart to Stout. Kant's equation of science with mesaurement, and his appeal to experience as the only foundation for the formulation of psychological laws, prepared the way both for the separation of philosophy and psychology, and the quantitative developments of the latter that have become so prominent a feature of the last hundred years.

In one respect, however, Kant's influence was probably negative rather than positive. It is generally agreed that he failed to bring to the problems of will and of morality the same powers of ruthless penetration and analysis that he had brought to the problems of perception and understanding. His refusal to consider the will in the light of the category of cause, and his ethical doctrine of the Categorical Imperative, were not calculated to encourage a psychological approach to the phenomena of desire, will, conscience, or moral obligation. His attitude in this sphere was one of "Hands off!", and tended almost certainly to strengthen the already existing intellectualist prejudice, rather than to direct endeavour to the relatively unexplored fields of feeling and striving. The apparent greater difficulty of investigation in these latter fields provides a convenient excuse for the backwardness of psychological knowledge with regard to them, but it seems not improbable that, had Kant been able to treat the problems of "practical reason" in the same thoroughgoing spirit in which he had dealt with those of "pure reason," the endeavours of psychologists in this direction might have been more proportionate to the obstacles to be overcome, and we should not have had to wait until the twentieth century for even the beginning of an adequate effort in this sphere.

Kant's *Critique of Pure Reason* appeared in 1781, his *Critique of Practical Reason* in 1788. In neither of these works was there more than the barest indication of the possibilities of psychology as a separate science independent of philosophy. In 1816, however, there appeared a work that struck a new note, both in title and in treatment—Herbart's *Text Book of Psychology*; to be followed in 1824–25 by his *Psychology as Science*. It is true that in 1812 Maine de Biran had published his *Essai sur les Fondements de la Psychologie*, but this book had kept pretty strictly to the subject-matter indicated by its title, being an acute and critical exposition of the fundamental presuppositions of psychology rather than a treatment of psychology itself. Herbart's two works were in a very real sense the first textbooks of psychology treated as a branch of study to be pursued for its own sake. At the same time the full title of the second book—*Psychologie als Wissenschaft, neu gegründet auf Erfahrung, Metaphysick und Mathematik* (it has never been translated) shows that the emancipation of psychology was not achieved at one stroke. Of the three bases of psychology thus postulated by Herbart, the first ("experience") was destined to be retained, and the two others not—at least in Herbart's sense. The very essence of the new psychology that was shortly to arise, lay in separation from metaphysics and adoption of the point of view common to the physical sciences. Mathematics, it is true, here played a by no means negligible part, but with this significant difference—that it has been employed almost throughout in connection with *experiment*—and experiment was quite definitely not part of the programme of psychology as conceived by Herbart. For him it was, rather, excluded by the very nature of the subject-matter; he failed to see how one *could* experiment on the mind. As Boring (in his *History of Experimental Psychology*) well suggests, Herbart was in much the same position as "the modern layman, who is puzzled as to what it can be that the experimental psychologist does." Divorced from experiment and even from systematic observation (for Herbart never brought together his two bases of experience and mathematics) Herbart's own imposing mathematical treatment remained sterile, and never played any appreciable rôle in the further development of psychology. To quote Boring again, Herbart "exhibited the not uncommon case in science, in which inadequate data are treated with elaborate mathematics, the precision of which creates the illusion that the original data are as exact as the method of treatment"—an illusion which did not, however, impose itself on his successors. We may therefore consider ourselves absolved in a chronicle of this kind from entering further into this aspect of his doctrine. Suffice it to say that his mathematics were called in to give quantitative expression to his doctrine of the interaction of ideas. Herbart was in one sense an associationist; his mental units were ideas, not faculties. But in at least two ways he differed very significantly from the majority of associationists, especially those of the dominant English school; he had no interest in, or use for, physiology; so that all explanations in neurological terms were excluded from his system; and his ideas (*Vorstellungen*), which we must interpret in Locke's sense as including both percepts and the non-perceptual "ideas" of modern usage), far from being linked together in a passive and mechanical way corresponding to certain "laws of association," were dynamic entities, struggling with one another for a place in consciousness and interacting according to definite quantitative principles.

This dynamic conception gave rise to a third important difference from classic associationism. Relations between ideas, as hitherto conceived by this latter school, had always been in the nature of *positive* connections linking up one idea to another. Herbart distinguished two kinds of interaction between ideas. On the one hand, ideas which are capable of so doing may combine into harmonious wholes, and the resulting composite ideas are then closely similar to those described by previous associationists from Locke onwards. When such ideas belong to the same "continuities" (modalities or sense departments), they produce a *fusion*, as red and blue combine to produce violet; when they belong to different "continuities," as would be the case, for instance, with a sound and a colour, they produce a unity of the kind called by Herbart *complication*; and through the influence of Wundt these terms have persisted to the present day. On the other hand, ideas which were in opposition could never combine but could only tend to inhibit one another. When they were of equal strength, the mutual inhibition was complete; when two or more mutually inhibiting ideas were of unequal strength, they contributed their resultant to consciousness, the content of which at any given moment could therefore be expressed in terms of the interplay of the competing ideas (it was here that the mathematics came in). Herbart was thus concerned with a quantitative treatment of the age-long problem of the "span of consciousness" —the remarkable fact that of all the impressions, thoughts or memories of which we are potentially aware, only a few paltry items can be clearly present in our conscious mind at any single time.

It is obvious that, since consciousness was describable in terms of ideas not themselves present in consciousness, or at any rate not wholly so, Herbart's psychology extended beyond the realm of the conscious to that of the unconscious. In this, as in many other respects, Herbart has much in common with Leibnitz, whose *petites perceptions* constituted the first clear statement of anything approaching the modern doctrines of the Unconscious. In fact Herbart distinguished three degrees of consciousness: the focal ideas which are apperceived or clearly apprehended ("attended to," as we should say in common modern parlance); the marginal ideas, which are dimly and unclearly present: and in the third place those ideas which have been forced out of consciousness altogether. For an idea that has suffered inhibition (or repression, *Druck*) does not thereby cease to exist. It merely joins the vast company of ideas that have gone from consciousness, but may return—either through a weakening of opposite ideas or by co-operation with an ally, the combined forces being able to overcome resistances that were formerly too strong.

Students of modern psychology will inevitably be struck by the resemblance to certain essential features of psycho-analytic doctrine. The notion of psychic quantities repressed from consciousness and struggling to re-enter it, is one with which Freud and his school has made us very familiar. It is perhaps worth while to try to state concisely the principal differences between the formulations of these two investigators, separated as they are by a period of wellnigh a century. These differences seem in the last resort to be reducible to two. In the first place, Herbart's theories bear a more *a priori* stamp than do those of Freud. Herbart stands at the very threshold of the scientific era of psychology. The conception of psychology as a science was beginning to form in Herbart's own mind and in those of a few others. But the methods of the new science had still to be worked out: the data actually available had not come from systematic observation or experiment but, as always hitherto, had been based merely on the psychologist's own more or less casual contemplation of the phenomena of human life and moulded by his theorizing thereon. No matter how insightful and ingenious the theoretical interpretation, the material itself was (as we now realize) necessarily limited, unorderly and biased. Freud's theories, however daring they might appear, had the immense advantage of being based on years of laborious and systematic investigation of individual cases. It is for this reason principally that one point in which Herbart's theory is inadequate is somewhat clearer in the hands of Freud. This concerns the reason for the opposition between ideas. With Herbart the opposition seems on the whole to be an intellectual one: with Freud it depends upon an opposition in the sphere of desire; certain desires are incompatible with other dominant tendencies of the personality, and for this reason are banished to the unconscious.

This brings us to the second main difference between the two writers. In conformity with the general tendency of his age (a tendency, however, to which his own work enormously contributed) Freud thinks of mental energy largely in terms of striving, of conation. Ideas, or cognitive elements generally, are for him only effective in so far as they arouse or modify desires (or determine the nature of the precise steps taken to gratify desires). Here, as elsewhere, modern psychology is tremendously influenced by the theoretical separation of cognition and conation, due in the last resort, as we have seen, to the attitude of

Kant. In Herbart's time this distinction was much less clearly made, and indeed part of our difficulty in interpreting Herbart today lies in the lack of this distinction, to which modern writings have so thoroughly accustomed us. With Herbart desire and will are both resolvable into the activities of ideas. When an idea gradually attains predominance in spite of opposition, we have the state of desire. If action is possible, desire becomes volition. Tension between ideas is a source of pain. When an idea, in making its entrance into consciousness, disposes of more forces than are necessary for the purpose, we have pleasure. In the course of development, certain combinations of ideas acquire a permanent predominance: it is this predominance, with its consequent regularity of mental functioning, that constitutes "character." Such a predominant combination of ideas exercises a powerful selective influence on the ideas which are struggling for access to consciousness, readily admitting congruent ideas, but presenting a barrier to those of an opposite kind: it constitutes an "apperceptive mass." The ego is itself some such apperceptive mass, which remains a constant element in all the varied processes in which we say "I see," "I think," "I feel." If we remember that to Herbart ideas are active forces, this doctrine bears also a distinct resemblance to Freud's formulations about the ego, which refuses admission to certain desires of a non "ego-syntonic" character: though in its later elaborations, especially in relation to the "super-ego," Freud's theory goes far beyond Herbart's in the detail with which it describes the process by which this censuring ego develops. Herbart's ego also bears considerable resemblance to McDougall's "self-regarding sentiment," which, for the latter author, is the ultimate determinant both of will and character. In both cases the ego develops as the result of a complex interplay of experience and internal forces: and the moral nature of man is thus accounted for in terms accessible to a purely scientific and empirical psychology, far removed from the transcendental obscurity in which Kant had wrapped this element of the human mind. The essential difference, here as with Freud, is that the modern writer is thinking primarily in terms of "instinct," i.e., of conation. McDougall's distinction between "emotions" as the affective aspects of instincts, and "sentiments," as complex and more or less permanent organizations of instincts, seems indeed to have a forerunner in Herbart's distinction between "emotions" as "transitory variations from the state of equanimity" and "passions" as "rooted desires" of a more permanent character.

It was in connection with the doctrine of "apperception" that Herbart developed the educational bearings of his psychology and became thus the "father" of scientific pedagogy. If the structure and function of the mind is such that some ideas are given a natural and spontaneous welcome, while others are resisted, it is obviously all-important for new information, if it is to be acquired easily and rapidly, to be presented in such a form and such an order that it will tend to be naturally accepted and assimilated rather than rejected. In his early life Herbart had visited Pestalozzi in Switzerland, and this, combined with two years' practical tutoring, had brought him into close contact with the actual problems of teaching. Herbart saw that Pestalozzi and Froebel were right in stressing the importance of observation and spontaneous interest rather than of formal instruction. He himself took a further step in emphasizing the significance of background, and by means of his doctrine of apperception provided a theoretical foundation for his precepts. We must make sure, he said, that each new fact is presented to the child only when the child has so co-ordinated his past observations as to be ready to assimilate it. This led naturally to the devising of scientifically ordered curricula, so arranged that the pupil should pass steadily from familiar to closely related unfamiliar elements of study. In its insistence upon order and interest, Herbart's doctrine has exercised an immense influence upon educational theory and practice in the last hundred years. True, it only provided a general principle, the detailed application of which had to be filled up by laborious specialized investigation. Even the principle has had to fight its way against much inertia and quasi-ethical formalism, based partly on a faulty faculty psychology and partly on a moral intuition to the effect that the mastering of difficult and uninteresting material had some especial virtue of its own. But a clear recognition of the connection between psychology and education was established once and for all by Herbart. His educational doctrines constituted the first clear example of "applied" psychology, and for this alone, apart from his many other contributions, his name will always be illustrious in the field of pedagogy as of psychology itself.

II. SYSTEMATIC PSYCHOLOGY OF THE EARLY NINETEENTH CENTURY—
THOMAS BROWN, JAMES MILL, BENEKE

If Herbart, beyond a doubt the most original figure in recent psychology (as our student of a hundred years ago would see it), represented a departure from the dominant associationist school, inasmuch as he conceived of the mind throughout in terms of dynamic forces rather than of passive mechanisms, the period was not lacking in eminent exponents of the more orthodox tradition. There were above all two Scottish writers who would have claimed the attention and coloured the thought of our student— Thomas Brown and James Mill. Thomas Brown was Professor of Moral Philosophy at Edinburgh from 1810 to 1820 and published his *Lectures on the Philosophy of the Human Mind* in the latter year. Brown's psychology is often said to represent a happy combination of Scottish, French and English ideas. From the Scottish tradition he inherited the religious and moral emphasis upon an active and controlling Ego, a tradition which became blended with the reaction against the mechanistic views of the arch-empiricist Condillac and the physiologically minded Cabanis that was just then taking place in France; while at the same time in much of his detailed work Brown adopted and extended the viewpoint of the English associationists. For him the mind could not be fully explained merely in terms of individual items of experience linked together by associations. There was emphatically a unity underlying the successive states of consciousness: in fact there was a soul.

Nevertheless it is to his contributions to the study of association rather than to his insistence on the soul that he owes the important place he occupies in the history of modern psychology: though doubtless the absence of the definitely mechanistic tendencies that had distinguished so many of the later associationists contributed to his success and influence among his contemporaries and made associationism respectable in places where it would otherwise hardly have been tolerated. Brown did, moreover,

20

make a very genuine contribution towards filling the gaps left unexplained by associationism in its cruder forms. Returning to Locke's position that we have ideas not only from externally given sensations but also from an inner activity of reflection—a position that had been quite definitely abandoned by such writers as Hartley and Condillac—he proceeded to enunciate two main principles of mental life, which he called respectively "simple suggestion" and "relative suggestion" (Brown substituted the term "suggestion" for "association," which he considered implied some process of unification between the ideas associated). It is "relative suggestion" that accounts for the creative aspects of the mind, the ability to supply non-sensuous data, as when the sight of a right-angled triangle suggests the proportions made famous in the forty-seventh proposition of Euclid. It was the same capacity for "relative suggestion" that enables us to judge and compare things, to see, for instance, that one object is larger or smaller than another—in fact, to notice the existence of relations between them.

This ability to see relations has been a regular will-o'-the-wisp in modern psychology. It has constantly been lost to sight, forgotten or neglected, and as constantly rediscovered. From our present standpoint it seems quite clear that Brown was here dealing with something of importance. It is equally clear, however, that he had not grasped the full import or applicability of his own doctrine. He does not seem to have realized, for instance, that this process of perceiving relations between things plays as big a rôle in perception as it does in judgment—a fact which had to wait many years before its true significance was realized. Nor did he indicate clearly the connection between "relative suggestion" and memory—a problem which is indeed only in quite recent years receiving the attention it deserves.

Nevertheless, by calling attention, as he did, to the creative aspects of mind, Brown remedied the association psychology of one of its deficiencies. At the same time his work on "simple suggestion" abolished much of its vagueness. From Aristotle onwards psychologists had enunciated and re-enunciated the main principles of association, occasionally adding a category to the Aristotelian triad of contiguity, similarity and contrast, occasionally endeavouring to reduce them all to one. Nobody had as yet seriously attempted to show in detail why association takes a particular course in any given case: why, for instance, the idea of "black" should make one man think of "blackballing" a candidate for membership of his club, another of "Black Maria," another of the "All Blacks" football team and yet a fourth of "white." This is what Brown set out to do.

His answer to the problem took the form of propounding the "secondary laws of association," as they later came to be called. We may perhaps be allowed to state these laws in the form in which they have been summarized by Warren (*A History of the Association Psychology*, p. 73):

(1) The relative duration of the original sensations: "The longer we dwell on objects, the more fully do we rely on our future remembrance of them."

(2) Their relative liveliness: "The parts of a train appear to be more closely and firmly associated as the original feelings have been more lively."

(3) Relative frequency: "The parts of any train are more readily suggested in proportion as they have been more frequently renewed."

(4) Relative recency: "Events which happened a few hours before are remembered when there is a total forgetfulness of what happened a few days before."

(5) Their co-existence in the past with fewer alternative associates: "The song which we have never heard but from one person can scarcely be heard again by us without recalling that person to our memory."

(6) Constitutional differences between individuals modify the primary laws: They give "greater proportional vigour to one set of tendencies of suggestion than to another."

(7) Variations in the same individual, "according to the varying emotion of the hour."

(8) "Temporary diversities of state," as in intoxication, delirium or ill-health.

(9) Prior habits of life and thought—the influence of ingrained tendencies upon any given situation, however new or irrelevant the experience may be.

The first four or five of these "secondary laws" have found a permanent place in textbooks of psychology under the heading of "Memory" (though as a rule without recognition of their original source in Brown's work). It is this which gives them, in

Murphy's phrase, "a peculiarly modern ring." Their formulation represents a real achievement, especially inasmuch as they all lent themselves to quantitative treatment in the hands of the experimentalists when they embarked on the study of memory towards the end of the century. Brown's laws had to wait many years before their full value could be recognized; nevertheless it must have been obvious to any discerning student, even from the start, that they cleared up many obscurities in matters of detail, and really signified a great advance of the associationist doctrine over a wide front.

The last four laws, although they have not been transplanted in the same immediately recognizable form into later psychological literature, represent an equally striking achievement in their own way. They show that Brown was willing to contemplate the importance for psychology of individual differences and of temporary and abnormal conditions. These also are aspects which were destined to be fully developed only at a much later date, when they blossomed out on the one hand into the immensely fruitful study of individual differences by statistical methods, and on the other joined up with the investigations into abnormal psychology, the action of drugs, fatigue and "the psychopathology of everyday life." In these respects therefore, as in others, Brown was a forerunner of tendencies that later on proved to be of great importance, but the full significance of which could scarcely be realized by himself or his contemporaries.

Another contribution of Brown's met, however, with much quicker recognition. This was his stressing of the importance of the muscle sense; a point on which he was not entirely an innovator, but which he carried over from physiology (where it was beginning to make some stir) into psychology. Aristotle, to whom is due the traditional classification of the senses into five groups, had himself seen that touch is somehow less unitary than the other groups. Physiologists had recently begun to realize that sensory impulses arise, not only from the outside world, but also from the interior of the trunk and limbs, and that these impulses are of importance in informing us of our movements and the general attitude of our bodies. To Brown the muscle sense was of particular importance in giving us our notion of resistance; an idea that had already been implied to some extent by the subtle philosopher Maine de Biran in his theory that the "self" is originally formed as a result of the resistance offered to the movement of our limbs in infancy. But Brown's treatment was free of the somewhat mystic considerations into which Biran had been lured in this connection. In virtue of his "downright simple" statement of the rôle of muscular sensation, Brown was also the first of the long line of psychologists who have recognized the importance of bodily movement in our mental life.

Herbart and Brown had both published their principal works some years before our period begins, and our student would therefore find them well known in the circles of like-minded persons in which he would naturally elect to move. There were, however, other important workers in his field, whose publications were so recent as to be still in the category of novelties, in process of being read for the first time, discussed and criticized as recent contributions. Indeed the turn of the thirties was quite a significant moment in the history of psychology. James Mill, who must next occupy us, had brought out his *Analysis of the Phenomena of the Human Mind* in 1829 (it appeared again, reedited and annotated by John Stuart Mill, together with comments by Bain and others, in 1869), while in the same year Weber began his experiments on the muscle sense, which were published in instalments between 1829 and 1834. These experiments were really epoch-making for psychology, since they established the tradition which may be said to have led directly to the creation of experimental psychology as an independent discipline, utterly freed from the hitherto almost universal philosophic foundations and implications. In 1832 appeared Beneke's *Textbook of Psychology as a Natural Science*, the title of which again indicated the direction in which things were moving, though Beneke himself was no experimentalist. This year was also distinguished by the birth of Wundt, unquestionably the greatest single figure among nineteenth-century psychologists. In 1833, as already mentioned, Wheatstone invented the first form of stereoscope, an instrument that greatly stimulated interest in the phenomena of binocular vision and space perception: and Johannes Müller, whose neurological work became of great importance in psychology, was made Professor of Physiology at Berlin—the first to hold such a chair in any University—and followed this by the publication, in the immediately succeeding years, of his great and influential *Textbook of Physiology*, the relevant portions of which may be regarded as constituting at the same time the first systematic treatise on "physiological" psychology.

For the present, however, we must confine ourselves to the purely psychological approach. We have seen how Herbart and Brown had been preparing the way for a more dynamic psychology than that which had been prevalent of late among the more scientifically inclined students of the mind. The great lesson of these thinkers (and particularly of Herbart), that mind was essentially active, was to play a striking part in the psychology to come. Nevertheless the next great writer in chronological succession, James Mill, was destined not to follow up this clue, but rather to represent the supreme and culminating effort of associationism of the mechanistic kind. It is generally recognized that James Mill's philosophical and scientific doctrines are in some sense an unusually clear expression of his personality. He is a good representative of those men, whose intellectual probity made religious belief impossible, but whose strongly developed sense of duty drove them, in the field of morals, to asceticism, hard work and self-renunciation, and, in the field of thought, to a pitiless and mechanical logic which would leave no loopholes for sentiment and caprice. His was the typical mentality, with all its advantages and defects, of the Puritan turned intellectual. Mill adopted the psychological hedonism of the more genuinely pleasure-loving Bentham, according to which people not only should, but do, consistently seek happiness; and yet he saw nothing incongruous or questionable in the fact that his mode of life confined him almost entirely to the pleasures of the mind— themselves pursued under circumstances (of his own making) that would have driven most men crazy. Nor did his hedonistic philosophy seem to him in any way in disagreement with the stern pedagogical principles which he applied to his son, principles which would have led most other children to rebellion, escape, or perhaps to suicide.

In Mill's psychology there is no room for any special creative activity of the mind. It is true that *ideas* represent, according to him, one primary state of consciousness, alongside of *sensations*, which constitute the other primary state; but "our ideas spring up or exist in the order in which the sensations existed of which they are the copies." In the last resort our minds are made up of sensory particles, which form the ultimate and irreducible elements of mind. It is natural, therefore, that Mill should devote considerable attention to the nature of sensation, and his analysis is carried a step further than was achieved by any previous psychologist—particularly as regards the breaking up of Aristotle's sense of touch. Mill recognizes in all eight classes of sensation; vision, hearing, smell, taste, touch, muscular sensation (which, as we have just seen, had been emphasized by Thomas Brown, and which Mill considered to have been "miserably overlooked" by earlier writers), sensations of disorganization (which included tickling and itching, together with a vague and ill-defined group of impressions subsequently included by Weber under the term "common sensibility," *Gemeingefühl*) and, finally, sensations from the alimentary canal.

Out of these elements, presented as actual sensations or re-presented as ideas (Mill did not clearly distinguish between ideas and what we now call *images*), the process of association was able to build up the whole complex structure of mental life. Association itself is of one kind only—contiguity; all other apparent kinds (even similarity) being reducible to this. It can, however, operate in two distinct ways, following the objective relationships of which associations are the mental counterparts. We must thus distinguish synchronous and successive associations. The latter determine the sequence of our ideas, as when a horse leads us to think of its owner, this in turn to the owner's occupation; or as when we recall the successive words of some well-known text, such as the Lord's Prayer. The former determine the perception of objects, as in the co-operation of sensory visual elements with ideal auditory elements when we "see" a violin; or in the combination of colour, hardness, shape, size and weight (from muscular sensations) when we see a stone. Mill recognized that associations might vary in strength, and indeed considered that sometimes associative links were so strong that they could not be separated, as in certain instances of colour and extension (from vision and the muscular sensations generated by movement respectively); whereas, in other cases, certain ideas could not be joined together (this latter a condition with regard to which he is often accused of confounding psychology with logic). But his account of the causes of these variations in strength is far less penetrating and elaborate than that of Brown; explicitly indeed he only recognizes the two main categories of "frequency" and "vividness," and it is difficult to make sure what exactly he included in the latter term, though he expressly says that he does not mean intensity.

Memory, in the sense of recognition, is for Mill a simple matter; it is merely the idea of an object *plus* an idea of our former experience of it. Nor is there any difficulty in accounting for the self or such phenomena as had been called by others "apperception." Mill practically says that the problems with which these concepts were called in to deal have no existence. Consciousness, for Mill, contains nothing more than feelings or ideas. "To say I am conscious of a feeling is merely to say that I feel it." The "I" is therefore quite superfluous; there is no such entity, except in so far as I have ideas of my own previous states. Apart from this, to have an experience is to be conscious of it, and there is no need of any mysterious or transcendental activity in accounting for this consciousness.

James Mill's system, as we have already indicated, represents the climax of associationism in its most rigorous and mechanistic form. Of the previous writers of this school, only Hartley and Condillac have approached him in the thoroughness and determination with which he set about the task of explaining mind as a mosaic of sensation built up by a series of purely mechanical processes. Of those that followed, none equalled him in the daring or ruthless consistency with which he applied his principles, unless it be a few of the more extreme behaviourists of a later age. It would seem indeed that it is among the members of this latter school that we must look for the true modern successors of those who sought, with Mill, to reduce all mental functioning to the operation of a single mechanical law. The film illustrating Pavlov's work, that has recently been shown to the learned world, ends with the dogmatic statement that all the complex life of man is but a series of "conditioned reflexes." This is in the true spirit of Mill and his companions in the field of rigid associationism—a spirit that will probably always manifest itself whenever men, in their intolerance of the vague, the mystic and the transcendental, and in their triumph in the discovery of some great principle or method, think they have obtained a master key which will unlock all doors in their own section of the treasure house of knowledge. To others, more tolerant of the unknown, less optimistic about the adequacy of human understanding, or

merely less enthusiastic in their estimate of the particular master
key in question, it has always seemed that closer inspection
revealed the fact that some doors remained locked, and that it is
merely the refusal to carry out such an inspection which has
permitted the illusion that all things were explained. Such on the
whole has been the judgment passed on Mill, as also on others
similarly minded. But this has not prevented Mill, together with
these others, from making real and lasting contributions to their
science. Their self-appointed task was to exploit a single line of
thought to its uttermost limits; it was left to workers of a different
spirit to determine just how far towards these limits the line in
question could comfortably and usefully be followed.

If James Mill's book had represented the extreme denial of
activity in mind, that of Friedrich Eduard Beneke, published
three years later, just as our imaginary student was contempla-
ting the beginning of his studies, was a very definite step in the
other direction. To Beneke the most essential fact of mind was
the presence of primal faculties or powers (*Urvermögen*), in
virtue of which the mind was able to do certain things—to
experience certain sensations or carry out certain movements. For
Beneke, in fact, the mind was active. The data expounded by the
associationists are recognized, but the complex process of the
development of mind from relatively simple elements is regarded
as the result of an inner mental activity reacting upon each new
element as it presents itself. The mind, moreover, is essentially
a unity, though in the beginning its activity is necessarily primitive, the complex behaviour of the adult being built up gradually
as a result of the unfolding and integration of the original powers
and the consequent development of new capacities. It is this
insistence upon the activity of the mind as a whole that distinguishes Beneke's dynamism from that of Herbart. In Brett's
descriptive words, the soul is treated "as a moving system of
forces rather than a place in which separate forces struggle
together." Herbart's "apperceptive mass," however, clearly has
functions that are not unlike those that Beneke attributes to the
mind as a whole, and Beneke was indeed accused by Herbart's
followers of being guilty of gross plagiarism—an accusation
against which he defended himself vigorously, at length, and, on
the whole, successfully.

Beneke's strength lies in the fact that he holds the middle road between the various byways of the special schools. He avoids the extravagances of extreme associationism, by refusing to deny the activity of the mind, and by maintaining that the living organism reacts to outer stimuli, not in the manner of a complicated machine, but in virtue of its own inherent vital tendencies. In modern terminology, he is a champion of Nature versus Nurture, and declines to neglect the rôle of innate capacities in behaviour and development. In his emphasis both on activity and on original endowment, he is utterly removed from Mill's notion of growth through the simple recording, blending, and connecting together of sensory impressions.

Beneke equally avoids the dangers of the faculty psychology, inasmuch as the powers or "faculties" with which he deals are not broad characteristics or abilities, such as Imagination, Reason, Will, each of which comprises a multitude of different acts grouped under one all-embracing head, but quite specific forms of apprehension, feeling or behaviour. He himself points this out very clearly in the case of Memory, which he describes as due to the operation of *traces*; when an idea vanishes from consciousness it leaves behind a trace, by means of which it can be brought back to consciousness later on in connection with another idea. The nature of the traces is not altogether clear; they are not, we are given to understand, unconscious in Herbart's sense, nor may they be regarded as physiological in nature; for Beneke insisted on the right of psychology to make its own laws without reference to the terms of other sciences. In this doctrine of traces he was the forerunner of many psychologists of later date, who have shown themselves very ready to operate with the notion of "memory traces," "psycho-physical dispositions" or "engrams," though usually with some degree of physiological connotation (for, even though we endeavour to avoid any specific neurological hypothesis, the word "trace" as applied to mental events almost inevitably suggests some kind of physical interpretation or analogy).

Finally, Beneke is no less opposed to the transcendentalism which takes refuge in a soul or in *a priori* categories removed from ordinary observation and analysis. It is true that Beneke speaks of the soul. But the soul is for him no more than a totality of powers—the powers that correspond to the activities that we can actually observe.

It was Beneke's opposition to the transcendental that lost him his right to teach at the University of Berlin. The decision in question, for which the Prussian Minister of Education seems to have been responsible, is a magnificent monument to academic prejudice and dogmatism, and deserves to be quoted, even though it had reference not to Beneke's psychological work but to his ethical doctrines (which for him, however, were intimately dependent on psychology). Speaking of a book by Beneke on *The Foundation of a Physics of Morality*, the Minister declared "that it was not a single passage which had given offence but the whole scheme, and that a philosophy which did not deduce everything from the Absolute could not be considered to be philosophy at all." The substitution of observation for "reason" or dogma is always liable to give offence: and thus the advocacy of empiricism is seldom without some opportunity for martyrdom, in great matters or in small. But it was scarcely just that Beneke, who was so very far from being an extremist, should be treated as though he were a daring innovator or a dangerous rebel.

LOOKING back from the vantage point that we ourselves enjoy after a hundred further years of work, we can see that the tragedy (if we like to call it such) both of Herbart and of Beneke was that, in considering psychology as a science, they were concerned far more with scientific form than with scientific method and procedure. They were too biased by the metaphysical implications of psychology and by the philosophical traditions in which it had been nursed to realize the applicability to psychology of the precise methods of observation and control which had already proved so fruitful elsewhere. They were still dazzled by the relative perfection of form that can be achieved by pure logic, and it simply did not occur to them that the next step should consist in abandoning this elegant speculation as to how the mind must work for the more humble and laborious method of studying in painstaking detail the way in which it does work. The time of this revolution in method and outlook was rapidly approaching even as they wrote. But, with one outstanding exception, it was to be brought about by men who had been brought up outside the strictly philosophical tradition, and who approached psychology in the spirit of some other science, especially in that of physiology. The beginnings of physiological research, in so far as they intimately concern the history of psychology, lie just outside our period. But we have taken the liberty of supposing that our student, through whose eyes we have been looking all this time, is a man of wide sympathies and interests, ready to avail himself of any light, however indirect, that may be thrown upon his chosen subject. We may, therefore, ourselves look back a few years to glance at such recent achievements in the realm of physiology as would naturally appeal to him.

At the beginning of the nineteenth century it had of course for long been recognized that there was some intimate connection between the phenomena of mind on the one hand and the

nervous system and the brain upon the other. It was, however, by
no means generally agreed that the brain and nervous system
represented the sole organs of mind; Bichat and other French
physiologists had maintained, for instance, that the emotions have
their seat in the internal organs. Still less was there a general
body of belief or knowledge with regard to any detailed correspondence between the different aspects of mind and the various
parts of the brain. Indeed, interest in such problems of the localization of function in the nervous system had, since the time of
Descartes, receded in favour of speculation about the seat of the
soul, in the sense of some particular part or organ especially concerned with the relationship between mind and body. All at
once, at the turn of the century, there arose a movement which
professed to have established the localization in detail of a large
number of mental traits and to have discovered a means by which
traits could be rapidly and accurately diagnosed in any given
individual by a simple examination of the external conformation
of the skull—the movement associated with "Craniology" or
"Phrenology," as it later came to be called. If the claim had
been justified, it would have been by far the most dramatic
event in the whole history both of psychology and brain physiology; it would have meant that problems, concerning which
we are even today, after 130 years of further research, still
largely in the dark, had been solved almost at a single stroke. It
would have meant in the first place, in the field of pure psychology, that we had become possessed of an apparently complete list
of human powers, faculties and tendencies, in terms of which the
whole human mind could be fully and accurately described; in
the second place, that our (at that time dawning and even today
still insecure) knowledge of the cerebral localization of mental
functions, had, quite suddenly and unexpectedly, given place to
a most exact and extensive scientific discipline, as the result of a
single great discovery: thirdly, that it had become possible to
diagnose individual ability and character, thus solving at once
and together the chief problems of the psychology of individual
differences and the dependent practical problems of vocational
guidance and selection. Mental tests, as we know them, would
hardly have been necessary: the problem of devising tests of
temperament and character, with which contemporary psychologists have been struggling for the last dozen years or so with

indifferent success, would also not arise. It is true that the *full* advantages that would have been derived from phrenology have only become clear with the further progress of psychology, and could scarcely have been realized when the doctrine was first put forward by its founders, Gall and Spurzheim; but, leaving aside any complete realization of its possibilities, the prospects, even at a first view and to the untutored eye, were sufficiently alluring, especially when to the uplift associated with a new marvel of science was associated all the thrill of a successful parlour pastime for the winter evenings! Small wonder then that the new doctrine aroused enthusiasm of an almost unprecedented kind: small wonder either that its claims were looked upon somewhat sceptically by the world of science.

Franz Joseph Gall, the originator of phrenology, was an anatomist by training, and undoubtedly possessed much real ability in this department. Even as a boy he had noticed what he took to be a certain correspondence between the mental abilities and characteristics of his schoolfellows and the shapes of their heads. Later he began to test and extend these boyhood observations, at first in prisons and lunatic asylums, then among his friends and on the head casts of prominent persons. His surmise as to the existence of a general correspondence between mental traits and the outward shape of the skull seemed to him to be amply corroborated; and his observations soon provided a mass of data, which allowed him to state the correspondence in detailed terms. He began lecturing on the subject in Vienna, and his views seem to have aroused interest from the start. But the full extent of the publicity subsequently obtained is due perhaps more to Gall's collaborator, Spurzheim, than to Gall himself. Their collaboration lasted from 1800 to 1813, after which Spurzheim continued vigorous propaganda both in Europe and America. The doctrines became known through their lectures for some considerable time before any authoritative exposition appeared in print. The first important publication on the subject was a memoir presented by Gall and Spurzheim in 1808, in support of their candidature for election to the *Institut de France*. A committee, including Cuvier, the biologist (who was chairman) and Pinel, the psychiatrist, was appointed to investigate the claims and gave a non-committal report; the candidates, however, were not elected, owing partly, it has been suggested, to the influence of Napoleon,

who did not approve of foreigners becoming members of the
Institut. Further and larger works appeared between 1810 and
1825. The British *Phrenological Journal* first appeared in 1823
and, after sundry changes and amalgamations, involving transference to America, ended with its 124th volume in 1911. Among
the most prominent supporters was the Scotchman, George
Combe, who was prolific in publication from 1819 onwards, and
who has left his mark on psychology by the founding of an annual
lecture at Edinburgh University, in which prominent psychologists and other scientists continue even today to make respectful
allusion to phrenology in honour of their pious benefactor. In the
first half of the nineteenth century, phrenology was, as some
of the historians of psychology have well suggested, somewhat in
the position of psychical research today. Its claims seemed, on
general scientific grounds, unlikely to be true, but had aroused
great popular interest and belief and had not as yet been confronted with any evidence that could be said to amount to
definite disproof. It was, moreover, frowned on by the principal
authorities, both in psychology and physiology, and therefore
never became in any sense one of the recognized teachings of
academic science. On the psychological side, Herbart, Brown, and
Sir William Hamilton, and among physiologists, Sir Charles Bell
and Pierre Flourens, all expressed their disapproval of it on one
ground or another. Indeed, in the light of later knowledge (not,
of course, available to these distinguished contemporaries of
Gall) it appeared that the grounds for rejecting phrenology in its
classical form were overwhelming.

Phrenology depended on three essential principles, none of
which have proved themselves true in the way and to the extent
that phrenological doctrine demanded. In the first place, it went
further than any other psychological system in its demands for
the splitting up of the human mind into faculties; indeed it was
the faculty psychology *par excellence*. As eventually formulated,
there were thirty-seven faculties. They were divided into two
main groups, affective and intellectual respectively. The affective group was subdivided into two classes, the Propensities (e.g.
Destructiveness, Amativeness, Acquisitiveness) and the Sentiments (e.g. Conscientiousness, Self-Esteem, Cautiousness); while
the intellectual group was subdivided into a Perceptive group
(e.g. Size, Configuration, Tune, Language) and a Reflective

group (with two members, Comparison and Causality). It is only in comparatively recent years that psychologists have learnt, chiefly through the work of Spearman, to deal scientifically with the question of faculties—that is, to discover by appropriate statistical means whether the various phenomena grouped together under a single faculty really do form a unity (e.g. whether a given individual can be said to be quite generally more "amative" or "acquisitive" than another, and, if so, to what extent). The whole possible field of faculties especially in the direction of propensities and sentiments is, moreover, very far from having been as yet adequately explored by the new methods now available. Nevertheless, the work already done in this direction seems to show clearly that the mind is in reality constructed on a very different pattern from that which the phrenologists supposed, and that a list of faculties drawn up on strictly scientific principles (if and when such a list can be drawn up) will be in its general principles quite other than that which figures on the familiar phrenological charts and tables; though, of course, it is quite possible that one or two of the phrenological items may eventually be corroborated and thus prove to have been happy guesses (this may well be the case, for instance with "Tune," which may correspond to a certain "broad factor" of musical ability, the existence of which is more than hinted at by modern experimental results). The reader who wishes to see the vast gap between the phrenological and the quite recent views on faculty, both in general conception and in method of approach, will do well to read Spurzheim's *Phrenology, or the Doctrine of Mental Phenomena*, published (just at the beginning of our period) in 1834, and then to turn to Spearman's *Abilities of Man*, published ninety-three years later.

In the second place phrenology claimed that each of its thirty-seven faculties was located in a definite area of the cortex—a scheme of localization known to most of us from the phrenological models of the head still to be seen occasionally at the present day. Unfortunately, the various more precise methods for studying the functions of the brain that have been devised since Gall's time have signally failed to corroborate Gall's findings, and have indeed shown that many parts of the cortex have functions quite other than those attributed to them by his system. Physiological psychology has indeed been no kinder to his doctrines than has the statistical psychology of individual differences.

Thirdly, the phrenologists believed that the degree of development of the various parts of the brain corresponding to the faculties could be ascertained by feeling the "bumps" or inequalities in the external contour of the skull. This presupposed that the outer cranial surface corresponded accurately to the surface (and, therefore, the degree of development) of the portion of the brain immediately below, a presupposition which is disproved by the fact, since ascertained by cerebral anatomy, that the thickness of the skull varies considerably and irregularly from one part to another. In so far as this is the case, the essential *method* of phrenology is inadequate for the purpose for which it was employed, and the evidence for the supposed correspondence based thereon must be regarded as fallacious.

By a piece of tragic irony phrenology was the most popular of all the doctrines of psychology in the whole history of the science, and at the same time the most erroneous. It affords a striking example of the danger of erecting a vast superstructure on inadequate observation and inexact methods, and the fact that Gall himself was no mere charlatan, but a scientist of admitted ability, only adds to the impressiveness of the lesson—a lesson on which psychologists even of the present day may do well to ponder. As Boring remarks in dealing with this subject in his *History of Experimental Psychology*, it shows the great scientific importance of a recognized technique, which is independent of the personal bias of the individual investigator, however brilliant. Both in his general notions, and in his detailed assumptions with regard to the correspondence of particular mental traits with particular features of the skull, Gall's observations started from striking, individual cases—a perfectly legitimate procedure, which, in the hands of genius, has often led to great discoveries. It was in *testing* the hypothesis suggested by these cases that Gall's and Spurzheim's procedure was inadequate—largely because the general scientific rules governing such a process of testing were as yet not realized, at any rate in their application to psychophysical problems of the kind in question. It was important, for instance, that, if the doctrine was to be regarded as of general application, the cases selected for testing the suggested correlations should be unselected. It was important, too, that the cranial

measurements should be fine and accurate enough to permit of
establishing significant differences between one individual and
another; that they should as far as possible be "objective" and
free from any subjectively determined "constant errors" of the
particular investigator; and that, in so far as this was not possible,
the two series of phenomena to be related should be observed
independently and "without knowledge," i.e. that the "bumps"
on the skull should be measured in ignorance of the mental
characteristics of the possessor of the skull and *vice versa*. In
these, and probably in other ways, the phrenologists' methods
fell far short of the rigid canons of scientific procedure, as they are
beginning to be understood, though not always accurately or
conscientiously followed, by the psychologists of today. The
failure of phrenology, with the implied immense amount of mis-
directed effort and ill-informed enthusiasm, was the price that
had to be paid for this neglect of scientific caution. No doubt,
many elaborate hypotheses that figure in present-day psychology
will have to be as ruthlessly discarded as the doctrines of phrenology; some of them are based on evidence that is but little
better, partly because the enthusiasm aroused by any wide and
novel generalization naturally and inevitably outruns the evidence available, partly because we do not as yet see clearly how
to apply the stricter scientific methods to all the psychological
problems of importance, partly again because the lesson of
phrenology has been inadequately learned and psychologists
have not always realized the necessity of using rigorous methods
of control in every case where they are applicable. These latter
instances show perhaps that psychology has not as yet become
entirely tamed by science over the whole of its wide and varied
field; a good deal of the speculative licence of the earlier days is to
be found here and there.[1]

But nowhere in psychology does there seem to be so vast and
dogmatic a body of doctrine based altogether on such slender evidence, as was the case with the whole school of Gall and Spurzheim. Schools there still are in plenty, often at cross purposes
with one another; but in their positive assertions (if not always

---

[1] As is the case with other disciplines, for instance, medicine, which is
notoriously subject to fashions and crazes founded on enthusiasm rather than
on evidence, and which, like psychology, has not always resorted to such
scientific methods of control (e.g. statistics) as were available.

perhaps in their denials) each school would seem to have a basis in facts ascertained with some degree of scientific care. We may reasonably hope that every important school existing today is making some solid and *direct* contribution to our knowledge; and that their doctrines will need to be revised and mutually supplemented rather than uprooted. Phrenology has been psychology's great *faux pas*; but we can at least console ourselves with the fact that no psychologist of note was party to the indiscretion, and that there is no immediate prospect of another lapse of comparable magnitude.

We emphasized the word *direct* above because, though phrenology does indeed seem to have made no direct contribution to our knowledge, there is general agreement that it was *indirectly* of some value. If it failed dismally in its particular contributions to the study of cerebral localization, it did not fail to draw attention to the general problem of the mind-brain relationship and to the *possibility* of the more detailed localization of specific functions. The failure of phrenology, if it had been fully realized at the time, might have led to a strengthening of the general attitude of neglect or distrust of physiology that distinguished the leading contemporary psychologists, and have deterred physiologists on their part from directing their efforts to the brain. Fortunately, it had neither of these effects. It seems rather to have diverted thought from the rather sterile speculations concerning the means or locus of interaction between mind and body to the much more profitable search for some specific form of psycho-physical correlation. Phrenology, with the widespread interest it aroused, established, once and for all, the belief that the brain was the essential and only organ of the mind; while, at the same time, it paved the way for more accurate attempts at localization (attempts towards which the general attitude had hitherto been hostile), by making these attempts seem mild and conservative as compared with its own vastly greater claims.

IV. EARLY PHYSIOLOGICAL PSYCHOLOGY

APART from the more dramatic developments of phrenology, the first third of the nineteenth century was a period of rapidly increasing knowledge about the structure and function of the nervous system, so that our imaginary student, starting work a hundred years ago, had at his disposal a considerably larger fund of well-established data on this aspect of his subject than would have been the case if he had begun his studies a third of a century before. This increased knowledge was principally due to the labours and insight of a few men, chief among whom were Bell, Magendie, Flourens, Rolando and Marshall Hall. The first and perhaps the greatest of these was Sir Charles Bell, another of the famous Scotchmen who figure so prominently in the history of psychology. Bell himself contributed a whole series of discoveries, chief among which were the distinction between the sensory and the motor nerves, the specificity of the sensory nervous impulses, the existence of the muscle sense and the facts of reciprocal innervation as shown in the relaxation of the flexor muscles during contraction of the extensors of the same limb and *vice versa*. In this last matter he prepared the way for the study of inhibition by later psychologists and physiologists. He was perhaps the first to draw attention quite explicitly to the existence of the muscle sense, though the notion was undoubtedly in the air at the time and was, as we have seen, espoused by several psychologists a few years later. Bell, however, undoubtedly had a priority in this, as in a number of other important matters. Owing to his method of publication however (some of his most significant discoveries were printed in the form of a privately published pamphlet of which a hundred copies only were available), the true nature of his work was for years unknown outside the circle of his students and his private friends, for though Bell was quick at announcing his results in lectures—even to describing his research work of the previous evening—he seems to have been slow at recording his

39

results in writing. This, however, did not prevent him from enjoying a big reputation in his lifetime. The pamphlet in question was published in 1811, but the conclusions became widely known only at a later date, when he summed up his researches in his *Nervous System of the Human Body* which appeared in 1830. It is partly for this reason that, in both the two first-mentioned discoveries, Bell's name is associated with others. In the case of the distinction between the sensory and motor nerves, he shares the honour with Magendie, a slightly younger French physiologist, who first announced what appears to have been a genuinely independent discovery in 1822. The Bell-Magendie law, as it is often called, is to the effect that the ventral roots of the spinal cord contain only motor nerve fibres, the dorsal roots and the spinal ganglia only sensory fibres. The distinction between the motor and sensory functions of the nerves had of course been known for very long—indeed since the time of Galen; but up till Bell's discovery all nerves had been supposed to perform both functions. Bell and Magendie showed that, while this was true of certain nerves, it was not true of all, since many had purely motor or purely sensory functions, while it did not appear to be true of any of the nerve *fibres*, each of which seemed to have an exclusive function of one kind or the other. This essential dichotomy of function has appeared so well founded that it has remained an implicit assumption of all subsequent work upon the nervous system. The Bell-Magendie law has, as its corollary, the "law of forward conduction," according to which conduction in a nerve fibre occurs in one direction only, a law which paved the way for the conception of reflex action which was soon afterwards to be formulated by Marshall Hall.

In the case of the specific nature of the sensory nervous impulse, Bell's name is associated with, or has rather been displaced by, that of Müller—for, as has been well said, it was Müller, who, in his great textbook published over twenty years after Bell's announcement, "placed the seal of orthodoxy" on the doctrine. It had, however, been referred to in an earlier publication of Müller's in 1826, and might therefore well be known to our student of 1833, if he were sufficiently alert. We may therefore perhaps be permitted to regard the law of the "specific energies of sensory nerves" as an integral part of psychophysiology at the latter date. The law, as finally stated, is somewhat complex and may be divided into several separate propositions.

The law starts from the fairly obvious assumption that, since our nerves are interposed as an essential channel of communication between objects and our knowledge of them, they inevitably colour this knowledge of ours and impart their own characteristics to the mind.

In the second place, assuming that there are differences in the quality of the various nerves, it follows that each nerve may impose its own specific quality on the mind.

In the third place, and this is the most essential part of the whole law, observation shows that certain nerves are in fact attuned to certain forms of stimuli—"adequate" stimuli, as they are sometimes called, to distinguish them from other and "inadequate" stimuli, which either produce no sensation or else a sensation corresponding in quality to that normally produced by the adequate stimulus. In other words, sensory nerves only produce the sensations which they usually produce, i.e. the sensations associated with the adequate stimulus to the nerves in question.

Two corollaries follow from this. First, one and the same stimulus may give rise to different impressions according to the nerve stimulated. A blow on the head may cause pain in the skin, at the same time cause the ears to ring and make sparks appear before the eyes, each set of nerves responding in its own peculiar manner. Secondly, different stimuli affecting the same nerve, if they cause any sensation at all, give rise each to the same kind of sensation. Visual sensations result not only from light, but from pressure on the eyeball, and section of the optic nerve in surgical extirpation of the eye has been reported to give rise to "the perception of a great light." The fact that excessive stimulation of the eye may also cause pain has since been accounted for on the ground that the outer coat of the eye contains pain nerves, and the same applies to the pain felt in operations on the eye. Similarly, touch and taste can be distinguished in stimulation of the tongue. Had they known the fact, Bell and Müller might have pointed to the striking instance of "paradoxical cold" that results from stimulation of a cold spot by a heated point. Subsequent criticism, observation and experiment have shown, on the whole, that such cases are comparatively rare and not always perhaps so easily interpreted as Bell and Müller thought; inadequate stimuli are, for the most part, entirely inadequate, i.e. they give rise to no sensation at all. Hence we are ignorant of whole aspects of the outer world, for the perception of which we are not endowed with the necessary organs—a fact that has been brought forcibly before us in recent years by radio transmissions, of which we become aware only when we can make use of receiving apparatus which will convert the ether vibrations into sound or light. Our wireless sets pick up the vibrations from the station to which we tune them, just as the eye picks up the rays of light from the object upon which it is turned, but we ourselves possess no organs for detecting the waves used in broadcasting; our sets, however, perform the double function of reacting to these waves and converting them into other waves which our own sensory apparatus *can* detect. Even when apparently inadequate stimuli do produce a perceptible effect, the stimulus itself may be complex and thus contain adequate elements, as when an edible object, which we value chiefly for its taste, nevertheless causes tactual or thermal sensations (and no gustatory sensation) when in contact with the outer skin, or when an object which we often handle but seldom (since our infancy!) put into our mouths yet arouses taste in virtue of its sapid qualities, if placed upon the tongue.

But these reservations have left the central doctrine intact, and as a general proposition the law of specific energies (usually associated with the name of Müller) has in recent times been almost as widely and unquestionably accepted as the Bell-Magendie law. There has been, however, and indeed still is, some doubt as to the precise way in which it should be interpreted. Where exactly does the specificity of the response arise? There are obviously several possibilities, e.g. the peripheral sense organs, the peripheral nerves, the spinal cord (in the case of nerve tracts that pass through this channel) or the brain.

In some cases an elaborate sense organ (such as the eye or the ear) seems clearly adapted to the reception of a particular stimulus; but the fact, already known to Bell, that when a nerve is severed, stimulation of the stump of the nerve nearest to the brain causes the usual sensation to arise, shows that there is a specificity of response (in the mature organism at any rate) that is independent of that of the sense organ. Is this further specificity in the nerve or in the brain? Neither Bell nor Müller definitely committed themselves on this point, though Müller's language often suggests that the specificity lies in the nerves, and (partly owing to the general opposition to phrenology) this was perhaps the more popular solution at the time. But later on, when improved methods of brain study began to afford good evidence for the existence of cerebral centres, opinion veered the other way, and in time this became quite definitely the predominant view, especially of course when physiology succeeded in locating the sensory centres themselves.

These last considerations bring us back once more to the brain itself. Here Pierre Flourens was doing pioneer work of a masterly character, his principal researches being published in 1824 and 1825. Flourens was the first to make a systematic attempt to determine the functions of the major divisions of the brain by the process of experimental extirpation, his chief observations being made on the brains of pigeons. In this attempt he was aided by a skilful operative technique, which enabled him to avoid the danger of unintentional mutilation of neighbouring parts of the cerebral substance and to reduce the shock of operation to a minimum. As a result of his experiments, he discovered that when the cerebral lobes were removed without damage to adjoining portions the birds displayed a lack of initiative, of memory and of understanding. They would react to direct stimuli of a violent kind, but were otherwise passive; at first sight they appeared to be blind and deaf, but they were yet sensitive to light, for the pupils still contracted under stimulation. To quote Flourens's own summary, as rendered by Boring, "the function of the cerebral lobes is willing, judging, remembering, seeing, hearing, in a word perceiving"; as regards the cognitive aspect of these functions, we may say, in modern terminology, that perception had been abolished, while sensation remained. As regards the cerebellum, Flourens concluded from his evidence that its function was the "co-ordination of the movements of locomotion." In this connection we may also mention that Flourens was the first to discover that the semicircular canals in the inner ear were somehow concerned with the same function, though he did not go on to draw the conclusion that this portion of the ear has nothing whatever to do with the process of hearing, but is quite another sense organ of a distinct kind. Pictures of the strange attitudes adopted by Flourens's pigeons after operative interference with the canals adorn some of our textbooks to the present day, though a more adequate theoretical interpretation of the results did not come until some fifty years after Flourens's work. The *corpora quadrigemina*, Flourens concluded, are concerned with seeing; without them the animal is blind. Finally, the *medulla oblongata* he considered to be the great organ of conservation, concerned in the fundamental and essential functions of life itself. In this he agreed with his contemporary and rival, the Italian Luigi Rolando, who had independently carried out experiments somewhat similar to those of Flourens, but who, possessing neither the operative skill nor the clarity of thought of the French investigator, had obtained results that were inconclusive and (as later appeared) in some respects erroneous.

Flourens's localization of function in the brain was a modest enough achievement in comparison with the vastly more ambitious claims of the phrenologists, but it was based on sound scientific methods skilfully applied, and has stood the test of time, needing amplification rather than amendment. Flourens himself regarded his conclusions as being of quite another kind from those of the phrenologists. He insisted only on the differences of function of the different main portions of the brain, whereas the phrenologists maintained that a single part of the brain—the cerebrum—had many different functions, each function separately localized in some small area. For Flourens the brain, over and above the distinctive functions of the main parts, still functioned as a unity, and this in two ways. First of all, in addition to what he called the *action propre* of each major part, as revealed in his experiments, he posits also an *action commune* of the whole organ, for he had observed that the removal of any one part, besides abolishing certain specific functions, reduced the energy of all the others. In his own words, "one point excited in the nervous system excites all the others; one point enervated enervates them all; there is a community of reaction, of alteration, of energy. Unity is the great principle that reigns." Similarly, within each portion of the brain, there is community of function, a view which, as applied to the cerebrum, is in direct contradiction with the doctrines of phrenology. "All the perceptions, all the volitions, occupy concurrently the same seat in these organs; the faculty . . . of perceiving or willing, constitutes thus only one faculty, essentially a unit."

Flourens's opposition to the phrenologists on this point represents (in so far as it was concerned with general principles rather than with particular instances of localization) one stage of a controversy that has been going on for the last hundred-and-fifty years, and which is still in progress. As Boring remarks, there seems to be a cycle of fashions with regard to this question of localization. In the days before phrenology, there was little if any suggestion of a precise localization of functions. The phrenologists at one step introduced localization of a highly specific order. Flourens, though his own work proved localization of a kind (a very different kind from that of the phrenologists), yet maintained that the brain functioned as a whole. His work was in a sense a compromise—"localization in the gross, but not in the fine." Some fifty years later, when the "new phrenology" was ushered in by the introduction of fresh techniques in the investigation of the brain, the search for centres corresponding to specific functions once again became the guiding principle and remained so for the last quarter of the nineteenth century. In recent years the work of Franz and Lashley in experimental neurology and of the "Gestalt" and "Factor" schools in pure psychology has again emphasized the importance of the more quantitative aspects of brain function as a whole. In general it would appear that, as in so many other things, Flourens's principle of compromise was right; in the light of the most modern knowledge it would appear that the existence of specific centres is a fact, but that, at any rate within any given major portion of the brain (the cortex, thalamus, cerebellum, etc.), the specificity resides in functional habit rather than in structural or innate peculiarity, and that each part, over and above any specific functions that it may perform, also contributes its quota of energy to the function of the whole.

The next great step in our knowledge of the nervous system came a few years later. In 1830 J. J. Lister, an amateur optician who had been successful in considerably improving the structure of the microscope, put his optical inventions to good use by discovering the cells in the blood stream and in animal tissue; and in 1833, just as our student was embarking on his studies, news might have come to him that Remak, using the improved instrument, had discovered that the grey matter of the brain is cellular; while, almost simultaneously, Ehrenberg had discovered that the white matter consists only of conduction fibres. The new discovery of the true nature of the distinction between grey and white matter paved the way for the further understanding of the nature of the units of the nervous system and of the function of these units; in due course it led to the formulation of the neurone theory and the related views as to the rôle of the synapse, that were destined to play a great part in later psycho-physical theory.

Still another achievement of the same year was the first clear formulation of the distinction between voluntary action and reflex action, a distinction due to the Scotch physician Marshall Hall. As a result of his observations on decapitated animals, Hall found that, by suitable stimulation, definite kinds of bodily movement could be produced with the help of the peripheral nerves and spinal cord, independently of the brain, and, therefore, quite distinct in character from conscious and voluntary movement. It is true that some observations pointing in this direction had already been made by earlier physiologists; the word "reflex" had been introduced nearly a century earlier by Astruc, and the pupillary reflex itself had been observed by Galen. But the widespread recognition of the general phenomena of reflex action dates from the time of Marshall Hall's work, which, like so many other physiological discoveries of the period, had the good fortune to be gathered together, catalogued and systematically ordered in that great treasury of knowledge, *The Textbook of Physiology* of Johannes Müller.

Before we leave the nervous system, we may call attention to a striking parallelism that must almost inevitably have suggested itself to our student; the parallelism between the structure of the brain that histological research was just revealing and the nature of the mind as pictured by the associationism which was the dominant psychological doctrine of the period and which had just found such a consistent and thoroughgoing exponent in James Mill. Associationism regarded the mind as composed of a great number of elementary units, the "ideas," linked together into combinations of varying degrees of closeness and complexity and continually forming new connections with one another; the phenomena of mind, as revealed by introspection, consisted indeed, it was supposed, in this very process of connection. Histology was now showing that the nervous system, on its side, was composed of innumerable simple units, the cells, linked together by a tangle of connecting fibres, admirably suited, it would seem, to serve as the physical substrate of the "associations" observed in consciousness. What more natural than to suppose that the individual cells somehow corresponded to elementary ideas and the nerve fibres connecting the cells to their associations? That complex ideas corresponded to a group of interconnected cells, and so on? The appearance of an idea in consciousness would then correspond to the occurrence of some process in the corresponding cell or cells, while an association of ideas would imply the passage of an impulse along the fibres linking the cells in question.

It is true that further reflection showed that there were difficul-ties in the way of such a very simple and obvious scheme of correspondence. On the psychological side, for instance, it was difficult to determine the precise nature of the really irreducible and elementary idea that would correspond to a single nerve cell. On the physiological side, cells were not confined to the nervous tissue, but were found throughout the bodies of animals and plants. Within the nervous system they were found not only in the brain but in the spinal cord and in various isolated ganglia, which did not appear to have direct relation to consciousness. Some cells moreover seemed pretty clearly to be concerned with purely motor functions. And, even within the brain itself, the cells in different parts were found to be of different shapes and sizes. These facts and others, seemed to show that the theory of correspondence that so readily suggested itself at a first view, required qualification and elaboration; so much so that the theory has scarcely ever been seriously maintained in its crude form. Nevertheless, the parallel between the complicated ramifications of the nerves and the complicated process of association was so striking that it indirectly exercised a powerful influence in favour of the association psychology, and has continued to do so to the present day. The eventual abandonment of simple associationism was due rather to a realization of its inadequacy on the purely psychological side than to any adverse evidence from physiology. It is true that physiological facts unfavourable to the psycho-physical correspondence just outlined were not far to seek. This view of the correspondence really presupposed a cerebral localiza-tion far more extreme even than that of phrenology, which only sought to localize some thirty-seven faculties, not countless num-bers of ideas; and although, as a scheme of localization it is quite independent of phrenology, and does not stand or fall with it or with any other doctrine of faculties, it was affected by the general arguments against localization, such as that afforded by Flourens's discovery that extirpation of any one region of the brain tends to weaken the function of all the others. Nevertheless, in spite of these difficulties, the view has persisted that the innumerable connections in the brain somehow mirror the equally innumerable relations continually formed within the mind, and further evidence, gradually accumulating through the century, both that from experimental investigations and that from the study of lesions in the human nervous system, is by no means altogether unfavourable to some general conception of this kind.

V. SENSATION AND THE SENSE ORGANS

OUR consideration of the nervous system leads us naturally to the allied subject of the sense organs. Here is a field which, by its very nature, belongs both to psychology and physiology; for it is impossible to deal with the psychology of sensation without taking into account the structure and function of the organs through which sensations come about, while it is profitless to consider these organs except in relation to the psychical impressions of the external world which it is their business to produce. The senses are "the gateways of knowledge"; without them the mind has no materials to work on (a fact which the associationists, especially, had stressed). It might have been supposed, therefore, that the psychologist would make every endeavour to understand the intimate structure and working of the sense organs. Such indeed has been the attitude of psychologists for the last half century and more, an attitude which we owe largely to the influence of such men as Fechner, Helmholtz and Wundt. At the present day, students of psychology learn about the sense organs as a matter of course. Indeed, for two or three decades, the problems of sensation and perception, considered in intimate relation to the function of the relative organs of sensation, constituted actually the major portion of experimental psychology; and in recent years these problems have only appeared to recede in importance, because of our increasing knowledge concerning what we are wont to call the "higher" mental processes. But a hundred years ago the philosophical bias of psychology was too strong to make such an attitude seem obvious or natural. Study of the sense organs clearly involved detailed observation, and psychology was still considered as a series of problems to be thought out at the desk or in the armchair rather than as a body of knowledge to be acquired in the laboratory, the hospital, the school, the consulting-room, the market-place. Hence, in the beginning, nearly all our early knowledge concerning the intimate structure and

49

function of the sense organs came from physiologists. It was only in the second half of the nineteenth century that the experimental psychologist made this department of knowledge peculiarly his own.

Our student, starting his work in 1833, would therefore probably encounter the detailed problems of sensation at a later stage in his studies than would a student of the present day. Nevertheless, when he did come up against these problems, he would find a very considerable collection of facts at his disposal; chiefly, however, in relation to hearing and vision, the available data concerning the other senses being relatively few and uncertain, as indeed (in spite of an all-round increase of knowledge) is still the case at the present time. The knowledge on this subject was, however, less conveniently ordered and summarized than it is for his successor today. Müller had published a book on vision in 1826, and in 1833 was engaged on his great *Textbook*, which, like subsequent textbooks of physiology (and later on of psychology) collected and systematized the information up to date. Treviranus had written a monograph on the senses in 1828, and Bell's *Anatomy*, published in 1803, also contained useful information. Apart from these, however (and Müller's *Textbook* was not yet available), our student would have had to search in a very considerable number of isolated treatises and papers.

What he would gather from these sources would be roughly as follows. The gross anatomy of the eye, including its optical properties, was pretty well understood; the same was true as regards the detailed structure of the retina. The existence of the blind spot had long been known, for King Charles II is said to have demonstrated it to his courtiers to show them what they would look like when their heads were off! At the beginning of the nineteenth century, Bell had shown that the different parts of the spectrum were of unequal brightness, and in 1825 Purkinje had described the phenomenon known by his name, i.e. the increase in the relative brightness of the greens and blues in dim light. The first two of the so-called three laws of colour mixture had been formulated by Newton, who thus knew the properties of complementary colours (the third law was announced by Grassmann in 1853). The use of rotating discs for producing colour mixtures was introduced by Musschenbroek in 1820, though they subsequently became known as Maxwell's discs, when the latter investigator took up and improved the method in 1853. Newton was also aware of the inertia of sensation, i.e. the continuance of a conscious sensory impression after removal of the stimulus. Müller gave a full description of both positive and negative "after-images" ("spectra," as he called them) and of the conditions under which they occur. He also understood the general nature of "light-" and "dark-adaptation," while the general facts concerning the lesser acuity and colour sensibility of the periphery of the retina had been discovered by Sir Thomas Young some thirty years before. Two main colour theories held the field, that of Young, according to which there were three elementary processes, and that of Goethe, who believed in four. These two theories, in a somewhat modified form, provided the basis of the subsequent theories of Helmholtz and Hering respectively, which have remained the two great rival interpretations right up to the present time. As regards the eye as an optical apparatus, the only major point about which there was still much uncertainty was the question of accommodation, or "adaptation" as it was then called. Numerous explanations as to how an image was focused on the retina had been put forward. Some had thought that the whole eyeball altered in length through the action of its muscles, others that the lens moved backward and forward, still others that the convexity of the cornea could change. Müller favoured the first of these views, though he also thought there might be alterations in the curvature of the lens. This last, the now accepted view, seems to have been first put forward by Young, though the mechanism responsible for changes in the lens was only explained later by Helmholtz.

All these facts concerned the function of the single eye. But it had, of course, long been obvious that considerable complications arise from the fact that we have two eyes, and a good deal of progress had already been made in the study of binocular vision. On the neurological side Müller had just given a correct description of the "partial decussation" in the optic chiasma, the fact that the nerves from the right halves of both retinae go to the right half of the brain (which, therefore, since the rays of light cross within each eyeball furnishes the centre for the left half of the total field of vision) and *vice versa*. The muscular mechanism underlying convergence of the eyes was also known, as were the facts of binocular colour rivalry and mixture. Naturally, the principal riddle of binocular vision concerns the question of why, given two eyes, we yet see objects single. Gall, unfortunately wrong as usual, had suggested that we only use one eye at a time —a statement which, as we have since learnt, is only true of certain particular persons and conditions (fostered, for instance, by miscroscopic work). Bell, again a pioneer, suggested the existence of "corresponding points" on the two retinae. It then began to be realized that the majority of objects are in fact seen double, but that we habitually neglect these double images, and that only a particular limited part of the visual field—the horopter—is seen single; Müller and others were, indeed, busy determining the precise form of the horopter at the opening of our period. The full part played by binocular vision in the perception of depth was not yet understood, and this had to wait until the invention of the stereoscope had brought these problems into greater prominence. Wheatstone's first stereoscope was, however, as we have already mentioned, actually invented in 1833, and Brewster's more convenient form followed shortly afterwards. Largely, no doubt, owing to this ignorance of the true significance of "disparation" (the fact that images not actually on the "corresponding points" of the two eyes, but very nearly so, exhibit a peculiarly convincing character of "depth" or three-dimensionality), Müller attributed a greater rôle to the purely psychological aspects of space perception than modern authors do. Even on the psychological side, however, the various factors had not been fully isolated and described.

As regards pathology, the chief purely optical defects of vision were of course known and capable of correction through glasses, but the full explanation of such defects as "old sight" (presbyopia), depending on diminished elasticity of the lens, could not be given, since the mechanism of accommodation was not yet understood. Some of the main facts of colour blindness had been known since the time of Dalton towards the end of the seventeenth century. Both Young and Goethe had discussed these abnormalities of vision, but the facts available were scanty, nor was it realized that there might be several distinct types of the disorder.

Turning now to the sense of hearing, the auditory functions of the outer and middle ear were in general well known, though it was supposed that the three auditory ossicles, the "hammer," "anvil," and "stirrup," which form such a curious feature of the middle ear, merely transmitted sounds like any other solid bodies, and it was not realized that they acted as a system of small levers. The grossest error concerned the functions of the semicircular canals, which, as mentioned earlier, were thought (very naturally) to form part of the auditory apparatus, though Flourens had demonstrated that operative interference with them produced disturbances of equilibrium. Nor was there such an intimate knowledge of the actual end-organs of sense (the terminations of the auditory nerve in the Organ of Corti) as existed in the case of vision. Probably owing to this, there was no well-known theory concerning the elementary qualities of auditory sensation to correspond with Young's and Goethe's colour theories. Helmholtz, when later on he came to formulate his famous theory of hearing, had no older theory of standing to build upon, as in the case of vision. Of the three great psychological correspondences between the nature of the stimulus and the resulting sensation (the amplitude of the air vibrations corresponding to intensity or loudness, their wave-length corresponding to pitch and their shape corresponding to timbre) the first two were known and clearly stated in Müller's *Textbook*, the last one not. With regard to pitch, the upper and lower "limits of hearing" had been determined with more or less exactitude; it was known that the ear could not appreciate air vibrations of less than sixteen or of more than approximately twenty-four thousand vibrations a second. The frequency ratios of the principal musical intervals were also known. With regard to the fact that we have two ears, it was recognized that the possession of this double organ was of assistance in the localization of sounds, and that the direction from which a sound reached the listener was largely, if not entirely, determined by the difference in the intensity of the sound at one ear and the other—a view which is still held today, though it is now recognized that other and subsidiary factors (e.g. phase and timbre differences) may also play a part in localization. Both in sound and vision, therefore, many of the essential facts, as we see them today, were already known, while some of the great riddles of 1833 still remain unsolved or only partly solved. The work of the last hundred years has consisted in the correction of a few serious mistakes and the accumulation of a great mass of further detailed knowledge, often of a quantitative kind. In particular the interest in the measurement of "differential thresholds" (i.e. the determination of the smallest perceptible difference between two stimuli) did not yet exist. This was a feature of the era that was just about to dawn, a feature that was of supreme import- ance, not only for the study of sensation itself, but for the whole development of the experimental method in psychology. For the rest, Helmholtz was the great figure, who, towards the middle of the nineteenth century, was to give the physiology and psycho- logy of sight and hearing, both as regards fact and theory, the general form which we find in our textbooks of today.

Regarding the other senses there is little to say. We have already referred more than once to the muscle sense, the full recognition of which was undoubtedly the principal recent event in this field. Mill, as we have seen, had drawn attention to what he called sensations of disorganization and sensations coming from the alimentary tract, while the sense of touch had been further split up by Bell's treatment of heat and cold as separate qualities of sensation. A new phase in the attitude towards touch was, however, shortly to begin. E. H. Weber, who was destined to play a remarkable rôle in the very earliest stages of experi- mental psychology, was professor of anatomy at Leipzig, and in 1833 was actually finishing a treatise on touch, the *De Tactu*, which appeared in instalments and was published as a whole in the following year. It was here that he reported experiments on the muscle sense, which not only afforded a demonstration of the fact that this sense is independent of touch, but laid the founda- tion of the most famous of all the "laws" of psychology—Weber's Law, as it was afterwards christened by Fechner. He was the first psychologist, so far as we know, to induce his subjects to indulge in the exercise of lifting weights. Owing to the interest and suc- cess of his experiments, hundreds of thousands of weights have since been lifted in psychological laboratories all over the world. In these early observations Weber showed: (1) that smaller differences in weight could be discriminated when the weights were actively lifted than when passively carried on the hand (thus demonstrating the influence of the muscle sense); (2) that in both cases discrimination depended, not upon the absolute, but upon the relative, difference between the two weights (the fraction corresponding to this difference being much smaller with lifted than with carried weights). In these discoveries, seized upon later by Fechner for his own purposes, lay the germ of experimental psychology, the great influence which was to combine empirical with quantitative methods, and to appear in due course as the "new psychology" of the second half of the nineteenth century. Our student could scarcely be expected to pay over-much attention to Weber's modest treatise in its antiquated Latin form. Nevertheless, had he known it, here was the book to which, more than all others, he should have looked for signs of some of the most significant of all the later developments of psychology.

As regards smell and taste, little was known, and indeed little was destined to be known until much later, while even today the data available are relatively meagre. In the case of smell, there were attempts at classification, notably that of Linnaeus, by an extension of which Zwaardemaker later constructed the best-known classification of the present time. Weber, with head bent back and a disregard of comfort that was to prove a permanent characteristic of experimental psychologists, was having eau de Cologne poured down his nose, in order to show that liquids are in themselves incapable of causing smell. Bell knew that the organs of taste were situated in the papillae of the tongue, and Horn, in 1825, had gone an important step further in showing that the various papillae are differently sensible to different tastes; the current classification of tastes into sweet, sour, salt and bitter had, however, not as yet been made. In the same year Brillat-Savarin had published (anonymously) his *Physiologie du Gout*, in which he made a remarkable attempt to treat gastronomy as a fine art. Though it contributed but little to our knowledge of the sensory basis of taste, this delightful classic is full of psychological wisdom, and may be regarded as one of the first essays in the field of scientific aesthetics—an essay which, in its own particular department, remains easily the foremost achievement even at the present day.

BEFORE we close this survey of psychology as it presented itself to our student a hundred years ago, we must take an extremely brief glance at one other aspect of the subject, the aspect that has since come to be called abnormal psychology. Not that there is much to chronicle. One of the most striking differences between the psychology of today and that of 1833 is that at the earlier date psychologists had as yet scarcely realized that they could learn anything of value from the study of the disordered mind. At that particular time the abnormal was indeed under an especially dark cloud, for Mesmerism had just been once again exposed, as not due to "animal magnetism" but to "imagination," and psychologists did not realize that what had failed to be a problem for the physicists might be a very important problem for themselves. Mesmer himself, after a stormy career, had died in 1815. He had in his lifetime enjoyed all the popularity of a healer who has new and occult methods at his disposal, had refused an offer of 20,000 francs from the French Government to reveal his "secret" (which indeed he did not understand himself), had been ignored or reported on unfavourably by the medical profession and had finally been denounced as an impostor. Mesmer was too firmly wedded to the theory of "magnetism" to envisage anything like the modern theory of "suggestion," and indeed the modern discovery (if it can be called a discovery: in a sense it had been known right down the ages) of enhanced suggestibility during a special sleeplike or "hypnotic" state seems to be due rather to one of his followers, the Marquis de Puységur than to himself. The first scientific commission on Mesmerism had been held in France in 1784, Lavoisier and Benjamin Franklin being members. It had correctly diagnosed the fact that Mesmer's so-called "magnetism" had nothing to do with the magnetism known to physics, but, as was to be expected, had not realized that the "imagination" apparently involved in Mesmer's cures might be an interesting matter for investigation in itself. Between Mesmer's death and the opening of our period two further commissions had been held. The first of these seems to have investigated with unusual care and impartiality. After several years' work, the members reported that the cures were genuine, but they refused to commit themselves as to the precise nature of "animal magnetism," and even indicated that they had evidence of quite a number of mysterious phenomena which they were not in a position to explain. This report was far too favourable for that large majority of the medical profession which, quite understandably, regarded Mesmerism as a nuisance. A third committee was appointed, and its report was much more in accordance with official expectations, in that the chief stress was laid upon the statement that animal magnetism itself was not so much an incorrect interpretation of the facts as a downright hoax. In 1833 our student would be living in the scientific atmosphere created by this last report, and it is unlikely therefore that he would include Mesmerism among the subjects of his studies.

As regards the more permanent conditions of abnormality there was very little knowledge of a scientific kind. The division into the three fundamental types of today, insanity (the psychoses), functional disorders (neuroses) and mental deficiency, had not yet been made, though a few of the more prominent types of insanity had been recognized and described. The father of scientific psychiatry was Philippe Pinel, who was appointed to the Bicêtre in Paris in 1792, and struck off the chains of its inmates. The current explanation of insanity was in terms of demoniacal possession, a condition for which the afflicted were regarded as at any rate in part responsible, so that treatment in their case consisted, as in that of criminals, in scourging and incarceration. Pinel taught his contemporaries to look upon insanity as a disease rather than as a manifestation of uncanny and diabolical powers which afflicted only the wicked. This abolition of the view that the psychoses were due to supernatural agency, inaccessible to ordinary human understanding, was an essential preliminary to the scientific treatment of insanity: at one step it brought the phenomena of insanity within the fields of psychology, physiology and medicine. But Pinel did more than this: he attempted to bring some kind of order into our conceptions of the different kinds of insanity, and thus worked out the first systematic classifications, a task in which he was followed by Esquirol, whose writings, which date from 1817 onwards, provided the real foundation on which the psychiatry of the nineteenth century was built. Pinel had also been indirectly concerned with the first attempts at the systematic study of mental deficiency, although Itard was really the pioneer in this field. Itard was originally concerned with methods of teaching the deaf, and in 1798 was consulted in the case of the "wild boy of Aveyron," who had been found by some hunters when he was about ten years old, and who had apparently been leading for some years a solitary existence removed from all human society. For five years Itard laboured to make a social and educated being of this savage foundling. Dominated as he was by the associationist psychology, according to which experience was the sole factor which needed to be taken into account, Itard had confidently anticipated success in this endeavour. Pinel, with greater insight, had been more doubtful of the outcome, and predicted success only in so far as the boy was free of intrinsic mental defect. As it turned out, Pinel's more modest expectations were nearer the truth. In spite of Itard's prolonged efforts, the wild boy never learned to play a normal rôle in civilized society. He was, however, able to acquire some habits more in keeping with his new environment and, although in itself largely unsuccessful, Itard's work was epoch-making, inasmuch as it constituted the first systematic attempt to train the feeble-minded. Largely through the efforts of Itard's pupil, Séguin, the work was carried on with increasing insight and success. In 1828 a special institute for the education of the mentally defective was established in Paris and in 1842 Séguin became its head. From that time onward the need of special pedagogic methods for this class of persons became widely recognized and special schools sprang up in many countries.

A century ago all these activities lay well aside from the traditional path of academic psychology. We have, however, all along taken the liberty of supposing our student to be gifted with a certain power of special insight for future developments. If thus endowed, he might have dimly recognized that these events in the field of abnormality were big with promise for the future.

II

1833–1860

I. THE HUNDRED YEARS—OUR PROGRAMME

WE have now completed the first portion of our task. Looking
through the eyes of our imaginary student we have studied in
main outline the psychology of a hundred years ago. We have
seen how, in the years immediately preceding our chosen date,
1833, a whole series of thinkers of distinction and originality had
consolidated old positions, indicated new problems, and hinted at
the possibility of novel methods and fresh points of view. We
have seen, too, how links were beginning to be forged between
psychology and other lines of study, hitherto distinct; how psychologists were beginning to realize the intimate connection between
their own discipline and that of physiology, a connection that
mirrors the intimate relationship between mind and nervous
system; how there had been a dawning insight into the possible
practical applications of psychology especially in the sphere of
education; and how a beginning had been made in the study of
mental disease and of abnormal conditions of the mind, though
the importance of these facts had as yet scarcely been grasped by
those who might have called themselves psychologists. A hundred years ago psychology was very much alive; there was a large
and growing body, both of fact and theory, which, as we now
see, was definitely "psychological." But as an independent science
it had only just come into being; its independence was recognized
by very few, even of the learned; and by them its boundaries
and possibilities were ill defined. Looking back, however, we can
see that it had started. Our business now is to follow its course
through the intervening century, to study its growth and its
gradually increasing recognition, its widening field and its
increasing diversity of outlook and of method, until it reaches

59

the stage of vigorous, sprawling infancy which seems to be its condition as a science at the present day.

This task itself may be conveniently undertaken in three stages—stages which appear to correspond to psychology's own phases of development. The first and shortest stage is from 1833 to 1860, a period in which the tendencies already noted continued to develop, but in which there are no startling new departures, no sudden changes of direction, no full realization of the potentialities already visible at the beginning of our "hundred years."

Two great events mark the inception of the second period; the birth of experimental psychology through the work and influence of Fechner, an influence which, in its distinctively psychological bearings is usually held to date from the publication of his *Elemente der Psychophysik* in 1860; and the advent of the evolutionary point of view following the appearance of Darwin's *Origin of Species* in the previous year. Together, the experimental and genetic standpoints gave a new stimulus and a new direction to the labours of psychologists and completed the separation of psychology from philosophy that was implicit in the work of so many writers of the first half of the nineteenth century. In this period, therefore, which lasts till 1900, we see the steady progress of the "new" experimental psychology, and the permeation of psychology by the idea of development—as manifested both in the race and in the individual.

The turn of the century may conveniently be looked upon as the end of this second period and the beginning of the third and last. From now onwards we find psychology embarking on the process of specialization incidental to the growth of new schools, each school having its own peculiar methods and outlook and even to a considerable extent its own peculiar jargon, so that the total picture becomes one of increasingly violent and bewildering activity; eventually, indeed, there are "psychologies" rather than "psychology," and students begin to complain that what is taught in one centre bears little resemblance to that which they have learnt in another. It is the period of psycho-analysis, behaviourism and *Gestalt*, of mental tests and the psychology of individual differences, of "factors," of reflexology, and of the application of psychological methods and concepts to the hitherto quite foreign fields of industry and commerce. The Great War cuts right across the middle of this period, but, beyond stirring up a general interest in "applied" psychology, seems merely to quicken the tempo of development without greatly altering its course. It is the period in which we are actually living, and which is, therefore, least easy for us to envisage in its true perspective. Our understanding of it must necessarily be imperfect and confused, not only because of its own inherent complexity, but because we see it out of focus. What we see, however, is sufficient to show us that psychologists are intensely busy on a multitude of new enterprises; how many of these enterprises will prove worth while, above all, how far they will go towards the construction of an enduring, coherent and satisfying scientific structure, it is impossible as yet to tell.

In surveying the first two, at any rate, of these three periods, we can, to some extent, avail ourselves of the main categories which served us in our review of psychology as it would have presented itself to the student of a hundred years ago. In the first place there is pure psychology, the direct descendant of the more philosophically tinged psychology of earlier times. In another category is the study of the brain, nervous system and sense organs, in so far as this study falls within the purview of psychology. In between these two may appropriately be placed the new psychology of experiment when this comes upon the stage. Only a few indications of it will appear in our first period, and both in this and in the second period it is a relatively easy matter to consider it apart from the continuing stream of the earlier psychology based on general observation, casual introspection and *a priori* speculation. In the third period, however, the boundary between experimental and "systematic" psychology (as the older tradition has sometimes been called) soon becomes obscured, and the majority of the schools that are such a feature of this period have not only their characteristic theories but their characteristic empirical procedures. In its early stages experimental psychology largely overlaps in subject-matter with the physiological study of sensation and the sense organs—but from the very start, as we shall see, the experimental psychologists had their own special interests, viewpoint and method of approach, which were different from, and in some ways much wider than, those of their physiological colleagues. A hundred years ago, indeed during the greater part—perhaps the whole— of the first of our three periods, it seemed as though most of the fresh stimuli to psychological development would come from physiology: it might even appear as though the psychologist were destined to become a humble picker-up of scraps from the physiologist's table, and some such anticipation was voiced from time to time. The advent of experimental psychology prevented any such development, and indeed made the "new" psychologist (as he later on came to be called) to some extent an invader of the physiologist's domain; for there is no doubt that, with his deeper interest in the sense organs as the very instruments of knowledge, the providers of the material of the mind (as the sensations were regarded by many), he carried on the study of these organs with greater pertinacity and ingenuity than the physiologist would have done, if left to his own interests and devices. In the fourth place comes the category of abnormal psychology. At the beginning of our first period this branch of our subject was, as we have seen, at a low ebb. After a good beginning in the hands of Pinel and Esquirol, the unfortunate attitude of the mesmerists and of their opponents had brought the whole matter into disrepute in scientific circles. Soon, however, fresh champions of mesmerism were to arise, this time of a scientific calibre to compel respect; while the uses to which the mesmeric trance was put made it inevitable that some serious attention should be paid to it by doctors and psychologists. A little later came a whole series of brilliant workers who linked up hypnotism (as it now was called) with the general study of mental disease; while eventually (especially in the hands of the psychoanalysts) the findings of psycho-pathology poured over, in a copious flow, into the field of normal psychology, so that what had started as a modest method for the treatment of certain forms of nervous disease became a powerful instrument apparently capable of throwing a strong (and often disconcerting) light upon the obscurer workings of the human mind in all or any of its manifestations. At the end of our last period, therefore, the boundary between abnormal and pure (normal) psychology is in turn becoming blurred—a reminder of the fact that all our categories and classifications are in the last resort mere arbitrary matters of convenience, and may at any moment require revision in the light of new developments.

II. SYSTEMATIC PSYCHOLOGY—J. S. MILL, BAIN, LOTZE

TURNING now definitely to the first of our three periods, we find that "pure" psychology during this period is dominated by a few principal figures, notably J. S. Mill, Bain and Lotze. If we were to insist on a strictly chronological account, we should have to include Herbert Spencer also; for the first edition of his *Principles of Psychology* appeared in 1855. But in spirit he belongs distinctly to our second period, for his whole outlook is in its very essence evolutionary, and indeed he became an influential figure in psychology only after the publication of the second and revised edition of his *Principles* (now incorporated as an integral part of his *Synthetic Philosophy*) in the early seventies. John Stuart Mill's work also falls partly in our first and partly in our second period, his chief contributions to psychology being found in his *Logic*, published in 1843, and in the *Examination of Sir William Hamilton's Philosophy*, published in 1865. In spirit, however, he belongs to the first period rather than the second. His most influential addition to psychological theory was, moreover, beyond all doubt, his doctrine of "mental chemistry" enunciated in the earlier work.

In conformity with his freer, tenderer and less pedantic nature, he set about, in this doctrine, to diminish the rigours of the uncompromising associationism of his father. For the rigid mechanical scheme of interaction between unitary ideas, in terms of which James Mill had described the working of the mind, J. S. Mill substituted a "chemical" conception, according to which complex thoughts and feelings were indeed generated by, but not in all cases merely composed of, simpler elements. In his own words: "the effect of concurring causes is not always precisely the sum of the effects of those causes when separate, not even always an effect of the same kind with them. . . . The laws of the phenomena of the mind are sometimes analogous to mechanical, but sometimes also to chemical laws. When many

63

impressions or ideas are operating in the mind together, there sometimes takes place a process of the same kind to chemical combination. When impressions have been so often experienced in conjunction that each of them calls up readily and instantaneously the ideas of the whole group, those ideas sometimes melt and coalesce into one another, and appear not several ideas but one. . . . The Complex Idea, formed by the blending together of several simple ones, should, when it really appears simple (that is when the separate elements are not consciously distinguished in it), be said to *result from* or be *generated by* the simpler ideas, not to *consist* of them."

This whole doctrine leads to an attitude of lesser dogmatism and cocksureness, a lesser confidence in the sufficiency of association as an all-explanatory principle. To James Mill everything was supremely simple, once you were in possession of the master key: his son, however, realized that the operation of this key was not always easy and straightforward; he even suspected there might be locks it would not fit at all. Thus in his *Logic* J. S. Mill expresses a doubt as to whether even mental chemistry can adequately account for the generation of *belief*, a mental state which he clearly sees to imply something more than mere inseparable association, and which he seeks to explain rather by "the power which an idea had obtained over the will by association." Here we see the beginning of that realization of the importance of conation, which was one of the chief rocks on which associationism was ultimately wrecked. Another adumbration of more modern psychology is to be found in his recognition of variations in clearness of mental content, a matter which was, of course, given full weight in Herbart's doctrine of apperception, but which had played but a small part in the doctrines of the associationists.

On the positive side, J. S. Mill emphasized the importance of attention in connection both with feeling and with will; but he endeavours to look upon attention as itself dependent on the laws of association. He does not see, as others later on began to see, that attention is itself a manifestation of conation, a selective power dependent on our reflexes, wishes and interests, that introduces a new, complicating (and, at first sight, arbitrary) factor into the relatively simple scheme of the association psychology. On the negative side, the passage we have quoted implies, even though it does not clearly express, another doctrine—that of *obliviscence*, according to which "when a number of ideas suggest one another by association with such certainty and rapidity as to coalesce together in a group, all those members of a group which remain long without being especially attended to, have a tendency to drop out of consciousness." They may even "disappear from consciousness as completely as if they had never formed part of the series." The way is here prepared for the problem of the unconscious and of the "psycho-physical dispositions" of a later date. Finally, Mill's lesser confidence in *a priori* principles shows itself in his insistence on the necessity of actual empirical study of the process of association. He here anticipates by several decades the experimental investigations into memory and association, investigations which he did not live to see, for he died in 1873, six years before the founding of the first psychological laboratory, and twelve years before the appearance of Ebbinghaus's epoch-making study *Über das Gedächtnis*.

Apart from these innovations (innovations which were perhaps of greater import than he himself even realized), Mill added little to the general associationist tradition. He was not satisfied with the laws of contiguity and similarity, still less with either one of these alone. In 1843 he added a law of "intensity" and in 1865 he spoke of "frequency" and "inseparability." But he did not clearly and consistently distinguish between primary or qualitative laws and secondary or quantitative laws, and his treatment of this part of his subject is less thoroughgoing, less influential, and above all far less modern in spirit, than had been that of Thomas Brown. By nature J. S. Mill was a brilliant and genial rather than a ruthless or consistent thinker. He saw the deficiencies of associationism as expounded by his father, but he did not dare to follow up his own revolutionary thoughts to the extent of abandoning or radically reconstructing the old doctrine where such a course seemed indicated by his own discoveries.

If J. S. Mill sometimes lacked courage and consistency as a thinker (though he was one of the most influential writers upon logic, he is one of the easiest to convict of logical fallacy), Alexander Bain on his part, though dogged and persistent, lacked originality. He owes his place in history to his power of laborious collation and classification of data and systematic expression of results rather than to any striking ability either to discover facts

C

or to interpret them. And yet Bain must for ever remain a figure of significance; for he was in a certain sense the first psychologist —the first, that is, to make psychology his life work, the first for whom the study of the mind appeared as a task worthy, in itself and for its own sake, of a man's best efforts. Hitherto psychology had been carried on by philosophers, physiologists, physicians and others, as a subject which they had come across, as it were, incidentally in the course of their main preoccupations. To Bain an understanding of the human mind was itself the end, not merely a branch of knowledge which had to be acquired or dealt with on the way to, or in connection with, some other undertaking. It is true, of course, that Bain was no professional teacher of psychology; he was merely Professor of Logic at Aberdeen. Even this chair was obtained by him only after much waiting and many fruitless applications for other posts—disappointments for which his liberalism and the fact that he was not a communicant of the Church are supposed to be responsible. Furthermore, he was not appointed until after his chief books were written. But so new a discipline as psychology, which was by tradition an accessory to other studies rather than a "subject" in itself, could in 1860 (the date of Bain's appointment) scarcely expect to enjoy the luxury of a teacher for itself. And in this respect Bain suffered no greater hardship than many psychologists of later date, for well into the twentieth century, and even at the present day, University teachers, whose main works and interests, like those of Bain, are psychological, are to be found occupying posts dedicated to Philosophy, Logic, Education, or some other subject of more ancient tradition or (supposedly at any rate) more urgent practical importance.

Bain is of significance not only because he was the first man to make psychology the major interest of his life, but also because he was the author of the first textbook of psychology written in the modern manner—a textbook to which (so far as other literary occupations would allow him) he devoted some ten years of his life and which appeared in two parts, *The Senses and the Intellect* in 1855 and the *Emotions and the Will* in 1859. Though the former work caused its publisher some worry by the slowness of its sale at first, both were eventually very successful, were revised and re-edited on several occasions and remained the standard British texts until superseded by the works of Sully and

Stout at the end of the nineteenth century. Bain, in fact, really determined the form in which the majority of general treatises, up to and including very recent years, were to be written. Thus Bain's books seem but little antiquated even to the modern student. And indeed they stand, as Boring so well puts it, "at a corner of the development of psychology, with philosophical psychology stretching out behind and experimental physiological psychology lying ahead in a new direction. The psychologist of the twentieth century can read much of Bain with hearty approval; perhaps John Locke could have done the same."

The essential feature of Bain's two textbooks can be indicated in relatively few words. In the first place Bain recognized the importance for psychology of the study of the brain, the nervous system and the sense organs. Hence a considerable part of his introductory section is physiological in tone. The physiology, moreover, is not general but specific: he is concerned, not so much with the nervous system as the general "substrate" of mental life, but rather with the structure and function of the particular parts of the brain, of the sensory and motor nerves, the sense organs, the reflex arcs, the muscles. From Bain's standpoint it seemed very clear that the psychologist of the future was to be more of a physiologist than a philosopher.

In the second place Bain adopted the view that mental events and the brain processes that correspond to them are two parallel series; there is no interaction of the one with the other, but the double series of events can be studied in either aspect. He thus made popular the doctrine of "psycho-physical parallelism," which in one form or another, explicit or implied, has dominated the majority of textbooks ever since. He was, it would seem, driven to this position by the law of the conservation of (physical) energy, which was being much discussed at the time he wrote. Any interaction between mind and body would break the continuity of the physical system and therefore constitute an exception to the law; such interaction, therefore, could not be admitted. The same arguments have weighed largely with all subsequent upholders of the parallelist theory.

In the third place Bain's psychology was associationist, tempered by the admission of mental activity and spontaneity. He adopted the two main laws of contiguity and similarity, but stressed conation more than any previous associationist had done.

In particular he dwelt in detail on the instincts, which, as a result of his treatment, held an undisputed place in the inventory of the human mind, until challenged by the American champions of reflexology in quite recent years. In his insistence on conation Bain laid great stress on movement. Movement gives rise to sensation and this explains the phenomenological aspect of the will. It is generally considered, however, that Bain hedged on the problem of the freedom of the will. He pointed out that under the influence of the instincts the nervous system is capable of spontaneous action—action which, therefore, seemed compatible with "freedom." On the other hand, this spontaneous action still takes place within the closed causal system of the physical universe and "freedom" can therefore at best apply only to the psychic side of the parallel series, and even here is apparently in the last resort reducible to the sensations of "innervation" that, he thought, accompany actual, intended, or contemplated movement. Perhaps, as has been suggested, Bain, with his painful experience of *odium theologicum*, was willing to leave a little ambiguity in the term "spontaneous action," a term which Darwin complained that he could never understand.

Though, like J. S. Mill, Bain had emancipated himself from the crasser over-simplifications of the associationists, their tradition still sometimes drags heavily at his feet and compels him to perform *tours de force* which have exposed him to the ridicule of later writers. Thus, writing some thirty years after the appearance of *The Emotions and the Will*, William James pours scorn upon the "silliness" of the attempt to derive sociability and parental love from the pleasures of touch. In Bain's view "touch is both the alpha and omega of affection," and he thought that, to account for the satisfaction we feel in "the companionship of other sentient creatures, over and above the help afforded by them in obtaining the necessaries of life," we need posit nothing but "the primary and independent pleasure of the animal embrace." James pertinently asks "why a satin cushion kept at about 98° F. would not on the whole give us the pleasure in question more cheaply than our babies do"; and most modern psychologists would call in the more complicated apparatus of instinct and sentiment before they would attempt to give an answer. Bain, in fact, we should now be inclined to think, was grossly over-estimating the power of association and under-estimating that of instinct. Nevertheless, as is shown by Freud's theory of the "component instincts," many of them related to specially sensitive zones of the body, and Watson's study of the "love" reactions of very young children, there may have been an important element of truth in Bain's contention, clumsy and strained as it appears.

Determining, as he did, to such a large extent the form in which modern psychological doctrine should be cast, our debt to Bain is greater than we sometimes realize. James himself, indeed, was indebted to Bain for the point of view so eloquently expressed in his famous section on habit (the finest piece of sermonizing to be found in psychological literature), for Bain stressed habit as it had never been stressed before; while Thorndike and others owe to Bain the first clear formulation of what later became known as the "law of effect" (the "stamping in" of movements under the influence of pleasure); though in both these cases Bain himself borrowed something from the work of Spencer.

Though Bain was not a great thinker, in the sense of being either brilliant or profound, he yet performed a very valuable task. He gathered up the new tendencies that were developing, related them to what had long been known, knit them into a whole, explained this whole in an attractive fashion, thereby creating general interest in it, and thus started modern psychology fairly on its way. Except among a few philosophers with special prejudices of their own, there was from his time onwards a general recognition of the fact that psychology was an independent branch of knowledge, with outlook, methods, problems all distinctively its own. His achievement shows how great may be the value of a quiet, persevering mind, which devotes itself to the task of collation and of synthesis in a critical early stage of the career of a new science.

Hermann Lotze cannot be said to be a psychologist in the sense that Bain was one. But he was, to a rather unique extent, both physiologist and philosopher, with psychology emerging as an important side issue from his major lines of interest. In 1844 Lotze, at the early age of twenty, succeeded to the chair of philosophy at Göttingen, left vacant by the death of Herbart. This chair has been a famous one, for Lotze in his turn was succeeded in 1881 by G. E. Müller, who held it until 1921. Lotze was a prolific writer in the field of philosophy, psychology, physiology and logic. He never himself published a general text-book of psychology systematically covering the whole field, as Bain did, but he lectured on the subject for thirty-seven years, and immediately after his death his lecture notes were published and even translated into English. His most influential work on psychology was, however, his *Medicinische Psychologie*, published in 1852. In this book he stressed the view, as Bain did three years later, that the mind and the nervous system must be studied in relation to one another. At the same time he held that physiology could never afford an explanation of mind—a position which, as Murphy remarks, seems a commonplace to us today, but which was perhaps a wise admonishment at a time when the rapid growth of new knowledge on the physiological side was beginning to prove a little intoxicating to the materialistically minded. To Lotze also belongs the credit of being among the first to realize the importance for human psychology of a study of the animal mind and of abnormal conditions; though his actual additions to our knowledge under these headings are of no very great significance.

His most famous single contribution to psychology was in the field of space perception, where he developed his theory of "local signs." Since the time of Berkeley and before, there had been .much discussion as to how far our perception of space is an un-analysable capacity or function of the mind (as, for instance, Kant had thought), or how far it can be analysed into simpler non-spatial elements, from which space perception is generated or built up; a discussion which, in some form or other, has been continued till our day. Although he held that we are endowed from the beginning with some capacity for apprehending the external world in terms of space, Lotze believed that our fully developed space perception is built up by a process of association from sensory clues, themselves of a non-spatial kind. In the case of vision, these clues were, he thought, to be found in the reflex tendency of the eye to move in such a way that the image of any object that interests us at the moment is brought into the point of clearest vision at the fovea. For every point on the retina this movement is a different one; hence we have an orderly and graded series of muscular sensations capable of being worked up into the orderly continuum that is space as we "perceive" it. In the case of tactual space, the "local signs" are provided by the peculiarities of touch on different parts of the skin. These peculiarities are dependent on the varying structure of the exterior of the body: some parts, lying above bony structures, are hard; others are soft. Tension and curvature, too, vary at different points. Each stimulus, therefore, produces a different sensory effect according to the point at which it impinges on the skin. Furthermore, in movement of an object over the surface of the body, the successive local signs come to indicate adjacent regions, so that here also a continuum is formed; which in course of time becomes linked up with the spatial continuum of vision. Both in the spatial and the visual sphere, actual movement eventually becomes unnecessary, the *tendency* to movement, even though unconscious, being sufficient for the purpose. Lotze thus came up against the necessity of positing unconscious mental processes; and subsequent research in the sphere of space perception has only served to increase the apparent inevitability of his assumption. Our fairly exact knowledge, under normal circumstances, of the relative positions of our trunk and limbs—a knowledge which enables us, for instance, to place our finger, even when blindfold, unhesitatingly upon a small point of the skin that has just been stimulated—really seems to be derived from a great number of sensory impressions from the skin and joints and muscles, impressions which are marvellously co-ordinated so as to permit of the desired movement, but co-ordinated in such a way that their integration seems to take place almost entirely below the threshold of consciousness.

Apart from this, however, Lotze's spatial theories have in later years been generally looked upon as ingenious rather than convincing. There are many points upon which they do not provide an altogether satisfying answer. Thus, to the objection that, owing to the bilateral symmetry of the body, corresponding spots on the right and left halves should often be confused, Lotze could only reply that the body is not perfectly symmetrical and the corresponding spots are in consequence never exactly alike in structure or in "feel." Perhaps in this, as in other matters, Lotze's achievement lay in stimulating interest in problems, rather than in finding their solutions. Coming at the time they did, his writings undoubtedly exercised considerable influence on the course of psychological thought. Even more so, perhaps, his

lectures and personal teaching. Among later psychologists, three
of note—Brentano, Stumpf and G. E. Müller—were Lotze's
pupils, and the two latter dedicated books to him. In the near
future many books were to appear from the standpoint of
"physiological" psychology. Lotze's *Medicinsche Psychologie* was
the prototype of these; although more metaphysically oriented
than the majority of its successors, it was this book that set the
fashion for systematic treatment of the detailed and intimate
relationship between the mind and nervous system.

III. PHYSIOLOGICAL PSYCHOLOGY—J. MÜLLER,
HELMHOLTZ, WEBER, FECHNER

TURNING now to our second heading of the anatomy and physiology of the nervous system, we find that, in the period 1833–1860, progress lay chiefly in the direction of a better understanding of the detailed structure and function of individual nervous units rather than in fresh discoveries concerning localization of function in the brain. We have seen how, just at the beginning of this period, improvements in the microscope led to a clear differentiation between cells and fibres and a realization of the fact that the grey matter of the brain was composed largely of cells. Histological work of this kind was carried on vigorously throughout the period, stimulated from time to time by the discovery of fresh methods of making microscopical preparations. In this way the details of cell structure gradually became clear. Meanwhile, physiological research was throwing light upon the functional relations of the different parts of a nerve. In 1839 Nasse found that if a nerve trunk is severed in the middle of its course, the peripheral end degenerates, while the central end does not. Thirteen years later, in 1852, Waller interpreted this fact to mean that every fibre was connected with a nerve cell and that the cell has some sort of trophic function. Waller also showed that the so-called "secondary degeneration" of the peripheral end of the severed nerve could be used as a very valuable clue whereby to trace the course of the nerve, by following the line of degeneration, wherever it might lead. In this way it became possible to plot the course of nerve, with an ease and accuracy hitherto impossible.

By far the most spectacular discovery within the field of nerve physiology was, however, the measurement of the speed of the nervous impulse by Helmholtz in 1850. Hitherto estimates of this velocity had differed widely, but had for the most part agreed that it was very high. In Müller's *Textbook* we even find one estimate, according to which it was eleven million miles a

second, or nearly sixty times the velocity of light! Figures of this
order were arrived at by assuming that the rate of flow for "animal spirits" in the nerves and for blood in the arteries would be
the same for vessels of the same size and would vary inversely
with the diameter of the vessel; a good example of the danger of
calculation by analogy, for of course nothing was known concerning the nature of the assumed animal spirits. Müller himself was
duly cautious of all such estimates and indeed suspected that
accurate knowledge on this subject would for ever be beyond our
reach. "We shall probably," he wrote, "never attain the power
of measuring the velocity of nervous action, for we have not the
opportunity of comparing its propagation through immense space,
as we have in the case of light." And yet a few years later the task
had been accomplished by one of his own former pupils. Helmholtz's procedure was in reality very simple and straightforward,
though it is one that would scarcely occur to anybody obsessed by
the prevalent idea that the speed was enormously great, for
Helmholtz's methods would have been inadequate, had the current estimates been true. He had recently invented the graphic
method of recording muscular contractions on a revolving drum.
The only further step was to take a muscle with its motor nerve
attached—a "nerve-muscle preparation"—and measure the
delay of the muscle twitch for different lengths of the nerve, the
time being recorded by the traces made by a tuning-fork upon
the drum.

The nerve-muscle preparation used in this case was provided
by the frog; but for his work on sensory nerves Helmholtz resorted to the human subject, and at the same time introduced a
method that was to become famous in psychology—the reaction
experiment. This, as is pretty generally known, was a contribution to psychology from astronomy. In 1796 Maskelyne, the then
Astronomer Royal at Greenwich, dismissed his assistant Kinnebrook because the latter appeared to be inaccurate in his observation of stellar transits. Some seventeen years later it occurred
to Bessel, an astronomer at Konigsberg, that the difference
between the observations of Maskelyne and Kinnebrook might
be due to personal factors. He compared his own observations
with those of fellow astronomers and showed that individual
differences in the speed of reaction indeed existed. This work led,
later on, to two definite lines of research in the young science of

experimental psychology: (1) the so-called "complication" experiment, in which an endeavour was made to say with which particular item in a series of auditory impressions a particular visual impression had synchronized, or *vice versa*; this being an experimental reproduction of the conditions involved in observing a stellar transit with the method then employed; (2) the reaction experiment, in which a particular voluntary movement is carried out as soon as possible after the perception of a particular prearranged stimulus. In 1850 early experiments along these lines, still chiefly conducted by astronomers, were sufficiently known to Helmholtz to suggest their application to his own problem of determining the speed of transmission in the sensory nerves. Helmholtz stimulated a man on the toe and on the thigh, and noted the difference in the time between stimulation and response by the hand in the two cases.

By these methods he found that the speed of transmission along the motor nerve of the frog was about ninety feet per second and for the sensory nerves of the man something between fifty and one hundred feet per second; far from travelling quicker than light, the nervous impulse appeared to be slower even than sound. It was shown by this discovery that man's body does not instantly obey his mind. Thought and movement follow one another at an appreciable interval, instead of being practically simultaneous as had previously been thought. Once this was realized, there was opened up a whole series of chronometric problems which eventually kept the experimenters busy for several decades—problems concerning individual differences (which had been the original point of departure), concerning the relative delays caused in different parts of the sensori-motor apparatus (sense-organ, sensory nerve, brain, motor nerve, muscle), or concerning the effect of different kinds and different intensities of stimuli. Helmholtz's discovery also had an effect of a more general order in emphasizing the distinction between mind and body. The conscious personality could no longer, by any stretch of imagination, be regarded as a matter of the entire organism; but became, even more definitely than before, correlated with the brain; while the functions of the nerves as conductors, linking the various parts of the body together, became all the more arresting. Now that it was known that they required a measurable period in which to perform the process of bringing one part of the periphery of the body into communication with another part or with the brain, interest was naturally stimulated as regards the *nature* of the nervous impulse, the *speed* of which was known.

Immediately after this striking discovery, Helmholtz began to turn his attention to sensation and sense-physiology, especially to vision. In 1851 he invented the ophthalmoscope, which permitted the observer to look directly into the eye. At about the same time he took over and amplified Young's tri-colour theory of vision, soon to be known as the Young-Helmholtz theory, and embarked on the task of writing a textbook on vision, which eventually appeared as the *Handuch der Physiologischen Optik*, the greatest classic in the whole domain of sense perception. This work gave full scope to Helmholtz's threefold gifts as physicist, physiologist and psychologist. The book was published in three parts, appearing in 1856, 1860 and 1866 respectively. Both chronologically and scientifically it belongs to the second of our three periods rather than the first; for it, together with an almost equally important textbook on hearing, *Die Lehre von den Tonempfindungen*, published in 1863, constitutes by general admission one of the great influences in the development of the "new" experimental method in psychology. More detailed consideration of Helmholtz's contributions to the study of sensation can therefore quite properly be deferred till we deal with this second period. One small matter, however, may be noticed here. His public adoption of Young's theory of vision dates from 1852, and in the course of his treatment of the subject Helmholtz made an extension of Müller's doctrine of specific energies, by applying the principle to differences of quality within a single sense department. In the present case three distinct sets of nervous fibres were postulated, the stimulation of which caused the sensations of red, green and violet respectively. Through his great influence this extension of the original doctrine has become associated with the name of Helmholtz. The credit for the first general statements of the extension belongs, however, to Natanson and Volkmann, who came forward in 1844 with the view that the doctrine logically implies that there must be separate nerves not only for every main modality of sense but also for every elementary quality that can be distinguished within each modality. Thus, they argued, the nerves of touch must be distinct from those of temperature, while the sensation of blue must involve different nerves from those involved in yellow, the sensation of sweet different nerves from those involved in sour or bitter.

The most important work of all, however, from the point of view of its influence on the future development of psychology, was that carried out by E. H. Weber in the sphere of touch. We have already noted his early work, the *De Tactu*, published in 1834, which contained the observations on the muscle sense which paved the way, in Fechner's hands, for the formulation of Weber's Law. Twelve years later, in 1846, appeared another book, *Der Tastsinn und das Gemeingefühl*, which contained a more detailed and extended study of this and other matters. According to Weber, touch (*Tastsinn*) is found on the skin only, while common sensibility (*Gemeingefühl*) is found both on the skin and in other (internal) regions of the body; for Weber recognized that, not only the surface, but also much of the inside of the body, was supplied with sensory nerves. Common sensibility included pain and sensations from the muscles (indeed, he considered the two to be allied, since strong muscular contractions, as in cramp or childbirth, can be intensely painful); while touch itself included sensations of pressure, temperature and locality. Weber recognized that the sense of locality (*Ortssinn*) was different and less elementary than the sense of pressure and that it depended to some extent on the activity of the mind. But he was evidently unwilling to embark on any full description of the "higher" functions; so that his views on this point were never quite fully developed. He was, however, much interested in temperature, and made many original observations in this field. He regarded heat and cold as opposite extremes within a single sense series, analogous to white and black in the field of vision. In this respect he differed from Charles Bell before him and from the great majority of writers after him. He noted that the apparent temperature of an object depends upon the area of the skin that is stimulated (we can comfortably immerse the tip of a finger into water of a temperature that would be intolerable in a hot bath), and that the apparent weight of an object depends upon its temperature (one thaler just removed from cold water and placed upon the forehead felt heavier than two thalers just removed from hot water). In the course of his observations he also came across the phenomena of temperature contrast, as manifested for

instance in the famous experiment in which both hands are
placed in a bowl of lukewarm water after one has been in very
hot and the other in very cold water. This led him to a theory of
temperature, according to which the sensations of cold and heat
correspond to a *changing* temperature of the skin in the direction
of falling or of rising respectively; a theory which in later times
has usually been abandoned, because of its inability to account
for the fact that at the more extreme temperatures cold or warmth
may be experienced for many hours on end ("adaptation" being
only possible, it would appear, to a middle range of temperatures).
As regards pressure, Weber continued the kind of experiment
already reported in his earlier book, and made a detailed study of
the various degrees of sensitivity that distinguish different parts
of the body. Moreover he extended his work upon the ability to
discriminate small differences to the fields of hearing and of
vision. In the former he studied the discrimination of pitch, while
in the latter he endeavoured, for instance, to discover the smallest
arc that would permit the discrimination of two lines or the smallest difference that would enable one line to be seen as longer
than another. He thus inaugurated the study of *thresholds*, which
has since played such a great part in experimental psychology.
In general, he corroborated his earlier findings to the effect that
the increase of stimulus necessary to be perceived as such was not
an absolute amount but was proportionate to the intensity of the
original stimulus—the actual proportion varying from one sense
department to another. He thus collected the material for the
enunciation of Weber's Law, when Fechner turned to the same
problem a few years later.

One particular experiment of Weber's was destined to excite
a quite especial interest; this was his "compass test"; an attempt
to find out how great must be the distance between two simultaneous touches on the skin in order that they may be just
perceived as two. It soon appeared that this two-point threshold
varied immensely in different regions of the body, the tips of the
fingers, for instance, being more than thirty times as discrimina-
tive as the upper arm. In interpreting these results Weber
thought that there must be at least one unstimulated nerve fibre
between the two stimulated points before they could be perceived
as two—the compass test serving, therefore, as a convenient
means of studying the richness of the nerve supply in various

parts of the body. This explanation was held to be a likely one until, some forty years later, the work of Blix, Donaldson and Goldscheider showed that there were many "touch spots" even within an area in which the two points appeared as single. Apart from this, however, it gradually became only too painfully clear that the threshold varied greatly according to conditions of training, attention and fatigue. The experiment in question is indeed an extremely difficult and trying one to carry out successfully, as generations of students in experimental psychology have since discovered to their cost. But, perhaps just because of its difficulties, the experiment has always exercised a fascination, and the little instrument required for it, later dignified with the impressive title of "aesthesiometer," has in the last eighty years been applied to the bodies of innumerable individuals of all races and all ages. Indeed the individual differences in the results eventually proved to be among the most interesting features of the experiment; for on the whole it is now possible to generalize and say that savages have a lower threshold (i.e. can perceive two points as such at a smaller distance apart) than the civilized while the same is true of women as compared with men and children as compared with adults. The variations that depend upon the condition of the subject have also proved a fertile field, and the threshold has even been used as a measure of fatigue, though here the results have proved less regular and less easy to interpret.

All such developments, however, were probably very far from Weber's thoughts as he carried out his pioneering observations. He could not foretell the use to which his methods would be put, nor realize that he was building the foundations of a new branch of science. Nevertheless, we ought perhaps to look upon Weber's patient and persevering observations as the true beginning of experimental psychology. With Fechner this new discipline became self-conscious, and with Wundt it began to claim a place (though, inevitably, still a humble one) among its sister sciences. But with Weber it may be truly said to have begun, even although its creator was not aware of the significance of his achievement.

While Weber was working, Fechner was all the time a near neighbour (and for the most part a colleague) in the town and University of Leipzig. The two men actually arrived there in the

same year, 1817, Weber as *Dozent* (to become Professor of
Anatomy a year later), Fechner as a student of medicine. In his
long life (1801–1887) Fechner contributed to many fields of
knowledge, being in turn physiologist, physicist, philosopher,
psycho-physicist and aesthetician. In 1834 he was appointed Professor of Physics, a post which he held till 1839. Throughout this
early period, he was busy writing and translating works on
physical science, having won his spurs by a paper of generally
recognized importance on Ohm's Law in 1831. In 1839 he suffered
from what we should now call a "severe nervous breakdown,"
aggravated by eye trouble brought on by staring at the sun in
order to study after-images (his first essay in the sphere of
psycho-physics). This was a "crisis" in his life, and after several
years of illness he turned to philosophy.

Philosophically, Fechner was an impassioned monist. But his
monism was itself the outcome of an attempt to solve the problem
of a double allegiance—one to the methods of materialistic science
in which he had become an adept, the other to the philosophy of
idealism, which in turn was based on an overwhelming convic-
tion of the importance of the human mind and indeed of consciousness generally.[1] In his earlier years he had been the author
of a number of satirical writings in which he expressed his aver-
sion to a one-sidedly materialistic viewpoint. These writings,
which appeared under the *nom de plume* of Dr. Mises, included a
Proof that the Moon is made of Iodine and a *Comparative
Anatomy of the Angels*. In his philosophical period, and indeed
throughout his subsequent life, he was constantly grappling with

[1] In an interesting psycho-analytic study of Fechner's life, Imre Hermann
(*Imago*, 1925, xi, p. 371) brings forward much evidence to suggest that Fechner's long illness was to a great extent determined by an unconscious desire to
produce a child. This desire was itself connected with the fact that Fechner's
father died a few days after the birth of his last child, birth thus becoming
associated in the young Fechner's mind with the death of the father and all the
ambivalent feelings naturally called up by this event; the desire being also
intensified by the fact that Fechner's own marriage was childless. His illness
was initiated by a long period of staring at the sun (father symbol); the illness
itself (during which he could live only in a much darkened room) was a symbol
of prenatal life, followed by an eventual rebirth (return to health). The same
tendencies, Hermann argues, are shown in his work. In his psycho-physics for
instance, stress is constantly laid on the *increment* of stimulus and sensation
(growth, children) and on the threshold (birth); while his general desire to
attribute life and consciousness to everything appears, from his own writings
to be derived from interest in the embryo. In *Nanna*, for instance, the mental
life of plants is compared to that of the foetus.

the task of showing that matter should be looked at in the light of consciousness, rather than consciousness in the light of matter —in advocating the "Day Viewpoint," as he called it, in opposition to the "Night Viewpoint" of materialism. But, since the existence of matter and the validity of material science could not be denied, the only solution was to regard the two elements— matter and consciousness—as one. It became the work of his life to collate the two worlds and to discover the laws of their interconnection. If men and animals had consciousness, why not the plants (in 1848 he published *Nanna, oder das Seelenleben der Pflanzen*), why not indeed the earth itself and the other heavenly bodies? Men and animals are bound up with the earth, and the earth-soul may be related to the individual souls of men and animals, as the earth-body is to their bodies. The earth, "our mother," is a being like ourselves, but far more perfect. In the last resort, too, all souls are part of the highest all-embracing world-soul, whose life and reality is manifested in the causal law. The methods of physical science are, therefore, adapted also to the study of the mental life through its manifestations in the body. What is needed is only to discover the law of the connection between mind and body.

On the morning of October 22, 1850, as he tells us, pondering this matter "in bed before getting up," it occurred to him that the secret of this law was to be found in the quantitative relation between stimulus and sensation. According to Fechner's own statement, this thought was not prompted by a knowledge of Weber's results, although something of the latter must surely have been known to him. Soon, however, he recognized that these results provided the beginnings at least of just the material he wanted. He proceeded to give mathematical form to the empirical data and enunciated Weber's Law, generously giving credit to his colleague for the principle (which he himself had been the first to realize), as well as for the facts on which this principle was based. Not content with this, however, Fechner drew up a programme of further work and promptly set out to put it into execution. The programme itself was announced in the *Zend Avesta* of 1851, and for the next few years Fechner worked on quietly by himself, developing the famous "psycho-physical methods" and performing the classical experiments on lifted weights, on visual brightness, on tactual and visual "difference

thresholds." A preliminary account of all this work first appeared
in two short papers in 1858 and 1859. Then in 1860 he published
the completed work, the *Elemente der Psychophysik*, which pur-
ported to be nothing less than an "exact science of the functional
relations or relations of dependency between body and mind"—
an event which is usually looked upon as marking the birth of the
new science of experimental psychology.

By an irony of fate the scientific world has cared little or
nothing for the motives which inspired Fechner in this work. It
adopted his methods and continued his investigations, gradually
extending their sphere, so that the exact procedures originally
devised for measuring the relations between stimulus and sensation have since been applied to ever wider aspects of the mental
life. But for the philosophy, which to Fechner was the true end
of all his labours in this field, scarcely a single subsequent
psychologist has shown the slightest interest or enthusiasm; indeed, it is perhaps true to say that no one has quite understood
how even the most brilliantly successful psycho-physical investigations could really provide the satisfactory basis for the philosophy that Fechner himself sought to establish. Fechner is one
of the very few philosophers who have endeavoured to found a
metaphysical system upon exact experiment. He failed in this
endeavour, but his failure was in its own way more fruitful than
success could possibly have been. No one believed that he had
proved his metaphysics, but many seized joyfully upon the new
weapon that he had created in his attempt to make this proof, and
thus armed, proceeded, not indeed to a final conception of the
nature of the universe, but to a slow, painstaking, systematic and
relentless attack upon the mysterious problems of the human
mind.

TURNING now to the category of abnormal psychology, we find
that almost the sole developments of real importance in the first
of our three periods are concerned with hypnotism, or mesmerism as it was still called at the beginning of this period. It will be
remembered that, when the period opened, mesmerism had
fallen into utter discredit in the learned world. At the end of the
period it had been rehabilitated and put upon a sound basis;
indeed in this particular field the period is one of rapid progress,
due largely to the work of a few enthusiasts, who willingly
jeopardized their scientific reputations in the search for knowledge and the attempt to ease the sufferings of their fellow-men.
Three names stand out in this connection above all others: John
Elliotson, James Esdaile and James Braid.

Elliotson, the first of these, was a man of unusual ability and
originality, a rare combination of scientist, philanthropist and
rebel, with great hopes of the future, great receptiveness towards
all things new and unexplored, and an almost equally great contempt for the errors and prejudices of the past. He was the first
physician to use the stethoscope in England and to introduce many
forms of treatment which later on were generally adopted. In
1831 he was made Professor of the Theory and Practice of
Medicine at the newly founded (1828) University College of
London. With Elliotson's enthusiastic support University College
Hospital was opened in 1834, the first hospital to be established
for the definite purpose of providing a centre for research and
demonstration in connection with a medical school. In 1837
Elliotson witnessed an exhibition of mesmerism by a Frenchman
styling himself Baron Dupotet, and his imagination was at once
fired by the possibilities of its use in the treatment of nervous
disease. He lost no time in putting his ideas into practice and soon
all sorts of cases were being treated by this method in the hospital. Unfortunately one of his patients, Elizabeth Okey by name,

developed an apparent faculty of clairvoyance, with the help of which she prescribed for her own ailments and those of others and claimed to "foretell the issue of disease and the advent of death." Mesmerism was not confined to the wards, but frequent *séances* were given in the theatre of the hospital, attended, we are told, "by crowded and fashionable audiences, which included among peers, bishops and philosophers, Thomas Moore and Charles Dickens." Mesmerism, however, was still regarded as a scientific scandal, and the authorities of the College, not unnaturally anxious for the reputation of what was still a relatively new and upstart institution, did all they could to stop these, as it seemed to them, highly unedifying exhibitions. The Dean, in advising Elliotson to desist, urged that the interests of the medical school ought to be placed before those of science and humanity, and that the risk of the loss of public confidence was of more importance than the alleged facts that were being demonstrated. Nothing could have been more calculated to arouse the Professor's most fiery indignation. In characteristic vein he replied that "this institution was established for the discovery and dissemination of truth; all other considerations are secondary; we should lead the public, not the public us." The Council of the College replied by forbidding the practice of mesmerism in the hospital, whereupon (in 1838) Elliotson promptly resigned his chair. To complete the debacle, Thomas Wakley, the editor of the *Lancet*, invited Elliotson to bring Elizabeth Okey to his own house, where she was carefully tested and it was found (as Benjamin Franklin had found some fifty years before) that the phenomena of "magnetization" depended solely on the belief of the subject in the reality of the supposed magnetic power.

Elliotson, however, was not to be discouraged. His writings on mesmerism having been refused by all the recognized medical periodicals, in 1843 he founded a paper of his own, the *Zoist*, which continued for about thirteen years. This provided an organ for all those who were working on the new lines. The paper was also hospitable to communications on clairvoyance (which was arousing much interest in connection with the rise of "spiritualism," which had spread over the world like wildfire, following the mysterious rappings that had taken place in the house of the Fox family in Hydesville in 1847), and on phrenology. This latter discipline was still largely practised, and about this time received the respectful attention of many eminent people. To please her friend Mr. Bray, George Eliot had her head shaved in order that her bumps might be studied more conveniently,[1] and Herbert Spencer contributed articles on "The Situation of the Organ of Amativeness" and "A Theory concerning the Organ of Wonder," though he later changed his views on these matters, maintaining that "however defensible may be the hypothesis of a localization of faculties, when presented under an abstract form, it is quite indefensible under the form given it by the phrenologists." Towards the end of the *Zoist's* career, however, Elliotson's own scepticism seems to have been aroused concerning the claims of the clairvoyants, who were, he declared, many of them, impostors. The magazine was described as a "journal of cerebral physiology and mesmerism, and their applications to human welfare," and under the latter heading Elliotson developed ideas concerning the treatment of criminals and children, which have a very modern ring. His sympathies were always with the weak and the oppressed, and he drew a vivid picture of the sufferings of children at the hands of harsh parents, brutal teachers or callous physicians. If properly dealt with, children were, he maintained, easy enough to manage, indeed in most respects morally far superior to their elders. Their faults resulted from cruel and injudicious treatment and could be rectified by greater sympathy and understanding. Grown-ups themselves often became obstinate and irritable even over petty matters and it was not surprising if children, with their greater sensibility and smaller experience, sometimes behaved in the same way. Similar considerations applied to many criminals, and Elliotson was fond of inveighing against the senseless brutality of most forms of legally inflicted punishment.

Largely through the influence of the *Zoist*, mesmeric clinics were opened in London, Edinburgh, Dublin and other places. At first the interest centred chiefly round the treatment of nervous disease, but before long attention began to be directed to the possibility of using the mesmeric trance for the production of anaesthesia in surgery. Numerous operations were performed— as it was claimed—painlessly. The medical press and the medical societies nevertheless almost consistently refused to take any

[1] Emilie and Georges Romieu, *The Life of George Eliot*, pp. 80 ff.

notice of these claims, though on one occasion Ward, a surgeon
of Nottingham, was allowed to report to the Royal Medical and
Chirurgical Society on a case of alleged painless amputation of the
thigh. It was variously suggested that the patient was an impostor, that he had been specially trained to resist pain, and that,
even if true, the alleged fact was unworthy of the Society's
consideration, since "pain was a wise provision of nature and
patients ought to suffer pain while their surgeons were operating; they were all the better for it and recovered better." Eight
years later Marshall Hall, the discoverer of reflex action, stated
that the patient had made a declaration to the effect that in
reality he *had* suffered pain at the operation in question. Hall
admitted, however, that he had heard of this declaration only
at third hand and said that he was not at liberty to divulge the
source of his information. The patient, who was still living, was
sought out, and signed a sworn statement that the operation
had been painless—a statement that was produced at the next
meeting of the society, but was ruled out of order and was never
read.

Meanwhile the anaesthetic use of mesmerism was being
exploited on an imposing scale in India by James Esdaile. Here
too, the medical profession was distinctly hostile, but the Indian
Government was far more tolerant, and Esdaile was allowed, and
to some extent indeed encouraged, to pursue his work. Between
1845 and 1851, when he left India, he performed some 300 major
operations and enormously reduced the number of deaths following such operations. On returning home, he settled in Perth and
found the inhabitants of Scotland no less amenable to mesmerism
than had been those of India.

Elliotson and Esdaile were friends, and both were constantly at
war with the other members of their own profession. James
Braid, however, chose another course, and it was he who eventually succeeded in getting some recognition for the facts of
mesmerism in orthodox medical circles. At the same time, he
discovered (or rather re-discovered) the true and more purely
psychological nature of the phenomena. Braid was a physician of
Manchester, and his first interest in the matter was aroused by
the visit of Lafontaine, a French mesmerist, to that city in 1841.
Braid started by being "loud in his denunciation of the whole
affair," but soon became convinced that it was not mere fraud.

He had committed himself as an opponent of mesmerism and was naturally cautious and conservative in temperament; yet he was curious and urged by a genuinely scientific desire to understand the phenomena that he had witnessed. This combination of circumstances caused him to get nearer to the true solution than any of his predecessors or contemporaries. He went home and experimented on the members of his own family. To his surprise, he found that he could induce an artificial sleep-like state by the simple process of making them stare continuously at a bright object situated slightly above the level of the eyes. He therefore concluded that mesmerism was but a kind of sleep "induced by paralysing the levator muscles of the eyelids, caused by their continued action during the protracted fixed stare." The theory of animal magnetism was, he thought, refuted, and the phenomena shown to depend entirely upon conditions in the subject, and not, as had been believed, by the transference of some force generated by the operator. In his enthusiasm for this discovery, Braid himself gave public exhibitions a few weeks after Lafontaine's departure, reproduced Lafontaine's phenomena, and gave his own explanations. These were, of course, easier to bring into harmony with orthodox views, and were acceptable as disproving the objectionable claim to special powers on the part of mesmerists. Besides, Braid had from the first been an *opponent* of mesmerism and was held to have "exposed" it, even though in reality he had only given it a new interpretation (albeit a more reasonable one). His sleep theory served, therefore, in some degree to reconcile medical and scientific opinion to the genuineness of the facts, which, from now onwards, became known under the new name of "hypnotism." Braid continued his work on the subject, and his views found ever-greater acceptance among the medical profession, while to the end his relations with the mesmerists and the writers in the *Zoist* remained predominantly hostile, even though he and they were dealing with precisely the same facts. In 1843 he published his principal work, which was entitled *Neurypnology, or the Rationale of Nervous Sleep, Considered in Relation with Animal Magnetism*, and this was followed by many other publications.

As the work proceeded, Braid modified and enlarged his views. From the start, however these views would seem to have been in advance of others. The chief steps in the recognition of the psychological and subjective nature of hypnotism appear to have been somewhat as follows. Puységur discovered that it was possible to throw the patient into a special sleep-like state; but in this state there remained an obvious special relationship between somnambule and mesmerist, inasmuch as the former "took no notice of anyone but the person who had magnetized him, replied to no one else and obeyed no one else." This phenomenon of *rapport*, as it afterwards came to be called, prevented realization of the fundamentally subjective nature of the process and, in view of the general theory of animal magnetism, naturally confirmed the idea that everything was due to some special power of the magnetizer. Puységur took a further step, however, in showing that trees could be "magnetized" and human subjects in turn magnetized through them. Benjamin Franklin then made the discovery that mere belief in magnetization of the trees was sufficient to produce curative effects. From this it really followed that the effects had nothing to do with magnetism, but so closely were the phenomena bound up with the theory of animal magnetism that it seems to have occurred to no one that there might still be something worth investigating, even though the magnetic theory were disproved. It was Braid's great service that he took up this last point, and showed clearly that the phenomena themselves were genuine, however erroneously they might have been interpreted. Not content with this, he proceeded to investigate the causes and conditions of the hypnotic trance. His first experiments naturally suggested that the trance was induced by fatigue of a sense organ, but later he became convinced that a narrowing of the attention, so as to produce a state of *monoideism*, was the essential factor, and that, provided this were present, the trance could be induced by any method. He also began to understand something of the true nature of the relation between hypnotist and patient, and of the peculiar and capricious effects of hypnosis upon memory. He thus opened up the way for the work on suggestion and dissociation that was to follow in the later periods. Braid died in 1860, just at the beginning of our second period; but before his death he had the satisfaction of knowing that his discoveries were becoming pretty generally recognized by the medical profession, and also that they were taken up by psychiatrists and neurologists of other countries, notably by Azam and Broca in France. The favourable reception given to the reports of the two latter investigators inaugurated the brilliant phase of French psycho-pathology that distinguished the second half of the nineteenth century.

From the purely psychological point of view, it was probably a misfortune that chemical anaesthetics were discovered just at the same time as the use of hypnotic anaesthesia in surgery. The first painless extraction of a tooth under nitrous oxide took place in America in 1844, and although there was a temporary setback owing to the failure of a public exhibition and to medical and clerical opposition (in this case, too, it was argued that the abolition of pain was an interference with the proper course of Nature or with the Divine Will), in a few years' time chloroform, ether and nitrous oxide were in general use both in Europe and America. The advantages of these anaesthetics over hypnotism were obvious; they were more in accordance with the materialistic trend of medical thought, were less of a mystery, surer and more calculable in their action, and could be used on anybody without previous training, whereas the hypnotic method required as a rule that the patient should have been successfully hypnotized at least several times before the operation was attempted. It was only to be expected, therefore, that the new methods should rapidly supplant those that had been so successfully employed by Elliotson, Braid and Esdaile. With the dying down of the practical interest in hypnotism as an aid to surgery, there was a general decline in the interest taken in the subject generally, and we can scarcely doubt that psychological science suffered heavily in consequence. Since the middle of the last century, progress in the understanding of hypnotic phenomena has been slow and sporadic. Many problems are still today unsolved. If hypnotism had been allowed to develop further as an essential element of surgical technique, a far greater amount of research would probably have been directed to it, and our knowledge about its nature and conditions would in all likelihood have been considerably greater than it is.

Two further series of developments must be briefly noted before we close the survey of our first period—this time not in the sphere of functional abnormality but in that of mental and moral defect. It will be remembered how the wild boy of Aveyron and his education at the hands of Itard had brought into prominence the problem of innate deficiency of mental power, and how the education of those afflicted with such deficiency had been made a subject of study and experiment by Séguin. As already mentioned, a special institute for the training of the feeble-minded had been founded in 1828, of which Séguin himself became director in 1842. Soon after this, feeble-mindedness began to arouse interest in other countries—though, strange as this may now seem, at first chiefly in connection with other disabilities of a more specific nature—blindness, for instance, in America, and deaf-mutism in Germany. Séguin himself was invited to America at the instigation of Samuel Howe of the Perkins Institute for the Blind at Boston, himself a romantic figure who, like Elliotson, was ever fighting for the feeble and oppressed whether in medicine or politics, and who in Europe had assisted both the Greeks and the Poles in their struggles for independence. Séguin accepted the offer, and for some twenty years afterwards was busy improving the methods employed in this branch of education. In 1848 the first institution for the training of the feeble-minded was established in the United States and thereafter others sprang up rapidly. The same year witnessed the opening of the first British institution of the same kind. Even before this, Guggenbühl in Switzerland had founded a colony for the care and study of the particular form of mental defect associated with cretinism, and the success of his system of segregation soon won widespread approval and imitation. By the middle of the century, therefore, it may be said that the principle of a special system of training for the mentally defective was well on the way to universal recognition.

The outstanding personality in the field of criminology was Dorothea Dix, who may be looked upon as the true successor of Howard, the pioneer of prison reform. A woman of extraordinary energy and power, she started in 1840 to reform the prisons of her own state, Massachusetts, both by ameliorating the lot of the inmates, and by endeavouring to get the insane and feeble-minded placed elsewhere than with the common criminals. She possessed unusual ability to arouse public feeling in matters of this kind, and almost wherever she went she was successful in bringing about at least some measure of reform, either in improving the conditions of life in prisons or in the establishment of special institutions for the insane and feeble-minded. In spite of poor health, she travelled extensively, at first in America and then in Europe, and in the course of her long and strenuous life she must, directly or indirectly, have benefited the lot of countless thousands. Her own field was philanthropy, rather than psychology. Nevertheless, her work was of considerable importance to psychology, inasmuch as it brought about a widespread realization of the fact that insanity, feeble-mindedness and criminality are conditions between which it is well to make a clear distinction, and the practical approach to which should be governed by separate and distinct principles. The mere segregation of these three main groups of persons made the problems peculiar to each group stand out in such a way as to demand attention. The treatment of the insane, the mentally defective and the criminal thus each became the subject of special study, with its own experts and its own methods. It became generally recognized that the adoption of a moral attitude towards the two former groups was ethically unjustifiable and practically absurd. The field in which purely punitive methods were applied was hereby greatly reduced, and that of medicine, education and psychology correspondingly extended.

III

1860–1900

I. EVOLUTION—DARWIN AND SPENCER

AT the very beginning of our second period stands the epoch-making work of Darwin, which was destined to revolutionize the whole science of life, and with it psychology. Not, of course, that the idea of evolution was altogether new. It was at least as old as Lucretius, and in recent times it had been put forward in one sphere or another by quite a number of distinguished writers— by Laplace (the originator of the "nebular hypothesis") in astronomy, by Hegel, Fourier and Comte in sociology, by Lyell (probably the most influential of all) in geology, and by Buffon, Lamarck, Goethe, St. Hilaire, Erasmus Darwin (Charles Darwin's grandfather), and Herbert Spencer in biology. It was Charles Darwin, however, who, by the collection of a vast mass of facts in support of the hypothesis and the formulation of the precise biological mechanisms through which evolution manifested itself, gave the theory a truly scientific form, and, by stressing the continuity of development throughout organic life up to the human level, expressed it in a way that appealed at once both to the learned and the popular imagination.

The general features of Darwin's theory, together with the main circumstances that led him to propound it, are too well known to need repeating here. We can at most remind the reader of a few of the most salient facts. In 1838, some two years after his return from the voyage of the *Beagle*, Darwin read Malthus's *Essay on the Principle of Population*, in which is propounded the idea that, since the natural fertility of all species is vastly out of proportion to their actual numbers, population must be controlled by natural causes quite other than actual power of reproduction, the chief of such causes being lack of food,

disease and internecine strife. Malthus, in elaborating his famous
theory, had been chiefly concerned with its application to mankind, particularly in its bearings on the problems of poverty and
social reform. Darwin was at once struck by its wider implications. If all species are constantly engaged in a struggle for existence in an unfavourable environment, this fact must, he thought,
have other effects than the purely quantitative one of keeping its
numbers within bounds. There must be a principle of selection
among any given species, in virtue of which some members of
the species are more likely to survive than others. Those individuals who possess some feature which is of advantage in the
struggle, will tend, more than others, to survive to maturity and
reproduce themselves; and in virtue of the laws of heredity they
will tend also to hand on their advantageous features to their
offspring. Furthermore, these offspring will vary among themselves, since variation is another general law of heredity; some
will have the advantageous qualities developed in a higher degree
than their parents. These, in turn, will tend to survive, and so on
indefinitely; and thus in the course of many generations, great
changes may occur, changes so great that they can even account
for the difference between species as they exist today. On these
two foundations, the struggle for existence and natural variation, was based the theory of the evolution of living beings, a
theory which, after twenty years of laborious and detailed testing,
was eventually given to the world in the *Origin of Species* in
1859. One great book thus, after an interval of sixty-one years,
begot another.

Just before publication of the *Origin of Species*, however, a
dramatic event occurred. Darwin received a communication from
a young naturalist in the Far East, Alfred Russell Wallace, in
which essentially the same theory was propounded as that on
which he himself had been so patiently working; and, what is
more, the inspiration here too had come from reading Malthus's
Essay. Darwin was naturally embarrassed; but both scientists
behaved with a dignity worthy of their calling, and no petty
squabbles about precedency were allowed to mar the announcement of the great discovery. Darwin consulted Lyell as to what
had best be done; and at the latter's advice Wallace's paper,
together with some portions of Darwin's forthcoming book, were
read together at a meeting of the Linnean Society in July, 1858.

In the following year *Origin of Species* appeared and immediately raised a stir that (in some parts of the world) has not even yet died down. From that time onwards all biological thought was permeated with the idea of evolution.

To Darwin himself *Origin of Species* was rather the statement of a thesis than a full substantiation of it. Though the great strength of the book lay in its detailed confirmatory evidence (a matter in which it differed fundamentally from previous expositions of evolutionary theory and also from Wallace's contemporary statement), Darwin saw that there were many fields in which the theory had still to be worked out, and the remainder of his life may indeed be said to have been devoted to a testing and elaboration of his theory in some few of these fields. His work in several of them was of direct importance for psychology. In the *Descent of Man* (1871) he emphasized the similarity between the mental processes of man and those of animals, and laid stress upon the importance of sexual selection as a further factor in evolution; and in the *Expression of the Emotions in Man and Animals* (1872) he suggested an evolutionary interpretation of the changes of feature and of posture that are characteristic of the major emotions. These changes, he endeavoured to show, are either themselves of biological utility, are associated with or are remnants of movements possessing such utility (e.g. the showing of the teeth in anger), or are the result of social tradition (as in clasping the hands in supplication, which Darwin looks upon as a mute offer to let the hands be bound). Although many of Darwin's individual interpretations still remain matters of speculation the book is a monument both of bold suggestiveness and patient inquiry, and remains to this day by far the most important single contribution to its subject. Although these two books, together with his *Biographical Sketch of an Infant*, an article published in 1877, are perhaps the most psychologically oriented of all his writings, throughout his work Darwin never lost sight of the importance of mental factors in evolution; and the same applies to Wallace. Cunning in attack, defence or flight, gregarious tendencies, the cry of warning from one member of the species to another, sexual attraction (with its influence on heredity), mimicry, parental and family affection, these and other conscious reactions in men and animals are frequently mentioned by both writers. Consciousness indeed plays an essential part in their evolutionary theory, so that in so far as Darwinism was accepted, psychology was itself compelled henceforward to adopt the evolutionary point of view.

Darwin and Wallace were, however, not the only protagonists of evolution. Herbert Spencer, as already mentioned, had published the first edition of his *Principles of Psychology* in 1855, and this had been preceded in 1852 by an article in the *Leader* on "The Development Hypothesis," which, we are told, was the direct outcome of an argument with a friend upon the possibility of the "transmutation of species." According to his own account, Spencer's interest in evolution dated from his reading Lyell's *Geology* in 1839, one year after Darwin had read Malthus's *Essay on Population*. The first indication of his truly synoptic view of the nature and importance of evolution was contained in an article on "Progress: its law and cause," which may indeed be looked upon as the Synthetic Philosophy itself in embryo. Shortly before the appearance of the *Origin of Species*, Spencer, now nearing his fortieth year, determined to devote the remainder of his life to the systematic exposition of the concept of evolution as applied to the whole field of knowledge, and asked for a state grant to carry out this purpose. The State did not see its way to contribute to the undertaking, but Spencer nevertheless embarked upon the work, which occupied him continuously from 1860 to 1893. The *System of Synthetic Philosophy*, the successive parts of which appeared at intervals throughout this period, is a mighty effort to bring all observable changes in phenomena under one all-embracing law; and, as such, is among the most daring and magnificent achievements of the human mind. Indeed, there can be no doubt, that, after Darwin, Spencer has done more than any other to introduce the developmental point of view into biology and science generally. In recent years Spencer's contribution to knowledge has, in the opinion of the present writer, been very greatly underrated. Much that was characteristic of his outlook has been quietly adopted without due acknowledgment, while his over-confidence and his mistakes of detail are frequently held up to scorn. And yet Spencer's general formula for evolution remains the most satisfying that has as yet been proposed. This formula, so familiar in the last quarter of the nineteenth century, is today worth quoting. "Evolution," he said, "is a change from an indefinite, incoherent homogeneity

to a definite, coherent heterogeneity through continuous integrations and differentiations." The very statement of this definition
perhaps reveals to us one ground at least of Spencer's waning
popularity.[1] His "semi-deductive method, speculative and ultra-
logical manner and dry unattractive style"[2] were combined with
a certain pompousness and more than a soupçon of *de haut en bas*
that are repugnant to a disillusioned modern world, which is
suspicious of wide generalizations, and intolerant of what seems
to it to smack unpleasantly of Victorian pedantry, complacency
and priggishness. And, indeed, Spencer's work lacks much of the
fresh and living quality of Darwin's; for the minds and methods
of the two men were very different. Spencer was a great thinker,
a thinker interested in discovering the connections between facts.
Darwin was a great observer and a man of brilliant intuition.
Spencer's general practice, as well expressed by a contemporary
writer,[3] was "to carry off his facts to some inner chamber,
where he might meditate upon them without distraction and at
very great length. He did not by choice, or habitually, live in that
close contact with Nature which was to Darwin the indispensable
condition of all activity." Nevertheless, the breadth and mag-
nificence of Spencer's vision has never been surpassed, and if the
reader is tolerant for long enough, he is gradually compelled to
awe and admiration, as the pattern of the universe unrolls itself
in seemingly inevitable sequence.

The second edition of Spencer's *Principles of Psychology* followed *First Principles* and the *Principles of Biology*, and constituted the fourth and fifth volumes of his "System." His
psychology is biological from start to finish. Life is defined as
"the continuous adjustment of internal to external relations,"
and the task of psychology is to show in detail how this adjustment tends, in the course of development, to become more
perfect; behaviour and consciousness becoming both more
integrated and more differentiated in the process.

Spencer is little interested in the distinction between body and

[1] The mathematician Kirkman thought his definition needed translating
into English, and suggested the following: "Evolution is a change from a no-
howish, untalkaboutable allalikeness, to a somehowish and in-general-
talkaboutable not-allalikeness, by continuous somethingelseifications and
sticktogetherations."

[2] Baldwin, *History of Psychology*, Vol. II, p. 82.

[3] L. C. Miall, *The Life and Work of Charles Darwin*, p. 45.

mind, and only secondarily interested in the classification or description of mental states. In conformity with his synoptic outlook he is concerned, not so much with the nature of any particular psychological manifestation in itself, as with the question of its function and place in the evolutionary scheme. He took associationism largely as he found it, and looked at it in the light of his own concept of adaptation. Hence the general law of association is described as follows: "The persistence of the connection between states of consciousness is proportionate to the persistence of the connection between the agencies to which they answer." Simple organisms react in a simple and undifferentiated way to gross and undifferentiated stimuli. Their behaviour, like reflex action in the case of higher organisms, is relatively simple and invariable, and therefore adapted only in a coarse and general way to the environment. Instinct is "compound reflex action," capable of adapting to more varying and complex outer conditions. In proportion as phenomena become more complex, they also become less frequent; the connection between the outer phenomena and the inner states of consciousness (and consequently also the resulting behaviour) is therefore, in accordance with the general law, less certain, rapid and invariable. In this way arise the phenomena we know as memory, reason, will, etc. For memory may be regarded as a sort of incipient instinct. When stimulus and response (to use the terms of a later school) have become sufficiently connected, the appropriate behaviour will become automatic, and there will be no need to recall previous situations; hence memory in the sense of conscious recollection will drop out. When a complex situation gives rise to a "confusion between nascent motor excitations, there is entailed a certain hesitation," and out of this hesitation between various possible responses reason begins to emerge. Ultimately, however, some one response prevails over the others that are possible, and the act of making this response is will—which has been thought to be mysterious merely because we cannot discover the full nature of the forces in action, which may be of extreme complexity. The ego that carries out the act is nothing but what is present to our consciousness at the moment of willing; this content of consciousness is beyond our control, hence the freedom of the will is an illusion. The feelings grow more complex *pari passu* with the complexity of thought and action, and our

D

deeper emotions derive their intensity from the multitude of motives involved; thus "the passion which unites the sexes is the most compound and therefore the most powerful of all feelings," composed as it is of elements connected with sensory desire, personal beauty, affection, admiration, love of approbation, self-esteem, proprietary feeling, sympathy, and finally the extended liberty of action that follows the overthrowing of habitual barriers.

It will be seen that Spencer is true to the best associationist tradition, though giving it a biological, and to some extent, as we might now say, behaviouristic setting. His ultimate elements are even simpler than those of any previous associationist, for he attempts to reduce all mind, in the last resort, to "nervous shocks" or waves of molecular disturbance, increasing in complexity as development proceeds. On the other hand, he admits, as many had not done, the existence of relations between feelings, brought about by the "momentary shock produced by the commencement of a new state," when one apparently uniform state passes to another; these relations themselves being classifiable into those of likeness and unlikeness, co-existence and sequence. Spencer also lays far more stress than most associationists on the narrowness of consciousness, which indeed for him is the most essential characteristic of psychological, as compared with physiological, phenomena, for whereas the latter include both simultaneous and successive changes (an "immense number of different series bound up together") the former tend to include successive changes only ("presenting themselves as but a single series").

By far the most radical change from previous associationist teaching is, however, his insistence upon heredity and racial factors. Spencer tries to reconcile those who stress the importance of heredity and those who consider that individual experience accounts for everything, by supposing that what is acquired by the individual tends, to some extent, however small, to become an innate possession of the race. In his statement of this doctrine he has laid himself open to attack on the ground that he has greatly over-estimated the tendency for acquired characters to be transmitted—if, indeed, they are transmitted at all. When, a little later on, owing to the work of Weismann, this latter question began to be answered in the negative, Spencer's views upon the matter lost much of their attractive plausibility, and this contributed not a little to the general decline of interest in his work.

There is no doubt that the evolutionary factors on which Darwin laid most stress have stood the test of further biological research much better than has Spencer's rather naïve acceptance of the transmission of acquired characters. It is also true that, as regards the human race, Spencer stressed heredity too much and the facts of social and cultural influence too little (in spite of the remarkable contributions to the study of culture in his *Principles of Sociology*). But many of Spencer's main contentions do not necessarily stand or fall with his particular views as to the nature of transmission. The view that the innate endowment of the individual is dependent upon racial history seems to be unassailable, whatsoever the particular factors in that history that we may hold responsible. Apart from this, as Baldwin says, "the transfer of emphasis to racial experience introduced once for all the social way of looking at mental states," and this was an immense gain that we owe to Spencer. From his time onwards psychology became refreshed by the bracing atmosphere of biology and sociology. The individual mind could no longer be considered in the artificial isolation of the philosopher's study. And although to some extent the laboratory was to replace the study for the investigation of detailed problems, the developmental aspect of consciousness and of behaviour, and the fact that man was a being with intimate relationships to his fellow-men and to other living beings could no longer be lost sight of. From now onwards psychology was related not only to philosophy (as it had always been) and to physiology (as it had more recently become), but to the general study of life in all its varied manifestations, both animal and human.

II. THE BEGINNINGS OF ANIMAL PSYCHOLOGY

ONE of the most immediate effects of the new outlook due to the doctrine of evolution was to direct attention to the minds of animals; and during the last thirty years of the nineteenth century the foundations of animal psychology were laid by Schneider in Germany and by a whole series of writers in England, all of whom were inspired more or less directly by the work of Spencer and of Darwin. To Spalding belongs the credit of being one of the very first to apply the experimental method to this sphere. He was interested particularly in the question of the extent to which the more complicated actions of animals could be accounted for in terms of pure instinct, as distinct from experience or imitation. Thus in one of his experiments, reported in 1872, he took young swallows at the moment of hatching and confined them in cages away from the sight of their companions until they had reached the flying age; he then released them, and discovered that they very soon learnt to fly, although they had not had the opportunity of observing the flight of other birds. G. H. Schneider, whose pioneering works appeared in 1880 and 1882, was an early exponent of the theory of "recapitulation," according to which the development of the individual is an epitome of the evolution of the race, a theory which was later on to play a large part in the writings of Stanley Hall. In 1883 Weismann propounded his theory of the continuity of the germ plasm, according to which "part of the germ plasm in the parent egg-cell is not used up in the construction of the body of the offspring, but is preserved unchanged in the formation of the germ cells of the following generation." This was a view which soon aroused great discussion in the biological world, and presently became of interest to psychologists also. Not only did it appear to confer a sort of immortality upon the human race similar to that enjoyed by the unicellular organisms which multiply by fission (an immortality, if not of person, at least of a portion of each individual's vital substance), but it appeared to be irreconcilable with the Lamarckian doctrine of the inheritance of acquired characteristics on which Spencer had laid so much stress in his psychology. Indeed, towards the end of his life Spencer engaged in a vigorous discussion with the Weismannists. Psychologists, like biologists, for the most part accepted the theory, and indeed the evidence is very strong against the transmission of acquirements to anything like the extent that Spencer seems sometimes to have imagined. No quite conclusive *a posteriori* evidence has, however, ever been advanced on either side, and in recent years discussion has become keener once again and McDougall has performed experiments on rats which seem to him to afford a strong argument in favour of the older, Lamarckian, view, so that, even at the present day, fifty years after Weismann first enunciated his theory, this all-important problem is by no means settled.

A little before this, Fabre had begun his long series of observations on insects, which, published under the general title of *Souvenirs Entomologiques*, appeared at intervals from 1879 to 1904. Soon after his first volume appeared, Lubbock followed with his *Ants, Bees and Wasps*, and ever since that time workers have been attracted to the field of entomology because the insects seem to present a high development of instinct together with a very low grade of intelligence. The field has seemed, therefore, a peculiarly favourable one in which to study instinct in its purity. Some of the original investigators, struck by the great uniformity and predictability of behaviour among the insects as compared with the "higher" animals, at first, perhaps, tended to exaggerate the fixity of instinct and the inability of insects to profit from experience. This was notably the case with Fabre, who was perhaps influenced by the Cartesian tradition associated with Catholicism—a tradition which had always emphasized the differences, rather than the similarities, between men and the other animals, and which had consequently tended to err, if at all, in the direction of under-estimating the powers of these latter.

In dealing with animals other than insects, however, the early workers have often been accused of the opposite error. This was especially the case as regards Romanes, who, writing also in the eighties, collected a great mass of facts by what has since come to be called, rather contemptuously, the anecdotal method, i.e. the utilization of casual reports concerning animal behaviour. Since many of these reports come from untrained and uncritical observers, it is clear that they may in certain cases be exposed to all the dangers of faulty observation, careless description and prejudiced interpretation, more especially, it would appear, in the direction of a reading into the animal of human motives and human processes of thought. Romanes himself was not unaware of this "anthropomorphic" danger, and employed certain criteria for judging the reliability of the accounts that he accepted. To him, moreover, belongs the credit of first clearly envisaging the possibilities of "comparative psychology" as a general study of the behaviour of animals, somewhat analogous to the already existing science of comparative anatomy. Subsequent investigators, however, while admitting that his initiative and point of view are of historical importance, have been inclined to believe that his criteria in judging individual cases were often not severe enough. The reaction started with Lloyd Morgan, who, in the nineties, endeavoured to combat the dangers of the anecdotal method by "the law of parsimony," according to which we must always explain animal behaviour in terms of the simplest mental processes that will account for the facts. In his own words, "in no case may we interpret an action as the outcome of a higher psychic faculty, if it can be interpreted as the outcome of the exercise of one which stands lower in the psychological scale." To Lloyd Morgan is also due the first widespread use of the experimental method in the animal field. It is true his experiments were not conducted, like those of later students, in the laboratory; they were rather in the nature of detailed and careful observations of the behaviour of animals in their normal environment but in special and artificially produced situations. While, of course, they do not permit of the same rigid control as laboratory experiments, they have nevertheless the advantage of being less remote from the ordinary conditions of animal life than are these latter; in any case they were a great advance in method over the simple collection of facts made by other (and often insufficiently critical) observers. Lloyd Morgan's work was continued by Hobhouse, whose *Mind in Evolution* was, however, not published until 1901, and therefore strictly speaking, belongs to our third period.

Meanwhile, dealing again with lower animals, Jacques Loeb in 1896 had propounded his theory of "tropisms," which emphasized once more the automatic aspects of animal behaviour and represented an attempt to explain this behaviour as far as possible in purely physical or chemical terms. Other workers in Germany took up Loeb's point of view, notably Beer, Bethe and von Uexküll, who adopted an extremely mechanistic attitude and in 1899 anticipated the behaviourist school by proposing to discard all reference to psychological terms, substituting for instance "reception" for "sensation" and "reasonance" for "memory." H. S. Jennings, however, in America (to which continent Loeb himself soon afterwards migrated), maintained that the behaviour even of the simplest organisms was too variable and modifiable to be explained in physico-chemical terms, so that, if variability and adaptability are signs of mind, mind is present also in these organisms.

Right at the end of our second period, in 1898, Thorndike took the momentous step of bringing certain higher animals into the laboratory and carrying out experiments with them as if they had been human subjects. These classical experiments were made with cats, dogs and chickens, and mostly took the form of enclosing the animal in a puzzle box, from which it could only escape by making a series of more or less complicated movements. His results pointed, he thought, to an absence of anything in the nature of "insight" into the nature of the mechanisms, and the effects of the movements which ultimately procured the animals their freedom. The "curve of learning" fell slowly, and nowhere showed the sudden drop that, with human subjects, follows the acquisition of an understanding of the reason why certain movements must be made rather than others. The animal's movements were characteristic of what Lloyd Morgan shortly afterwards called the "trial and error" method of learning, the method, for instance, adopted by most human beings in learning to ride a bicycle, a process in which they too have no "insight" into the reasons why certain balancing movements should be carried out. Thorndike concluded from his results, that, until evidence to the contrary should be forthcoming, we were not justified in attributing "insight" to any animal below the

primates—a challenging contention that was well calculated to
lead others to perform further series of experiments on animals.
Thorndike's work was a good augury for the vitality and success
of animal psychology in the new century that was just about to
open.

III. GALTON AND THE STUDY OF THE INDIVIDUAL

In the applications of evolutionism to the human race one of the first in the field after Darwin and Spencer, and one of the most influential of all workers in this sphere, was Darwin's half-cousin Sir Francis Galton. In his wealth of novel ideas Galton is indeed without a parallel in the whole of modern psychology; but his genius was of a roving rather than of a persevering order. His insatiable curiosity constantly attracted him to new problems, to each of which in turn he brought to bear his characteristic energy, originality and courage, though inevitably leaving much to be filled in and followed up by others. From fashions to finger-prints, from the geographical distribution of female beauty to the application of statistics to prize-giving, from weight-lifting to the future of the race, nothing lacked interest to this ingenious, versatile and all-inquiring mind. He made an investigation into the efficacy of prayer, from which it appeared that this method was of little use for healing the sick or controlling the weather. He experimentally adopted a religious attitude towards the figure of Punch, and eventually succeeded in inducing in himself "a large share of the feelings that a barbarian entertains towards his idol." On another occasion he voluntarily and with much effort brought about a paranoia-like condition "in which every horse seemed to be watching him, either with pricked ears or disguising its espionage."

His first important book from our present point of view was *Hereditary Genius*, published in 1869, just ten years after the appearance of *Origin of Species*. In this he applied statistical conceptions to the problems of heredity and endeavoured to rank celebrated men into classes according to the frequency with which their particular grade of ability would appear in population samples of a given size, grade "F" being attained by one man in 4,300, grade "G" by one man in 79,000, and so on up to grade "X," attained by only one man in a million. He endeavoured to show that genius is hereditary and runs in certain families, a matter in which he is now generally considered to be right, and furthermore that there is inheritance not only of the general tendency to genius but of specific forms of greatness, a matter as regards which there is still some difference of opinion. It is no doubt true, that, as Galton's pedigrees indicate, eminence in science, medicine, law, etc., does to some extent, tend to run in families. But here, as so often elsewhere in problems of human heredity, it is an exceedingly difficult matter to assess the relative importance of innate qualities on the one hand and of nurture and tradition on the other. Furthermore, the problem has been complicated in recent years by the attempt of Spearman and his school to divide up human capacity into factors. If we accept for a moment the formulations of this school, we may say that at present there is good evidence for the inheritance of "general ability" and some evidence even for the inheritance of certain specific abilities, though it is doubtful whether these are always of the kind that show themselves in eminence in a particular profession. Though writing at a time when, through the interest aroused by *Origin of Species*, biological factors naturally attracted most attention, Galton did not altogether overlook the influence of environment, and he endeavoured later to separate the two by a study of twins, since from general observation it seemed clear that, on the physical side at any rate, twins have more in common than have other children of the same parents. Here, however, Galton's work remained on the "anecdotal" level, though some of the anecdotes concerning similarity of history, disease, etc., were very striking. Much later Thorndike returned to the question, this time experimentally, and proved that there was in truth a more than ordinary family resemblance between the abilities of twins. Galton followed up *Hereditary Genius* with *English Men of Science* (1874) and *Natural Inheritance* (1889) and almost innumerable papers on the same subjects. His interest in heredity extended from the individual and the family to the race; he became more and more preoccupied with the possibilities of improving the human stock by selective breeding, and in 1883 came forward with definite proposals for eugenics, the applied science of heredity in the interests of the race, proposals which ultimately resulted in the creation of a technical journal *Biometrika* (1901), the establishment of the Eugenics Laboratory at

University College, London (1904), with Karl Pearson as director, and the foundation of a propagandist society for spreading the ideal of racial betterment, all of which are still flourishing at the present day.

Galton's more purely psychological contributions were contained in *Inquiries into Human Faculty*, which appeared in 1883. This book consists of a series of short essays, nearly all of which broke new ground and many of which are of real historical importance. Only a few of them, however, can be noticed here. The most famous of Galton's investigations was that concerning imagery, which took the form of the now much-used questionnaire method. As is well known to every student of psychology, Galton asked his subjects to call up before the "mind's eye" a picture of their breakfast table and then note the illumination, definition and colouring of the resulting image. His first results, as he tells us, "amazed" him. To begin with, he addressed his questionnaire to scientific men, "as they were the most likely class of men to give accurate answers." Their answers may have been accurate so far as they went, but there was little to report, for, as he tells us, "the great majority protested that mental imagery was unknown to them, and they looked upon me as fanciful and phantastic in supposing that the words 'mental imagery' really expressed what I believed everybody supposed them to mean. They had no more notion of its true nature than a colour-blind man, who has not discerned his defect, has of the nature of colour. They had a mental deficiency of which they were unaware." One member of the group even went so far as to suggest that "some fallacy" must underlie the whole investigation. Further inquiry, however, soon showed that visual imagery was indeed to be found often enough among other kinds of persons, and particularly among the young. It was clear, however, that the power of imagery stood in no direct relation to the power of thought, and tended to atrophy among those who devoted much of their time to abstract thinking. Galton thus started the long line of researches which have subsequently been carried out upon the power of imaging, and in the main his results have been amply corroborated. His pioneer investigation was an illustration of the value of experimentation, even in the very simple form provided by the questionnaire. It at once brought to light a mass of interesting data concerning the extent, function and frequency of an important feature of the human mind—facts which the more casual methods of inquiry hitherto adopted had completely failed to elicit.

From visual imagery Galton went on to deal with "synaesthesia" and "number forms." He discovered that in some persons there exist close associations between elements of different sense departments; sounds, names, letters or musical notes constantly evoking the images or ideas of certain colours. For other persons, too, the number series appears to be arranged spatially in some constant but individually characteristic form in two-dimensional or three-dimensional space. Here again remarkable individual peculiarities were revealed for the first time.

Another section of the book deals with an experimental study of association. Galton drew up a series of words, presented them to himself one at a time, and noted the associations to which they gave rise, recording the time taken to perform the operation. He here anticipated the work of numerous subsequent experimenters, and it was not long before the method began to bear fruit in Wundt's newly founded psychological laboratory at Leipzig. In these experiments of Galton is also to be found the embryo of the method of systematic introspection to be developed later, especially by Külpe and the Würzburg school; for it was his habit, as soon as some associated ideas had arisen and while "their traces were still lingering in the brain, to turn the attention upon them with a sudden and complete awakening, to arrest, to scrutinise them, and to record their exact appearance." A feature of the results that caused him some astonishment was the large proportion of aroused ideas that belonged to an earlier period of life, often indeed that of boyhood or early adolescence. We may perhaps allow ourselves to see in this a first indication of the psycho-analytic findings by use of the association method, findings, which, as is well known, emphasized even more dramatically the great influence of early life and the way this influence has of directing the course of our ideas whenever we withdraw ourselves from immediate interests or preoccupations.

In other experiments Galton was concerned with the study of the human sense organs and their functions, and here too he left his mark, particularly in the "Galton whistle," which has become a familiar feature of the laboratory. It was devised for testing the sensitivity to very high-pitched notes, and Galton employed it extensively both on men and animals, having a special form of the apparatus for use in the Zoo. The whistle would be fastened to the end of a stick, and blown by means of a rubber bulb attached to the whistle by a small tube. When an animal in repose had got used to the presence of the stick in its cage, the whistle would be blown and the presence or absence of reaction noted. It was found that there were great differences in sensitivity between different species and different members of the same species. Some men could hear these high notes much better than others, and in general there was a considerable falling-off of the ability with age. Small dogs were better at the task than big dogs, and cats were the most acute of all (perhaps, as Galton suggests, because of their interest in the high-pitched noises made by mice). Although this is the best known of his sensory experiments, practically all the sense departments, vision, touch, smell, muscular sensation, etc., were at one time or another the subject of inquiry.

Memory and fatigue likewise fell within his purview; nor was the orectic field neglected; gregariousness, in particular, aroused his interest, both in men and animals; and one interesting essay on the domestication of animals opened a line of work, which has as yet been very inadequately followed up on the psychological side; for it is rather surprising how little animal investigators have been concerned with the psychological relations between man and the animals with whom he lives as members of his intimate environment. Two especially noteworthy contributions of Galton's, those dealing with composite photography and finger-prints respectively, are perhaps matters of "anthropometry" rather than psychology. But in his anthropometric laboratory, which was open for some six years at the South Kensington Museum, and where, during this time, nearly ten thousand people were examined, psychological tests played some part.

And this brings us to the consideration of Galton's essential rôle in the history of psychology. Galton was from the start interested not so much in the general laws governing the mind, as in *individual differences*. Hitherto regarded by psychologists merely as a nuisance to be eliminated as far as possible, or at best as a curiosity, the difference between individuals in capacity and character presented for Galton a fascinating problem on its own account. If to Wundt, building on the foundation made by

Fechner, belongs the honour of definitely establishing the reign of experiment in general psychology, to Galton falls the almost equal credit of pointing the way to an individual psychology on an experimental basis. Galton is the true father of the mental "test" and of all that later sprang from it—of the practical application of testing to problems of deficiency and aptitude, of vocational guidance and selection, of statistical analysis and the discovery of "factors" by the correlation method. Galton himself began the study of correlation between mental traits, work which was continued by a series of brilliant investigators, chief among whom were Pearson, William Brown, Cyril Burt, God-frey Thomson and (by far the most important) Spearman—all, it will be noticed, British; though (except in Pearson's case) most of this work only began in the twentieth century, some very considerable time after Galton had finished his, and under the stimulus of German experimental psychology, which was then being introduced into England. Had it not been for the work of Binet, we might indeed have said that this branch of psycho-logy was almost entirely British and American in its origin, just as the experimental psychology of general laws was almost entirely German in its early phases.

By Pearson, the biographer of Galton, and his successor in the statistical and eugenic fields, we are asked to look upon Galton as one whose claims as a founder of a new method in psychology are no whit inferior to Wundt's. So far as originality, ingenuity and versatility are concerned, there is much to be said in favour of this contention. If his work proved less immediately fruitful and inspiring, it was probably because the wide dispersal of his energies did not allow him time or patience to follow up the clues that he himself provided, or to collect followers or found a school to carry out this purpose. Except in the matter of eugenics (which was, it is true, his most absorbing interest, to which all else was in some degree contributory or subservient), he was a wanderer in the realms of science, who scattered riches by the roadside as he passed, careless of the use to which they might be put or whether any use was made of them at all. In due course most of them were picked up and some have borne full interest. But, so far as immediate utilization was concerned, his discoveries were at a disadvantage as compared with those of Wundt, whose chief interest was psychology throughout his life, who founded an institute and worked there steadily for forty years, attracting thither all who were anxious to learn and practise the new science. Galton, however, remains a unique figure in psychology. Never again in the history of the science up to the present time do we meet an investigator so brilliant, so versatile, so wide in his interests and abilities, so little bound by prejudice or preconception. Compared with him, all others (with the one exception perhaps of William James) are apt to appear a little ponderous and pedantic, a little blinkered in their outlook. Men of Galton's temperament are comparatively rare in the world of science, for they seldom possess the qualities necessary for the development and employment of truly scientific methods. Modern psychology as an independent science is fortunate in having such a man, and one of such calibre, in its brief history.

IV. CHILD PSYCHOLOGY AND SOCIAL PSYCHOLOGY

Two further developments of evolutionism may be noted here, before we pass on to a consideration of the further progress of systematic psychology after Bain and Spencer. The first and most important of these is child psychology, the second the anthropological study of the mental life of primitive peoples. We have seen that Darwin himself, in his *Biographical Sketch of an Infant*, made a start with the detailed and careful observation of the behaviour and development of young children. Some four years later appeared a more ambitious study of the same kind by W. Preyer, a friend of Fechner and Wundt, and a worker in experimental psychology in its very early days. Preyer observed the development of reflexes from birth and the gradual complications ensuing as a result of experience and learning, particularly the influence of imitation. Although much criticized, because of its inadequate separation of observation from interpretation, the *Mind of the Child* is one of the great classics of child psychology, and fresh editions of the book have been called for until quite recent times. In the early nineties the new interest in children began to develop apace. In 1891 Stanley Hall, who had recently returned to America from Wundt's laboratory in Leipzig, founded the *Pedagogical Seminary*, the first journal to be devoted to the subject, while Sully in England established the British Association for Child Study in 1893. Both journal and association have played a considerable part in the development of the "new education" in their respective countries. The year 1893 also saw a further important study of individual development, Shinn's *Notes on the Development of a Child*, while K. C. Moore a few years later prolonged the period of observation through several years of childhood. Another influential book was Sully's *Studies of Childhood* (1895), while in 1896 a very important practical step was taken by Witmer in founding, at Philadelphia, the first Psychological Clinic for maladjusted children. The full significance of this last step has only been apparent in quite recent years, during which a multitude of similar institutions has sprung up in several different countries. The sudden blossoming forth of this movement since the Great War is undoubtedly due, on the one hand, to the increased understanding of nervous disease, its prevalence in childhood and its connection with delinquency, and on the other hand to the ability to distinguish clearly with the help of mental tests between functional disturbance and hereditary mental defect. The foundation of Witmer's original clinic nearly forty years ago was, however, a step indicating remarkable insight and courage and marks an epoch in the history of applied psychology.

Through all this work the genetic background is constantly apparent. Without the evolutionary point of view, these branches of psychology could scarcely have developed as they did. From time to time, moreover, the common aspect of development in race and individual was definitely stressed. Stanley Hall early adopted the doctrine of "recapitulation," according to which the individual passes through the stages which have characterized the evolution of the race—a view which he consistently expounded in many of his contributions, and which may perhaps be said to culminate in his great work on *Adolescence* published in 1904. Stanley Hall believed, for instance, that in its play activity the child exhibits a series of phases corresponding to cultural phases of human society, a hunting period, a building period and so on. Another writer, Karl Groos, in two well-known books on the *Play of Animals* and the *Play of Man* respectively, both published in the nineties, advocated a different theory of play; namely that play was in the nature of a preparation for the future activities of the adult individual, that in his play the child, as it were, rehearsed and practised the tasks that he would later perform in all seriousness as a man, and that the individuals who enjoyed this practice (through their play) would have a corresponding advantage over others in the struggle for existence, and would therefore be more likely to survive and reproduce themselves. These two theories, together with the less popular theory of surplus energy that was advanced by Spencer, have remained the chief theoretical contributions to the study of play—unless we extend the conception of play to include art also, in which case the whole of aesthetic speculation becomes relevant to the discussion.

In his endeavour to bring together the development of the individual (ontogeny) and that of the race (phylogeny) Stanley Hall was ably seconded by James Mark Baldwin, the title of whose work on *Mental Development in the Child and the Race* (1895) sufficiently explains its standpoint. This leads us naturally to the other sphere we mentioned at the beginning of the preceding paragraph, i.e. the mental life of primitive peoples. The development of the anthropological and sociological aspects of psychology—like that of child psychology—was an achievement of our 1860–1900 period, though here, as elsewhere of course, earlier beginnings are not wanting. In sociology, especially, the influence of Comte, whose work became widely known both in England and France through the writings of John Stuart Mill, had familiarized thinkers with the idea of developmental stages in society even before the *Origin of Species*. His three stages, the theological, the metaphysical and the positive, have undoubtedly helped to mould thought in the sociological sphere among a host of writers, most of whom have not avowedly belonged to the "positivist" school. In the anthropological sphere Bastian and Ratzel began to describe human customs in terms of adjustment to varying environments. Already Waitz, Steinthal and Lazarus had published works in the fifties which were positivist in spirit and endeavoured to combine empirical analysis with historical perspective. Though written before Darwin's *Origin of Species*, their outlook was largely developmental, as was also to a great extent that of the *Zeitschrift für Völkerpsychologie und Sprachwissenschaft*, founded by Steinthal and Lazarus in 1860. To these two writers belongs the credit of being among the first to realize the psychological implications of philology. These implications were soon to be followed up by Max Müller and others, and in later times have been illuminatingly treated by the philologist Jespersen and by certain of the psycho-analytic writers; they have however, it would seem, not even yet received the more systematic and extensive treatment which will give philology and psychology full mutual benefit of one another.

The most important writer in the whole sphere of anthropology was undoubtedly E. B. Tylor, whose *Primitive Culture* (1871) marked an epoch in the development of what later came to be called "cultural" anthropology. Tylor's most celebrated contribution was his doctrine of animism, the view that primitive man tends to look upon all things anthropomorphically, to treat them as though they had a consciousness and "soul" not unlike his own—in short to regard Nature as a mass of conscious forces, benevolent or hostile, to which all human happiness or sorrow, success or failure, are ultimately due. Religion itself is a development of animism, and is, therefore, in the last resort based upon the same delusions, though Tylor himself did not push the implications of his doctrine with the same fire and aggressiveness as some of the more biological evolutionists had done. His doctrine, nevertheless, proved a very influential one and was indeed but little called in question until close upon the end of the century. It then began to appear that there were degrees and kinds of animism which had to be distinguished, and that sometimes the objects and forces of Nature were not so much personalized, as regarded as vaguely defined powers, possessed by, or connected with, visible and tangible things—powers which were helpful or dangerous as the case might be. This latter concept of "mana," originally introduced into anthropology by Codrington in his study of the *Melanesians* (1891) and later popularized by Marett, was perhaps the most important factor in leading to an eventual qualification of Tylor's animistic views; his general influence, however, has been a very potent one in the psychologizing of anthropology, and in the main we may perhaps say that several of the greatest subsequent writers, including Wundt and Frazer, have followed in his tradition. As in the case of these latter writers, his predominantly psychological approach blinded him to some extent to more sociological and historical considerations, as was presently to be pointed out very forcibly by the "diffusionist" school. Tylor himself was a "parallelist," i.e. inclined to think that, given a certain level of cultural development, the same customs tend to arise spontaneously among different groups, however widely separated; whereas the "diffusionists" laid greater stress on the geographical transmission of cultural elements, this naturally leading them to enphasize historical rather than psychological considerations. Tylor's attitude is one that is natural to the psychologically-minded student of anthropology, and, though it has its very real dangers, it is no more perilous than that of the opposing school, who, in their enthusiasm for "culture contact," are only too ready to neglect mental factors altogether. It seems clear that for a complete understanding of a given cultural element we require to know both its historical derivation and its psychological significance; in truth, the two schools are carrying on work that is complementary rather than antagonistic. In any case Tylor's (and Frazer's) general outlook was one that later on became adopted and developed by the psycho-analysts, in whose hands the general similarities between the different aspects of "primitive mind"—whether in the child, the dreamer, the neurotic or the savage—have recently undergone an elaboration which seems likely to establish a successful and progressive "comparative psychology" upon a very wide basis.[1]

The term "comparative psychology" was used by Herbert Spencer as the title of an essay in 1876, and between 1880 and 1896 there appeared the three volumes of the *Principles of Sociology*, based on several further volumes of *Descriptive Sociology*, compiled by a number of assistant hands. Here the general scheme of development already worked out in *First Principles*, in biology and in psychology, is applied to the growth of human societies. Though writing from a more *a priori* standpoint and in the interests of a general theory of evolution, Spencer corroborated and amplified many of Tylor's findings as regards animism and religion. Thus both authors are in agreement as to the importance of dreams and abnormal states in fostering the belief in the existence of the soul as an independent spiritual entity separable from the body and surviving after death, while Spencer elaborated the animistic theory of the origin of religion by showing the way in which the souls of ancestors gradually become converted into gods. The three great volumes exhibit the same magnificent breadth of vision and detailed application of the evolutionary theory as the earlier parts of the *Synthetic Philosophy*. Indeed they are in some ways even more impressive, inasmuch as they are based on fuller data (obtained with the aid of the compilers of *Descriptive Sociology*) and are less marred by exaggerated or mistaken biological doctrines, such as that concerning the inheritance of acquired characters, which played so large a part in the *Psychology*. The *Principles of*

---

[1] We may note in this connection that J. Piaget has recently endeavoured to show that Tylor's animistic theory is true also of the young child, though in view of criticisms now being made it would appear likely that Piaget's views may be in no less need of qualification than were Tylor's.

Sociology definitely and irrevocably introduced the concept of evolution into anthropology, social psychology and sociology itself, and however little Spencer's influence is actually acknowledged, there have been few books since written in any of these fields that do not to some extent bear the impress of his work.

Spencer's *Principles* may be justifiably looked upon as the first book on "Social Psychology" as now understood, though it was much else besides. Several other works of importance followed, however, in the course of the nineties. Of these the first was Gabriel Tarde's *Laws of Imitation* (1890), in which there is an attempt at a logical analysis of the various forms of social interaction, for in Tarde's sense "imitation" embraces practically all influence exercised by one human being on another—whatever the mental level involved. A great number of general situations were considered in which it is evident that "imitation" plays a part in the structure and development of human conduct: the formation of groups through the assimilation of behaviour, belief, and attitude, the influencing of one group by another, as when country people copy townsmen, the socially inferior copy their superiors, or the conquered copy their conquerors, and so on. In all these matters the treatment is more explicitly and intimately psychological than in any previous work upon such subjects. In one sense Tarde's standpoint represents a passionate reaction against the sensationism of the associationists. He distinguishes three kinds of mental activity: the mind's reaction to external objects, to other minds, and to itself respectively. Whereas the associationists had attached most importance to the first, Tarde stresses the two latter. As a result, sensation plays in his work an unimportant part as compared with belief and desire. We here find the emphasis on the conative aspects of the mind which has ever since been a characteristic of books on social psychology. While it was comparatively easy to write textbooks on the individual mind in which knowledge received a far more extensive and elaborate treatment than feeling or emotion, this seemed almost from the beginning to be an impossible task to carry through, when psychologists began seriously to concern themselves with the action of men in groups. The fiction that man was a consistently rational animal could no longer be maintained when he was looked at from this new point of view, and psychologists had now perforce to look to the orectic, rather than the

cognitive, elements of the human mind, to account for the strange
and unreasonable behaviour that was everywhere so much in
evidence. This element of irrationality was even more stressed in
the writings of Sighele and Le Bon, who devoted their attention
not so much to permanent groups as to crowds. Le Bon's work on
The Crowd (1895) has become a classic. It presents the reader
with a vivid picture of the collective madness that may take
possession of undisciplined and fortuitously formed assemblies.
Emphasis is laid upon the fact that the moral and intellectual
level of such assemblies tends to be that of its lowest rather than
of its average or highest members, and this is explained in terms
of loss of individuality. The individual feels himself swamped in
the group and at the same time is conscious of a sense of brute
strength through belonging to the group. There is no need for
him to use his intellectual powers, no call for him to awake his
sense of moral responsibility, for the group is in a sense all powerful, and therefore not in need of intellect or morals. Such crowds
are at the mercy of the more primitive instincts that all its
members have in common, or of such suggestions as are given
by their leaders. A leader indeed occupies much the same position in relation to the crowd as the hypnotist does in relation to
the patient he has hypnotized. In fact Le Bon carried into crowd
psychology the knowledge recently gained by Charcot, Liébault,
Bernheim and other French psychiatrists in the domain of psycho-
pathology, much as Freud some twenty-five years later employed
in the same sphere the concepts he had formed in his psycho-
analytic work.

Together with these important developments in social psychology, the nineties witnessed also the beginnings of the psychology
of religion. In some ways these beginnings may be traced to
Stanley Hall's studies of childhood, which included inquiries into
the child's notions of God, his ideas of right and wrong and any
sudden "conversions" or changes in his moral attitude. By far
the most significant event in this field, however, was the appearance of Starbuck's *Psychology of Religion* in 1899. This book was
based essentially on a series of personal documents in which the
writers described their own, often very remarkable, religious
experiences, Indeed this collection of manuscripts has been correctly described as the first great inductive approach to this
unique aspect of human life. Starbuck himself used his material

chiefly for the purpose of a study of religious conversion. He showed that conversion is in the nature of a sudden resolution of a conflict between mutually antagonistic elements within the personality, a resolution in which certain concepts all at once acquire a new value and, through the intense satisfaction they afford, enable the individual to settle down with a stability hitherto unknown. Starbuck thus found himself brought face to face with the phenomena of mental conflict, which at just about the same time were being studied by Freud in the early days of psycho-analysis. Indeed, it seemed clear from the start that religious psychology, no less than social psychology, might have much to learn from psycho-pathology, and, if any investigator had been bold enough to draw the inference, it might even then have been maintained that here again there was room for a broadly conceived "comparative psychology," embracing many at first sight very distinct aspects of human behaviour and experience. In fact, however, the need for collaboration and mutual assistance over a wide field is only now becoming realized. The multiplicity of claims on the attention of the infant science of psychology has up to now prevented anything like a satisfactory plan of development or adequate co-ordination of the work carried on in various fields and by various methods. Such co-ordination, we may hope, will characterize the adolescence of psychology, which has yet to come. For the moment, and throughout the century that is covered by our present survey, we have to be content with the enterprising, though often inharmonious and erratic, efforts of a youthful discipline that has not yet gained a full understanding of its own powers and limitations, and has yet to learn how to use these powers to its own best advantage.

IT is now time to pick up the story of what from want of a better
term we have called "systematic psychology," i.e. psychology
which was not predominantly experimental, physiological or
biological, but which may be looked upon as in the tradition of
the older psychology established by the earlier, more philosophic
writers. Within this field the first important writer after Bain
was Franz Brentano, whose *Psychologie vom empirischen Standpunkte*, published in 1874, proved to be a very influential work,
though actually it is one that is but little read today by English-
speaking students. Brentano is looked upon as the founder of
"act psychology" as distinguished from the "content psychology" that was predominant among the early experimentalists.
We have seen that for long there had been two dominant,
though not always clearly differentiated, conceptions of how the
mind worked. According to the one notion, which found its
fullest expression in the extreme associationists, the mind was
essentially a mechanism, automatically elaborating the material
provided for it by the senses. According to the other, it was
itself an active and creative agency. Those who favoured the
first view endeavoured to conceive of mind in terms of material
causality, those who held the second believed that the most
essential phenomena of mind were left out of account in any
such reduction. Since the experimenters had physics and physiology before them as their ideals, it was only natural that they
should tend to adopt the former, mechanistic, standpoint. Accordingly they were interested in the content of the mind at any
moment and the laws which governed the appearance of successive contents; the simple scheme of associationism suited them
well enough, especially since associationism regarded mind as
built up of sensory elements, and sensations were relatively easy
to experiment upon. The "activity" of mind on the other hand
appeared as something uncontrollable, unpredictable, and even

mystical—and as a matter of fact had often enough been emphasized by those who invested the mind with certain transcendental powers, which removed it altogether from the domain of strictly scientific treatment. It is perhaps not surprising, therefore, that Brentano should have been a priest, and that the "Austrian school" with which he is associated should have flourished in the more southern part of central Europe, where Catholic influence prevailed. Brentano's originality, however, consisted in uniting an insistence on activity with a strict empiricism. "Experience," he said, "alone influences me as a mistress." And certainly he was no docile follower of dogma; for, though it cost him his chair, he resigned from the Church rather than accept the doctrine of papal infallibility, against which he had fought as the champion of the liberal party. For Brentano, however, experience revealed, not an inert content of sensations and their combinations, but mental "acts." Sensations exist, but they themselves are not mental; what is mental is the activity that occurs when a person "sees" a colour, "hears" a sound, or "smells" an odour. There are, according to Brentano, three fundamental classes of psychic activity; ideating (as in sensing or imagining), judging, and the processes loosely to be described as love or hate (which, in more modern terminology, may be said to embrace the whole category of orexis). Moreover, the objects of an act may be another act, so that the mind can actively contemplate its own activity.

We need not enter here into the complexities of Brentano's psychology. It is perhaps sufficient for our present purpose to state that his great contribution was the emphasis he laid upon activity, and to indicate some of the principal ways in which his influence was felt in subsequent psychology. The most immediate effect of his work was on the Austrian school of writers who dealt with *Gestaltqualität*, about which we shall say a few more words in a moment. Later on, his influence passed to England and, in the persons of Ward and Stout, led to the final overthrow of associationism in its classic form. In the early twentieth century it appeared in the work of the Würzburg school on the "psychology of the thought processes," a little later in that of the very prolific modern school of *Gestalt*, and quite recently the work of Brentano and other members of the "Austrian school" appears as a directing element in Spearman's ambitious attempt to formulate the "principles of cognition." Brentano himself, though an empiricist, was no experimentalist, but in the three last developments, we find that the forces set in action by his work eventually penetrated to the laboratory and there produced results of great importance.

We may now turn our attention to Brentano's immediate successors in the Austrian school. The most important of these were his pupils von Ehrenfels and Meinong, to the former of whom is due the first clear formulation of the doctrine of form-quality (*Gestaltqualität*). Already in 1886, in his *Analyse der Empfindungen*, Ernst Mach had propounded the view that there existed sensations of "space form" and of "time form," meaning thereby that the form is independent of particular sensory quality, e.g. that a circle may be either red or green, or that a tune is the same in whatsoever key it may be played. Five years later, in 1890, von Ehrenfels maintained that form in space or time is a new element or quality, independent of the sensory *fundaments* on which it rests. The form of a square, or circle or a tune, is as immediately experiential as the purely sensory elements concerned. Such form qualities, moreover, are not confined to space and time, but are to be found in tonal fusions, in the flavours of taste and smell, and in the perception of movement. Furthermore, they may themselves be of various levels, the higher levels having as their fundaments the form qualities of lower levels, as when we became aware of the relationship between two figures or two tunes. Much the same views were also urged by Meinong in the following year, though with a different terminology,[1] with more emphasis on the importance of relations, and with a distinction between form qualities on the perceptual and ideational level.

Since their novelty consisted in a new element, the views of both these writers might possibly have been expressed in terms of "content" psychology; but, principally owing to the influence of their teacher Brentano, both von Ehrenfels and Meinong conceived of their new elements as "acts," and saw in them dynamic creations of the mind. Meinong's terminology, however, already indicates a tendency to return to the old view; and this tendency was carried still further by the next member of the school, Cor-

---

[1] Meinong called the fundaments "founding contents" and the form qualities "founded contents," the two together forming a "complexion."

nelius, for whom a form quality was not a founded *content*, as it was for Meinong, but a founded *attribute*, an attribute that itself came into being as the result of an analytic process of attention—a view which was expressed in terms that were more familiar to the experimentalists and which was for the most part in harmony with the results of extensive investigations into perceptual forms carried out shortly afterwards by Schumann, von Aster, and others. Schumann, however, in stressing the effects of the varying direction of attention on these forms, considered attention itself to be an act. The Austrian school is usually held to include also Witasek and Benussi, who to some extent carried on the "act" tradition into the twentieth century; Benussi, moreover, was definitely an experimentalist, whose psycho-physical work on space and time perception was expressed in the concepts and theories elaborated by the earlier members of the school. Meinong himself, though no experimenter, had founded the first Austrian laboratory at Graz in 1892, and it was here that Benussi carried over the "form quality" tradition into the experimental field.

The revolt started by Brentano against the associationist outlook, as found in the "content psychology" of the laboratories, in one way or another influenced most of the important writers of textbooks or systematic treatises in the last twenty years of the nineteenth century. We have already mentioned Ward and Stout in this connection. We might, however, with almost equal justice have referred in the same way to Th. Lipps, Höffding, James and Külpe, who (excluding for the moment Wundt) were among the principal writers of textbooks or general expositions during this period. Of the others, Volkmann's *Lehrbuch*, published in 1876, was almost purely Herbartian, Sully's works may be regarded as continuing the tradition set by Bain, while Titchener's *Outline* was Wundtian in spirit. Theodor Lipps's *Grundtatsachen des Seelenlebens* (1883) was the first general textbook, other than Wundt's own, to take account of the new developments in the experimental field; but it was in no sense a copy of Wundt's. Lipps took into consideration the data provided by Lotze, Helmholtz, Wundt and others, and endeavoured to incorporate them in a new system which had much in common with that of the Austrian school, for to Lipps also the mind was essentially active. In Boring's words, he was "just on the edge of experimental psychology—but not quite within it." This applies particularly to his work on space perception and aesthetics, for which he is perhaps best known at the present day. He is especially associated with the doctrine of "empathy" (*Einfühlung*), to which he was led by his studies of optical illusions,[1] and according to which we tend to "feel ourselves into" the objects of our contemplation, a circumstance that determines many of our aesthetic reactions. A vertical line seems to be contending against gravity, the end lines of the celebrated Müller-Lyer illusion make the whole figure expand or shrink together as the case may be, a column with too large a capital seems to be oppressed with a heavy burden, whereas another with too small a capital gives a sense of unnecessary effort. In Lipps's work the act psychology is fused with an insistence on the importance of the self, and both of these elements find characteristic expression in his views on aesthetics.

Next in historical order to Lipps's *Grundtatsachen* came Sully's *Outlines of Psychology* (1884) which was an immediate success, and took its place as the foremost English textbook, supplanting Bain's two books which had been written about a quarter of a century earlier, and were now growing out of date. Sully had a gift for clear and ordered exposition, and he followed up his first textbook by several others, of which the *Teachers' Handbook of Psychology*, published in 1886, was the first psychological book on modern lines written expressly from the educational point of view. Sully, in his earlier years, had written books on more special aspects of psychology, and his *Illusions* in particular was a stimulating essay on a subject that was at the time arousing the greatest interest among writers of all schools. Later on, as already noted, he devoted himself principally to child psychology and published several volumes on this topic also.

James Ward was the true successor of Brentano and of Lipps, for the most essential elements of his system are the two concepts of activity and the unity of the self. Ward's fame as a psychologist is based on his article on "Psychology" in the ninth edition of the *Encyclopaedia Britannica* (1886), subsequently elaborated in the eleventh edition (1911). Seldom has an encyclopaedia article aroused so much interest or enthusiasm. It was immediately treated and reviewed as though it were a book, and one

[1] *Raumaesthetik*, 1897, *Aesthetik*, 1903–6, and many individual papers.

of the principal reviewers was Bain, whose associationism it attacked. The appearance of the article was indeed an event of considerable importance. First, because it represented the first occasion on which the Encyclopaedia had honoured psychology with the treatment accorded to sciences recognized to be of importance in their own right (in Mansel's article, which Ward's supplanted, psychology was treated under "Metaphysics"); secondly, because of its own merits as an exposition; and thirdly, because it delivered a blow to associationism from which this doctrine has never yet recovered. Ward literally put associationism in its place, by showing at once its justification and its limitations. Association was important as a mechanism, but was far from being able to account either for the unity or the creativeness of mind. For both of these the "subject" was an indispensable desideratum; the complexity of mind comes about, not "through the combination and re-combination of various elementary units," but rather as the result of a gradual differentiation of a primary unity. In this respect Ward's conception was biological rather than physiological or physical. Though he had studied considerably in Germany, it was not for nothing that he was a countryman of Darwin and of Spencer. Ward eventually gave his system fuller form in his *Psychological Principles*, which appeared, over thirty years after the original article, in 1918. As if to anticipate an inevitable criticism, he himself suggested that his later book would seem to many a "belated patchwork." Belated it undoubtedly was, for, though containing many of the merits of the article, it failed utterly to take account of the great mass of data that had accumulated in the intervening years. To the majority of psychologists, busy with new methods and the discussion of new standpoints, the book seemed an anachronism and served as little more than a reminder of the important rôle that Ward had played a generation earlier.

Influential as Ward's encyclopaedia article had been, it was not altogether easy reading; nor was its mode of publication calculated to bring him many other readers than those of the professional or specialist class. The wider popularization of Ward's point of view was, however, brought about by Stout, whose *Manual* (1898) is well known to every English student, and who combined the influence of Ward and Brentano with that of Herbart and of traditional associationism in a happy way that appeared to extract the best elements from them all and make them complementary rather than antagonistic. The *Manual* was preceded by the *Analytic Psychology*, in which the biological attitude implied in Ward (and before him explicitly adopted by Spencer) is elaborated. Both Ward and Stout made new and fruitful use of Kant's distinction between the three aspects of mind: cognition, affection and conation. It was Stout who popularized the last word and who most clearly defined the relation of these aspects to one another. Both thinking and willing, he maintained, were ways in which the organism seeks to maintain itself and to regain its lost equilibrium; whereas feeling is dependent on the success or unsuccess of these efforts, pleasure accompanying success and its opposite accompanying failure. The mind thus seeks a goal, and its development cannot be accounted for except in terms of an active unity. In dealing with this process of development in the *Analytic Psychology*, much use is made of the concept of apperception, though the word is never mentioned in the *Manual*. On the whole the earlier work, though less often read today, is the more suggestive and original of the two. It is well worthy of greater attention than it usually receives from the modern student, for it is at once an acutely penetrating and profoundly satisfying book, and it is astonishing how many anticipations—or at least adumbrations—of later twentieth-century developments are to be found in it. It contains a good deal of what is more explicitly stated later on by the *Gestalt* school, and even some things that are characteristic of psycho-analysis, while the general biological view of the mind endeavouring to preserve its equilibrium in spite of disturbing circumstances is one that has become increasingly popular in recent years.

Textbooks or general treatises came fast round about 1890, and between Ward's article and Stout's *Analytic Psychology* there were no less than seven such works of an important character, Dewey's *Psychology*, Höffding's *Outline*, Ladd's *Elements of Physiological Psychology*, James's *Principles*, Sully's *Human Mind*, Külpe's *Outline* and Titchener's *Textbook*. It is clear that there was now a demand for books on the mind of a scientific but not too technical a nature. The public and the ordinary student had awakened to the fact that new life was astir in this field which had so long been regarded as being a territory reserved strictly for the philosophically erudite. Their demand for knowledge in a palatable form was very adequately catered for by the above-mentioned series of volumes, which together provided a treatment suitable for every reasonable taste. Sully's book was perhaps the least original but the most generally instructive. Höffding's was mainly in the tradition of Brentano and Ward rather than of Wundt, for it laid great stress on activity in a biological sense, combining this with an emphasis on the unconscious and the adoption of a pan-psychic attitude that would surely have pleased Fechner (who died the same year, 1887, in which this book was published). The *Outline* was very popular and was translated into several languages, making a wide appeal both to English and German-speaking readers. Külpe's *Outline*, published six years later, was a rather more academic production. Külpe was Wundt's pupil, the book was dedicated to Wundt, and was definitely an attempt to write a textbook on an experimental basis. On the whole Külpe succeeded in turning out a much more readable presentation than his teacher. The *Outline* was indeed the first short presentation of experimental work in a systematic setting that had been attempted. It was, however, written before Külpe's own intellectual maturity and before he himself had embarked on the new experimental adventures of the "Würzburg school" with which his name is now chiefly associated. In later years he was often urged by his pupils to bring his early *Outline* up to date, but he never gave way to their entreaties. A revised *Outline* might have become a textbook of very considerable importance in the early twentieth century. As it is, the book is now little likely to be read, unless it be from the historical point of view.

Dewey's *Psychology* was the first American textbook of the "new" psychology, but it still approached its subject from the philosophical point of view and devoted some space to the discussion of philosophical presuppositions. Perhaps for this reason it was, after a few successful years, superseded by other texts that dispensed with these preliminaries. Ladd's *Elements of Physiological Psychology* was a definite attempt to produce an English equivalent of Wundt's *Grundzüge*. Like the latter work, it deals at much greater length than most psychological texts with the brain and nervous system. It was successful in its aim, and was also far more readable than its great original. It was revised by Woodworth in 1911, and is indeed worthy of being periodically revised in the same way as the *Grundzüge*. Titchener's *Outline* (published in 1896, four years after he had finished his studies with Wundt at Leipzig) was somewhat similar to Külpe's and only just missed the honour of being the first English treatise written definitely from the laboratory standpoint. In any case, however, it was soon eclipsed by the same writer's unique *Experimental Psychology*, which appeared in the early years of the new century.

Meanwhile, however, William James had written what is almost certainly the greatest classic of psychology. It took twelve years to write, during which time James, who had started as a physiologist, became a psychologist, and was on the way to becoming a philosopher. The *Principles of Psychology* was never really planned as a systematic treatise, and, when it eventually appeared, large portions of it had already been published in various journals. It is not even quite internally consistent; but these defects are more than outweighed by compensating virtues. Its qualities are essentially those of the man who wrote it. James was forcible, yet kindly and tolerant; he possessed a very real and lively interest in human beings, their thinkings and doings (for he was certainly not one of those psychologists who adopt their profession as a compensation—in the Adlerian sense—for their inability to understand their fellow creatures in ordinary life); he was a philosopher, but one who held that philosophy should not be divorced from the actuality of human hopes and strivings; and he possessed a challenging, compelling and attractive literary style. There are phrases and passages in the book which, when once read, are apt to become part of the permanent equipment of the budding psychologist—as many generations of students have discovered. When we add to this the fact that James's general attitude seems to have been in harmony with the predominant tendency of American psychological thought, i.e. towards activism and functionalism, the study of the living person and of the difference between persons, rather than the investigation of fundamental laws or the discovery of elementary qualities, then it is not difficult to understand the influence exercised by this book. James, too, had many subsequently distinguished psychologists (including Angell, Calkins, Healy, Sidis, Thorndike, Woodworth and Yerkes) among his pupils, though he founded no school as Wundt had done (probably because he was too unsystematic); if anything, he was indeed, as Brett puts it, "systematically erratic."

One of the curiosities of James's position was his attitude towards experimentation. He was the first to teach the subject in America, for when instructor in physiology at Harvard he gave some training in it to his students in 1875—four years prior to the foundation of Wundt's laboratory. He was always the champion of the experimentalists, and was somehow convinced of the ultimate importance of their work; but personally he disliked it, was impatient of its limitations, and felt admiration mixed with wonder and contempt for those who were able to tolerate its drudgery. He solved the difficulty in his own case by bringing Münsterberg (with whom he sympathized as the most dashing and "advanced" of the experimenters) to Harvard in 1892, to take charge of this side of the subject. James disliked pedantry in any form, and the experimenter all too easily became a pedant—especially in the early days when he was inevitably to some extent self-conscious about his newly achieved methods of precision.

On the other hand, James was one of the first psychologists to realize the importance of the "abnormal" phenomena of mind and the lessons to be learnt from them. He took his pupils to visit mental hospitals, and though at first he was hostile to the idea of subconscious mind (saying that it threatened to turn "what might be a science into a tumbling ground for whimsies"), he later on became more than reconciled to the notion, and even went so far as to declare that the discovery of mental processes outside the sphere of consciousness was the "most important step forward" that had occurred since his own student days, revealing as it did "an entirely unsuspected peculiarity in the constitution of human nature."

James's general attitude was one not far removed from that of Ward and Stout. He had no use for elementarism, but looked upon the mind in a way that combined Brentano's insistence on activity with the evolutionary outlook of biology. "Consciousness," he said, "has in all probability been evolved, like all other functions, for a use." Anticipating his later pragmatic attitude in philosophy, he held that even "necessary truths" which appeared to be inevitable, such as geometrical relations or logical structures, are not really inevitable in any absolute sense but only because

E

for countless ages our ancestors were selected by virtue of their possession of certain modes of apprehending and reacting to the universe. Such "necessary truths" in the biological sense are contrasted with the effects of (individual) experience, which have been dinned into us by repetition, but which still appear as arbitrary rather than inevitable. Poles asunder as the two men were, we may yet here see something very similar to Spencer's endeavour to combine the empirical theory that all experience is individually acquired with the theory of innate dispositions by assuming that what is learnt by the individual tends eventually to become the natural heritage of the race—except that Spencer presupposed the inheritance of acquired characters, whereas James did not. James's biological outlook is shown also in his insistence upon instincts. It was he who really started the fashion for classifications and catalogues of instincts, though his own list is somewhat crude, including as it does tendencies of very various levels of complexity, without any adequate statement or explanation of their differences in this respect (compare, for instance, the very vague and ill-defined instinct of "secretiveness" at one end with the very specific mechanisms of "sucking" or "hiccoughing" at the other).

The most famous—or perhaps one should say the most notorious—of James's more specific doctrines was his theory of emotions—originally propounded in 1884, and independently put forward in a very similar form by the Danish physiologist C. G. Lange a year later. As is well known, this theory endeavours to explain emotional experiences in terms of their bodily accompaniments. He reversed the usual assumption as regards cause and effect, and maintained that the perception of the bodily changes *is* the emotion, not that the changes take place as a consequence of the emotion. If we analyse out the various bodily factors in fear, anger, etc., the changes in the heart beat, the goose flesh, the tensions in the muscles and so on, there is nothing left of these emotions. In his original statement of the theory he over-emphasized the influence of the voluntary muscles, but it is clear that from the start he intended to include visceral changes also, and it is these changes that have been chiefly stressed in subsequent expositions of the theory. The theory has always been spoken of respectfully and is admittedly not easy to disprove; nevertheless few, if any, have ever believed it to be really true—

or at any rate to be the whole truth (for no one disputes the great importance of bodily changes in emotion). Apart from more general appeals to experience, two special lines of evidence have been brought against it in recent times—the first by Sherrington, who tried to sever all afferent nerves that could convey impressions from the viscera to the brain and who found that under these conditions the emotional expressions of the dogs on whom he operated remained unaltered; the second by Cannon, who, although he discovered a well-marked series of physiological changes (connected especially with the secretion of adrenalin) in fear and rage, could find no difference corresponding to the subjective distinction between these two emotions. Neither of these arguments is decisive, and the theory still stands much as it did when it was propounded. But however adequate or inadequate it may be, it has undoubtedly served a valuable purpose in calling attention to a neglected factor and in stimulating thought, discussion and research—which is exactly what James would have wished.

James's revolt against the elementarism of Wundt comes out most clearly in his doctrine of the "stream of consciousness." Temporal subdivisions are, he maintained, purely matters of convenience, and the attempt to split up consciousness into a number of discreet ideas or presentations is bound to prove misleading. At most we may grasp a span of a few seconds' duration as a unity (the "specious present"), and distinguish between the more "substantive" states—which are, so to speak, the stopping-places of thought and are easily observed—and other more "transitive" states, which are so vague and fleeting that they usually escape notice altogether.

James's activism comes out strongly in his treatment of the will. He gives a characteristically vivid description of various types of choice and decision—a description the correctness of which has to a remarkable extent been borne out by subsequent experimental investigations, though in the last resort he calls in a somewhat mystical *fiat*, which most other psychologists would prefer, if they could, to reduce to more familiar terms. He has been accused, too, in this connection, of being inconsistent with regard to the mind-body relation. He repeatedly says that psychology has no use for the concept of the soul, and yet he contends elsewhere that there exists some integrating and organizing force which looks very like the soul. But James never regarded consistency as among the most important of the virtues.

We may possibly consider it inconsistent also that, although he thought there was no real inevitability about "necessary" truths, which in the last resort only represented what had proved to be convenient and useful methods of apprehension, he yet held that space perception was not entirely a matter of experience, as Lotze, for instance, had maintained, but that every sensation had a certain intrinsic spatiality or "crude voluminousness" which provided the substance out of which is built the complex spatial order as we actually know it.

Of the many other well-known features of James's *Principles*, we can mention only one, his treatment of memory. He sought to reconcile the traditional view of the faculty psychology, according to which memory is an ultimate unitary power of the mind, with the associationist view, according to which it is only a loose name for a vast number of quite independent traces or connections. There is, he suggested, on the one hand a general power of retentiveness, dependent on the structure of the brain, a power that varies from one individual to another, while on the other hand it is equally true that the retention of a specific item depends on one particular neural path, so that learning one thing will not help us to learn another. To test this latter point he conducted what was really the pioneer investigation into the "transfer of training," and actually found that the memorization of certain kinds of poetry did not improve the ability to memorize others. He concluded that general retentiveness cannot be improved by training, and that such transfer as occurs is due only to the carry-over of improved methods of learning, where this is possible. The many subsequent experimental inquiries on the same lines have on the whole overwhelmingly corroborated the view that there is no general transfer; but they have tended to show also that there is no general power of retentiveness in the sense that a given individual is equally retentive for all kinds of material; they have indicated rather that there are a number of narrowly specific but overlapping abilities, and that the further removed two kinds of learning are from one another (as regards either material or method) the less safe it is to predict from ability in one to ability in the other.

VI. FECHNER AND PSYCHO-PHYSICS

IT is more than time that we started to deal seriously with the developments of experimental psychology in our second period, for, as the reader will have observed, the experimental method has for some little while been constantly intruding itself into our discussion, though we have on the whole endeavoured to avoid it and to confine ourselves to evolutionary and systematic psychology. We have seen, for instance, how Galton's fertile mind linked up psychological experiment with the evolutionary outlook, and how the same fusion was later on made by Thorndike in the case of animal psychology. We have seen, too, how James, the literary genius of psychology, was both attracted and repelled by the new school. It is now our business to examine the birth and progress of this movement, which we have hitherto sensed as an important background to the developments we were considering.

The first nineteen years of our second period (from the appearance of Fechner's *Elemente* in 1860 to the foundation of Wundt's laboratory in 1879) differs from the later part of this period in that interest centres round some half-dozen names only, of whom three, Fechner, Helmholtz and Wundt were stars of the first magnitude. With the work of the two first of this trio we are already to some extent familiar. We have seen how Helmholtz measured the speed of the nervous impulse and how Fechner arrived at the ideas embodied in his *Elemente*, the work which is usually regarded as marking the definite beginning of the "new" psychology. A full history of modern psychology should doubtless deal *in extenso* with the problems and conclusions of this historically most important book and with the discussions to which they are, after more than seventy years, still giving rise (discussions which continued in full flood for at least half this period). But as soon as we begin to treat these points in detail, they take on an academic and forbidding air, so that we may well be excused from attempting such a treatment here, for this is not a book for specialists in psycho-physics. Besides, there are psychologists of eminence who maintain emphatically that the task is in any case not worth while. Of these, James was the one who expressed himself most vigorously and strikingly. He took up the extreme view that the intrinsic merit of all this work amounted in the end to "just *nothing*." It is almost impossible to forbear quoting some of his own words in this connection:

"The Fechnerian *Maasformel* and the conception of it as an ultimate 'psycho-physic law' will remain an 'idol of the den', if ever there was one. Fechner himself indeed was a German *Gelehrter* of the ideal type, at once simple and shrewd, a mystic and an experimentalist, homely and daring, and as loyal to facts as to his theories. But it would be terrible if even such a dear old man as this could saddle our science forever with his patient whimsies, and, in a world so full of more nutritious objects of attention, compel all future students to plough through the difficulties, not only of his own works, but of the still drier ones written in his refutation. Those who desire this dreadful literature can find it; it has a 'disciplinary value'; but I will not even enumerate it in a footnote. The only amusing part of it is that Fechner's critics should always feel bound, after smiting his theories hip and thigh and leaving not a stick of them standing, to wind up by saying that nevertheless to him belongs the imperishable glory of first formulating them and thereby turning psychology into an exact science."

Most students will agree with James that much of the discussion and a good deal of the experimental work on psychophysics is of an arid kind that has borne little fruit commensurate with the labour spent on it. Few, however, have been ready to believe that this work has historical value only. At this distance of time it is becoming relatively easy to see what were the points of real value established by Fechner and his more immediate successors, over and above the stimulus their work provided for the attack on "more nutritious objects." These we can accept with gratitude, leaving the rest to those who have the necessary courage to make closer acquaintance with the "dreadful literature," either because, as James ironically suggests, of its disciplinary value, or because they have caught a few sparks of Fechner's original enthusiasm, which (strange as it may seem to those of James's persuasion) saw in these patient measurements a means of transforming the appearance of the universe in a manner comparable only to the change from night to day.

Fechner's contributions of permanent value to psychology can perhaps best be stated briefly under three closely related headings: he gave clear expression to Weber's Law, he elaborated the concept of the threshold, and he worked out three independent psycho-physical methods for the measurement of thresholds. The first two of these were of course implicit in the work of Weber himself, but Fechner, as we have seen, approached the problem independently, and there can be no doubt that it was he who gave Weber's work its full significance. Weber's original discovery was to the effect that the increase in any stimulus necessary to be perceived as such was not any absolute amount, but was proportionate to the intensity of the original stimulus. Fechner, after much further experimentation, thought and calculation, gave this discovery a new and more precise mathematical form, to the effect that the sensation increases according to the logarithm of the stimulus, or, expressed differently, that in order for the sensation to increase in arithmetical progression the stimulus must increase in geometrical progression. This stated the relation between sensation and stimulus more generally, and made of it more than a mere matter of thresholds. But the assumptions involved in this extension have given rise to endless controversy and to the literature that James deplored.[1]

On the whole, however, Fechner's statement has shown itself

[1] It is curious to note that, in spite of all the discussion about Weber's Law, there has been scarcely any treatment of the psychological applications of the law outside the sphere of perception. Yet such applications are, beyond doubt, possible. One case that has a bearing on this was mentioned long before by Bernoulli (to whom Fechner admits much indebtedness). Bernoulli's interest in the theory of probability as applied to games of chance led him to distinguish between *fortune morale* and *fortune physique*. An increase of physical fortune (e.g. money) brings an increase of mental satisfaction that does not stand in relation to the absolute amount of the increase but is relative to the previous total fortune of its possessor. A gain of £100 may mean little to a rich man, but may make all the difference in the world to a beggar. The same considerations apply to the use of luxuries quite generally, a fact that may profitably be borne in mind in all civilizations in which, as in our own, great importance is attached to material possessions.

to be approximately true over a large scale of intensities. Of subsequent additions and modifications resulting from the controversies, we need perhaps only mention one. Fechner thought
that, if sensations are to be measured, every sensation must have
an absolute magnitude measured from a zero point. Now magnitude is not introspectively obvious in sensory experience (a
lamp for instance is not just so many times as bright as a candle);
nor is it obvious, as Fechner had assumed, that the just noticeable differences that constitute the psychological aspects of successive thresholds should be equal to one another. Delboeuf in
1873 to some extent short-circuited these difficulties, and at the
same time invented a new psycho-physical method, by showing
that we can judge the size of the interval between two sensations
immediately and directly, and compare it with another interval
("method of equal-appearing intervals"). Given three sensations,
A, B, C, of the same modality but of different intensities, we can
say, for instance, that the difference in intensity between A and
B is greater than, equal to, or less than, the difference between
B and C. This being so, there is no need, in the measurement of
sensations, to presuppose zero points or to depend on thresholds.
We can, in fact, arrange sensations on a measurable scale in relation to one another, without worrying about absolute magnitude
at all. Many needless and difficult theoretical questions were
thereby abolished.

Fechner's second important contribution was also one that had
been implicit in Weber's work, i.e. the concept of the limen or
threshold itself. From the beginning it was clear that it was
possible to distinguish theoretically between two kinds of threshold: (a) the initial threshold, i.e. the intensity of stimulus that
is necessary for the stimulus to be perceived at all, and (b) the
differential threshold, i.e. the amount by which a stimulus must
be increased or decreased in intensity in order that it may be
perceived as different. The initial threshold, as Fechner understood it, required the theoretical existence of negative (subliminal) sensations, too feeble to affect consciousness, while the
same applied to subliminal differences of sensation in the case of
the differential threshold. A summation of subliminal sensations
may, however, produce a supraliminal sensation—an idea that
led back to the doctrine of *petites perceptions* of Leibnitz, who
asked us to believe that the sound of the breakers on the beach

is compounded of the sensations produced by countless individual falling drops of water, no one of which would be audible alone.

It soon became apparent that in practice the initial threshold has in many cases some of the characteristics of a differential threshold. This is notably so in the case of hearing. Even in a completely soundproof room (a very rare feature even of the modern psychological laboratory) a sound of minimal intensity is heard, not against a background of complete silence, but against one of physiologically determined sound of low intensity; and the same, to some extent, is true of vision, for it is impossible to do away with the "retina's own light." Nevertheless, the background sensations are in such cases usually of different quality, or have different temporal and spatial characteristics from those of the experimental stimulus proper, so that some important distinctions between the initial and differential thresholds still remain.

It is scarcely necessary to say that the threshold has, since Fechner's day, proved a fruitful concept, with many applications, both in psychology and physiology, that are outside the original field of interest in connection with Weber's Law. We may, therefore, be justifiably thankful to Fechner for having brought the matter into prominence.

Whatever view we may take as to the value of his own psychophysics, Fechner's concept of the threshold was emended, in a way that had some real practical and theoretical significance, by G. E. Müller in his *Zur Grundlegung der Psychophysik* in 1878. Among other important comments on Fechner's work, Müller showed that the concept of a fixed threshold is in reality a fiction. The varying results obtained when (even under favourable circumstances) a just noticeable stimulus is applied a number of times in succession should, Müller thought, be looked upon, not so much as due to mere errors of observation, as to real differences in the threshold value—i.e. in sensitivity itself. The "threshold," as measured, is, therefore, according to this view, merely an average measure of something that in its very essence varies within certain limits. Thus no single measurement, however accurate, can be adequate, for there is no single thing to measure. Psychology was thereby shorn of a metaphysical abstraction, though the concept of the threshold remained as useful as before.

Fechner's third contribution, the development of the psycho-physical methods, was more purely his own. We have already related how he devised these methods in the ten years' work that preceded the appearance of his *Elemente*. These famous methods have, ever since, been a most valuable part of the experimental psychologist's armoury. As every student knows, they are three in number, though each possesses more than one name (a) the "method of minimal changes" (or of "limits"), in which the variable stimuli are given in a continuous ascending or descending series; (b) the "method of average error" (or the "production method"), in which the subject himself adjusts the variable stimulus so as to fulfil the instructions given to him; and (c) the "method of right and wrong cases" (or the "constant method"), in which a series of variable stimuli are presented to the subject in irregular order. Each method has its advantages, according to the varying circumstances of the particular experiment—time at disposal, fatiguability or endurance of the subject, nature of the apparatus employed, degree of accuracy required, and so on. The psycho-physical methods are the essential instruments for the measurement of thresholds, and so long as thresholds are of interest, they will doubtless continue to be used. The method of minimal changes is the most accurate of the three, and has aroused the greatest interest. It has at various times been developed and refined by G. E. Müller, Urban, Spearman and others. Among the other modifications of Fechner's original methods we may mention the bold step, taken by Jastrow and Peirce in 1884, of eliminating the judgments of equality between the two stimuli to be compared, thus compelling the subjects to make a definite judgment in terms of "more" or "less," even though this judgment might appear to be based on guesswork only. It has been suggested that we may see in this an early example of the characteristic American distrust of introspection and tendency towards behaviourism. In any case, the new departure is justified in that (not to speak of facilitating calculation) it eliminates individual differences in confidence—which are irrelevant factors in many investigations. It was also instrumental in showing that what appeared to the subject to be mere guesses were often based on some genuine ability to give the correct answer, since the proportion of correct "guesses" was often significantly greater than what might have been expected by pure chance. This seems to point clearly to the existence of something like subliminal sensation, as Fechner and Leibnitz had conceived it, and to the ability of such sensation to affect consciousness—a fact which is in harmony with much further evidence, both from everyday life and from experiment (notably perhaps in recent times the experiments of Coover, in which it was shown that subjects could make correct guesses with regard to spoken words that were apparently inaudible, and with regard to written letters so far removed from the eye that they appeared only as small spots). Early in the twentieth century a further development of some note consisted in the elaboration—in the first case, it would appear, by McDougall—of a new method, the "method of serial groups." This is a modification of the method of minimal changes, the stimuli being presented in steps of ascending or descending order, but a number of stimuli of the same intensity (sometimes with "catch" stimuli of theoretically zero intensity interposed) being given at each step (instead of only one stimulus at each step as in the original procedure).

Almost immediately after the appearance of the *Elemente*, Fechner ventured into a new field, that of aesthetics. Here also, as in the case of the mind-body problem, which had given birth to psycho-physics, Fechner applied quantitative methods. He began by measuring pictures, and his first article on the "golden cut" appeared in 1865. He was then drawn into a discussion at that time in progress as to the authenticity and relative artistic merits of two closely similar pictures, the "Holbein" Madonnas of Dresden and Darmstadt respectively. The two pictures were exhibited together and Fechner asked visitors to record their judgments. The experiment was in itself a failure, as scarcely any of the twenty-one thousand people who came to see the pictures ventured or troubled to write down their views in the book provided; nevertheless it has sometimes been looked upon as the beginning of the "method of impression," which was later to become a regular procedure in the laboratory investigation of affective stimuli. Undeterred, moreover, by this lack of sympathetic interest, Fechner carried on his studies, and eventually, in 1876, published his *Vorschule der Aesthetik*, which is to experimental aesthetics what the *Elemente* had been to psycho-physics, and which contains the fundamental methods on which all quantitative work in this field has been based. Fechner thus introduced mathematical conceptions into two fields from which they had hitherto been almost totally divorced. In a very real and true sense we may say that he founded two quantitative sciences.

IF Fechner was many sided in his interests and activities, so, too, was Helmholtz, who was as much physicist, physiologist, and psychologist as Fechner was physicist, philosopher, psychophysicist, and aesthetician. But fundamentally the two men differed greatly, for, whereas Fechner was primarily a philosopher, with not a little of the mystic in his disposition, Helmholtz was wholeheartedly a scientist and an empiricist. Indeed his empiricism was of a kind very similar to that of the great British associationist writers, for whom he had much admiration. He was intolerant of the element of mysticism and transcendentalism in German philosophy, and, in the associationist tradition, he endeavoured all his life to explain psychological phenomena in terms of individual learning and experience rather than in those of inheritance or faculties. (He does not seem to have been aware of Spencer's attempt to combine these standpoints.) Such a view seemed to him the only one consistent with a truly scientific attitude. He was indeed a scientific giant; his output, his grasp, his originality, his power of systematic exposition, were alike prodigious. He alone, perhaps, of modern scientists has had the honour of having his chief work translated and republished (with, of course, additions) sixty years after its appearance, not merely as a "classic" of historical interest, but as the leading manual and book of reference on its subject. For that is what happened to his *Handbuch der Physiologischen Optik*, the three successive volumes of which first appeared in 1856, 1860 and 1866 respectively, and which was translated into English in 1924–5. In this book, and in his smaller but almost equally important *Lehre von den Tonempfindungen*, he did for the two most important sense departments what Johannes Müller had previously done for general physiology; he carefully collected and sifted the available data, added important contributions of his own, and gave the whole a systematic form.

141

We have already encountered Helmholtz in connection with his measurement of the speed of nervous impulse, his reaction time experiments undertaken in the course of this work, and his extension of J. Müller's doctrine of specific energies to elementary qualities within a single sense. It remains for us now to deal with the further additions to knowledge contained in his two great textbooks and such other works as have a psychological bearing (many matters, such, for instance, as his connection with the theory of the conservation of energy, fall outside our scope). One of his most important discoveries in vision concerned the mechanism of accommodation. It will be remembered that Müller was still in uncertainty upon this point. Helmholtz described the way in which the lens alters the curvature of its outer surface under the influence of the internal eye muscles. In another research he determined the complicated functions of the external muscles of the eye, which enable the eye to be turned in the desired direction. He corroborated Bell's doctrine of "corresponding points," and maintained that it is by a process of "unconscious inference" that we learn to see objects single even when they do not fall on the horopter. This theory of "unconscious inference" is one that plays a considerable part in his whole treatment of perception. It was also adopted by Wundt for a time, though subsequently dropped. In general, the doctrine is based upon the resemblance between integrations that are achieved automatically and without our knowledge and those other explicit integrations that result from the conscious processes of reasoning. "An astronomer," he says in illustration, "computes the positions of the stars in space, their distances from the earth, etc., from the perspective images he has of them at different times and at different points in the earth's orbit. [He] bases his conclusions upon a conscious knowledge of optics. In the ordinary acts of seeing, such a knowledge of optics is lacking; still it may be permissible to designate the psychic acts of ordinary perception as *unconscious inferences*, as this name distinguishes them sufficiently from the ordinary, so-called conscious, inferences. While the similarity of the psychic activities in the two cases has been doubted and will perhaps always be doubted, still no doubt can remain of the similarity of the results of such unconscious inference and of the conscious inference." Stated in this way, Helmholtz's view, as applied to many cases, seems reasonable enough, especially with regard to illusions and to space perception; in other cases, however, for instance with regard to visual contrast and after-images, his explanations have seemed very forced, and even the staunchest upholders of Helmholtz's visual theories in general (such as McDoulgal) have felt obliged to reject his views on these points and to give fresh explanations of their own.

Helmholtz's sponsoring of Young's three-colour theory of vision is of course one of his most famous contributions in the field of sight. He tried to show that all visual phenomena can be accounted for on the assumption that there are three, and only three, elementary retino-cortical processes, corresponding to the sensation of red, green and blue respectively. The way in which his theory attempts to deal with the various critical cases, and the manner in which it contrasts with the great competing theory, that of Hering, have been expounded in so many textbooks that it would be quite superfluous to enter on these questions here. Suffice it to say that modern opinion almost unanimously considers that the theory, as originally propounded, is inadequate to account for all the facts, especially for those of colour blindness and (as already indicated) contrast and after-images. There are, however, still psychologists and physiologists of note who believe that with the necessary emendations and supplementations the theory is still at least as good as any other.

No less famous is Helmholtz's theory of hearing. Here he made even bolder use of the theory of specific energies. Finding that complex sounds can (with the help of resonators) be analysed into their constituents of fundament and overtones, and that after practice we can even make this analysis introspectively without artificial aid, he concluded that there must be a large number of elementary sensation qualities of different pitch, from the lowest to the highest of those that are discernible. The next step was to look for an equivalent anatomical organ of perception. At first he fixed upon the rods of Corti, later (at Hensen's suggestion) on the transverse fibres of the basilar membrane, which appeared capable of vibrating "sympathetically" to tones of different pitch in the same manner as the strings of a harp or piano. The boldness of this theory consists in the fact that the doctrine of specific energies is here stretched so as to postulate, not three independent specific qualities within the same sense department (as in the case of his theory of vision), but several thousand. At the time when the theory was first propounded the fibres of the basilar membrane were estimated at 4,500, but later research indicates that double or even treble this number more nearly represents the truth. The great difficulty of the theory is that the differences between the length of the fibres is relatively very small; for, whereas the longest fibres are barely three times the length of the shortest, the highest audible pitch has many thousand times the vibration rate of the lowest, and such inadequate differences in fibre-length could only be compensated by almost inconceivable differences of loading. For this reason, Helmholtz's "resonance theory" has been opposed by a number of other theories, most of which have in common the view that the perception of single tones of a definite pitch corresponds to the production of a particular vibration pattern on a whole relatively large vibrating membrane, rather than to the specific response of a single unit fibre; in other words, these theories work on the analogy of the telephone rather than the harp. The vibrating membrane in question might, as Ewald has tried to show, still be the basilar membrane, and in that case Helmholtz would still be right in one important particular, though his theory would have lost its really characteristic feature. It is generally admitted that, both here and in the case of vision, our knowledge is not yet adequate to allow us to accept finally any of the theories that have been propounded. The main function of such theories at the present stage is not to give final and dogmatic explanations but to stimulate further research. Judged by this standard, Helmholtz's theories, both in vision and in hearing, have been eminently satisfactory.

Besides the elaboration of his well-known theory, Helmholtz's work on hearing included investigations on pitch discrimination, on "difference tones" and "summation tones"—all of which are familiar enough to us through our textbooks—and (most important of all) on "timbre," "clang colour," or "tone quality," as it is variously called. Before his time the characteristic difference between the same note (say the middle C) as played on various instruments (say the piano, the flute and the violin) was of course familiar enough to everyone; but the physical cause of this difference was not understood. It was Helmholtz who discovered that this perceptual difference corresponds to the fact that different instruments, even when producing the same fundamental note, give off different overtones. Most vibrating bodies vibrate not only as wholes but as parts; and these latter vibrations differ characteristically from one case to another. Hence the shape of the wave (which depends on the kind and number of these overtone-producing partial vibrations) varies with each instrument, and these variations in wave-shape are apprehended by the mind as "timbre"—just as variations in wave-length are apprehended as pitch and variations in wave-amplitude are apprehended as loudness or intensity.

By a further process of analysis Helmholtz showed that the differences between the various vowel sounds are (partially at any rate—modern work seems to show there may be other influences in the shape of independent tones or "formants" produced by different positions of the tongue and mouth) due to the same cause. Taking still another step, he went on to explain discord and harmony in terms of overtones. Discord, he believed, was due to the presence of "beats," either between the fundaments or between the overtones of two or more simultaneous tones, whereas harmony was due to the absence of such beats. Harmony, however, in the last resort is a relative and purely psychological matter, and Helmholtz, who was much interested in the development of music, believed that there was a general tendency in this development towards the toleration and enjoyment of ever greater complexity in the relations between the tones used for purposes of harmony. Starting with the simple octave ($1 : 2$) men have gradually come to appreciate such increasingly complex mathematical intervals as the fifth ($2 : 3$), the fourth ($3 : 4$), the major third ($4 : 5$), and the minor third ($5 : 6$), a theory which, as Murphy reminds us in his history, has been shown by recent experiment to be strictly true, so far at least, as the more accessible facts of *individual* development are concerned; for by practice individuals may come to be less satisfied with the simpler intervals they liked at first, while they grow to appreciate more complex intervals that seemed at first unpleasant.

The only figure comparable to Helmholtz in the history of psychology is Galton. Helmholtz had all Galton's restless energy, curiosity, originality and ingenuity, but far greater power of consistent application. Both men covered a vast field in their investigations and left their mark on nearly all the problems that they touched upon. But whereas Galton, for the most part, was content to indicate the problem and to show a method of approach, leaving the detailed work to others, while he himself proceeded to open up new fields elsewhere, Helmholtz carried his investigations through to a successful finish, saw their relation to the whole mass of existing knowledge, and had the patience to build this mass, together with his own additions, into a coherent whole. Galton was invaluable as a pioneer, whereas Helmholtz was not only a pioneer but an exceptionally capable settler and administrator of territory already won but not yet organized. He comes down to us not only as a great investigator but a great writer of textbooks, one who co-ordinated knowledge and made it generally accessible. Under both heads he is among the foremost figures of the "new" psychology.

WILHELM WUNDT, the last of the three great figures who are
responsible for the birth of the new experimental science, was a
man of different mould. He was certainly inferior to Helmholtz
both in his scientific flair for the choice of problems and methods
and in the sureness of touch with which he handled them. But he
combined courage and originality with an immense capacity for
work and taking pains. The mere enumeration of his writings
is thoroughly impressive. The bibliography collected by his
daughter runs to close on five hundred titles, from standard
works in several portly volumes to one-page articles. According
to Boring (who warns us not to lose our sense of humour in
statistical investigations of this sort!), it appears that Wundt
wrote 53,735 pages from his twenty-first year onwards till his
death in 1920 at the age of 88, and that he wrote or revised at
the rate of 2·2 pages a day—a striking record, considering that
the questions with which he dealt were for the most part far
from easy and his treatment far from superficial. For psychology
he was undoubtedly the most important of the great pioneers,
and this for three chief reasons. In the first place he was, unlike
both Fechner and Helmholtz (but like Bain, who, however, was a
lesser man), *primarily* a psychologist, his physiological and
philosophical writings, important as they were, being subsidiary
both in interest and in ultimate significance to his psychology. In
the second place it was he who was the first to conceive of experimental psychology as a science and to give it that name. In the
third place he founded the first psychological laboratory as a
home for the new branch of science in its tender years, a
home in which a whole school of psychologists were trained, and
from which they went forth, eager and equipped, to carry on
the new tradition wheresoever they might be appointed.

Wundt, like Helmholtz, started as a physician and soon
became a physiologist. He began work at Heidelberg, spent a

semester with Johannes Müller in Berlin, and then returned to take his degree and to teach at Heidelberg, where for thirteen years he was assistant in Helmholtz's Institute of Physiology. In 1871, the year in which Helmholtz left Heidelberg for Berlin, Wundt was made Extraordinary Professor, but was not appointed Helmholtz's successor. During the seventeen years in all that he spent at Heidelberg Wundt, from being a physiologist, became a psychologist. The outward sign of the change was the publication between 1858 and 1862 of the *Beiträge zur Theorie der Wahrnehmung*. In this book, besides reporting original experiments, he laid down his views as to the methods of psychology. "All psychology begins," he said, "with introspection," but there are two auxiliary methods, experiment and the natural history of mankind (*Geschichte*). He remained true to this conception, and indeed his two major psychological works, the *Physiologische Psychologie* and the *Völkerpsychologie*, may be said to constitute the fundamental treatises on the two auxiliary methods in question. It was in the *Beiträge* too that Wundt first spoke of "experimental psychology." He himself tells us that it was Herbart who convinced him of the necessity of treating psychology as *Wissenschaft*, though as a physiologist, trained in the experimental methods of that science, he was from the start in disagreement with Herbart as to the impossibility of psychology being experimental. This book, therefore, together with Fechner's *Elemente*, which appeared two years before its completion, may be taken to mark the literary birth of the new discipline. It was followed, one year later, in 1863, by another and more important work, the *Vorlesungen über Menschen und Tierseele*, a book which was translated into English thirty-one years after its first appearance and which has remained popular almost to the present day. It contained a preliminary attack on many of the problems that were later to begin the subjects of systematic observation and experiment. It can be regarded as a statement of the principal achievements and the more obvious tasks of experimental psychology as they presented themselves three years after the date to which its "birth" is usually assigned.

In 1867 he began to lecture on "physiological psychology," and in 1873–4 there appeared what is often considered to be the most important book in the whole history of psychology, the *Grundzüge der Physiologischen Psychologie*. The *Grundzüge* may, in many respects, be considered the bible of experimental psychologists, though, like the bible itself, it is nowadays not read as often as its alleged importance might perhaps lead us to expect. It is not an easy book to read, and its more theoretical contributions have in many cases found but little support. Nevertheless, there can be no doubt that its historical significance has been very great. For many years it served, and to some extent still serves, as a central storehouse of information and a record of progress with regard to the new science. The early workers naturally looked on Leipzig as their headquarters, and in starting, under Wundt's inspiration or direction, each on his own problems, it was no small incentive to realize that their results might modify or add to this or that section of the great book which endeavoured to knit all their labours into a coherent system. For it was a feature of the book, as of all Wundt's major literary undertakings, that it continued to appear in ever revised and amplified editions.[1]

In the year in which the first edition of the *Grundzüge* was completed Wundt went to Zürich as Professor of Inductive Philosophy. He was there but one year, however, and in 1875 went to occupy a chair of philosophy at Leipzig, where he stayed for the remaining forty-five years of his life. In 1879 he founded his laboratory at Leipzig, and immediately, as if in justification of this momentous step, there flowed to it a steady stream of students to work in the laboratory and to take their doctorates in this new branch of knowledge (though of course, in the Faculty of Philosophy). His pupils during the first twenty years include many names which subsequently figure in our history, and the most remarkable feature of the list is the large number of Americans, practically all of whom returned to teach psychology in their own country, many of them to found or direct laboratories of their own. The "almost complete" list of such Americans given in Boring's history consists (in chronological order of

---

[1] In this case the successive editions appeared in 1874 (one volume), 1880, 1887, 1893 (two volumes each), 1902–3, 1908–11 (three volumes each). Of Wundt's other psychological works the *Vorlesungen* (published in 1863) appeared in five revised editions up to 1919, the *Gründriss der Psychologie* (published in 1896) in nine revised editions and five subsequent unchanged reprintings up to 1911, and the *Völkerpsychologie* (published in 1900) in five revised and much expanded editions up to 1920 (the work eventually running to ten volumes).

their visit) of Stanley Hall, Cattell, Wolfe, Pace, Scripture, Angell, Witmer, Warren, Patrick, Stratton, Judd, Tawney. Among the best-known continental Europeans were Kraepelin, Münsterberg, Störring, Kirschmann, Lehmann, Külpe, Meumann, Marbe, Kiesow, Lipps, Krüger, Merkel, Lange, Martius. There was, moreover, the Englishman Titchener, who went to Leipzig from Oxford (which, of all great universities, has consistently remained the most hostile to psychology) and who eventually followed the American friends whom he met at Leipzig to the United States, where he remained. It is an imposing list—one of which any university department in whatever subject might very justifiably feel proud. For an institute founded for the study of a new and upstart subject it was a great success, and very naturally the Leipzig laboratory, in which so many of its exponents had won their spurs, came to exercise an immense influence on the whole development of experimental psychology and, as new laboratories were founded, it was inevitable that they should be modelled for the most part on the Leipzig one.

The care of the new laboratory and the direction of research were, however, by no means sufficient to exhaust Wundt's energies. No sooner was the laboratory founded than he turned to philosophy, and in the next ten years produced large treatises on Logic and Ethics as well as a *System of Philosophy*. These in turn were followed by two more psychological books, the *Grundriss* (1896) and the *Einführung in die Psychologie* (1911). The two most important psychological events following the founding of the laboratory were, however, undoubtedly the following. First, the establishment of a journal—*Philosophische Studien*—in 1883, to contain the publications of the laboratory. (This was the first purely psychological journal to be founded. It is true that *Mind* had already appeared under Bain's editorship seven years before, but ever since its foundation this periodical has been predominantly philosophic and, important as it is in its own sphere, has never proved a very congenial home for work of an experimental character.) Secondly, the appearance of the *Völkerpsychologie* in 1900 and later. This latter event, however, belongs to our fourth period, in considering which we shall return to it.

Before carrying on the general history of experimental psychology, we must say a few words about Wundt's own psychological system, though it is difficult or impossible to do justice to this system in a small space. One of the difficulties here is that, as already indicated, his works were constantly undergoing revision, a revision that was by no means confined to the treatment of isolated facts, as work in the laboratory provided them, but which often introduced profound modifications of theory—though it cannot be said that these modifications ever went quite far enough to overthrow the original system. Perhaps we may, following Boring, distinguish four main stages in the evolutionary process. The first corresponds to the period before the writing of the *Grundzüge*; it is a relatively unsystematic period. Large use was made of the doctrine of "unconscious inference," as found in Helmholtz. In the second period, after the first edition of the *Grundzüge*, unconscious inference disappears, and Wundt's general tendency to elementarism becomes clearly evident. He had much in common with the English associationists and particularly J. S. Mill; the mind is depicted as describable in terms of elements like those of sensation. These elements may themselves have attributes and are connected by association. They are, however, by no means mere inert static units, but are conceived as processes (a point which has been sometimes lost sight of by Wundt's later critics, though there is some excuse for this in Wundt's own exposition; while the whole notion of elements as processes implies, as Boring remarks, "a difficult and somewhat ambiguous concept"). In his description of association, Wundt is largely Herbartian in his ideas and terminology. There are "fusions" within the same sense department and "complications" between elements of different sense departments, while there is also a process of "assimilation" in which one element annexes, so to speak, another—as happens in the cases of "confluence" or contrast, on which so many optical illusions depend. In addition to these, however, there is a more active process of "apperception," which was destined to grow more important as Wundt's views matured. At this stage feeling was only an attribute of sensation, comparable to the attributes of intensity and duration. But in the next (third) period it undergoes a great development in the shape of the celebrated "three-dimensional" theory. According to this theory (first announced in the *Grundriss* of 1896) it is possible to distinguish six main qualities of feeling, arranged in three pairs of opposites: pleasure–unpleasure, strain–relaxation, excitement–calm—a theory that can be crudely represented by three lines all intersecting at the "zero" point. Feeling was no longer an attribute; rather, each of these feelings was itself an elementary process, so that the total number of elements (sensory and effective) was approximately doubled. The tri-dimensional theory aroused immediate interest and gave rise to considerable research in the effort to confirm or to confute it. In the last and fourth period (beginning with the fifth edition of the *Grundzüge* in 1902) the tri-dimensional theory and the doctrine of apperception are more fully developed, both in themselves and in relation to each other. Feeling becomes "the mark of the reaction of apperception upon sensory content"—a doctrine that appeared to get over the old difficulty connected with mental activity (and, therefore, also with the special activity of apperception), i.e. that it is not easy to observe or to experiment upon. If feelings are, so to speak, the phenomenal representatives of apperception, observation of the feelings will enable us to some extent to study indirectly the more elusive process of apperception itself. But there is also another method of approach —this time on the cognitive side. Consciousness has roughly two levels, for within its general field there is a small region of clearer "focal" consciousness; the processes within this region are, Wundt thought, apperceived. Thus "attention" is also a phenomeno-logical aspect of apperception, and attention admits of being experimented on. In particular, the experiments undertaken on the "span of apprehension" have a bearing on the process. In this way the doctrine of apperception, though it has never yet admitted of direct attack, has nevertheless proved very stimulating to research in at least two directions.

We may now return to the work of the laboratory and indicate some of the main problems that were studied there. In so doing, we immediately become aware of a very significant aspect of the change that psychology underwent as soon as it became a laboratory science. Instead of a few men working independently and publishing their results in books, we find a large number of individuals working in co-operation or at any rate in close contact with one another (for the most part, too, under the same direction, if they are working in the same laboratory), and publishing in journals (though, of course, their results are ultimately synthesized in books; as in the case of the Leipzig laboratory, where the results were brought together in successive editions of the *Grundzüge*). As fellow laboratory workers, psychologists are indeed almost inevitably brought more closely together than students of other sciences. In most psychological experiments a "subject" or "observer" is required as well as an experimenter and (except in the "mass" experiments that were developed later on) it soon became usual for the experimenter in one investigation to become the "observer" in another. Indeed, things could scarcely have developed otherwise, especially in the early days; for nowhere, except among his colleagues, could an investigator hope to get persons (a) sufficiently qualified by training, and (b) sufficiently patient and understanding, to act as his observers. Experimental psychology is undoubtedly one of the most trying and the most exposed to ridicule of all the sciences. At first sight its apparatus—its aesthesiometers, tachistoscopes and chronoscopes—may be impressive. But as soon as they are put in use, the whole procedure, to the untrained mind, is apt to become humiliating and absurd. It is difficult to retain a due sense of our own dignity, when we are having sharp points poked into our arms, when we are trying to count an elusive group of dots exposed momentarily during the fall of a shutter, when we are learning rows of syllables purposely deprived of all ulterior use or meaning, or when we are exerting ourselves, as though our lives depended on it, to depress a key the moment that a certain colour is exposed. As James said, there is little of the grand style about those who resort to such expedients, and, especially when the young science had no prestige behind it, it must have been difficult (as indeed it often still is) to induce people to expose themselves to such ordeals. Only those who are willing to sacrifice ease and dignity to a prospect of intellectual adventure of a not too enthralling kind, those who masochistically seek self-humiliation and see in such practices a convenient and well-rationalized means of satisfaction—with, of course, the inducement of inflicting this humiliation on others in their turn, or those who (as has been still more unkindly suggested) are woefully deficient in a sense of humour, will be ready to submit their minds and bodies to the experimenter without undue discomfort. No wonder that experimental psychologists are thrown back upon themselves. No wonder, either, that the philosophers in the early days tended to look (as they still do in Oxford and some other places) upon their confrères of the "prism, pendulum and chronograph" with amazement and with scant approval. The philosopher is often incomprehensible to the plain man, but he is seldom undignified. The experimental psychologist may easily be both. On the whole, it is surprising how quickly the new methods spread, and how many pupils of promise and ability came and worked with Wundt as soon as his laboratory was opened. The early history of experimental psychology would indeed probably make an interesting subject of historical study along psycho-analytic lines.

But to return to the facts. Throughout the first twenty years' activity of the Leipzig laboratory there was, as might have been expected, a preponderance of work on sensation and perception. A considerable proportion of this was psycho-physical in Fechner's sense, i.e. concerned with the quantitative relations between stimulus and sensation, though the more qualitative aspects of sensation were not neglected. Within these fields the sense of vision claimed most attention. Besides the psycho-physics of colour, peripheral vision, visual contrast, after-images, colour blindness, night vision, binocular vision, the visual perception of form and, finally, optical illusions (which last began everywhere to arouse great interest in the nineties)—all find a place in the reports of the laboratory's work contained in the *Philosophische Studien*. Hearing came next in order; here also there was much psycho-physical work, together with the investigation of beats, combination tones, tonal fusion, and the analysis of clangs and tonal intervals (this last being a subject which brought Wundt into violent and undignified conflict with Stumpf *à propos* of a paper by Lorenz).

In the second decade the problems of touch also began to figure in the programme. Both touch and vision led naturally enough to the investigation of space perception, which early showed itself amenable to the new experimental methods. The importance of various "physiological" factors in three-dimensional visual space perception (particularly disparation, convergence and accommodation) became ever clearer, so that the "psychological" factors, which had been assigned such a large rôle by J. Müller, though still important, became relatively less so. Time, however, was a comparatively new field of investigation, though of course it had been the chief factor in Bessel's studies on the "personal equation" made many years before.

Soon there were in progress three kinds of experiment on time. There was, first of all, the "complication experiment"—the direct continuation of Bessel's work, though the term "complication" was Herbartian; here it was shown that the results obtained in the classical astronomic setting of the experiment depended upon the disposition of attention, in the sense that the stimulus to which the attention was principally directed enjoyed the "prior entry" into consciousness.[1] The second method consisted in a direct attack on the "time sense" by various studies on the ability to compare intervals. Here the laboratory was carrying on work that had already been begun in the sixties by Mach and others, who were in turn inspired by Fechner. In this field quite a little host of problems revealed themselves as eminently suitable for experimental treatment, e.g. the ability to reproduce intervals of varying lengths, the influence on the estimation of an interval of the stimuli that marked its beginning and its end, the comparison of "filled" and "unfilled" intervals, of intervals "filled" in a variety of ways (by mental work, sensory stimuli, etc.). In all these problems the psycho-physical methods, originally elaborated for dealing with *sensory* thresholds, could be applied practically without change, as soon as the necessary apparatus (the celebrated "time sense apparatus," which is now to be seen in all laboratories) was devised.

The third method, that of the "reaction experiment," was the most fruitful of all. Indeed, in the early days it appeared to be perhaps the greatest triumph of the new psychology. The reaction experiment was, as we have seen, a legacy both from the personal equation problems of the astronomers and from Helmholtz's measurement of the speed of the nervous impulse in the sensory nerves. The experiment had, however, been elaborated and pursued for its own sake, before the opening of the Leipzig laboratory, by the Dutch physiologist Donders, who in 1865 published, together with de Jaager, a classical experiment on "simple," "discrimination" and "choice" reactions. In the "simple" reaction the subject was instructed to react as quickly as possible to the perception of a light, in the "discrimination"

---

[1] It has recently been shown that the results obtained with the classical complication pendulum, in which a moving hand passes across a clock face, are to some extent affected also by eye movements, but that prior entry, as determined by attention, still persists when these have been eliminated.

reaction to react to a red light but not to a green light, in the
"choice" reaction to react with the right hand to the red light
and with the left hand to the green light. The times were found
to be greater for "discrimination" than for "simple" reactions
and greater for "choice" than for "discrimination," and it was
thought that the difference in time measured the processes of
discrimination and of choice respectively.[1] This was the famous
"subtractive" procedure. The experiment was soon taken up
again at Leipzig, and confirmatory evidence for the general
validity of the procedure seemed to be forthcoming from some
experiments of N. Lange, in which it was shown that even in
the "simple" reaction, the times would differ according to the
attitude of the subject. If his attention were directed chiefly to
the task of moving his finger with the greatest possible speed (the
"muscular" reaction), the time was shorter than when he
directed his attention primarily to the stimulus, allowing the
reaction to take place more or less automatically (the "sensory"
reaction). It seemed clear that the difference here was due to the
time required for the full perception of the stimulus (the time of
apperception, as Wundt interpreted it). This encouraged further
resort to the "subtractive" method, and before long it appeared
as though the times for "discrimination," "will" and "association" were all on the way to being measured. The large variable
errors found in such measurements proved, however, to be an
unexpected obstacle, and in 1891 a great blow to all these hopes
was delivered by Külpe, who showed that the assumption underlying the subtractive procedure was not really justified, since,
when the conditions of reaction are complicated, there is no simple
addition of one mental process, the other processes remaining unchanged. Rather, the whole conscious task is changed throughout

[1] Murphy draws attention to the relatively crude technique employed in this
pioneering investigation. Donders does not seem to have realized the significance of either the "variable" or the "constant" errors in experiments of
this sort. Thus, on the one hand, he was content with less than thirty trials
with some of his subjects, neglecting the question of the statistical significance
of such small samples, while, on the other hand, he made no allowance for
the effects of practice and fatigue and for the influence of these factors on the
order in which the experiments were conducted. These and other pitfalls of
quantitative treatment were matters to which psychologists gradually learnt
to give due weight, as the consequence, for the most part, of discordant results
obtained with different subjects or by different experimenters. It is, however,
just the great advantage of the experimental method that it gradually compels
attention to such factors by the necessity of accounting for discrepant results.

its course. Interpreted behaviouristically, the quantitative results of course still retained their value; the additional time required for the performance of tasks of increasing complication could indeed be measured (within the limits of the variable errors); but this was long before the beginning of behaviourism, and the disappointment at the breakdown of the purely mental analysis was naturally a somewhat bitter one. Külpe's contentions were in harmony with some experiments on perception carried out by Cattell, which showed that there was considerable overlapping in the perception of a series of letters or colours successively presented, inasmuch as with an arrangement that allowed several items to be seen at once, the subject could name the whole series appreciably quicker than when he could only see one item at a time.

In some ways the most remarkable of the Leipzig reaction experiments were those on association. Wundt took over the word-association experiment from Galton, and Trautscholt in the first volume of the *Philosophische Studien* made the first inductive classification of associations (based on an initial dichotomy into inner associations—depending principally upon meaning; and outer associations—depending upon habits and on extrinsic, superficial or accidental connections). Important as this might seem theoretically, the full value of the association method has so far been found to lie (unexpectedly enough) in the orectic sphere, in abnormal psychology and in the study of individual differences. Cattell was chiefly responsible for discovering the importance of "control" in association, i.e. the determination to react with a word that stands in some definite relation to the stimulus word (a superordinate, a subordinate, etc.). He found that "controlled" associations are for the most part quicker than "free" associations, and that, even among the former, the narrower the limits of possible response the quicker as a rule was the association made. In general, it appeared as though, in cases where there were many possible responses, none of which were more closely associated or more permissible than others, there was a process of interference which delayed the reaction. This seems indeed to be a finding of considerable importance and wide applicability. The mutual interference of "divergent associations" is a fairly frequent occurrence; it is, for instance, painfully familiar to some persons who know several foreign languages, especially when these languages themselves are very similar, e.g. Spanish and Italian. Kraepelin, following shortly after Cattell's first work on reaction times, showed that the process of association was characteristically altered in (experimentally induced) abnormal conditions, such as those of fatigue, hunger, alcoholic intoxication, etc., especially in the direction of increasing the number of "outer" associations—an effect which appeared to be similar to that produced in mania.

Cattell played a part also in another important aspect of the Leipzig activities—namely, in the study of attention. Attention was investigated chiefly in two ways—as to its "range" and its "fluctuations" respectively. As regards the first of these, Cattell carried out the classic tachistoscopic experiments on "span," and found that some four, five or six units (whether lines, letters or words) could be apprehended in a single exposure too short to allow of any "movement" of attention. Dietze correspondingly investigated the range of attention for *successive* stimuli (as regards which rhythm was found to play an important part). This led Wundt to look upon attention as existing in two dimensions, as embracing not only simultaneous but successive events. The second method consisted in the study of the appearances and disappearances of minimal sensory stimuli—a phenomenon which had already been noted by Hume, but which had been first investigated scientifically by the Viennese aurist Urbantschitsch. Wundt interpreted these fluctuations as due to central causes—a view which gave rise to much controversy. Peripheral factors (especially in the case of vision) undoubtedly play some part, but experiments which have endeavoured to eliminate the causes of fluctuation in the sense organ itself seem to show that Wundt was at any rate partially correct.

Later, with the development of the tri-dimensional theory of feeling, the laboratory investigations extended also to the affective aspect of the mind, and during the nineties (and in the first year or two of the twentieth century) there appeared a number of studies in which the classical methods of "impression" and "expression" were worked out. Cohn started with the procedure used by Fechner in his experimental studies of aesthetics and elaborated the very *gründlich* but somewhat cumbersome method of "paired comparisons," in which every stimulus in the series investigated is compared with every other. On the "expression" side came studies on the bodily accompaniments of feeling, as manifested in alterations of pulse, breathing, muscular strength and so on. All these researches aimed at corroborating the tri-dimensional theory, an aim in which they are now generally considered to have failed. Indeed, none of the expression methods has quite fulfilled the hopes of those who started them. Some few results of value have, nevertheless, been forthcoming (especially in connection with blood pressure and the psycho-galvanic reflex which, however, were not products of Wundt's laboratory), and work is still being carried on, with here and there encouraging results. It may well be that, with greater refinement of technique and the discovery of the exact nature of the psycho-physical correspondence involved, some of these methods may eventually prove to be of great value. But in any case the attempt had clearly to be made, and, as in so many other matters, Wundt's laboratory has the credit of taking the initiative.

IX. FURTHER STUDIES IN SENSATION

In our last chapter we studied the work carried on in the "home" of experimental psychology in the important first two decades when the new science was on trial. From Leipzig Wundt's students went out to carry on the work in other quarters of the world. But before we follow these adventures, we must pause a little while to study the contemporary developments in Germany—for, although Leipzig was beyond all doubt the centre of the new work, it had by no means an exclusive monopoly, even in the early days. Before 1879 experimental psychology had largely come into being in the laboratories of physiologists. This work still to some extent continued. While, quite apart from Wundt's tradition (though of course not uninfluenced by it) there arose in the seventies and eighties one or two important figures who were quite definitely and primarily experimental psychologists, at least during a part of their lives or as regards a part of their endeavours.

We may begin with the physiology of sensation. There were at least four major events in this sphere during the period 1860–1900, outside the work of Helmholtz and of Wundt. Three of them were, however, primarily concerned with theory rather than with the discovery of new facts, and two of these were in the field of vision. In 1866 M. Schultze discovered the separate function of the rods and the cones in the retina, i.e. that the rods appear to be concerned primarily with vision at low, the cones with vision at higher intensities of illumination. In 1894 A. König and Else Köttgen discovered that the "visual purple", which is found over the rods, is, in light of weak intensity, absorbed most readily by colours of just those intensities which are seen as brightest in such light. This seemed to afford a satisfactory physiological explanation of the Purkinje phenomenon. In the same year von Kries elaborated the full "duplicity theory," according to which the cones only are concerned with the seeing of colours and generally with vision in a bright light, while the rods are the organs of twilight vision. This theory is supported by such a strong array of evidence (including some from comparative anatomy, in that night-seeing animals possess exclusively rods) that it has for a good many years enjoyed almost, but not quite, universal support (Edridge Green, for instance, believes that the rods are purely trophic in function).

The duplicity theory, however, obviously gives no satisfactory account of the detailed facts of *colour* vision, and to account for these one of the other theories has to be invoked. The chief rival to Helmholtz's theory in this field is that of Hering. As is well known, this theory postulates six primary colours and three types of receptor in the eye. The six colours are arranged in pairs, white-black, yellow-blue, and red-green, in such a way that the first member of each pair produces a dissimilative process, while the second member of each pair produces a corresponding assimilative process in the same receptor. The theory accounts very well for the fact that yellow and blue, red and green, do appear as connected in a certain relation of oppositeness in a number of phenomena. They are "complementaries," i.e. when mixed in the right proportions they produce a neutral grey (though unfortunately, so far as the immediate introspective appeal of the theory is concerned, the complementary red and green are not the colours usually selected as appearing to be the simplest and most elementary); they have a reciprocal function in after-images and in colour contrast; in peripheral vision red and green disappear at a certain distance from the centre, yellow and blue at a certain further distance; and, finally, in some forms of colour-blindness red and green of a certain brightness are confused together, in other (rarer) forms yellow and blue. Among the chief objections to the theory are the facts: (*a*) that the white and black pair do not appear to stand in the same relationship to one another as do the other pairs (since they never cancel one another, their fusion always producing a sensation of grey); and (*b*) that the theory of assimilative changes giving rise to sensations is not in harmony with our usual assumptions as to the physical and chemical functions of the nervous system, since, so far as our present knowledge goes, it seems more likely that all sensations and indeed all conscious processes (like other active functions of the organism) have katabolic rather than anabolic processes as their physiological concomitants. These causes of

F

dissatisfaction have led to the formation of numerous other theories, none of which, however, has won general acceptance or has been able to produce positive evidence in its favour. Historically considered, the theories of Helmholtz and of Hering are unique in the amount of discussion and research which they have aroused. The data for a complete and final theory are not yet to hand, and will doubtless have to wait until a more refined technique is available for the physico-chemical investigation of the retinal and nervous processes.

The third important theoretical achievement in the domain of sensation concerned the functions of the labyrinth of the inner ear. This had been shown long ago by Flourens to be somehow concerned with the maintenance of equilibrium, but no satisfactory explanation of how the organ worked had been forthcoming. In the early seventies Mach made an elaborate experimental study of the effects of rotation, by placing the whole body on a frame which could be fixed at any angle and then turned. As a result of these experiments, he was able to investigate in detail the perception and the negative after-image of rotation, and described them in a monograph on *Grundlinien der Lehre der Bewegungsempfindungen* published in 1875. As so often happens in such cases, others were beginning to occupy themselves simultaneously with the same problem. Mach, Crum-Brown and Breuer, all within a few months of one another, formulated practically the same theory, which has since been known by their joint names. According to this theory, changes in the position of the head cause (through inertia) currents in the endolymph—the fluid in the semicircular canals. These currents bend the hairs on the ampullae of the canals or at least modify the pressure on them, in this way setting up nerve impulses to the corresponding centres in the brain. The three semicircular canals are placed roughly in the three planes of space, and no matter in what plane a movement of the head takes place, the fluid in one canal or the other will lag behind at the beginning of movement, at any change in the speed or direction of movement, and at the cessation of movement. This theory, supplemented by a view suggested by certain experiments of Kreidl[1] as

---

[1] In which he substituted iron filings for the otoliths of fish and was thereafter able to produce forced movements in the fish by placing magnets near them.

to the functions of the otoliths in the utricle and saccule, which he supposed to act by pressure on the underlying nerve endings and thus indicate (by reference to gravity) the position of the head, has become the accepted theory of the function of the labyrinth.

The last of the four outstanding events to which we referred above resembled the third in one remarkable particular, i.e. in that it represented the independent but almost simultaneous work of three men. It differed from the other three events, however, in that it was definitely a discovery of new facts, and not merely the elaboration of a theory. In 1884 and 1885, Goldscheider, Blix and Donaldson explored the surface of the skin with pointed stimuli and were rewarded by finding that cutaneous sensibility was not distributed evenly over the whole exterior of the body, but was to be found in certain "spots", each spot giving rise, when stimulated, to a sensation of specific quality. There were four kinds of spots, connected with sensations of pressure, pain, heat and cold respectively. The problems concerning the relative fequency, threshold value, etc., of the spots, in relation to one another and to different parts of the body immediately opened up a further interesting field of research. In this research the most prominent rôle was played by Goldscheider himself and by von Frey. The latter (some ten years after the original discovery of "spots") demonstrated the existence of "paradoxical cold" resulting from the stimulation of a cold spot by a hot metal point, seeming thus to provide further striking evidence for the doctrine of specific energies.

Following on this work, Alrutz in 1897 tried to show that the sensation of heat is distinct from warmth and is really a fusion of warmth and cold. Von Frey also endeavoured (though with but indifferent success) to correlate the four principal sensations with particular types of sense organ. He carried out, too, a series of psycho-physical experiments which tended to show that the intensity of pressure sensation corresponds, not to the simple pressure of the stimulus nor to the area of skin stimulated, but rather to $\frac{pressure}{area}$.

In the nineties taste and smell began to receive some attention. Kiesow had begun to work on taste in Wundt's laboratory, and continued after he had left. He and Oehrwall established definitely the existence of the four primary qualities of taste—sweet, sour, salt and bitter—with the possibility of a fifth quality, in-sipidity—which was supposed to be a mixture of sweet and salt in much the same way as heat was a mixture of warmth and cold. In smell Zwaardemakar, a Dutch physiologist, was the chief investigator. He restated (with some modifications) the old classification of Linnaeus. He invented the olfactometer, a familiar (but not much used) feature of almost every laboratory, studied the phenomena of mixture, adaptation and contrast, and in his *Physiologie des Geruchs*, published in 1895, brought together such scientific knowledge as was generally available.

In sound, much the most important event was the publication in 1883 of Stumpf's *Tonpsychologie*; and with Stumpf we leave the physiologists and come to the psychologists proper (though they were also to some extent philosophers, and—as is still cus-tomary in Germany—held chairs of philosophy). Outside the Leipzig tradition there were three outstanding figures in this class—in addition to those whom we have already mentioned under the heading of systematic psychology. These were Stumpf himself, Hermann Ebbinghaus and G. E. Müller. Carl Stumpf, a pupil of Brentano, had from early years exhibited an interest in two things—philosophy and music. These he ultimately com-bined in the psychology of sound. His first psychological writings dealt with space perception, in which he ranged himself with Hering, as a nativist, against Helmholtz and Wundt, who were the chief empiricists. His great work, the *Tonpsychologie*, appeared in two volumes, one in 1883, the other in 1890. This was soon recognized as the most important book on hearing after Helmholtz's *Tonempfindungen*, and it has remained a classic. Like the latter book, it contained accounts of much original observa-tion (especially on tonal fusion—experiments which were carried out with the forks obtained by pulling to pieces an old tuning fork piano, which Stumpf found in the physics laboratory at Munich). It marks the beginning of the psychological study of music—a branch of knowledge which was at first carried on by Stumpf himself, and subsequently by Seashore. After many wanderings from one university to another, Stumpf went to Ber-lin in 1894 and took over a laboratory that had been started by Ebbinghaus. Here he became active in a number of fields : he continued to write on music and acoustics; he founded an insti-tute for the collection of phonographic records of primitive music from all parts of the world; he founded also the Berlin Association for Child Psychology; he published a well-known theory of feeling, in which he tried to reduce all feeling to sensation, though on different lines to the James-Lange theory of emotion; and he investigated the celebrated horse Der Kluge Hans, who appeared to be able to carry out arithmetical operations of some complexity, and who was eventually shown by Pfungst to be responding to small unconscious movements on the part of those present. Stumpf retired from his chair in Berlin in 1921 and was succeeded by Köhler, a leader of the new *Gestalt* school.

HERMANN EBBINGHAUS was to a large extent a self-made psychologist, and started as an experimentalist with no university training or tradition in the subject. His inspiration, however, came from Fechner. After taking his doctor's degree in Bonn in 1873, with a thesis on von Hartmann's philosophy of the unconscious, he spent seven years in private study and in visits to France and England. In a second-hand book shop of Paris he came across a copy of Fechner's *Elemente*. He was seized with the idea of applying experimental methods to the "higher mental processes," and the influence of the English associationists probably caused him to make the attempt in the field of memory. During the next few years he carried out long series of experiments entirely on himself, and in 1885 reported his results in his epoch-making *Über das Gedächtnis*.

The associationist writers had gradually been attributing more and more importance to the principle of *frequency* of association as a condition of recall. Ebbinghaus adopted this principle as his fundamental measure for the experimental study of memory. From Fechner's psycho-physics he realized the necessity of eliminating the influence of variable errors by a sufficient number of experiments. In order to repeat the same experiment, he required material of the same difficulty to learn in his successive experiments. As everyone knows, however, some pieces of poetry and prose can be learnt much more easily than others. Here was a problem that the psycho-physicists had not encountered; Ebbinghaus solved it ingeniously enough by the use of nonsense syllables. The fact that his native German was a language of long words, enabled him to construct some 2,300 syllables like *mon*, *gid*, *var*, which had no previous meaning and thus proved much more equal in difficulty from one syllable to another than any list of words. With such material and with poetry, Ebbinghaus set out on his experiments.

He proceeded according to the "learning method" (in which he noted the number of repetitions necessary for one faultless reproduction of rows of syllables of varying length) and the "saving method" (in which he noted the number of repetitions needed for relearning a given material after varying intervals). By the first method he was able to construct curves showing how the number of repetitions that were required increased as the material was lengthened. He found that the increase was very rapid, for whereas he could, on the average, learn seven syllables at one repetition, he required fifteen repetitions to learn twelve syllables and thirty repetitions to learn sixteen syllables. By means of the second method he found that the curve of forgetting is asymptotic: it falls very rapidly at first, then more slowly and it would appear as though associations once formed are never entirely lost. Thus, to take an extreme case, Ebbinghaus found he could learn stanzas of Byron's *Don Juan*, previously learnt twenty-two years before, with a saving of seven per cent as compared with other stanzas he had never learnt. He also investigated the effects of over-learning, i.e. of repeating the material after it had been sufficiently learnt to be correctly recalled in *immediate* memory. He found that the ratio of overlearning to subsequent "saving" was approximately constant for rows of syllables of very varying lengths. After twenty-four hours the number of repetitions saved was consistently about one-third of the number of excess repetitions. Ebbinghaus also investigated the most economical methods of learning. He found that, with a given number of repetitions, more was learnt when the repetitions were not given all at once, but were separated by intervals of time; and that the more numerous the intervals the better was the result. One more investigation of his may be mentioned. He found that, in learning a series of syllables, associations are formed not only between the immediate neighbours in the series but also between the more distant members of the series; that they are formed, moreover, not only in the forward direction (i.e. as learnt) but in the backward direction—the so-called "remote" and "retroactive" associations respectively.[1]

---

[1] Ebbinghaus found that the retroactive associations are about one-third as strong as the forward associations. It was later shown by Wohlgemuth that this difference is only found with material learnt by motor memory; and that in visual memory the forward and backward associations are of equal strength.

Ebbinghaus's monograph represents perhaps the most brilliant single investigation that has ever been made in experimental psychology. At once a wide new field was made available for study, a field that has not even yet, nearly fifty years after the appearance of his *Gedächtnis*, been exhausted. The work not only opened up new territory; it was itself a striking example of both technical skill and dogged perseverance. No other single investigator working alone, as Ebbinghaus did, has subjected himself over a period of years to such a rigid régime of experimentation; for the experiments were not only exacting in themselves but also required that he should keep his habits of life as constant as possible. The achievement is all the more surprising in that Ebbinghaus was by no means a simple plodder, one of those who, in James's phrase, "could not be bored." On the contrary, he had a versatile and ingenious mind, and when, later on, he came to write a textbook, it proved to be unique in German literature, "the only readable, kindly handbook of psychology, that nevertheless fell not a whit short in scientific care and exactitude." Probably on the strength of his work on memory, Ebbinghaus was in 1886 made Extraordinary Professor in Berlin, where he had been *Dozent* since 1880. Stumpf, however, was in 1894 promoted to the full professorship over Ebbinghaus's head, and Ebbinghaus himself took over Lipps's chair at Breslau. Apart from his work on memory, he worked on colour contrast and on Weber's Law as applied to brightness. He also put forward a theory of colour vision of his own. More important perhaps than any of these activities was his foundation (together with Arthur König) in 1890 of a new journal—the *Zeitschrift für Psychologie und Physiologie der Sinnesorgane*. By that year there was too much material in the new psychology to find a home in Wundt's *Philosophische Studien*, which had also from the start been the rather exclusive organ of the Leipzig laboratory. The new *Zeitschrift*, as Boring puts it, "represented in a way a coalition of independents outside the Wundtian school," and has ever since continued to flourish, though the two parts (for *Psychologie* and *Sinnesorgane*) are now issued in separate numbers. Apart from this, Ebbinghaus's most famous achievements are the invention of his "completion test" (which was devised at the request of the Breslau municipal authorities) and his textbook, to which we have already referred. In a small way the completion test showed the same originality and permanent value as the memory experiments of earlier years. It was the first successful test of the "higher" mental capacities, and (sometimes in slightly modified forms) has remained a feature of many "batteries" of modern tests of "general intelligence." The completion test and the first part of the textbook, the *Grundzüge der Psychologie*, appeared in the same year, 1897. The completed first volume did not appear till 1902. It was a great success, as it deserved to be, and unfortunately Ebbinghaus devoted himself to revising this first volume rather than to getting on with the second. His *Abriss der Psychologie*, published in 1908, was originally the section on psychology in a large omnibus volume of *Die Kultur der Gegenwart*. Ebbinghaus died suddenly of pneumonia in 1909, without even finishing the *Grundzüge*—a considerable misfortune for psychology, for, as far as it went, it was perhaps the most satisfactory textbook on psychology that had ever been written. The second volume was eventually completed by Dürr, but Dürr did not possess the facility, charm and clarity of style that had distinguished the first volume, so that in a sense the work remained a magnificent torso. Apart from this, Ebbinghaus's comparatively early death probably deprived psychology of further valuable contributions. His productiveness was not great, but the quality of his work was always of the highest standard, and it is unlikely that, if he had lived another ten or fifteen years, his original mind would have let this time pass by without finding some fresh field of endeavour, in which he would have still further enriched his chosen science.

Georg Elias Müller was born in the same year as Ebbinghaus (1850) and was a pupil of Lotze at Göttingen, to whose chair he succeeded in 1881.[1] During his long occupancy of this chair Müller became, as has been said, "something of an institution," as Wundt had done at Leipzig. In fact his influence on psychology is in many ways comparable to Wundt's, though of course on a lesser scale. His laboratory became a centre of activity which attracted many distinguished students, among the best known being Schumann, Pilzecker, Jost, Henri, Martin, Rupp, Gamble, Katz, Spearman, Jaensch, Rubin and Kroh. Müller, however,

[1] We have already mentioned the distinction of this chair, which was held in succession by Herbart, Lotze and Müller for eight, thirty-seven and forty years respectively.

was more purely an experimentalist than Wundt. He wrote only one small general textbook (and that only in 1924) and elaborated no system of psychology. His own contributions were made in three principal fields, in psycho-physics, in visual sensation and in memory. His doctorate thesis was a book, *Zur Theorie der Sinnlichen Aufmerksamkeit* (1873), which had considerable influence on all subsequent treatments of attention, and (especially through the work of Titchener) is still familiar to many students of today. His second book, *Zur Grundlegung der Psychophysik* (1878), we have already noticed. This, more than anything else, caused Fechner to return to psycho-physics after a long interval and write his *Revision der Hauptpunkte der Psychophysik* (1882), in which he took account of the chief criticisms that had been made upon the *Elemente* in the twenty-two years since its appearance. Müller's further work on psycho-physics was carried out in collaboration with his pupils Schumann (1889) and Martin (1899). Together they produced exhaustive studies of the factors determining the judgment of the heaviness of weights— that most popular of all psycho-physical experiments. Müller also applied the psycho-physical methods to the study of tactual space perception, work which was subsequently carried on by V. Henri (a pupil of Binet), when he came to the Göttingen laboratory in the nineties. Müller somewhat enlarged the Fechnerian sense of the term psycho-physics, so as to include investigations of a primarily physiological nature. Thus his most important work on vision (1896–7) was published under the title *Zur Psychophysik der Gesichtsempfindungen*. Here he brought forward, among other things, his modification of Hering's theory of colour vision. According to this theory the three pairs, white-black, yellow-blue, red-green, depend, not upon an opposition between katabolism and anabolism, as Hering had supposed, but upon reversible photo-chemical substances. He supplemented Hering's theory also by the supposition that a constant grey (the "cortical grey") is produced by the molecular action of the cortex. In this he sought to overcome two of the principal difficulties in Hering's theory as at first propounded. Müller's modifications have been accepted by many upholders of Hering's theory, and in some modern books the theory is now definitely stated in the form given it by Müller.

Müller's most famous investigations, however, lie in the field of memory. He and his collaborators took up the work where Ebbinghaus had left it. They improved Ebbinghaus's technique by using instruments which allowed of any desired speed of presentation of the material to be learnt and by introducing certain rules as to the choice of syllables. New methods were devised and many fresh problems were attacked. On the side of method, the "method of hits" (*Treffermethode*) proved particularly useful; according to this a syllable is presented to the subject, who has then the task of recalling the one that had originally followed it. It permits the measurement, not only of the number of items correctly recalled, but also (with suitable apparatus) of the speed of the recall of each item, which Müller and Pilzecker showed to be an important indication of the strength of the association. Müller and Pilzecker also took over the "method of paired associates" originally devised by Calkins, a method which has been found valuable for the investigation of many problems of memory. In the course of all this work many fresh results of value were obtained. It was found, for instance,[1] that the attitude of the learner was an all-important matter; intention to learn was essential to quick learning, mere repetition without such intention being very ineffectual (a point which showed the inadequacy of the more mechanistic forms of the association doctrine). It was found that the initial and final members of a series were learnt more quickly than those in the middle of the series; that when two associations are of equal strength but of unequal age, a repetition strengthens the older more than the younger ("Jost's law," which was considered to afford an explanation of Ebbinghaus's discovery of the advantage of "spaced" repetitions); and (perhaps the most famous of all the results and one that has given rise to much further experimentation and discussion) that, in general, it is more economical to learn in "wholes" (by reading the material through from beginning to end without interruption) than in "parts" (by splitting it up into sections and mastering each part before proceeding to the next). These and other similar achievements constituted a great triumph of the experimental method, which in a relatively few years was able to give exact quantitative expression to the "laws of association" that had been discussed for centuries. They showed very

[1] By Müller and Schumann (Müller published a good many joint papers with his assistants and collaborators).

conclusively that this method was applicable, not merely to sensation and perception, but to the "higher mental processes," and thereby provided some compensation for the failure of the reaction experiment as a means of throwing light upon those processes.

Before retiring from his chair in 1921, Müller summarized and systematized his work on memory in three large volumes entitled *Zur Analyse der Gedächtnistätigkeit und des Vorstellungsverlaufes*, which occupies somewhat the same position with regard to memory as Stumpf's *Tonpsychologie* does with regard to the psychology of sound and music. Since his retirement he has devoted himself principally to the problems of vision, to writing the above-mentioned small textbook, and to a controversy with Köhler, the *Gestalt* psychologist, in which he questions the novelty of the *Gestalt* point of view. Müller is today the *doyen* of experimental psychologists. Except for the great founders, his work has probably done more than that of any other single individual to establish the new method of approach.

XI. THE EXPANSION OF PSYCHOLOGY—WUNDT'S PUPILS
IN EUROPE AND AMERICA

WE may now return to the main Wundtian school, and deal very
briefly with the expansion of experimental psychology by the
students who were trained in the Leipzig laboratory. One of the
very first of these, who came in the year of the laboratory's
foundation, was G. Stanley Hall, whom we have already considered in connection with the development of the evolutionary
doctrine. Stanley Hall is one of the most remarkable figures in
the history of American psychology. Born on a farm in Massachusetts, even in boyhood he began to develop the succession of
intense interests that was a permanent feature of his mental life.
Farming had no attraction for him and he was therefore sent to
train for the ministry. An admiration for J. S. Mill's philosophy
and an interest in the doctrine of evolution were, however, of no
advantage in this calling, and when Hall came to give his trial
sermon, the member of the theological faculty whose business it
was to criticize found comment useless, and resorted to prayer as
the only adequate way of meeting the situation that the sermon
had created! Nevertheless, after a visit to Europe young Hall
took his degree in divinity. In 1874 Wundt's *Grundzüge*, then
just published, fired him with enthusiasm for the new psychology
and he started out for Leipzig. But he had no money, and was
therefore unable to refuse an offer of a tutorship in English at
Harvard. Here he met William James (only two years his senior),
studied psychology with him and took what was probably the
first doctorate in that subject to be granted in America, his thesis
being on the rôle of the muscles in space perception. In 1878 he
was able to return to Europe, where he worked at Berlin with
von Kries and Kronecker, and arrived in Leipzig just in time to
make use of the new laboratory, though he did not stay there
long.

In 1881, on his return to America, he was given a lectureship
and then a chair at the recently created John Hopkins University.

Here, in 1883, he founded what is usually considered as the first
American laboratory for psychology, and for some years it seemed
as though he might make of it a western Leipzig, for he sur-
rounded himself with a number of able students, many of whom
afterwards played a part in American psychology, among the best
known being Dewey, Cattell, Sanford, Donaldson (who, while he
was there, made the discovery of the "spots" in the skin) and
Jastrow. Four years after the opening of his laboratory, Hall
founded (just as Wundt had done after the same interval) a
journal—*The American Journal of Psychology*—the second all-
psychological periodical in the world, and still the most important
in America. This journal differed, however, from Wundt's in
that it was, from the start, connected with no one laboratory,
but open to papers from any quarter. In 1888 Hall left John
Hopkins to become President of the new Clark University at
Worcester, Massachusetts. At the same time he was Professor of
Psychology, though the laboratory was soon handed over to Sanford, who in 1898 published the first laboratory *Course in Experimental Psychology*. In 1891 Hall founded another journal,
this time devoted especially to educational psychology, *The
Pedagogical Seminary*, which likewise still survives, while in the
following year he was instrumental in founding the American
Psychological Association, of which he was first President.

Hall was always favourable to experimental psychology, but
was impatient of its limitations. The psychological aspect of
growth and development was the field where his interests really
lay, and they found full expression in his educational work, in
his great *Adolescence* (1904) and in his favourable attitude to
psycho-analysis when he came to hear of it. His mind was of the
kind that is characterized by a succession of enthusiasms for fresh
objects rather than a steady devotion to a single cause; evolution,
however, remained for him a master key throughout his intellectual wanderings. He took over Galton's questionnaire method
and made extensive use of it, while at another time he became
much concerned with Pavlov's conditioned reflex and the psychology of food. During his thirty-six years at Clark, he gave no less
than eighty-one doctorates, which include many of the most
important names in American psychology today. In his last
years (if we may here anticipate what really belongs to our next
period) he became interested in religion and wrote a book on

Jesus the Christ in the Light of Psychology (1917), a work which is, unfortunately, difficult to read, because of the vast number of Greek neologisms which it contains. When the time came for Hall to retire, he characteristically became interested in the phase of development that this implied, and ended his list of major publications with a volume on *Senescence* (1922), dying two years later.

James McKeen Cattell, another American pioneer, came to Wundt from Lotze. His work at Leipzig was interrupted by a brief return to America, where for a term he was Hall's pupil at John Hopkins. On coming back to Leipzig in 1883, where he now stayed for three years, he boldly told Wundt that he needed an assistant and that he (Cattell) proposed to take on the job (which he did). From the very beginning, Cattell showed an independent mind and a predominant interest in individual differences. Wundt said this was *ganz amerikanisch,* but allowed the young man to have his way. Wundt's remark was very justified, for an interest in individual differences—an interest that was a natural outcome of the evolutionary point of view—has ever since been a feature of American, as distinct from German, psychology. On returning to America he founded a psychological laboratory at the University of Pennsylvania in 1888, after three years left it in Witmer's charge, and founded a new one at Columbia, where he remained till 1917, when he was dismissed because of his expression of pacifist views. He afterwards founded the Psychological Corporation, an organization for psychological service for industrial and public ends.

In 1914 six of Cattell's students drew up an account of his original work (which was scattered in many short papers) under six main heads, as follows: reaction time, reading and perception, association, psycho-physics, the "order of merit" method, and individual differences. Of these the last, as already indicated, represented Cattell's most fundamental interest. He is, however, in addition, the foremost authority on the reaction experiment, which he started with James at Johns Hopkins, took with him to Leipzig (where he was one of the very few students who determined the nature of his own research) and continued all the earlier part of his life, devising new procedures and apparatus, but always with the statistical and individual standpoint more or less in mind. The reaction experiment led naturally to the association experiment, and here, quite early, Cattell anticipated some of the later findings of Jung, when he said that associative reactions "lay bare the mental life in a way that is startling and not always gratifying." He also realized that this experiment might be used for the classification of individuals, as others have subsequently used it.

In 1892 he published (together with Fullerton, a philosopher "temporarily bewitched," as Boring puts it, "by experimental psychology") an important psycho-physical monograph *On the Perception of Small Differences*, in which he brought statistical refinements to bear upon the psycho-physical methods, criticized several general points of procedure, and endeavoured (in the method of right and wrong cases) to substitute the conception of the probable error for that of the threshold. Another innovation in methodology was the invention of the order of merit method— a great simplification on the method of paired comparisons as used in Wundt's laboratory. He applied this new method both to the ordinary stimuli available in the laboratory and to the ranking of individual persons, as in his studies of "Eminent Men" and "American Men of Science," in which the central position of each individual together with its probable error, is worked out on the basis of many rankings by different judges. Finally, Cattell was a pioneer in mental testing. In 1896 he published (with Ferrand) a classical study of physical and mental tests of the Columbia students—a forerunner of the entrance tests subsequently carried out regularly at Columbia and elsewhere. When Thorndike (a student of Cattell) was experimenting with his puzzle boxes on animals, Cattell advised him to carry out the same sort of thing with children, and from this beginning Thorndike became the foremost exponent of mental testing in America.

Through the position he held, Cattell, moreover, exercised an immense influence on the younger generation of psychologists (the list even of the more distinguished of his pupils is too long to mention) and inspired in them his own fundamental interest in the differences in human nature and capacity.

Cattell is now, by general consent, America's senior psychologist, and was appropriately enough elected president of the first International Congress of Psychology to be held in America, in 1929.

Stanley Hall and Cattell are in many ways of exceptional importance among Wundt's pupils, because of the very influential part they played in the development of American psychology; and the rapid rise of American psychology is beyond all doubt one of the most striking scientific events of the last two decades of the nineteenth century. By 1892 there were fifteen laboratories in America and by 1900 twenty-six, in both cases distinctly more than there were in Europe at those dates. The hospitable attitude of America to the new science is shown also by the fact that those who were appointed to teach it were usually called Professors of Psychology, whereas in German universities, although there might be a *Psychologisches Institut*, its director still, as a rule, carried (as he does even today) the title of Professor of Philosophy. But in taking over psychology, America distinctly modified the German attitude. From the very first the principal features of this modification were clearly apparent. They can be summarized very briefly under three heads: (1) a much greater interest in the genetic standpoint; (2) a distrust of introspection, and (3) an emphasis on individual differences rather than on the general characteristics of the human mind. The first feature was a direct inheritance from the work of Darwin and of Spencer, which profoundly modified the whole Anglo-Saxon outlook in the biological sciences, the second was to show itself presently in a very acute form in the rise of behaviourism, while the third began to manifest itself very soon in the rise of mental tests, a form of experimentation that has never made a great appeal to German psychologists.

Wundt's other pupils must be disposed of more briefly, not because they were less able, but because circumstances did not conspire to give them the important historical position held by Stanley Hall and Cattell.

Emil Kraepelin was one of the earliest and most original, though he is better known as a psychiatrist than a psychologist. Both on the descriptive and the classificatory side, he has been one of the most influential figures in the study of mental disease. Perhaps his greatest single contribution lay in the recognition that there exists a certain fundamental similarity between several, at first sight, distinct types of psychoses—types which he proceeded to class together under the common head of *dementia praecox*. But Kraepelin was also an experimental psychologist of originality. We have already referred to his work on reaction times under abnormal conditions. Another field in which he was a pioneer was the study of continuous work, such as that involved in adding (his "adding sheets," specially prepared for this kind of experiment, have become part of the permanent equipment of the psychological laboratory). By checking the amount done in successive short intervals of time, he was able to construct a "work curve," showing the fluctuations in output as the work proceeded, and enabling him to attempt an analysis of the chief factors determining the shape of the curve, the opposing influence of practice and fatigue, "warming-up," voluntary "spurts," etc. These were the classic experiments on which nearly all subsequent investigations on this subject have been based. In later times, owing to their obvious importance in education and industry, the measurement of practice and fatigue has aroused especial interest. Two pioneering nineteenth-century studies in this field may be mentioned here, although they were independent of the Wundtian tradition: Mosso's work on the ergograph, an instrument for measuring fatigue by means of the decline in muscular efficiency, and Bryan's and Harter's work on practice in telegraphic sending and receiving. The ergograph has shown itself less useful than was hoped, and altogether the subject of fatigue has proved to be full of difficulties and complexities. Practice, however, is easier to deal with, and, from the time of Bryan and Harter's work onwards, considerable progress has been made in analysing the factors that determine the rate of practice with various kinds of work and under various conditions.

Hugo Münsterberg was another early pupil of Wundt, but one who was less permanently influenced by the great Leipzig master than were most others. He soon established a laboratory of his own at Freiburg, where he produced some studies of originality, the *Beiträge*, which attracted the favourable attention of William James. James thought he had found in Münsterberg an experimentalist who was less stodgy than the rest, and invited him to Harvard, first for three years (1892–5) and then permanently (from 1897 onwards). James was glad enough to hand over the laboratory to Münsterberg, and to have his own title changed back to "Professor of Philosophy." But Münsterberg never developed into an important psychologist, so far as original research was concerned. His influence, however, in one way and another was considerable. He developed a so-called "action theory" of consciousness in which he stressed the significance of motor discharge (always an attractive subject to American readers, who, even at that time, were behaviouristic in tendency, if not in theory). The details of Münsterberg's views are now unimportant and are open to serious criticisms, but the fact of the theory coming when it did gave it some significance. Later, Münsterberg's activities were largely directed to the popularization of applied psychology in various fields, in psychotherapy, criminology, industry, etc., and there can be no doubt that his efforts in this direction, by creating a widespread interest in the possibilities of practical psychology, indirectly assisted in the actual task of application, though he himself contributed but little on the purely technical side.

E. W. Scripture was another student of Wundt who contributed to the popularization of psychology, though earlier, for his two chief books, *Thinking, Feeling, Doing* and *The New Psychology* appeared in 1895 and 1897 respectively. At this distance of time, they seem perhaps to betray an element of exaggerated confidence and optimism. But in those days, when new laboratories were being founded in all the chief American universities, optimism was a very natural thing. Scripture was in charge of the Yale laboratory from 1892 to 1903, during which time he edited ten volumes of *Studies from the Yale Laboratory*, on the model of Wundt's famous periodical. But (in contrast to what happened with Cattell at Columbia) comparatively few distinguished psychologists were trained at the laboratory (though Seashore was a striking exception) and Scripture's own interests presently turned predominantly to phonetics.

Only a few other of Wundt's students can be mentioned here, for anything approaching a full account of the subsequent work of those who received their psychological training in Leipzig would be far too big an undertaking. Ernst Neumann has been known chiefly as an educational psychologist, and his most famous investigations deal with various aspects of learning, though in the years preceding his death in 1915 he was beginning to deal with aesthetics. Alfred Lehmann, for many years director of the laboratory at Copenhagen, was the foremost exponent of the "expression" methods in their relation to the study of the feelings. Later on, he published a general treatise of much originality, the *Grundzüge der Psychophysiologie* (1912), in which he recorded many of his own experiments and endeavoured to look at mental phenomena consistently from the point of view of energy. It is a book that has perhaps not received the full consideration it deserves.

Among the early workers in Leipzig whom it is impossible to pass over were Külpe and Titchener, whom we have already mentioned. Angell also must be referred to, but the most important work of all these three was done in the twentieth century, and it can therefore be conveniently reserved for the treatment of our third and last period.

It will have been noticed that our account has shown that in the nineteenth century experimental psychology was almost entirely a German and American science. As regards the origins of the experimental method, the initiative was overwhelmingly German; in fact, the only exception of any real importance was the work of Galton, and in England there was a complete failure to continue what Galton had begun—until experimentation was reintroduced from Germany by McDougall, Spearman and others early in the twentieth century.

THE way in which America seized hold of the German methods,
adapted and acclimatized them so successfully that in ten years
from the foundation of the first laboratory the American effort
was at least equal to the German and was soon to surpass it, is
one of the most interesting features of the whole history of
psychology. America, however, was not quite alone in realizing
the possibilities of experiment as applied to human mind and conduct. Several other countries were making a beginning, though
in none of them did the movement flourish in any way at all
comparable to the wave of success that carried it to triumph in
America. The most important of these countries was France, and
a reference to the French laboratories and those who founded and
worked them affords a convenient means of transition to the subjects of brain physiology and abnormal psychology, with which
we must conclude this review of our long second period—convenient because in both these fields, and especially in the latter,
France was one of the leading contributors to progress.

Modern psychology (as distinct from brain physiology) in
France may be said to begin in 1870, when two important books
were published, Taine's *De l'Intelligence* and Ribot's *La Psychologie anglaise contemporaine* in which the prevailing associationism was well and clearly expounded. Ribot followed up his book
nine years later (the year in which Wundt's laboratory was
founded) with another book on *La Psychologie allemande contemporaine*, in which he brought the new departures of Fechner,
Helmholtz and Wundt to the knowledge of his countrymen. In
1885 he was placed in charge of a course in experimental psychology at the Sorbonne, where, in 1889, a laboratory was established
under Beaunis and Binet, Ribot himself being given a chair of
experimental and comparative psychology at the Collège de
France; while in 1890 another laboratory was founded at Rennes
under Bourdon.

But, as we have just said, the principal work of the French investigators during all this period lay in the field of abnormal psychology. On an earlier page, in dealing with the development of hypnotism in England, we mentioned the fact that at Braid's death in 1860 his discoveries had already been taken up in France. Soon there were two great schools of thought with regard to hypnotism. The Paris school, under the leadership of Charcot, took a view that can be described as primarily medical and physiological. They thought that hypnotism was a phenomenon characteristic of hysteria, and could only be induced in persons suffering from, or at least prone to, that disease. Furthermore, various "stages" of hypnotic sleep were described, and regarded as of general validity for all hypnotic subjects: lethargy (in which there is little beyond drowsiness), catalepsy (in which there is rigidity of the limbs with subsequent forgetfulness of what has happened) and somnambulism, in which there is a dissociation or splitting of the personality, so that one part is ignorant of what the other is doing or thinking. The Nancy school, under the leadership of Bernheim and Liébault, followed up more closely both the practice and the theory of Braid. They believed that, by suitable methods, hypnosis could be induced in nearly everyone, and maintained that it was a phenomenon due, not to a particular diseased condition of the nervous system, but to the general psychological trait of suggestibility. Subsequent research has shown that, on the whole, the Nancy school were nearer the truth, though, as we have said in dealing with hypnotism in our first period, the problems connected with this subject have been very much neglected in more recent years.

Charcot, however, the head of the Paris school, was himself the most eminent figure in French psychiatry and attracted many pupils, among them Janet and Freud, the two foremost representatives of psycho-pathology today. Janet carried on the studies of dissociation in hystericals, and made many experiments which eventually brought him to the concept of *integration* as one of the most important characteristics of personality. In hysteria the integration is imperfect and unstable as compared with that achieved by normal persons, and in extreme cases there may actually come about a "dissociation of personality" into two or more selves with different character and memories. A number of interesting cases of this kind began to be reported both in France and in America, where interest in the subject was aroused by the writings of James and Morton Prince. French psychologists generally, however, were much more in touch with abnormal conditions than those of other countries. Psycho-pathology served them as a general background, comparable to that provided by biology in England and philosophy in Germany. Ribot, the principal figure in the earlier years, wrote constantly on psycho-pathological topics, to which the titles of some of his most famous books, *The Diseases of Memory* (1881), *The Diseases of Will* (1883) and *The Diseases of Personality* (1885)—all of them translated into English—bear testimony. Alfred Binet's first book, *The Psychology of Reasoning* (1886), also stresses the abnormal, and was based largely on the results of hypnotic experiments, a method of approach which it is difficult to imagine in the case of an English or German author dealing with this topic. A little later he began cultivating experimental psychology, though with an outlook that was never confined to his laboratory. He investigated aesthesiometric thresholds, tactile sensibility and optical illusions as a German might have done, but at the same time he wrote books on *The Alterations of Personality* (1891) and on *Suggestibility* (1900), and investigated the methods of great arithmetical prodigies and famous chess players. His most celebrated work, however, was done at the beginning of our next period, and we shall have occasion to refer to him again.

TURNING, finally, to brain physiology, we know that at the beginning of our "hundred years" there had been a strong movement away from the theory (implied in phrenology) that various mental functions or capacities were connected with narrowly specific areas of the brain, in favour of the view that there existed only a much more general correspondence between certain levels of activity and certain major divisions of the brain—a view for which Flourens, more than any other single individual, was responsible. In our first period, from 1833 to 1860, there had been no evidence of sufficient weight to change this belief, though the fairly frequent observation made in hospitals that sensory, motor and intellectual functions were independently or unequally affected was not easy to harmonize with Flourens's view that all parts of the cortex were equally concerned in all these functions. Phrenology, too, still had its followers (as indeed it has today), but such further arguments as were brought in its support quite failed to convince the learned world even of its general thesis of the precise localization of functions in special areas.

All at once, at the beginning of our second period, the situation altered. Discoveries were made, and continued to be made throughout the earlier part of this period, which pointed once again to localization of specific functions, though not of the kind that the classical doctrines of phrenology demanded. In 1861 there died in a Paris hospital a man who had been an inmate for thirty years, and whose only defect was that he could not talk. A few days before his death he had been carefully examined by the surgeon Broca, who satisfied himself that the patient's inability to talk was not due to defect of the articulatory organs or to muscular or intellectual incapacity. Immediately the patient died, Broca examined his brain also, and found a lesion in the third left frontal convolution—in a region ever since known as

"Broca's area." Broca concluded that here was the cerebral centre that controls the processes of speech, and his evidence was soon supported by that from other cases. And if there was a centre for speech, why not centres for other functions also? Flourens's views began to totter, and received blow after blow in the succeeding years.

The clinical method of correlating lesions in the brain observed after death with defects manifested by the patient while he was alive, was soon supplemented by two other methods of an experimental nature that could be applied in the case of animals—the method of extirpation (that had already been employed by Flourens) and the method of stimulation. As regards the latter, it had usually been supposed, on the basis of the evidence then available, that the brain was insensitive to direct stimulation. But in 1870 Fritsch and Hitzig applied for the first time an electrical stimulus. Hitzig first noticed that electrical stimulation of the cortex of a man caused eye movements, he verified this observation on a rabbit, and then, in collaboration with Fritsch, made a detailed study with dogs, as a result of which he found that, by stimulation of certain parts of the anterior portion of the cortex at appropriate strength (too powerful stimuli produced general convulsive movements), specialized movements of particular parts of the body could be elicited. Both the general fact and the detailed findings (making reasonable allowance for experimental errors) were soon afterwards corroborated by Ferrier and others. Indeed by 1876 Ferrier, in his well-known *Functions of the Brain*, was able to give a fairly detailed map indicating the discoveries of the "new phrenology," as it was sometimes called. As a result of these and many later studies, it soon became abundantly clear that, in the portion of the cortex immediately in front of the fissure of Rolando, there was an area which controlled voluntary movement, and that there existed special centres within this area which were correlated with movements of particular parts of the body.

Similarly, the clinical and extirpation methods were producing evidence as to the localization of sensory functions, and although for the most part they did not allow of such detailed exploration as could be carried out by the stimulation method on the motor side, knowledge of the general boundaries of the principal sense areas steadily accumulated, so that by the end of the century it became possible to draw the maps with which all students are now familiar, indicating the body-sense area just behind the fissure of Rolando, the visual area in the occipital lobe, the auditory area in the temporal lobe, the olfactory and gustatory areas in the hippocampus.

Evidence similar to that of Broca's was, meanwhile, indicating the existence of other specialized forms of disease, analogous in many ways to the case he had reported. They have received special names according to the nature of the particular disturbance, but "aphasia" is a term widely used, sometimes with qualifying terms, to all cases of this kind. Broca's was a case of "motor" aphasia. Soon afterwards, in 1874 Wernicke described a case of "sensory" aphasia, in which the patient was able to speak but not to understand the speech of others. This led to the identification of "Wernicke's area," a little below the sensory auditory area. Soon, quite a number of such disorders were reported, both on the motor and the sensory sides, interfering sometimes with reading, sometimes with writing, sometimes with the manipulation or tactual recognition of objects, and so on—though it has for the most part not been possible to establish special areas for these with any degree of precision. Indeed, in spite of the enthusiasm for cerebral localization which these discoveries naturally aroused, there were not wanting, throughout this period, students who continued to stress the function of the *whole* cortex in the way that Flourens had done. Flourens's operation of removing the cerebral lobes from lower animals was repeated, and his statement concerning the general sluggishness and lack of initiative of such animals was confirmed. An interesting triangular contest took place between Goltz, a pupil of Helmholtz, who tended to return to Flourens's position, Munk, a champion of specific localization, and Luciani, who looked upon the brain as a complex of overlapping areas, and according to whom, therefore, localization would be possible but not in so definite a way as Munk maintained. It is interesting to note that, at the present day, analogous views are being eagerly discussed on the purely psychological side, as regards the question of general, specific or overlapping abilities or functions.

The clinical, stimulation and extirpation methods of determining the localization of functions were supplemented by others; to some extent by arguments from comparative anatomy, in which the brains of different animals distinguished by specialized functions or abilities could be compared, and to a greater extent by the tracing of nerve paths through the nervous system to the various centres, a task which was greatly helped by observing the effects of "secondary" or "Wallerian" degeneration when a nerve was severed. This latter method, as already mentioned, was of assistance also in determining the course of individual nervous units.

In this last field, however, most progress was made by the introduction of improved methods of staining microscopic preparations, particularly Golgi's nitrate of silver method, introduced in 1873. In 1889 Ramon y Cajal discovered that each nerve cell and its processes is apparently separated from other units by a gap or "synapse," and two years later Waldeyer gave much prominence to the "neurone" theory based on this discovery, the theory which regards the nervous system as consisting of a vast number of independent elements, the "neurones," each composed of a cell (its trophic centre), together with an axon and dendrites. This theory suggests that great importance attaches to the synapse or junction between neurones—a suggestion that was later on to be followed up by Sherrington and other neurologists, who showed that, in fact, great complications occur to the passage of a nervous impulse as soon as a synapse is involved. Psychologists, in turn, have not been slow to seize upon these discoveries, and the view has been put forward (notably by McDougall) that the ultimate physiological equivalent of consciousness is to be found in the synaptic processes.

Considerable progress was made in this second period as regards an understanding of the general distribution of function in the various parts of the nervous system. Hughlings Jackson's notion of "levels" was perhaps especially important in this connection. He distinguished three principal levels. At the lowest level only the spinal cord was operative, but this was sufficient to effect integration of the sense organs and the muscles below the level of the neck. At the intermediate level the medulla or midbrain was involved, as in turning towards a light, or sound, or orienting the body to the influence of gravity; while, at the highest level, the cortex is the centre for voluntary and intelligent behaviour.

The concept of levels was destined to acquire additional importance later on, when it was realized, through the work of

Sherrington and others, that the higher centres, and especially the cortex, normally exercise an inhibiting effect upon the function of the lower centres. This is apparently a discovery of very great significance, since if there is failure on the part of the higher centres, or the nervous paths through which their control is exercised, the lower centres, released from this control, begin to function with unusual vigour and freedom. This "over-reaction" may be useful for determining the existence of higher level defect, and also for ascertaining the specific functions of the lower centres, which are revealed more clearly in their exaggerated form. Quite generally, the concept of control or inhibition was coming to be of increasing importance both in neurology and psychology, and in the hands of such writers as Sherrington, McDougall, Head and Freud, was soon to become one of the most essential elements in the whole modern picture of the mind.

PART IV

1900–1933

I. MODERN PSYCHOLOGY AND THE "SCHOOLS"

IT is clear that our third period from 1900 onwards will need a rather different treatment from that which we have given to the two preceding periods and to our initial survey. For one thing, the number of workers and the quantity of work done is so much vaster, that, if we were to continue our examination on the same scale, our account of this third period would be longer than the three other sections of this book together. Our sketch must therefore be on broader lines, an indication of general tendencies rather than of particular achievements or investigators.

In the second place, the conduct of the science itself takes on a different complexion. The movement inaugurated by Wundt has had its inevitable consequences. Not content with his own colossal output, Wundt founded a school and inspired a number of workers with his own ideals. Henceforward, the history of psychology must take account of schools and teams of workers rather than of isolated individuals. Not, of course, that the individual is unimportant; a school requires a leader, or at least a founder—an individual with the ability and initiative to strike out a new course and to make others follow him. In the last thirty years, psychology has certainly not been lacking in such outstanding personalities; but for the most part they do not stand alone, as they would have done at an earlier period. They have attracted followers, who have adopted their outlook and their methods, who have, as it were, carried on both propaganda and research on their behalf; and the contributions of the leaders to the total picture are due (of course in varying degrees), not only to their own labours, but also to the stir and bustle created by their followers.

In the third place we can scarcely proceed with the same assurance as when dealing with the earlier periods. It is notoriously difficult to form an accurate estimate of our contemporaries. We may easily mistake for an epoch-making discovery an innovation that turns out to be nothing but a nine days' wonder; while, on the other hand, we may pass by scarcely noticing the beginnings of events which later on show themselves to be of quite revolutionary significance. So far as concerns the contending schools which have played such a great part in recent years, the dust of conflict is still in our eyes. Moreover, our estimates of relative importance are necessarily determined by our own position in the total field of action; things going on immediately about us inevitably concern us more, and therefore seem of greater moment, than what is happening farther off. Thus any one observer can but try his best to be impartial; however well-meant and conscientious his report may be, in the end he must resign himself to the fact that he can achieve but indifferent success in any attempt to give a clear and undistorted impression of the tangled mêlée of conflicting tendencies that make up present-day psychology.

The question of the order and manner of our treatment is itself far from easy to decide. Schools, methods, fields of work—these three suggest themselves as possible bases of classification that would allow of a consistent and logical approach. But all these show a partial overlapping that makes consistent treatment on such lines, if not impossible, at least difficult, confusing and wearisome. Each school has to some considerable extent its own method and field of work, but naturally and inevitably it seeks both to develop its method and to enlarge its field; in the course of this endeavour it often enters a field already worked over by another method and mapped out from another point of view; and the same field sometimes looks very different according to the method by which it has been cultivated and the point of view from which we look at it. Even the same methods may be employed with different preconceptions and different aims in view. If we are to avoid tiresome and pedantic repetition, we must, therefore, sacrifice logical order and consistency to convenience, dealing sometimes chiefly with a school, sometimes with a field of work, and sometimes even with a method—hoping meanwhile that this unsystematic approach will not too greatly prejudice our understanding or lead us to pass over too many matters of importance.

In order, however, to get some kind of general orientation—however vague and inadequate—concerning the main questions at issue, we may attempt, as a preliminary step, to arrange certain tendencies, which distinguish a number of the schools, in pairs of opposites. There have always been antithetical tendencies in psychology (as probably in all other sciences), and it is sometimes conducive to clearness to make them as explicit as possible, and to see just how and where they operate, in the clash between any particular writers, schools or doctrines.

A hundred years ago there were perhaps two main antitheses in psychology, as follows:

Mechanism	Activity
Association	Faculties

We have seen these antitheses at work, especially in the earlier parts of this book, and the reader will probably have noticed that there was a general, though by no means an invariable, tendency for associationism to be mechanistic, whereas a resort to faculties or "powers" has nearly always meant an explanation in terms of the mind's activity. While these two opposing pairs had by no means disappeared, we found that, during our second period (1860–1900) three other pairs were becoming of importance, and that psychology was tending to become either

Systematic	or	Experimental
Contentual	or	Actual
General	or	Differential (devoted to the study of individual differences)

In this period we may perhaps distinguish five main contrasting tendencies:

Structural	Functional
Associationist (Elementaristic)	Configurationist (*Gestalt*)
Introspective	Behaviouristic
Mechanical	Purposive
Conscious	Unconscious

We could easily add other pairs to the list, such as Sensation—Thought, Two Factors—Many Factors, Individualistic—Sexual,

Pure—Applied, and so on. Some of the older antitheses, moreover, still play a part; notably that between General and Differential, though of late years it has become pretty generally recognized that both are useful and legitimate, whereas this degree of toleration is still absent in some other cases. Fortunately, too, there are a few schools or doctrines which are more or less *au dessus de la mêlée,* in the sense that they have as yet discovered scarcely any vested interests that are opposed to them.

II. "STRUCTURAL" AND "FUNCTIONAL" PSYCHOLOGY

THE conflict between *structural* and *functional* psychology may be regarded as the natural continuation of the older antithesis between Content and Act (which itself, to some extent, but not entirely, represented the still earlier contrast between Mechanism and Activity). In its modern form this conflict began in America, and was connected with (indeed to a considerable extent arose out of) the antithesis between general and differential psychology. We have seen how the predominant American tendency was to deflect experimental psychology away from the study of general mental laws (which had been the aim of Fechner and Wundt) to that of individual differences. To this deflection, which was manifested in Wundt's own pupils (especially, as we have seen, in Cattell) no less than in others, there was one striking exception—Titchener. Throughout his life, Titchener (who, it will be remembered, was an Englishman) remained true to the Wundtian tradition. He wanted to experiment on the normal human mind, and had little interest in the features that distinguish one individual from another, or in those still wider fields of comparison presented by abnormal, racial or animal psychology. A characteristic dispute arose between Titchener and Baldwin (who in this matter represented the predominant American position) about reaction times. In 1895 Baldwin had challenged the interpretation of the difference between "sensorial" and "muscular" reaction times, maintaining that this difference was due rather to the existence of "sensory" and "motor" types of observer than to differences of attitude. In the following year Angell and A. W. Moore showed that there was nothing really incompatible between Lange's interpretation of his original results with practised subjects (which Titchener defended) and Baldwin's explanation of his own findings; differences of voluntary attitude and of natural tendency might quite well both exist. The controversy, however, was of importance in that it served to bring out very clearly the difference between Titchener's position and that of the majority of American psychologists.

This difference in the point of view of general and of differential psychology soon became a difference between the upholders of "structure" and of "function." Modern "functional" psychology is often said to have begun in the next year, 1896, with a paper by Dewey on *The Reflex Arc Concept in Psychology*, in which he criticized the analysis of the reflex arc into stimulus and response, insisted that the entire arc was the minimal unit that could profitably be considered in isolation, and that, in general, attempts at detailed analysis were misleading, in that the key to understanding lay in function. Stimulus and sensation alike exist *for* the act, and have little meaning unless considered in relation to it. Titchener, in his reply, adopted from James the phrase "structural" psychology, and contrasted it with the functional psychology of Dewey, by saying that the datum of the former is an "Is," that of the latter an "Is for." In what followed, Angell was the principal champion of the functional point of view, which remained important until interest was transferred to the even more radical revolt against Wundtianism that was implied in the rise of behaviourism in the second decade of the twentieth century.

Statements of the aims of functionalism have varied according to the year in which they were made and the writer who made them. But, in general, two differences from structuralism stand out very clearly: (1) functionalism deals with acts of operations (e.g. with seeing, tasting, conceiving, believing) rather than with contents or elements (visual or gustatory sensations, concepts, beliefs); (2) it considers consciousness as an activity with a biological end, an activity of special use in allowing the organism to adapt itself to novel circumstances. Two further characteristics of functionalism are often implied, though they can perhaps be looked upon as mere corollaries of (1) and (2) respectively. They are: (a) that functionalism allows itself to take account of "meanings" and of the functional relationship between conscious phenomena, and (b) that, in its biological outlook, it need not confine itself to clearly conscious reactions, but can consider also automatic or well-habituated responses in which consciousness is absent or at a minimum.

Structuralism, or existentialism, as it has sometimes been called, mapped out for itself a much narrower and more rigid path. Its limits seem, in the last resort, to be largely determined by its method, and, as regards the latter, structuralism is essentially an introspective psychology, aiming at an analysis of experience into elements. It is, therefore, prevented from entering the wider biological sphere, which is inaccessible to introspection. Even within the individual mind of the trained observer, however, much is excluded that might at first sight seem within its province. As is implied under claim (a) of functionalism, above, the kind of introspection demanded by the strictest structuralism must make no reference to meanings or to things. To deal with meanings involves us, Titchener would say, in the "stimulus error"—an error into which the psychologist is all too prone to fall, because his linguistic and his thinking habits have alike been formed with reference to things and not to thoughts or percepts. In ordinary life we constantly refer to objects and relatively seldom to our feelings or experiences. Hence we might naturally say, "the path is getting more uneven," whereas a person would seldom naturally introspect as follows: "the pressure on the soles of my feet is tending to get more uneven and irregular at each step, while the sensations around the joints and the skin of my knees and ankles are also varying more and more from one step to another," though this might be an accurate and "existentially" correct introspection of his experiences, when parted from their meaning (by exclusion of all reference to the path). We have, in short, according to Titchener, to describe our experiences themselves, and not the objects to which they may refer. An austere, and even an arid doctrine, it might appear; for experiences, thus robbed of outer reference, seem at first sight little more than the dry husks of mental life. And yet, for its own purpose, the instruction is undoubtedly correct; the question is, rather, whether the purpose is one of universal application in psychology, even as regards the method of introspection. That the method is at any rate not sterile, is shown by the volume of useful work that has been done at the Cornell laboratory during the thirty-five years when Titchener was in charge there. It is well to remember, too, in this connection that Titchener is the author of what Külpe is said to have described as "the most erudite work on psychology in the English language"—his great *Experimental Psychology* in

four volumes, published between 1901 and 1905 (the last
volume delayed by the appearance of Müller's final summing-up
of psycho-physics—his *Gesichtspunkte und Tatsachen*—in 1903).
As a laboratory handbook it is quite unique in its thoroughness,
and must ever remain a classic text as regards the methodology
of experimentation, as it existed at the beginning of the century.

FULLY to understand Titchener's standpoint with regard to
structural psychology, with which we were concerned in the last
chapter, we must turn to another controversy in which he played
a part—that which centred round Külpe's "Würzburg" school—
a controversy in which the chief antithesis lay between sensation
and thought. It was a controversy in which the method of introspection (and certain new developments within it) also played a
major part. The Würzburg school, of which Külpe was throughout the leader and director, though he himself wrote comparatively little, employed "systematic experimental introspection"
as it had never been employed before. To Wundt introspection
(*Selbstbeobachtung*) had meant little more than having an experience and subsequently describing it. In the hands of the Würzburg workers it meant, rather, a special attitude, the adoption of
which enabled the observer to study his experience in detail as
though under a microscope. The whole experience was described
methodically and systematically, if necessary being divided into
periods for this purpose (the method of "fractionization"). Similar
tasks would be performed again and again, so that the accounts
might be corrected, corroborated and amplified. Finally, the
spontaneous reports might be supplemented by the answers to
questions asking the subject to direct his attention to special
points. In effect, this work really provided psychology with a new
tool, which has to some extent been subsequently used by all
schools which employ introspection at all; and a special training in
the use of this tool has become a feature of many laboratories. It
is a tool, however, that has been severely criticized. Wundt himself, though he had all along admitted that introspection was the
most essential method of psychology, was very sceptical as to the
value of the new refinement of the method. It involves, as he
correctly pointed out, a double task; the subject must judge,
memorize, feel, or whatever else the experiment calls for, and

must then turn round, as it were, on himself, and examine just *how*
he judged, memorized or felt. In this respect it differs from other
scientific observations. Furthermore, in experiments on relatively
complicated processes of thought, for which it was eventually
employed by the Würzburg school, the subject does not know
exactly what it is he will have to observe, nor is it possible to
observe the *same datum* in repeated trials, as can be done with
sensory stimuli. To these charges the only reply was that it was
possible to perform *similar* tasks again and again, in the course
of which the essential common features of the mental processes
involved could be repeatedly inspected; that, as a matter of fact,
the double task did not seem to present any insuperable difficulties; and that, furthermore, the reliability of the method was
shown by the large measure of agreement between the reports of
different subjects. On the whole, psychologists have of course
come round to the point of view of the innovators, so far at least
as to agree that if introspection is employed at all, it should be
thorough and systematic.[1] The objections that are heard today are
directed against introspection as a whole, rather than against the
attempt to make it more refined or to use it more methodically.
It is pretty generally conceded, moreover, that the Würzburg
school did achieve some very real advance in our knowledge of
the "higher mental processes," although the exact interpretation
of their findings is still to some extent a matter of dispute.

The first contribution of importance from this school was a

---

[1] The point of view of the modern introspectionist is perhaps best expressed
in the following words of Aveling: "All these abstract phenomena (involved in
will, choice, emotion, etc.) can be discriminated introspectively, provided care
be taken to arrange suitable conditions in which one or the other is emphasized,
and the experiments repeated a sufficient number of times to allow of adequate
characterization of the phenomena in question. This is a *sine qua non* of all
serious introspective work, since what in reality is introspected is (cognized)
experience, and not all that enters into a single given experience can ever be
taken to be cognized adequately—a fact due to the law of the limitation of
mental energy. We are directly aware only of an infinitesimal part of our
external sensory experience at any given moment. Our span of consciousness is
likewise limited for any aspect of experience whatever. Very many observations, accordingly, may be necessary to disentangle the phenomena of the
simplest mental process" (*Feelings and Emotions*, p. 52). The distinction here
made between cognized and uncognized experience, a distinction which seems
to afford a fresh justification of the introspective technique, is taken from
Spearman, who himself reported some remarkable introspective experiments
bearing on this distinction in his *Nature of Intelligence and Principles of Cognition* (1923), a book to which we shall refer again later.

study of judgment by Marbe (who eventually succeeded Külpe at Würzburg). The results here were primarily negative, though the negation itself was of a somewhat startling kind. Marbe found that in comparing weights the subject did not know how the judgments "heavier" or "lighter" came into his mind. Images and sensations and other easily introspectible contents there were in plenty, but these appeared to play no essential part in the process of judgment itself. Here, as in some other cases of experimental work, a little careful experimentation and introspection sufficed to shatter the belief of centuries. It had usually been supposed that judgment was a definitely conscious process and that, in comparison of the kind here in question, the subject retained an image of the first object, compared it with the impression of the second, and formulated his verdict. Marbe's experiments, taken in conjunction with those of G. E. Müller and his pupils, showed that the supposed comparison of image with impression was usually absent, that the process of judgment was a much more elusive thing than had been imagined, and that, in the case of weights, the most essential factor was the speed with which the weight was lifted—this itself depending upon the relation of the muscular contraction to the objective heaviness of the object raised (as anyone who has ever lifted an empty water-jug, thinking it to be full, will be able to confirm for himself).

But though the elements thought to be essential in judgment were for the most part absent, other conscious states were found which had not previously been suspected—such states as doubt, hesitation, confidence, searching for (or waiting for) an answer. These states were, it was thought, neither sensations, images nor feelings, and were provisionally called "conscious attitudes" (*Bewusstseinslagen*). As reported, they seemed indeed to correspond to James's "transitive states" more than to anything else previously described. In a subsequent paper Orth tried to show that Wundt's supposed feelings of "strain-relaxation" and "excitement-repose" are reducible to these same obscure and intangible "conscious attitudes."

Having attacked judgment and feeling, the new school went on to deal with association and will. Marbe had shown that there was little that was really relevant to report as regards the conscious process of judgment; Watt went on to show that much the same was true of partially controlled association (as when the subject is asked to find a subordinate or a superordinate of, say, "bird"). But here systematic introspection reaped its reward in an important discovery. Watt found that in many cases his subjects reacted correctly (with a superordinate, e.g. "animal," or a subordinate, e.g. "linnet," as the instructions required) but without being conscious of intending to do so at the moment of reacting. The conscious work was done earlier, when the instructions were given and assimilated. The subject then determined to react in the way required, and, upon the stimulus word being presented a little later, he carried out the instructions without further conscious effort. It appeared as though the determination had set up an unconscious "determining tendency" (as it came to be called), as a result of which a person acts in a particular way when the appropriate stimulus is given. As was pointed out by Ach, who carried on the work, these determining tendencies seem to be factors of great importance in our daily life; we constantly set out on a given course of action, e.g. to walk to a given place, and take the necessary steps for carrying out the act without any further conscious direction of these steps. The same thing happens when persons with polyglot accomplishments start talking in a given language—the appropriate words come in this language and not (barring exceptional cases) in any other. Perhaps the most striking case of all is when, in reading music, the actual notes sung or played depend upon the key in which the piece is written, a matter which is determined once for all by a glance at the signature at the beginning; any one printed note being played natural, sharp or flat, according to the indications of this signature. The determining tendency is also clearly akin to what happens in so-called post-hypnotic suggestion, in which the hypnotized person is told to carry out an act on a given sign being made some time after he has been awakened. Once more in his normal state, he may remember nothing of the instruction; which he will nevertheless obey, as though impelled by some unconscious urge (often inventing some trumped-up "rationalization," if the act be one that seems in need of justification).

Indeed these determining tendencies would seem, in their way, to be almost as important as the associative tendencies which had so much earlier aroused the interest of psychologists. By a very ingenious procedure, Ach succeeded in creating a conflict between "determining" and "associative" tendencies, and endeavoured to measure the intensity of will acts by the strength of the associations that they were able to overcome. On the purely quantitative side his work has not been followed up in the way that it deserves; but he made a very important contribution to the introspective study of the will process, analysing this process with a delicacy never before attempted, and discovering one apparently characteristic feature of powerful volition, which, he said, could best be described in the words "I really will." This analysis of will (sometimes combined with a study of the processes involved in choice) was subsequently taken up by Michotte and Prüm and by Boyd Barrett in Belgium, and, in recent years, by Aveling and his pupils in England.

As a result of all this work it is becoming fairly clear that, in difficult actions, the will act itself is not conative, whereas the carrying out of the decision frequently is. The will act is rather a process *sui generis*, which under certain circumstances may be a condition of the release of conation, and which consists in "the adoption by the Self, the identification *with* the Self of the motive or motives for the selection of one of the alternatives." The experimental work on will, as already mentioned, seemed to fit in well with some of the conclusions already arrived at by James. More especially, however, did it harmonize with McDougall's treatment of will in his *Introduction to Social Psychology*. Approaching the problem from a difficult angle (the place of will in the general organization of the instinctive and affective life) and by a different method, he defined volition as the "supporting or re-enforcing of a desire or conation by the co-operation of an impulse excited within the system of the self-regarding sentiment." Here, in words very similar to those of Aveling's just quoted, we get the same insistence on the self that was originally brought out in Ach's formula—a striking enough corroboration. Since will is generally regarded as having a peculiarly close connection with the psychological aspect of morality, we should naturally expect that this discovery of the rôle of the Ego would throw light upon the moral factors also. The experimentalists have had as yet little to say upon this point, but for McDougall the "self-regarding sentiment" is really the essential mechanism of morality; and it is instructive to note that McDougall's "self-regarding sentiment" is in turn very similar in many respects to Freud's "super-ego," which is the concept in terms of which the psycho-analysts describe morality—again a concept arrived at by a very different method of approach. Finally, Spearman has not hesitated to bring the introspective findings of Ach and Aveling into relation with a more statistically oriented research by Webb, which showed the existence of a general moral factor in character organization, described by the author as "consistency of action resulting from deliberate volition or will." Such a convergence of four completely independent lines of work (systematic experimental introspection, the psychology of the affective life undertaken as a preliminary to social psychology, psycho-analysis, and the statistical analysis of individual differences in character) is one of the most impressive results that modern psychology has to offer.

Returning to the work of the Würzburg school, the most important remaining writers are Messer and Bühler. These two (and especially Bühler) pushed their researches further on the cognitive side, and developed the doctrine of "imageless thought," the view that the actual processes of thought, though introspectible, are not sensory or imaginal in character. The same conclusion had really been arrived at a few years earlier by Binet in his remarkable *Étude Expérimentale de l'Intelligence* in which he reported the results of a series of simple but ingenious experiments carried out on his two daughters. This latter work is of importance, both for its bearing on the psychology of thought, and because it heralded Binet's interest in individual differences and mental tests. The two young ladies happened to present a striking contrast in character and ways of thinking, and Binet's description of the manner in which this contrast emerged under his skilled and patient treatment makes one of the most delightful contributions to the literature of experimental psychology. He supplemented his objective records by introspective reports, and found that in many cases the girls denied that they were helped by images in solving the problems that he set them. Thinking, therefore, he was obliged to admit, was often carried on by mere thoughts, *pensées*.

Ever since the work of Bühler, who presented his thesis in a more challenging way than Binet had done, controversy has raged around this question. Titchener, who took up the matter in his *Experimental Psychology of the Thought Processes* in 1909, was critical of the whole Würzburg school; and as the result of somewhat similar experiments carried out in his laboratory, it was maintained that, with proper care in the method of introspection according to existential principles (as described above) the so-called thoughts could all be reduced to sensory or imaginal elements of a faint, fleeting or obscure kind. Others, however (notably Woodworth), have corroborated Bühler's findings, and a further argument for the separate existence of "thoughts" was furnished in 1915 by T. V. Moore, who found that the meanings of words tend to arise more quickly than the corresponding images. At the present moment it may be said that the conflict has abated rather than that it has been decided. The question is still a live issue, and will doubtless break out again afresh when interest once again turns in that direction or a new method of attack upon the problem is devised. The Würzburg school came to an end with the work of Bühler, and the conflict between elementarism (of which Titchener was undoubtedly the champion throughout this period) and the anti-association movements took on another form soon afterwards, coresponding to the rise of a new school, that of Configurationism or *Gestalt*.

IV. CONFIGURATIONISM (*Gestalt*)—WERTHEIMER, KÖHLER, KOFFKA

THE new school of configurationism had, of course, its historical background, like any other movement (von Ehrenfels's doctrine of *Gestaltqualität*, and—in the more philosophic field—Husserl's phenomenology being particularly important in this connection); but, as a school, it started very definitely with a particular research carried out by Wertheimer (a pupil of Külpe) at Frankfurt am Main in 1912. Wertheimer was concerned with the perception of movement. About eighty years earlier Plateau had invented the stroboscope—the forerunner of the modern cinematograph— an instrument by which apparent motion could be produced by projecting rapidly a series of different pictures on the eye, the "moving" objects in each picture being slightly displaced from their position in the immediately preceding picture. Wertheimer reduced this phenomenon to its simplest terms by presenting only two pictures, each with a single line, the first one vertical, the second, one sloping somewhat in one direction or the other. By varying the length of the blank interval between the two pictures, he could study at leisure the conditions under which the perception of movement arises. Thus, when the interval was one-fifth of a second or longer, the observer saw first one line, then another; when the interval was as short as one-thirtieth of a second, the two lines appeared to stand side by side; but in between these limits the observer had the impression of a single line moving from one position to another, an impression for which there was, of course, no justification in the objective stimuli. Although both time and space perception had been the subject of considerable investigation, movement, which implies a combination of the two, had been relatively very much neglected. To Wertheimer it appeared as something which could not be properly reduced to simpler terms; it is in its way as elementary as sensation, and yet it obviously differs from sensation; above all, it cannot, Wertheimer thought, be reduced to a mere sum or succession of sensations. It is rather a phenomenon *sui generis*, and as such he gave it a new name of its own, calling it the phi-phenomenon.

Conventional analysis into sensory elements being ineffective here, the question naturally arose as to whether other phenomena could not profitably be studied in the same manner—i.e. simply as phenomena, rather than as supposed compounds of *atomic* sensory units. In this way there arose the idea of an experimental phenomenology. Actually, in our mental life we find ourselves dealing with whole objects of particular shape, size and position, not with elements such as those into which the associationists and their modern followers were endeavouring to analyse the mind. Even when we have a homogeneous experience, as in looking up into an unbroken expanse of blue sky, we experience a single whole impression, not a mass of blue points. May it not be then that this whole search for elements is misleading?

Inspired by such considerations as these, Wertheimer and two other investigators who had taken part in his experiments, Köhler and Koffka (both of them pupils of Stumpf), set out to wage war on the elementarist-associationist psychology. These three men have remained the leaders of the movement, a movement which has inspired an astonishing amount of experimental research and has attracted a considerable number of very able workers, of whom Lewin of Berlin and Rubin of Copenhagen are deserving perhaps of special mention. This research has lain predominantly in the field of perception, though it has extended also to the spheres of behaviour (human and animal), of learning and of intelligence, and has even made excursions into the domain of physiology, biology and physics; for the whole living organism is, it is maintained, a *Gestalt*, as is also, for instance, the solar system. In these, as in the configurations of perception, it is useless to attempt to consider the parts in isolation; for a change in any one part inevitably changes the whole. On the other hand, the whole can persist when all the parts are changed, as when the same tune is played in different keys. Animals show clearly by their behaviour that they too perceive in "configurations" and not in terms of elementary sensations—as is shown in a celebrated experiment in which an animal is taught to seek food in a medium grey box in distinction from another box of light grey; when a dark grey box is substituted for the light grey one, the animal now goes to the new, dark grey, box—and not to the medium grey one, as it should, if it were judging by the absolute colour of the food-containing box rather than by the total situation.

The most famous animal experiments of the *Gestalt* school were, however, those carried out on apes by Köhler, while he was isolated at Teneriffe during the Great War. Here also the results were interpreted in terms of "insight" into a "whole" situation. Thus an ape would unhesitatingly pull into its cage a banana attached to the end of a string, but if several other strings led from its cage in the general direction of the banana, it would not at first realize clearly which string to pull. The first situation was one that could be easily grasped as a whole, the second was beyond the ape's ability to envisage clearly all at once. Similarly, if the banana (now unattached) were situated just outside the animal's reach, but a stick were placed near the bars of the cage, stick and banana would be seen as parts of a single situation, so that the stick would immediately be used to rake in the banana. But if the stick were placed at the back of the cage, the two objects could less easily be realized as part of a whole situation; while only the most intelligent animals could fit several (specially constructed) sticks together, so as to rake in a banana that was beyond the range of a single stick, or pile several boxes upon one another to reach a banana suspended from the top of the cage. The solutions of such problems, when they came, appeared to come suddenly, as though a new "configuration," embracing the whole complicated means to the desired end, had suddenly sprung up in the animal's consciousness; it was exactly as though the appropriate action followed on a "flash of insight," and, as in the case of all insightful behaviour, the insight remained a permanent possession, enabling its possessor to act at once appropriately on a subsequent occasion.

Arguing from such cases, Koffka subsequently challenged the whole theory of trial and error learning, as expounded, for instance, by Thorndike. Learning of this type, as Koffka interprets it, is not a purely mechanical process, for Thorndike's curves themselves, he maintained, showed evidence of insight, albeit often of a low order. The mere noticing of *where* to pull or scratch or claw, in order to get out of a cage, is insight of a primitive kind. If a button is seen as something to be pushed or a loop as something to be clawed, this is insight of a higher order (about as high, for instance, as many of us get with regard to an electric door-bell); while an understanding of the way in which the mechanism works implies insight of a higher order still. Varying degrees of intelligence are thus to some extent correlated with varying levels of insight or complexity of *Gestalt*; while the problem of learning is that of forming "configurations" of sufficient extent and complexity for the purpose in hand.

The doctrine has therefore a very considerable bearing on the problems of education and is in harmony with the general modern tendency to expound things in their proper setting, rather than to teach each item separately and then combine them into a whole, which was the procedure naturally suggested by the associationist psychology. Thus, in reading a Shakespeare play, the old method would be to explain it line by line (or even word by word, when the words were difficult), whereas it would now be begun by a preliminary treatment of the whole play in its historical setting; in learning the piano, the pupil would formerly begin by scales, but would now be allowed to acquire the necessary dexterity in the course of playing pieces; and even in the case of psychological textbooks themselves, whereas those written under the influence of associationism began with sensory elements and from them worked up gradually through perception and conception to reasoning, emotion and social behaviour, new treatises written from the *Gestalt* point of view (such as Wheeler's *Science of Psychology*) start from the most complex structure of all, the social organism, and proceed steadily in the opposite direction, so as to end up with the senses and the nervous system. It follows that the social sciences, too, must be treated in the same way, and in the psychological approach to social and cultural phenomena attempted by the "developmental" school of Felix Krüger, a treatment of the whole cultural level (the *Kulturganze*) to which a given institution belongs is held to be a pre-requisite for the understanding of this institution. Krüger was Wundt's successor at Leipzig, and it is interesting to note that Wundt himself seems to have had some anticipatory intuition of the new point of view, for though the monumental *Völkerpsychologie* treats of its subject according to such conventional headings as Religion, Myth, Law, etc., in 1912 (the year of Wertheimer's epoch-making paper) he published a shorter work, the *Elemente der*

Völkerpsychologie, in which he divides human culture into four
main levels or stages of development ("Primitive Man," "The
Totemic Age," "The Age of Heroes and Gods," and "The
Development to Humanity"), treating each institution in the
light of the *Kulturganze* of each level.

And this may serve to remind us that, as a number of writers
(among them G. E. Müller) pointed out, the *Gestalt* psychology
was not really as novel as the words of some of its exponents
would often lead us to suppose. Ward and Stout, for instance, had,
a good many years earlier, enunciated some of the main principles of *Gestalt,* as when Stout says in his *Analytical Psychology*
that "noetic synthesis owes its peculiarity to the introduction of a
distinct kind of mental factor, the apprehension of the whole,
which determines the order and connection of the apprehension
of parts," words which (as M. Hammond in a recent article
rightly remarks)[1] "might very well have issued from the lips of
an approved configurationist"; while the great majority of
associationists were in practice far from being as obstinately
atomistic as the configurationists attempted to make out, or,
perhaps, as their own more formal utterances might lead us to
expect. It was true, however, that earlier psychologists had not
followed up what they themselves had dimly realized concerning
wholes. It required perhaps a complete breakaway from the
associationist tradition before these aspects of the mind could be
given the attention that they undoubtedly deserve; and the fruit-
fulness of the research that it inaugurated has very amply justified the revolt from psychological convention that gave birth to
Gestalt.

On the whole it is astonishing that this revolt did not give rise
to greater opposition. Perhaps the most vigorous and thoroughgoing critic was the Italian psychologist Rignano, who complained: (1) that the term *Gestalt* was used in several different
ways, more especially as signifying the occurrence of simple
spatial and temporal relations between sensations on the one hand,
and the formation of meanings and "things" upon the other;
(2) that (like the associationist psychology, which it seeks to
combat) it fails to perceive that meanings are achieved through
the workings of our affective tendencies, that it is the constant
operation of our interests and desires that makes us construct,

[1] *British Journal of Educational Psychology,* 1932, II, p. 159.

out of a given mass of sensory data, this or that "thing," rather than another. As regards the latter criticism, it is true that configurationism has paid relatively little attention as yet to the more detailed study of conation. Instincts and reflexes are alike somewhat foreign to it, though in modern psychology as a whole this deficiency has been amply made up by other schools, by behaviourism, "hormic" psychology and psycho-analysis, with the findings of which it will ultimately have to harmonize. Nevertheless, as regards fundamentals, it presents us with an essentially dynamic picture of the mind. The perception of configurations brings about, it maintains, a relief of tension and a re-establishment of equilibrium, and those particular configurations are most likely to be formed which relieve tension in the most satisfactory way. This emphasis on tension and equilibrium goes back in modern psychology at least as far as Herbert Spencer, and has in quite recent times been a feature of many writers, including Rignano himself. At bottom then the configurationists have not lost sight of conation, though in detail Rignano's criticism may be sometimes justified.

As regards the spatial or temporal grouping of sensations, which, according to Rignano, is the other fact included under the general heading of *Gestalt*, the whole matter has been carried an important stage further by Spearman, to whom Rignano submitted the dispute that had arisen between himself and the configurationists as represented by Köhler. In 1923 Spearman, the director of the Laboratory at University College, London, had published a remarkable book entitled *The Nature of Intelligence and the Principles of Cognition*, in which he had endeavoured to comprehend all the cognitive processes of the mind under three qualitative and five quantitative principles. Mind, Spearman emphatically maintained, is creative, and creates new mental content according to the three, qualitative laws of the "apprehension of experience" (by virtue of which we not only feel or strive or know, but know that we are doing so), the "eduction of relations" (by virtue of which we can relate ideas) and the "eduction of correlates" (by virtue of which, when we have in mind an idea and a relation, we can bring to mind a correlative idea—as when, given a line of a certain length and the relation of equality, we draw another line equal in length to the first). Of these three laws, the third may be said to be a creative product of

Spearman's own genius, but the other two were more precise formulations of what was very old. The first is really implied in all doctrines of attention and subconsciousness, the second we have already come across a good many times in our allusions to the "relations" posited by many modern authors. It is this second law which is of most importance in the present connection. Spearman would make all configurations a matter of relations. But relations can be on various levels (in complex configurations there is a whole hierarchy of relations, as in an intricate geometrical figure or a complicated fugue) and in various degrees of explicitness or clearness. When the relation between two things is explicit, we see that they *are* related; when the relation is less clear we see them *as* related. The formation of new configurations corresponds to the eduction of fresh (and often more complex) relations—as when, in seeing again the figure or listening once again to the fugue, we notice relations that had not been evident at first; while differences in intellectual ability correspond to differences in the ease with which relations or correlates can be educed. Spearman admits that for the adult the seeing, even of complex configurations, may seem to be a single process. But then there is another law; this time a quantitative one—the law of retention, according to which "cognitive events by occurring tend to occur with greater ease"—and according to this we may well believe that the more familiar relations tend to occur so rapidly as to be almost, if not quite, unintrospectible as separate processes; in this way the unitariness of the configurations, upon which the *Gestalt* school had laid such stress, is, Spearman thinks, satisfactorily explained. Furthermore, the difference between figure and ground, which is another matter much emphasized by the configurationists, is describable in terms of Spearman's first law, according to which we can become clearly aware of some part of our experience, though our minds are so constituted that this field of clear awareness is inevitably of a restricted character (the well-known phenomenon of "span" or the "narrowness of consciousness"). Spearman is even willing to admit, with the configurationists, that perhaps even at birth there may be some awareness of relations, and therefore some configuration also, but this does not mean that the unity of the configuration is unanalysable; on the contrary, where there are no relations, there can be no configurations.

In the hands of Spearman's student Gopalaswami, these same ideas were applied to trial and error learning. A careful analysis of the movements made in the unfamiliar process of "mirror drawing" (tracing a figure which is seen, not directly, but only through a mirror, so that the normal movements have to be reversed) showed that these too could be reduced, either to the effects of retention or "habit" (which, of course in this case, led to wrong movement), or else to processes of relation or correlate finding. These latter processes, however, were for the most part rapid and of low conscious intensity; whereas in learning by insight these same processes are relatively slow and enter fully into consciousness—this difference in speed and clearness constituting the chief difference between the two kinds of learning. Trial and error learning can, indeed, often be converted into insightful learning by a slowing-down and a clarification of the eductive processes, with great benefit to the learning (though in some cases this conversion is rendered difficult or impossible by the fact that it is not possible to slow down the processes appreciably, as, for instance, in learning to ride a bicycle). Thus Thorndike's view of learning is harmonized with Koffka's.

If we accept Spearman's view, the *Gestalt* psychologists went too far in their insistence on the unitariness of the configurations. But even if we agree that configurations are ultimately analysable in terms of relations, we must admit that the *Gestalt* point of view has led to a great increase in our knowledge of the circumstances under which relations are educed. It is scarcely too much to say that the configurationists have done for perception what the earlier experimental psychologists of the Leipzig school and their modern successors have done for sensation. Above all, their principle of "closure," according to which there is a natural tendency to fill up gaps (as shown, for instance, in the fact that, even with one eye closed, we are not aware of any interruption of the visual field corresponding to the "blind spot" of the seeing eye) is one which, because of its wide application, because of its easy explanation in terms of equilibrium, and because of the analogies which, through this, it presents to many physical phenomena, seems likely to prove a concept of the greatest value in psychology. The new school has amply justified itself and by its vigorous prosecution of psychology in terms of consciousness has proved a valuable counterweight to behaviourism, that other revolt against "traditional psychology," which came into existence about the same time and which, in its extremer moments, threatened to do away with psychology as the study of consciousness altogether.

V. BEHAVIOURISM AND ANIMAL PSYCHOLOGY—BECHTEREV, PAVLOV, WATSON

CONFIGURATIONISM was a revolt against the excessive appeal to the classical principle of association and the elementarism to which this had given rise. Behaviourism was also a protest—this time against an exaggerated dependence on the classical method of introspection and the consequent tendency to look upon psychology as the science of consciousness. It is true that observation of *behaviour* had always found a place in psychological literature and had for long been growing increasingly important. But the general view that psychology was concerned primarily with the *mind* had made it appear as though the objective study of behaviour was rather in the nature of an auxiliary method of but secondary importance, and had led to a tendency to interpret objective observations in terms of consciousness, as though such observations were insufficient in themselves. We have seen how in America there had been from the first a certain distrust of introspection, and a corresponding desire for objective measurement, particularly in connection with the study of individual differences. Behaviourism was the extreme development of this tendency. Its coming was heralded, not only by the general characteristics of American psychology, but also by a tendency to lay more stress on behaviour even in the definition of psychology and in the statement of its aims. Thus in 1905 McDougall (later the most important opponent of behaviourism) had defined psychology as "the positive science of the conduct of living creatures," while in 1911 Pillsbury in his *Essentials of Psychology*, one of the most popular textbooks in America, had said roundly that "psychology is the science of behaviour," though he added that it "is to be studied through the consciousness of the individual and by external observation." The most important avenue of approach to behaviourism, however, was through animal psychology, where introspection *cannot* be applied and where interpretation in terms of consciousness is bound to be

213

precarious. The developments of animal psychology in America may, therefore, be appropriately referred to in this connection, though behaviourism itself has, in the twentieth century, tended to break down the sharp division between human and animal psychology that formerly existed.

We have seen how, at the end of our previous period, Thorndike had inaugurated a new era by his systematic experiments on animals. At the very beginning of the new century fresh workers came into the field that he had opened. Thorndike had invented a useful piece of apparatus for animal psychology, the puzzle box. In 1900 Small introduced another that was destined to be even more important, the maze, taking as his first model the famous maze at Hampton Court. The most persevering worker in this field was, however, Yerkes, who started his researches about the same time and continued them for many years, climbing steadily up the evolutionary scale from crustaceans through turtles, frogs, dancing mice, crows, pigs, monkeys to the anthropoids. He is undoubtedly the senior experimentalist in the animal field, and an immense number of facts have been accumulated as the result of his labours and the labours of those who followed up his work. Together with an extension of the field to experimentation, there went a gradual development and refinement of method. Two instances of this may be mentioned: the "multiple choice method" (chiefly used by Yerkes) according to which an animal has to choose one stimulus which is distinguished by its position in relation to others—a procedure which admits of any desired degree of complication, and which is very similar to some of the methods adopted by the *Gestalt* school: and the "delayed reaction method" of Hunter (afterwards a leading behaviourist), according to which a stimulus is shown indicating the direction in which food is placed, the animal, however, being prevented from moving in its direction until a certain interval has elapsed. By this latter method it was shown that animal behaviour is not dependent on the immediate presence of a stimulus, for rats, raccoons and dogs would react successfully after intervals of ten seconds, twenty-five seconds and five minutes respectively, though as to the exact way in which the result should be interpreted (more particularly as to whether they imply the existence of free "ideas") there is still much difference of opinion. In general, however, the extensive experimentation that has been carried out on perception, discrimination, learning, and the modifiability of response, has resulted in a more generous estimate of animal intelligence than Thorndike had allowed. As regards the apes, at any rate, Yerkes is quite in accord with Köhler. "The evidence," he says, "for the solution of problems ideationally is now both abundant and convincing . . . the great apes exhibit ideational behaviour; they act with insight," while the title of his last book on this subject, *Almost Human*, clearly indicates his general attitude towards the anthropoid subjects of his experiments. As with human beings, however, there are "gifted and stupid individuals, good and bad days, favourable and unfavourable conditions," so that the training of these animals, like that of the child itself, requires insight, tact and patience.

The fact that experimental animal psychology had definitely "arrived," and had to be treated respectfully as an important branch of the whole science, was attested by the appearance of the first textbook on the subject, Margaret Washburn's *Animal Mind*, in 1908—an admirable, though somewhat condensed summary, which was subsequently republished, in revised editions in 1917 and 1926. To Yerkes, however, animal psychology was only part of the larger field of "comparative psychology," including the study of individual differences in both animals and men, differences between species and between races, between normal and abnormal mind and conduct; and in 1913 he put forward a plea for the use of the term in this wide sense. Such a linking-up of animal with human psychology was also one of the essential features of behaviourism, which was born in the same year.

In an article in the *Psychological Review* entitled "Psychology as the Behaviourist views it," J. B. Watson, an animal psychologist of distinction who had worked with Yerkes on the subject of vision, definitely came forward with what we have since come to recognize as the behaviouristic challenge. He not only asserted the justifiability and usefulness of the objective methods of animal psychology, but seriously questioned whether they were not the only useful methods. "It is possible," he said, "to write a psychology, to define it as Pillsbury does (as the 'science of behaviour'), and never go back upon the definition: never to use the terms consciousness, mental states, mind, content, will, imagery, and the like"; and he went on to state that the various branches of psychology had made progress just in so far as they had freed themselves from the trammels of consciousness and introspection. Next year he made a more formal and systematic statement of his position in *Behavior: An Introduction to Comparative Psychology*, to be followed after the war, in 1919, by a still more general textbook *Psychology from the Standpoint of a Behaviorist*. He has since remained the leader and chief spokesman of a school which soon aroused immense enthusiasm and attracted large numbers of recruits; though these recruits have varied greatly in the thoroughgoingness with which they have adopted or proclaimed the gospel. Many have merely taken up a generally behaviouristic attitude towards their work and justified this attitude by their results. Some few have stated bluntly that (in the words of Lashley) "the behaviourist denies sensations, images and all other phenomena which the subjectivist claims to find by introspection," or at any rate maintained that these things have no meaning for him. One enthusiast—Hunter, whom we mentioned above in connection with the "delayed reaction"—even proposes to scrap the word "psychology" altogether and to substitute the new term "anthroponomy"—a curious choice in view of the fact that Hunter himself had won his spurs in *animal* research. Actually, however, as matters have worked out, the changes introduced by the behaviourists have not been quite so drastic as might at first have been expected. Though it is true that some matters, such as imagery, have remained on the proscribed list, they have yet found ways of dealing with certain other phenomena, such as sensation, after-image, thought and emotion, which at first sight might seem to be inevitably excluded from their programme.

But before we deal with this, we must mention a further fact of the greatest importance in the history of behaviourism—the fact that, early in its career, it fell in with a powerful ally from an unexpected quarter—namely the doctrine of reflexology or the "conditioned reflex," which had meanwhile been developing quite independently in Russia. Russian reflexology was the creation of two men, Bechterev and Pavlov. The former, a pupil of Flechsig, had from 1880 onwards been working on brain physiology, and about 1907, while collaborating with Spirtov, reported experiments on an "artificially associated respiratory motor reflex" in the dog. If cold be suddenly applied to the skin, there occurs in dogs (as in ourselves, as is familiar enough to those who indulge in cold baths) a well-marked reflex catching of the breath. Bechterev noticed that, if another stimulus is repeatedly applied at the same time as the cold, it will eventually start off the same reflex when given by itself, will in fact act as though it were a substitute for the "natural" stimulus of the reflex. Similar experiments were successfully carried out with other reflexes, notably with defensive paw movements provoked by electrical stimulation, and a corresponding "associated reflex" was found with stimulation of the sole of the foot in human beings. In 1907 he wrote a book on *Objective Psychology* (translated into French and German some years later) in which he urged, much as the more moderate behaviourists have done, that it is worth while seeing how far psychology can be carried by purely external observations, without reference to the mind and using the reflex as a fundamental concept. Strictly speaking, this book, rather than Watson's, should be regarded as the first systematic exposition of behaviourism. In later life, up to his death in 1927, Bechterev continued to write books in the same tenor, but with more stress on social factors—a point which he has in common with Weiss, a well-known American behaviouristic exponent of the "bio-social" point of view. Bechterev's later writings, however, remained for a long time untranslated and were in consequence less known in the western world than they deserved to be.

Even before Bechterev's discovery of the "associated reflex," Pavlov had found a similar phenomenon in what he called the "conditional reflex." He was a specialist in the physiology of digestion, and while working on this subject he found that a dog would secrete saliva, not only when given food, but when presented with a stimulus that was associated with food. Pavlov's salivary method had the disadvantage that, since it necessitated a fistula by which the saliva from one of the salivary glands could be drawn off into a receptacle, it could not be used with the ordinary human subject—that is until, much later on, Lashley devised a method by which the saliva could be drawn off directly. On the other hand, it had the great advantage that it permitted of a quantitative measurement of the response in terms of the amount and rate of salivary secretion. Armed with this weapon, Pavlov and his pupils attacked a great variety of problems, their work being eventually made accessible to the English reader by

the translation of his *Conditioned Reflexes* in 1927. The work of
Pavlov's laboratory, indeed, affords one of the most magnificent
examples of co-ordinated research over a long period that the history of physiology or psychology has to offer. We can only indicate
here in a word or two some of the more important matters dealt
with in this way. The first and most obvious problem was of
course the *creation* of conditioned salivary reflexes. Practically
any stimulus, it was found, could act as a conditioning stimulus,
provided it were given before, and not after, the natural or innate
stimulus (in this case food); even pain stimuli being no exception
to the rule. This, however, was itself a cause of difficulty, since
any unintended movement on the part of the experimenter could
also act as a conditioning stimulus (as Pfungst independently
discovered in the case of the mathematical horses of Elberfeld).
To avoid this a special laboratory was eventually built for Pavlov
by the Soviet government, and here the work is still vigorously
proceeding. The dogs could also be trained to salivate at *varying
periods* after the conditioning stimulus (the so-called "trace
reflex"), and such astonishing accuracy in the measurement of
time was shown that a suitably trained dog would salivate exactly
thirty minutes after the stimulus, no reaction being obtained
even at the twenty-ninth minute. Next in order were experiments on *extinction* of the reflex (by continuing to give the conditioning stimulus but without its being followed by the natural
stimulus). More important, however, were the experiments on
sensory acuity and discrimination. Thus it was found that, when
care was taken to avoid differences of brightness, dogs have
apparently no perception of colour as distinct from light and
shade (a result that has been independently corroborated by
E. M. Smith at Cambridge by a different method). On the other
hand, as was to be expected, their power of distinguishing smell
was shown to be very great; they can easily detect very feeble
olfactory stimuli, "even though disguised in most horrible mixtures of odours." As regards hearing, Galton's conclusion that the
dog's auditory range is higher than the human range was confirmed. Men can hear high-pitched notes only up to 50,000
vibrations a second, at the very most, whereas dogs can often
hear notes of 100,000 vibrations a second. Conditioned reflexes
cannot be built up during sleep, and extirpation of appropriate
areas of the cortex produces loss of conditioned reflexes or in-

ability to form them, though the latter ability may be reacquired, at any rate in some degree, showing that the function can be taken up by other areas. By refined methods of experimentation extending over a long period, it was even possible to determine a sort of differential threshold of the dog for various sensations. Thus if food is always given after a note of a certain pitch, and never after notes of any other pitch, the dog may eventually be able to distinguish intervals even up to one-eighth of a tone, which amounts to saying that he has acquired "absolute pitch" of a very delicate kind for the note which constitutes the conditioning stimulus. If pushed beyond its limits, however, the dog breaks down altogether and appears to lose all power of discrimination, becomes agitated and irritable, seems in fact to develop a sort of artificially induced "neurosis."

The conditioned reflex has gradually become one of the principal methods and working concepts of behaviourism. Indeed it would seem to afford an almost unlimited field for research, which may profitably occupy a host of workers for many years. The method, however, undoubtedly has pitfalls, and it is only with the help of a properly equipped laboratory, and an elaborate technique that reliable results are forthcoming. Want of adequate precautions doubtless accounts for some of the discrepancies observable in the work done up to the present. Nevertheless, some highly suggestive results have already been obtained with various kinds of reflexes. Thus Mateer, using a method devised by Krasnogorski, trained young children to open their mouths to receive a chocolate drop whenever they received a touch on the arm. The children, who ranged in age from three to seven, were also submitted to intelligence tests, and it was found that both the development and the extinction of the conditioned reflex were more rapid in the case of the more intelligent children. On the conative side, Watson has been able to establish conditioned fear reactions to a number of stimuli, as when he showed the child an animal at the same time as a loud noise was made, and found that a fear reaction subsequently occurred at the appearance of this animal. Conditioned "reflexes" of this kind were very difficult to extinguish, and Watson himself believes that such experiments reveal to us the way in which are formed the irrational phobias of the neurotic. Indeed by many behaviourists the conditioned reflex is regarded as the pattern on which all modifications of

conduct are acquired; for the behaviourist the conditioned reflex
has thus taken over the part formerly played by the "association
of ideas." Behaviourism, as thus interpreted, is indeed a sort of
objective associationism; Watson may perhaps be looked upon as
the twentieth-century representative of the position occupied in
the nineteenth century by James Mill, and much the same objections may be, and have been, brought against both attempts at
the abolition of purpose or activity of mind.

Watson's own most famous experiment in animal psychology
was carried out as early as 1907, six years before he definitely formulated his behaviouristic programme. Having trained white
rats to run a maze, he eliminated one sense after another by
suitable operative interference and found that the rats could still
run the maze when only kinaesthetic sensation was left. He concluded that the process by which these animals found their way
consisted of a chain of muscle reflexes. Subsequently Lashley
eliminated this sense also by cutting its conduction path in the
spinal cord, and, astonishing as it may seem, the rats were still
able to get through the maze. In trying to explain this curious
result, Lashley fell back upon some observations to the effect that
the rats seemed to obtain a sort of general orientation in the
direction of the exit from the maze—an explanation that savours
more of *Gestalt* than of the associationistically inclined interpretations of behaviourism. Such a result serves to remind us,
however, that, great as has been the influence of the conditioned
reflex concept on behaviourism, this doctrine—especially if we
regard it rather as a methodological postulate rather than as a
metaphysical dogma—is by no means tied down to the atomistic
stimulus-response notions which actually figure so largely in its
literature. As already indicated, behaviourism has found a way
of including in its programme many matters which we are accustomed to look at only from the point of view of consciousness. It
does so, often enough, by adopting an attitude that seems at first
a little strained, and a terminology that is apt to appear unnatural
and uncouth. The sceptical may even be tempted to think that
the insistence on such an attitude is a pure piece of pedantry
made merely in the interests of a system. Time alone will show
how justifiable the new position is; but even though it prove that
the behaviouristic approach is really less convenient and fruitful,
in many aspects of psychology, than the conventional one of

introspection, there is, nevertheless, a pretty clear indication that the ingenuity required for making such an approach will by no means be altogether unrewarded.

The treatment of sensation and after-image actually adopted by many behaviourists does, however, seem to amount to little more than verbal quibbling. The word "sensation" must of course, according to their terminology, be scrupulously avoided, but the facts themselves can be dealt with under the terms "auditory response," "response to light," etc., while the same considerations apply to "after-images" which are, of course, only forms of delayed response. Since, however, sensation and after-image gave rise to no directly observable behaviour, recourse has to be made to a special method, that of "verbal" report, which is, it would appear, nothing more than what others would call a recorded introspection. But if it is permissible to employ "verbal report" in the case of subjectively observed sensations and after-images, why not also in the case of the image (which is the bugbear of behaviourists)? And if in the case of image, why not also in the case of thought, feeling and emotion?

Actually, however, the behaviourists have found more congenial methods of dealing with these latter. The ordinary interpretation of images as something in the nature of "centrally aroused" sensations is denied altogether, and an endeavour is made to describe them in terms of kinaesthetic impulses and verbal responses. Feelings are regarded as incipient movements of approach or retreat, together with impulses from the sex organs or other erotogenetic zones. In these and similar matters an important distinction is made between "explicit" behaviour, visible to an outside observer, and "implicit" behaviour, which takes place inside the body and can therefore only be observed, if at all, by indirect or special methods. Thus thought, according to Watson, consists in "implicit" movements, chiefly those of the speech organs, but perhaps to some extent of other parts of the body also. This hypothesis gains some plausibility from the fact that the child often describes in words what he is doing, that we all sometimes "think aloud," and that, even when there is no audible or visible function of the speech organs, it is easy to observe that we often think in terms of "inner speech" (if it is permissible to use an argument from introspection in favour of a behaviouristic proposition!). This is, of course, in contradiction to the findings of the Würzburg school with regard to the occurrence of "imageless thought"; and several investigators have endeavoured to test Watson's view by registering the movements of the tongue and larynx during thought. The apparatus as yet devised for such experiments is not entirely satisfactory, but so far as they go, the results have failed to produce evidence in favour of the theory—the movements of the speech organs, even in deliberate "inner speech," showing no regular correspondence to the corresponding movements when the same words are said aloud.

Emotion is also held to consist largely in "implicit" behaviour on the part of the viscera—so that the behaviourist explanation is not very different from that of James, except that all reference to sensation is omitted. The modern behaviourists have, however, an advantage over James, in that they have at their disposal a great amount of investigation that has been carried out in recent years on the function of the ductless glands. More especially Cannon (in a well-known book on *Bodily Changes in Pain, Hunger, Fear and Rage*, 1915) and his followers have, in a very remarkable group of researches, shown that there exists a characteristic series of bodily changes accompanying the major emotions of fear and anger. These changes are connected particularly with the function of adrenalin, the secretion of the adrenal glands situated just in front of the kidneys. The adrenal glands and the "sympathetic" or central division of the autonomic nervous system work in harmony with one another, and together produce a general condition of the body which prepares it for violent exertion in combat or escape. Such a condition includes an increase in the rate and amplitude of the heart beat, an increased supply of blood sugar (enabling the muscles to work harder and resist fatigue) and more rapid coagulation of the blood (minimizing loss of this precious fluid in case of wounds). This portion of the autonomic nervous system works in opposition to the upper or "cranial" portion, which is chiefly concerned in nutrition and digestion, and the lower or "sacral" portion, which is concerned rather with the sexual and excretory processes, activity of the central portion inhibiting activity of the others. Unfortunately it has not as yet been possible to find any visceral differences corresponding to the subjectively distinct emotions of fear and anger, so that if we would explain the difference in behaviouristic terms, we must fall back here on the "explicit" differences in posture, action and expression, or await further refinements of technique in the recording of visceral changes.

As the result of observations on the "explicit" behaviour of the very young child, Watson considers that there are only three well-marked emotions in early life, "fear," "rage" and "love," and that each of these are aroused in connection with very definite situations: fear when the child suffers loss of support by slipping or falling or when it hears a loud noise, rage when its movements are impeded, and love when it is stroked or gently patted. All other emotions he considered to be in the nature of habits induced by conditioning. Indeed, Watson attributes an extremely wide influence to this factor of conditioning, so that he is naturally hopeful as to its practical use, when scientifically applied to education and the remoulding of human nature generally. He has already written a small book of practical advice on this matter for those who have the charge of young children, and the ultimate possibilities in this direction are known to the general reader through Aldous Huxley's brilliant but satirical treatment of the subject in his *Brave New World*. Indeed, if conditioning is really as all-powerful as is sometimes suggested, the chances of rapid racial improvement (in the sense of adjustment to social environment) are much more rosy than was previously supposed, even by those who stressed the influence of environment rather than that of heredity. Some such prospect as this has, no doubt, played a part in the remarkably enthusiastic reception which has been given to behaviourism in America—an enthusiasm which is scarcely justified by the results as yet achieved. Thus an important New York paper said of Watson's *Behaviorism* (1924) that "It marks an epoch in the intellectual history of man," while another, going yet further, ventured to suggest that it was "perhaps the most important book ever written." Western Europe, on the other hand, has been far more critical in its judgment, and has as yet shown little inclination to adopt the behaviouristic outlook. Indeed, the difference of attitude towards behaviourism on the two sides of the Atlantic will provide the material for an interesting chapter in a psychologically oriented history of psychology when this comes to be written.

SINCE behaviourism, with which we were concerned in the last chapter, necessarily lays more stress on the nervous system, and the physical organism generally, than on the mind, we may be permitted, before passing on, to deal very briefly with a few of the more important achievements of the modern period in the field of neurology and brain physiology. Two of the foremost American workers in this field have actually shown strong behaviouristic sympathies. The first of these was S. I. Franz, who took to neurology as a result of his dissatisfaction with his own initial research in after-images, which he had carried out under Cattell's direction at Columbia. To Franz belongs the credit of combining the extirpation methods of the brain physiologist with the training methods of the animal psychologist; in other words he trained his animals in certain performances, noted their achievements, produced an artificial lesion affecting a given area of the brain, and then studied the effect of this lesion on the performances. While confirming by this method the general distribution of the sensory, motor and "association" areas, as mapped out in the second half of the nineteenth century, his work, as it went on, tended more and more to show that the localization of function in the brain was not so precise and definite as the upholders of the "new phrenology" had supposed; extirpation of a limited area, although it might destroy some habits, did not as a rule prevent the habits being re-acquired. In this, Franz (whose investigations extended from 1902 onwards) was in agreement with Pavlov. From the beginning of the twentieth century, therefore, evidence once again began to accumulate in favour of the position taken up by Flourens, that the cortex functions as a whole. In later years this position was still further strengthened by the work of Lashley, who, pursuing Franz's methods, showed, not only that the localization of precise functions was uncertain, but that the power of learning was decreased in proportion to the total amount of cerebral destruction. He endeavoured to summarize his findings under two main principles: the principle of equipotentiality, according to which any part of the cortex, other than the sensory or motor areas, has potentially the same ability as any other to take part in any learned performance; and the principle of mass action, according to which the cortex acts as a whole, so that the more cortex there is available, the more effective is the animal's performance.

While Franz and Lashley were thus corroborating Flourens's view as to the general function of the cortex, Head and Holmes, in a brilliant series of clinical researches which they carried out in collaboration, and reported in 1911, were carrying further the other main part of Flourens's doctrine, to the effect that the various major divisions of the brain have distinct functions. The most important aspect of these researches concerned the functions of the thalamus. Since Hughlings Jackson's work, it had been fairly clear that a higher centre of the nervous system exercises two functions in relation to a lower centre. In the first place it takes up the impulses arriving at the lower centre, deals with them selectively and elaborates them; in the second place it exercises a certain degree of inhibitory control over the lower centre. Head and Holmes studied carefully a number of patients in whom a lesion on one side of the brain had interfered with the normal exercise of this latter (inhibitory) function on the affected side. The resultant changes were, they argued, due to an over-reaction of the thalamus, freed from its normal control. The over-reaction took the form of an exaggerated intensity of feeling and emotion. Stimuli which were normally unpleasant became intolerably so; thus one patient had to give up going to church because of the impression made by the hymns upon his sensitive side. A warm bath, however, would be much more agreeable on the affected side than on the normal one. Similarly as regards the emotions, which were somehow felt more keenly on this side; thus one patient found that since the lesion had occurred he had grown more sexually excitable on this side, and also experienced there a greater need of sympathy.

Head and Holmes concluded that one of the essential functions of the thalamus is to act as the seat of feeling and emotion—a conclusion that is in harmony with much other evidence from pathology, from extirpation experiments and from comparative

H

anatomy. On the pathological side there are some organic diseases of the brain where we are fairly sure that the thalamus is the seat primarily affected. Perhaps the most striking case of such disease is that of common epidemic encephalitis. In these cases the higher functions of thought and intellect are relatively unaffected, but the emotional and instinctive life shows either an exaggeration (resulting in an unduly impulsive behaviour, often, as we might expect, of an immoral or unsocial kind) or a depression (the patients showing little spontaneous interest or initiative, though when sufficiently stimulated they can adapt themselves normally). In the former case there is, probably, either (as with Head's and Holmes's original patients) loss of normal inhibition, by destruction of nerve fibres leading from the cortex to the thalamus, or else irritation and over-excitation of the thalamus itself by an active infection. In the latter case the functions of the thalamus appear to have suffered as a result of intra-thalamic destruction; while in many instances the disorder passes from the former condition to the latter, probably owing to a gradual extension of the infection.

Extirpation experiments show that, when the cerebral cortex of the higher animals is removed, instinctive and emotional behaviour of a primitive type, nutritional, sexual, maternal, combative, etc., continues to manifest itself (while if the brain be cut across below the level of the thalamus, the animal becomes little more than a reflex automaton). Finally, comparative anatomy shows that there is a close correspondence between the development of the cerebral hemispheres and the possession of intelligence, as manifested in the power of adapting behaviour to varying circumstances.

The view that has been widely accepted in recent years, on the basis of all this evidence, is that the cortex is primarily—and perhaps entirely—a cognitive instrument, whereas the thalamus has primarily an orectic function. If this view is correct, it would appear that the distinction made by psychologists between cognition on the one hand and orexis (including affection and conation) on the other, corresponds to some extent to a real difference of function between two major portions of the brain.

Only one other worker in the neurological field can be mentioned before we pass on: C. S. Sherrington, whose work on *The Integrative Action of the Nervous System*, published in 1906, has become the great classic on the interaction of reflexes. In this book Sherrington reports his very detailed studies of the processes of facilitation, summation, inhibition, after-discharge, etc., as they occur on the reflex level, and shows that reflexes stand in a certain relationship to one another, some reflexes being "allied," others mutually "antagonistic." Sherrington made clear how much of the ordered functioning of the organism depends upon such interaction of reflexes, particularly perhaps in the case of the mutual and alternate inhibition of certain antagonistic reflexes, such as those involved in the alternate flexor and extensor movements of the limbs in locomotion. He also demonstrated very clearly the numerous and very important changes that occur in the transmission of a nervous impulse whenever it crosses a synapse—thus emphasizing the significance of Waldeyer's neurone theory. Transmission along a single unbroken nerve fibre is a relatively simple matter, but as soon as a synapse is involved the whole process becomes more complex, such phenomena as latent period, after-discharge, summation, fatigue, variability of threshold, susceptibility to drugs and to variation in blood supply, all becoming both more marked and more irregular. The synapse is also, of course, the place of interaction between one neurone and another, so that it is here if anywhere that we must look for the neurological changes involved in the modification of behaviour as the result of experience. It looks as though the next great step in our understanding of the nervous system—a step that must be of exceptional interest to the psychologist—must lie in an increased knowledge of what happens at the synapse. Unfortunately, at the present day, nearly three decades after Sherrington's great attack, we are still in ignorance as to the real nature of the physical, chemical and physiological processes at the synapse itself.

AMONG the psychologists who, in the early years of the twentieth century, were most in touch with the neurological work with which we have just been dealing, the foremost was undoubtedly McDougall. In a small but influential book on *Physiological Psychology* and in an important series of papers in *Mind, Brain,* and elsewhere, he suggested that the synapse was the seat of consciousness, and developed a theory of inhibition by drainage (on a physical analogy with the mutual interference along the various channels of supply which constitute our household water, gas and electricity systems—as when the stream of water issuing into our hand basins is lessened when we turn on the tap of our bath). According to this theory, inhibition is always the negative aspect of a positive process—the whole event consisting in a re-distribution of energy rather than a mere prevention of something that would otherwise occur. Although it has perhaps attracted less general attention than it deserves, it is, almost beyond doubt, the most successful neurological theory that has ever been propounded. In his earlier works McDougall applied it to a great variety of phenomena at all levels of the nervous system: the reciprocal inhibitions of the spinal level, inhibitions on the sensory level (especially in the case of vision, in which he employed it in the course of an elaborate defence of the Young-Helmholtz theory), the mutual inhibitions of instincts, and finally many well-known features of the "attention process." The theory seems to fit in admirably, too, with the "displacement" and "sublimation" doctrines of the psycho-analysts and also (as McDougall himself has pointed out in a recent paper) with the phenomena of the conditioned reflex as demonstrated by Pavlov.

Although McDougall was thus in his earlier work largely concerned with the subject of nervous energy, there was, in his opinion, nothing incompatible between this and the adoption of a strongly teleological or purposive view of life and mind—a view that in later years, largely under his influence, has come to be spoken of as the "hormic" theory. It is this latter view that has brought McDougall into conflict with the mechanistic theories of the behaviourists and has indeed made of him their chief opponent in America, where he went to take up a chair at Harvard at the conclusion of the war, after having taught previously at Cambridge, London and Oxford.[1] McDougall's championship of the hormic point of view may be said to date from the appearance of his *Introduction to Social Psychology* in 1908, a book which has since gone into more editions than any other work on psychology. His intention in writing the book was to provide a psychological basis for the social sciences. He realized that, chiefly through its neglect of the orectic aspects of the mind, modern psychology, in spite of the undoubted progress it had made in so many directions, was still largely useless to the historian, the sociologist, the anthropologist and the economist, who therefore were compelled—with very unsatisfactory results—to construct an *ad hoc* psychology of their own, so far as it was essential for their purpose. McDougall's attempt to provide for the wants of workers in these sister sciences, though only partially successful in its ultimate aims (for the psychology of the sociological disciplines is still very far from being satisfactory, as he himself has pointed out in a recent small book), nevertheless resulted in a remarkable achievement in the psychology of conation and affection. His *Social Psychology* undoubtedly represents a great advance in the treatment of instinct, emotion and character, inasmuch as the analysis of these factors was at once more systematic, more delicate and more in touch with real life than in any previous attempt in this direction.

For McDougall a realization of the rôle of instinct is all important for the understanding of behaviour. Instincts are hereditarily determined channels for the discharge of nervous energy—they are "psycho-physical dispositions," to use a favourite term of his. They may be considered to have three aspects—an afferent or perceptual aspect, by virtue of which we have a tendency "to perceive and pay attention to objects of a certain class,"

---

[1] It is interesting to note that the two men who have most consistently opposed predominant American tendencies in America—Titchener and McDougall—have been British psychologists, and that both went to America from Oxford, largely as a result of the generally antagonistic attitude of this University to psychology.

a central, affective or emotional aspect, by virtue of which we tend "to experience an emotional excitement of a particular quality" on perceiving such objects, and an efferent or motor aspect, by virtue of which we tend to react to such objects in a particular manner. The most novel feature of this conception of instinct is the inclusion of the central portion, which involves a close correlation of instinct with emotion—every major instinct having its own characteristic emotion, the arousal of which is an essential part of the function of the instinct. Thus the emotion of fear corresponds to the instinct of escape, the emotion of disgust to the instinct of repulsion, "tender emotion" to the parental instinct and so on. An obvious difficulty arises from the fact that certain tendencies, usually regarded as among the most import-ant instincts, have nothing on the affective side that we are accustomed to call "emotion," e.g. nutrition and sex. In a later work—the *Outline of Psychology*, published in 1923—McDougall attempts to meet this difficulty by pointing out that instincts vary in the complexity of bodily adjustment and that emotions vary in their specificity. Now if we rank the instincts in a scale, in descending order of complexity of bodily adjustment we find that the quality of emotional excitement correspondingly diminishes in specificity. Common speech possesses definite terms for the more specific emotions, such as fear, anger and disgust, which are found at the top of the scale, while there are no well-recognized terms for the less specific emotions at the bottom of the scale, where we find the "instinct of acquisition" with, on the emo-tional side, the "feeling of ownership," the "instinct of con-struction" with the "feeling of creativeness," and the "instinct of laughter" with "amusement," "jollity," "relaxation." Besides these we have such minor instincts as scratching, sneez-ing, coughing, urination, defaecation, etc., which "are so simple in their bodily expression that we cannot recognize as specific qualities the excitements which accompany their exercise."

There are clearly difficulties here, both in the general concep-tion and in the particular classification, though the two problems are linked together, for our classification of instincts must neces-sarily depend upon our view as to what constitutes an instinct. Apart from the difficulty already mentioned as to the relation between instinct and emotion, there are further problems (com-mon to this and all other classifications of instinct) as to where to draw the line between reflexes and instincts and how to distinguish between instincts and habits. McDougall's conceptions have been subject to much attack on all these points. Emotion, it has been said (for instance, by Drever, whose *Instinct in Man*—1917—may be regarded as another important contribution from the hormic point of view), only arises when an instinct is obstructed, and then only in the case of some instincts. The latter objection is perhaps met by McDougall's distinction between the varying specificity of the different emotions. To the former it may perhaps be replied that instinct, too, is only aroused when there is some obstruction, at least in the sense that the organism is subjected to some stimulus which has produced a disturbance of psychic equilibrium. Instincts would thus be brought under the "tension" view of mental activity that we have met with in Herbert Spencer and in the *Gestalt* school and which is beginning to play a big part in psychology generally. McDougall himself, in spite of his interest in "psycho-physical" energy, has scarcely dealt with this view; but nothing would seem to forbid us to apply it to his conception of instinct.

The other difficulty mentioned above—the distinction between instinct on the one hand and reflexes and habits on the other—has been the chief battleground between McDougall and the behaviourists. In recent years a number of behaviouristically inclined writers—Josey, Bernard, Kuo, Kantor and others—have launched able and vigorous attacks upon the whole concept of instinct, with the result that this term is now almost banished from some of the psychological departments of American universities. These behaviourists regard instinct as a vague and mystery-breeding concept which should have no place in a scientific terminology; and it is easy for them, in support of this contention, to point to the different ways in which the term has been used and the very various classifications of the human instincts made by those who still believe in them. The fundamental difference between these writers and McDougall is that they are willing to consider as instinctive actions only those that are performed by virtue of the innate equipment of the individual and that owe nothing to experience (in which case instincts become practically synonymous with reflexes), whereas it is of the essence of the hormic view that instincts provide us with primitive desires and purposes which continue to express themselves in *various ways* (according to past experience and the present situation) until they are satisfied. In the course of this process of seeking satisfaction, instincts undergo complication and modification, so to speak, at both ends; they come to be aroused by objects other than those by which they are innately set in motion (as the behaviourist would also admit, though he would probably use the term "conditioned reflex" in this connection); and they express themselves in behaviour different from that which is innately determined. According to the behaviourist, all the more complex behaviour showing the effects of learning through experience must be explained by reference to the *stimuli* which have produced the modifications of response, i.e. in terms of the environment. To the hormic psychologist, on the other hand, instinct is essentially modifiable, differing in this respect from the reflex, and it seems justifiable and useful to trace the developments of behaviour in terms of *variations in expression of the same fundamental urge.* Thus if an angry man whips out his revolver, unsheathes his sword, or merely utters a sarcastic remark, these actions are all, from the hormic point of view, just as much manifestations of the instinct of combat as would be the more primitive manifestations of kicking and crying in which the infant would indulge. In tracing out the series of changes which have led from the more natural and primitive to the more developed form of response, the hormic psychologist thinks it is profitable to keep in mind the nature of the original urge; indeed he would be inclined to think that the whole process of development cannot be properly understood unless it is looked upon as a series of new outlets for the same fundamental energy or *purpose.* Thus instinct is a natural concept for the purposivist; whereas for the behaviourist, who has no use for purpose, and likes to look upon the organism as a machine played upon (and in the process of this, built up) by external stimuli, "instinct" is useless, or even harmful, since it seems to him to introduce a dangerous element of mysticism.

On the basis of instinct, McDougall has built up a systematic psychology of conation and affection. Not only does an instinct tend to become canalized in a particular direction or with reference to particular objects (as happens, for instance, with the sexual instinct, in successful adaptation to monogamy), but various instincts become organized with reference to particular objects by means of sentiments. Thus a mother who loves her child will feel fear when it is in danger, anger when it is hurt or threatened, sorrow when it is lost, joy when it prospers, and gratitude to those who help it. The principal sentiments are those of love and hate, though we can, of course, also classify sentiments according to their objects, which, in turn, may be an individual (as when we love a particular person or a particular country), a class (as when we are "interested" in wireless sets or horses) or abstract qualities (as when we "love" virtue or sincerity). It is this organization of instincts into sentiments that brings order and consistency into our orectic life. Of particular importance in this connection is the "self-regarding sentiment," a sentiment in which the various instincts and emotions are organized round the idea of self. In a well-integrated personality the sentiments themselves are organized into something like a hierarchy, with the self-regarding sentiment in the supreme position. The moral nature of the individual is largely determined by the nature and strength of this sentiment. In the highest types of character a strong self-regarding sentiment is determined, as to its nature, by some ideal of conduct—an ideal that is itself, of course, largely determined by admired persons who are known in real life, in religious or ethical teaching, in history or literature. In the particular form of conation we call will, the conations organized within the self-regarding sentiment add themselves to the weaker ideal motive and enable it to win the mastery over some, in itself, stronger and more primitive desire. This theory we have already referred to in connection with the experimental work on volition initiated by the Würzburg school.

In dealing with the personality as a whole, McDougall distinguishes between "disposition," which corresponds to the sum total of the instinctive qualities and is determined by heredity, "temperament," which is the sum of the effects upon the mental life of the metabolic or chemical changes occurring in the body (including, of course, the effects of the ductless glands now recognized to be of such importance), and "character," the sum of the acquired tendencies built up on the basis of disposition and temperament.[1] Here, as elsewhere, McDougall has succeeded in

---

[1] In the later *Outline of Psychology* McDougall also includes a fourth factor, "temper," which corresponds to "the way in which the instincts work." This factor, however, seems much less clear and much more open to criticism than the others.

bringing some sort of provisional order at any rate into a region of psychology that, before his work, was in a most chaotic state.

Space forbids us to deal with the many further contributions which McDougall has made to the psychology of orexis. It must suffice to say that he has given us a systematic treatment of conation and affection that, in completeness and thoroughness, is without a rival, and in penetration is second only to the work of Freud. Doubtless, many details of his system will require modification and re-statement as our knowledge grows; but some kind of orderly presentation covering the whole ground is often essential to a science at a certain stage of development, and McDougall's attempt in this direction would seem to be a more hopeful one than any other to serve as scaffolding with the help of which a more firmly established edifice may eventually be built.

McDougall's *Introduction to Social Psychology* was originally undertaken in the hope of providing the necessary psychological foundation for the social sciences. In his subsequent *Group Psychology* he applied his orectic system to the actual task for which it was intended, and produced another book of the greatest value. Taking up the work where Le Bon and other writers at the end of the nineteenth century had left it, he proceeded to deal with the psychology of crowds, of group loyalties and group ideals, leading upward to the psychological peculiarities of that bigger group we call a nation. Subsequently, in a smaller book, *National Welfare and National Decay*, he applied his findings to certain practical problems, with particular reference to eugenics, an application of biological science which had interested him from the beginning.

His biological interests have also led him in recent years to carry out an elaborate series of experiments with a view to testing the Lamarckian theory of the inheritance of acquired characters. He trained rats for twenty-three generations to escape from a tank by the more dimly illuminated of two exits, on pain of receiving an electric shock if they attempted to escape by the other exit. In each generation, training was confined to approximately half the number of rats born. He found that, in spite of precautions to avoid selective breeding, the rats of the successive trained generations displayed an increasing facility in mastering the task, so that, according to his last report, whereas rats of the control stock, whose ancestors had not been trained, made on the average 165 errors before learning to avoid the shock, those of the twenty-third generation of the trained stock made on the average only 25 errors. He concludes that the experiment at last provides some real evidence in favour of Lamarckian transmission. The theoretical interest of such a result, both to biology and psychology, can scarcely be exaggerated. Indeed, it may eventually turn out that it will be by this work rather than by any other that McDougall will be best known to posterity.

OPPOSED to behaviourism in somewhat the same way as the hormic psychology (and indeed treated by McDougall as in this respect a potent ally) is another important school—that of psycho-analysis. Psycho-analysis, however, differs in turn from the hormic psychology (and from all others) in the stress that it lays on the *unconscious*. A full understanding of human behaviour, this school maintains, is impossible unless we take into account certain mental factors, which can be directly observed neither by introspective nor behaviouristic methods, but which can be inferred from their effects. The general idea of unconscious or subconscious mental states was, as we ourselves have seen, far from being a new one. The notion, in one form or another, had been common in psychology almost from the earliest times. At the dawn of modern philosophy it had been emphasized by Leibnitz, and in the second half of the nineteenth century it had come into prominence in connection with the French studies in psycho-pathology. In its origin, psycho-analysis itself developed from this latter source.

More perhaps that any other school, it is the creation of a single man, Sigmund Freud, of Vienna. Freud, in the eighties, studied with Charcot in Paris, and he and Janet were Charcot's most distinguished pupils. But, whereas Janet may be said to have carried on the French tradition, Freud, soon after leaving Paris, met with another investigator, Breuer (whom we have already mentioned in connection with his theory of the sense of equilibrium), and this turned his thoughts in a slightly different direction, which he has followed ever since. Perhaps the most striking of all the phenomena of psycho-pathology is the lack of integration shown by sufferers from practically all forms of functional nervous disease. The consciousness of these patients does not seem wide or strong enough to embrace all the mental happenings that in more "normal" persons would become conscious. Both Janet

and Freud are in agreement as to the importance of "dissociation," but would explain it differently. Whereas Janet considers
that it is due to a "lack of power, on the part of the feeble subject,
to gather together, to condense his psychological phenomena, and
assimilate them to his personality," Freud thinks that dissociation is due to an active incompatibility between the dissociated
elements and the rest of the mind. Janet, following the lead of
Charcot, showed that these dissociated elements could often be
recovered in hypnosis and could then be dealt with therapeutically by means of suggestion. Breuer, with whom Freud collaborated on returning to Vienna, demonstrated, on an interesting
case that has since become historic, that the mere bringing back
and discussing of memories that had been dissociated might itself
act therapeutically. This was the "talking cure," which the
patient in question humorously referred to as "chimney sweep-
ing," and which Freud and Breuer called subsequently "abreaction" or "catharsis." This procedure obviously has some
resemblance to "confession" as practised by the Roman Catholic
Church (though freed from the moral and theological implications of this latter) and—going further back—to the function of
tragedy, as expounded by Aristotle, who had taught that
tragedy produces a healthful "purging" by intense arousal of
the emotions of "pity" and "terror."

The history of psycho-analysis is usually considered to begin
with the publication of Breuer's and Freud's researches published in their *Studies in Hysteria*, which appeared in 1895. Continuing the work alone, Freud's next step was to abandon the
method of hypnosis and to substitute for it a process of free
association in the waking state. His reason for doing so lay partly
in the fact that he (like other hypnotists) could not succeed in
easily inducing the hypnotic state in all his patients, partly in his
impression that some obstacles or barriers were circumvented,
rather than overcome, by the hypnotic method. The new method
of association, in which the patient was simply asked to say everything that occurred to him, abandoning all conscious control of
his thoughts and all reference to the usual canons of what appears
relevant, logical, seemly or polite, soon revealed these obstacles
in plenty; it was thus that Freud perceived, as he thought, that
there was some active force opposing itself to the entry of the
dissociated elements into consciousness. Eventually, however, in

so far as the procedure was successful, the patient did become
conscious of these elements, which proved to be of a highly
emotional nature. At first the stress was laid upon particular
experiences, experiences which seemed to have aroused an intolerable degree of affect and which were therefore "repressed" into
the unconscious. Later, it was seen that these "traumatic" experiences (as they came to be called) were important rather
because they stirred up certain "wishes," desires or tendencies
which were out of harmony with the dominant moral trends of
the personality. These "wishes" (a term which has always
aroused opposition among English readers) showed themselves to
be chiefly of two kinds—aggressive and sexual, with the latter
greatly preponderating.

According to Freud's own statement, he had been anticipated
in the latter discovery by Charcot, who once said *à propos* of a
young woman who had developed neurotic troubles as a consequence of her husband's sexual inefficiency, "in such cases sex is
always the most important thing—always, always, always!"
Charcot, however, was discreet enough never to express this
view officially. Freud, on the other hand, knew no discretion, and
with a certain ruthless *naïveté* and disregard of conventional susceptibilities, which is an essential feature of his character, proceeded, as he tells us, "without any apprehension" to describe
his findings. "But," he says, "the silence with which my
addresses were received, the void which formed itself about me,
the insinuations directed towards me, caused me gradually to
realize that one cannot count upon views about the part played
by sexuality in the aetiology of the neuroses being treated like
other communications."

Thereafter, for some years, Freud worked in isolation, quietly
developing his views, with only a few papers to mark the progress
of his thought. In 1900, however, he definitely appeared as a
writer of importance in psychology by the publication of his
Interpretation of Dreams, in which he endeavoured to show that
dreams were the distorted expression of repressed wishes, dis-
playing many of the same psychological mechanisms as are found
to be operative in the case of neurotic symptoms. By this time he
had also elaborated the fundamental concepts of "condensation"
(unconscious fusion of ideas), "displacement" (transference of an
affect from one idea to another), symbolism, etc. (The best known

of all—"complex"—was introduced by Jung, though the fundamental facts of the "nuclear" Œdipus complex were adumbrated in the *Interpretation of Dreams*.) Only very gradually did the views here presented find any considerable measure of acceptance. To most readers they seemed both "far fetched" and repulsive. Nevertheless, from about 1902 onwards, a small band of followers came into being, resulting in the first psycho-analytical Congress in 1908 and the founding of an International Psycho-Analytical Association in 1910, which, ever since, has served as a central organization of psycho-analysts throughout the world. Abraham, Ferenczi, Jung and others on the Continent developed the more clinical aspects of psycho-analysis, while Rank made important applications of the new knowledge to the spheres of art, literature and sociology. Ernest Jones and Brill introduced psycho-analysis into North America, and in 1909 both Freud and Jung accepted an invitation from Stanley Hall to give a series of lectures at Clark University. Later on, Reik and Róheim, supported by contributions from some of the writers already named, established a contact between psycho-analysis and anthropology, while the establishment of psycho-analytical clinics in a few big cities eventually brought the medical benefits of the method within the reach of a wider class of patients, and thus considerably increased its practical utility.

Meanwhile, Freud had applied his views to three other fields, as reported in his *Psycho-pathology of Everyday Life* (1904.), his *Wit and Its relation to the Unconscious* (1905) and his *Three Contributions to the Theory of Sex* (1905). In the first two of these he showed that the mechanisms he had found in neuroses and dreams were also operative in many of the small slips of the pen, tongue, hand or memory that we all experience in daily life, and that are generally attributed to "chance," to faulty association, or to some general factor like fatigue; also in jokes, wit and humour.

In the third book he expounded a theory of the development of the sexual instinct from a number of "component instincts," which manifest themselves in the child from birth onwards, which are for the most part connected with some particular part or organ of the body, which at first (in the "auto-erotic" stage) seek each their own satisfaction in relative independence of one another, but which later on in so-called "normal" development

become integrated under the hegemony of the instincts connected with the genital organs and thus are put into the service
of reproduction. Sexual "perversions" in adults were, Freud
thought, brought about by the failure to achieve such hegemony
and by the consequent undue predominance of some component
instinct other than the genital one; the child could therefore be
described as a "polymorphous pervert"—a conception which, as
was doubtless to be expected, added to the unpopularity already
aroused by his views on sex.

Later on, in 1914, he considerably (but, as judged by its fruitful results, very justifiably) complicated his picture of sexuality
and its development by interposing a stage of "Narcissism" between the unintegrated stage of "auto-erotism" and the fully
developed stage of "object love"—in which the sexual impulse is
directed outwards to a person (or, in its displaced form, a thing)
external to the self. In this "Narcissistic" stage, the libido (the
term given to the sum of the component instincts) is directed to
the self; there is integration, but no direction of the impulse to an
object other than the self. Of course, neither the auto-erotic nor
the Narcissistic stage is ever fully outgrown, any more than are the
other primitive functions of mind and body. A certain amount of
libido always finds its satisfaction auto-erotically; we all enjoy sensations from the erotogenetic zones and organs of the body—
genitals, mouth, anus, skin, muscles, etc., and in the case of the
mouth gastronomy has developed their production into something almost approaching a fine art. We all, too, normally direct
a certain amount of "love" to our own persons, though there are,
even within the range of the "normal," immense individual
differences both in the relative strength of the different component instincts and in the relative proportion of Narcissism to
object love, "normal" development in the female implying a
somewhat higher degree of Narcissism than in the male (as
shown in the greater importance we attach to bodily beauty and
decoration in the former sex). Full development, however,
implies a high degree of outward direction of the libido; and, of
the libido thus turned to object love a large portion is "sublimated," or directed away from sexual ends to the various
objects and activities which together make up human "culture";
each component instinct having its own characteristic forms of
sublimation and thus making its own particular contribution to

civilization. Even within the sphere of "object love" itself there normally occurs a process of progressive displacement from one object to another. The earliest love objects (as also the earliest recipients of jealousy and hate) are necessarily found within the family circle. Thus the small boy loves his mother and to some extent inevitably regards his father as a rival—hence the Œdipus complex; for Œdipus, in killing his father and marrying his mother, does but translate into the terms of adult life the primitive wishes of the boy child. But in course of time the libido tends to find new objects, though perhaps these latter always remain to some extent representatives of, or, as it were, reincarnations of the old; the loved woman, school, town, or country, is still in a sense regarded with feelings that were originally directed to the mother; the authorities placed over us, teacher, employer, policeman, magistrate, priest, prime minister and king, are still the recipients of the medley of love, admiration, awe, and hatred that were first aroused by the father—and similarly *mutatis mutandis* in the case of the girl, and in that of the mixed sexual attitudes which are found in so many individuals of both sexes.

Freud thus attributed immense significance to sex. An impulse of obvious importance which had long been neglected by psychologists had at last received full justice (or, as some think, more than justice). The pragmatic warrant for his views on sex and the unconscious lies in the astonishing illumination that they have thrown upon so many obscure problems of mind and behaviour. Starting out as a simple therapeutic method, there is now scarcely a single important aspect of human activity to our understanding of which psycho-analysis has not in some degree contributed. As a form of treatment it has now taken a recognized place in most civilized countries, and a new field has been opened in quite recent years by the extension (with a few modifications) of the analytic method to young children. But, in its present form, it has the serious disadvantage of being slow and costly— and the attempts that have been made to shorten it have so far met with but doubtful or indifferent success. It is still too early to pass final judgment, but at present it looks as though the contributions of psycho-analysis to psychology, and through this to social science, are destined greatly to outweigh its importance in the purely medical sphere in which it had its origin. With

McDougall, and still more with Freud, psychology first began to bear some semblance to a science to which men could look for real help in unravelling the puzzles presented by their own and others' behaviour. Here was no mere system of general laws, too abstract and remote to be of any use in dealing with practical problems, and on the other hand no mere study of isolated reflexes or sensations, extracted from their setting. Here, at last, was some real light on the motives underlying our loves and hates, our interests, our longings, our work and play, our difficulties, failures, maladjustments and general unreasonableness. It is small wonder, perhaps, that psycho-analysis has on the whole met with a more ready acceptance among literary men and novelists than among professional psychologists or physicians. The former had, all along, been concerned with these real psychological problems of everyday life, which the psychologists themselves, in their intellectualism or their atomism, had avoided, and which medical men were prepared to deal with only in the physiological terms for which their training had prepared them. The full benefit of psycho-analysis can come only when it has been properly assimilated by psychology and sociology, and that is still far from having been accomplished. In many countries there is as yet comparatively little *rapport* between psycho-analysts and "academic" psychologists of the other schools, this being particularly the case in continental Europe (except in Switzerland). To the present writer there seems no doubt that general psychology is capable of being made more fruitful than it is by a liberal infusion of psycho-analytic insight, while psycho-analysis on its side stands equally to gain by the application to its findings and problems of such of the more exact methods of experimental psychology as may be suitable. The trouble with psycho-analysis at present is that there is too much of the art about it, and too little of the scientific method that can be applied in experimentally controlled and repeated observations. To many, including the present writer, a large number of the major conclusions of psycho-analysis appear to be very well established; but the fact that its fundamental clinical methods are less easy to teach or to set down in exact terms than those of experimental psychology not unnaturally renders it suspect to many of those whose principal training has been in the latter discipline.

Something like a new era in psycho-analysis was inaugurated

by the appearance of Freud's *Ego and the Id* in 1923. Hitherto, paradoxically enough as it might seem, psycho-analysts had had much more to say about the repressed forces of the mind than of the forces that produced the repression. It had appeared that these latter forces were vaguely connected with the "self," and that they had something to do with the moral aspects of the personality; otherwise little enough was known about them. In this book Freud began to throw some real light upon this subject. He divided the mind into three main parts, the (conscious) ego, the "id" (the unconscious reservoir of instinctual urges), and the "super-ego" (the moral elements). The last named has proved the most important concept of the three, and a great deal of subsequent psycho-analytic work has been devoted to its elaboration and clarification, as a result of which it now appears that the super-ego is a vastly important element of human nature, an element, however, which is itself largely unconscious. So far as present knowledge goes, it would seem to be formed chiefly as the result of three distinguishable processes: (1) the "introjection" into the self of the external moral authorities, as represented especially by the parents and other important persons in early life; (2) the direction on to this introjected or internalized morality of some portion of the Narcissistic libido, so that the individual comes to love himself not merely as he *is*, but as he "ought" to be; (3) the recoil upon the person's own self of hostile and aggressive impulses which could not be outwardly expressed.

The first of these three factors is one which had been dimly envisaged by many writers on ethical questions, who had often emphasized the importance of "ideals" as exemplified in the lives and characters of influential persons. The second factor has obviously much in common with the "self-regarding sentiment" of McDougall (who, it will be remembered, also stressed "ideals" as important in this sentiment). The two factors together explain how an internal moral sanction is, in the course of development, substituted for an external one, and how this internal sanction comes to be a highly valued and influential portion of the personality. They do not, however, fully explain another finding of the psycho-analysts, namely, the severity of the super-ego, which often revealed itself as more exigent and cruel in its demands than were the original external authorities themselves. It is here that the third factor comes in—a factor that was discovered rather

later, by a number of investigators. It is simply one instance of
the general rule that instincts that cannot find external satisfaction tend to work themselves out within the organism itself. In
this case the instinct is aggression. Aggression is inevitably
aroused by the frustration of primitive impulse necessitated even
by the most gentle forms of education; and, when the authorities
are mild and tolerant, it may become even more difficult than
when they are harsh to direct this aggressiveness upon them
(who appear so little to deserve it), so that, failing alternative outlets, it must be directed back upon the self. It there allies itself
with the introjected morality of the authorities, and gives this
morality a harsh and cruel flavour which it may not have had in
its original form. Often there is added another, and fourth, factor,
not always easily distinguishable from this last. This consists in an
admixture of the cruel or "sadistic" elements which are a
normal constituent of the libido and which Freud distinguishes as
one of the "component instincts." In such cases there may be
said to be an erotic element in the exercise of a cruel morality.
This is seen clearly when—as often happens—the whole complex
of moral tendencies embodied in the super-ego is projected outwards (the opposite process to the original introjection), in which
case a cruel delight may be taken in the moral condemnation or
punishment of others—a process to be observed almost daily in
any educational establishment run on conventional lines, and
exemplified still more strikingly in our punitive systems, or in
such special moral or religious institutions as the Inquisition.
Indeed, when we come to think of it, almost all cruelty is exercised with a moral or quasi-moral motive or excuse.

The fact that (as recent work on child analysis has more
especially emphasized) the super-ego has its roots deep in the
unconscious and begins to be formed at a very early age makes it
relatively insusceptible to later experience or thoughts. There is,
therefore, often enough a conflict between reason and conscience (which is merely the conscious part of the super-ego), and
psycho-analysis shows that, in a progressive and rapidly changing
civilization like our own, our over-rigid and archaic morality is
in some respects just as big an obstacle to successful adaptation as
our instincts are. This is true both in the individual and in the
community as a whole. In the individual the successful solution
of a neurotic conflict always implies some renunciation on the

part of the super-ego of the more extravagant among its claims, as well as readjustment on the part of the libido in the form of sublimation. Left to itself the super-ego would prefer to see the patient fail in health, in love, in his career, or even driven to suicide, rather than that he should achieve success at the cost of infringing the primitive but drastic morality of the unconscious. In the community we can also see that one of the chief obstacles to progress is to be found in loyalty to Draconian and archaic moral codes. We would rather face the horrors of over-population, with its attendant poverty and wars, than encourage birth control among the poorer classes, rather endure the ravages of syphilis than give instruction in the means of its prevention, rather allow thousands of women to harm themselves or die than legalize abortion in the hands of qualified practitioners—because in all these cases the removal of the evil would offend against the sexual taboo and abolish some of the penalties which attach to sexual pleasure.

And this brings us to another point, namely, that there is often formed, both in the individual and the community, a kind of alliance or agreement between the super-ego and the id; as a result of which, indulgence of a kind that is disapproved of by the super-ego is permitted on condition that this indulgence be paid for in terms of suffering. The suffering may be of many sorts; failure in professional life, physical ill-health, poverty, an unhappy marriage, or a neurosis, being perhaps the most common forms. But the compromise thus arrived at is apt to be a very stable one, and the analyst, endeavouring to break it down, is frequently opposed in his efforts by both aspects of the personality, the moral and libidinal; much as in America both the Churches and the gangsters formed a curious and, at first sight, unnatural alliance in favour of Probibition, from which they both derived satisfaction in their different ways.

These new discoveries of psycho-analysis would seem, at the very lowest estimate, to be at least of equal importance to the earlier findings with regard to sex. They have cast a new light upon an all-important aspect of human personality, the moral aspect, in virtue of which man has learnt to control his individualistic impulses and become a social animal. Having already shown, in Freud's words, that man is "far more immoral than he believed," psycho-analysis has in its more recent developments made us realize also that "he is far more moral than he had any idea of." This "morality," however, is of a crude and undiscriminating kind, often out of touch with the realities of present life, and therefore productive of much unnecessary suffering and inefficiency—both individual and social. Just as analysis of the individual brings about a greater harmony between man's desires and his moral tendencies, making him both more capable and more reasonably moral, so also, we may expect, in its ultimate consequences, psycho-analysis must surely prove of inestimable benefit in straightening out the tangled social life of man. Other branches of psychology may make—are indeed already making—intensely valuable contributions to the detailed study of the proper use and development of human abilities for any given purpose. But nowhere else than in the psychology of the unconscious is there to be found the knowledge which may enable us to employ these abilities in a fundamentally more reasonable way; so as to find a means of escape from the predicament—at once ridiculous and tragic—in which, by general consent, civilization finds itself in the present critical moment of its history.

Whatever value we ultimately place upon his work, there can be no doubt that Freud is one of the most remarkable figures in the whole history of psychology. In mere bulk of publication he surpasses all but Wundt (and possibly Helmholtz), the *Psychological Register* of 1932 recording no less than 222 books and papers (excluding translations) on psychological and neurological subjects. In originality, and in intuitive psychological insight, he is undoubtedly a greater man than Wundt. Wundt saw the logical implications of the work of his predecessors, Herbart, Weber, Fechner, and proceeded to develop them by making psychology an independent science; in this respect his position is unique. Freud, however, created in his turn a definitely new approach to the problems of the mind, in showing how the unconscious could be studied. And in so doing he owed surprisingly little either to his predecessors or to his contemporaries. On the purely scientific side his stimulus came, of course, chiefly from Charcot and Breuer, but his views generally, it would seem, have been more influenced by the great pessimist philosophers, Schopenhauer and von Hartmann. Freud's work may perhaps even be looked upon as a scientification of von Hartmann's philosophy of the unconscious. But though he could no more escape the influence of philosophy than other German or Austrian psychologists, Freud was—like Darwin—above all a great observer. He was, like James, somewhat careless of consistency in theory, and used his theories as little more than provisional and temporary (though doubtless very necessary) structures for the understanding and classification of his data. If, in recent years, his writings appear in places to have taken on a more dogmatic or philosophic tone, this is because, as he grew older, he seems to have felt himself more pressed for time, rather than because of any fundamental alteration of his attitude. Thus Freud (unlike McDougall) has no well-rounded system, and his more theoretical contributions are often puzzling to read on that account. His charm and his ability lie rather in his deep intuitive understanding of psychological facts as they present themselves to him. It must be granted that his methods are less precise than those of the experimental psychologists. But his conclusions seem to be, in some respects, far more momentous. The study of those aspects of the mind to which he devoted himself has not yet entered the stage where the precision and control of experiment is possible. But it is an outstanding achievement to have opened up a vast region, which before him had been suspected to exist, but never entered by the scientist. It would be absurd to refuse to follow him into this region, which appears to be so full of promise, merely because the methods of exploration are still relatively crude. Available methods inevitably to some extent determine the direction of research, but, on the other hand, methods will never be devised to cope with problems until these problems have been shown to exist; and Freud has revealed to psychologists a whole host of new problems of the utmost theoretical significance and the gravest practical concern.

In 1912, some ten years after the appearance of psycho-analysis as a school, two leading members of this school, Alfred Adler and C. G. Jung, broke away from Freud, subsequently to found schools of their own. At first the difference seemed mainly one of the relative degree of emphasis placed on various points of psycho-analytic doctrine, but before long it became apparent that the divergence of opinion was really one that affected fundamental matters, and was too great to permit of common work together or the use of a common name. Adler's doctrine then came to be called Individual Psychology, Jung's Analytical Psychology (though these terms have at times held other meanings). Both differ from Freud in attributing less importance to sexual factors, but apart from this the two new schools diverge as widely from each other as they do from the parent school of psycho-analysis itself.

The fundamental feature of Adler's doctrine is an insistence on the desires that are connected with the assertion of the individual self and of its superiority over other selves—desires which themselves arise largely from a fear of inferiority. In his early life each individual is inevitably impressed with his weakness when confronted with the powers surrounding him. Human life, in fact, is devoted to the struggle for superiority as a compensation for this sense of insufficiency; the "will to power" is the essential human urge. Indeed, Adler's psychology corresponds closely in many ways to the philosophy of Nietzsche. Since, in the human race, the female sex is the weaker and for the most part in a subordinate position, the quest for superiority often takes the form of "an overstrained desire for masculinity"—the "masculine protest" as Adler has called it. Furthermore, each individual has some special point of weakness or inferiority, either in body or mind. When he has discovered this, the direction of his search for power is largely determined by an attempt to compensate for this "organ inferiority," as it is sometimes broadly called. This may be done directly, the original inferiority being converted into a superiority by constant exercise and effort; as when Demosthenes, the stammerer, became one of the greatest of orators, when Sandow, the weakling boy, became a recognized strong man of his day, or again, when a person gifted with exceptionally little insight into the thoughts and motives of his fellows compensates by becoming a psychologist. Another method is by developing superiority in some other sphere, as when Nietzsche, prevented by physical infirmity from being a soldier, substituted pen for sword, and wrote a philosophy of power, to compensate for the physical exercise of force that was debarred him. According to a third solution, the individual may take refuge in external difficulties, in disease or in neurosis, and thus avoid the demands of the environment. In this way he saves himself from the painful realization of inferiority, and sets himself a "fictive goal" which corresponds to no real achievement in the outside world; paradoxically enough, he may even take refuge in a notion of his own unworthiness, one inferiority being substituted for another and more painful one. Therapeutic treatment must aim, first and foremost, at discovering the patient's "style of life," his general trend of compensation. Such an individual style of life, which is determined at an early age and in reference to the family circle, is usually found to be the same in all the great fields of human endeavour, in social life, in work, in love between the sexes. If the compensatory striving is to be satisfactory, however, it must be useful and socially approved—a notion clearly analogous to Freud's "sublimation."

Indeed, in much of this there is nothing intrinsically opposed to the findings of the psycho-analytic school; much even will be found in the writings of this school, though usually expressed in other terms; for Freud has never denied the ego, and in his later writings it has taken up an ever more important place. It is rather in what Adler denies, than in what he asserts, that the incompatibility of Individual Psychology with psycho-analysis is found to lie. Adler has made many valuable contributions to the study of self-assertion and aggression. But, judged by psychoanalytic standards, there is little place for sex, or love, or sympathy within his system. And, together with sex, he has thrown out much of that rich insight into the complexities of mental life that psycho-analysis had won. Intra-psychic conflict, repression, condensation, displacement, even the idea of the unconscious itself—these have all vanished, or very nearly so, from the later expositions of Individual Psychology. To the psycho-analyst, Adler appears to have sacrificed the whole for the sake of an exaggerated insistence on a part. Small wonder that there is at present little possibility of understanding or co-operation between the two schools.

Adler's psychology, as distinct from Freud's, has made considerable progress recently, especially as regards popular estimation in America, where it has enjoyed a distinctly favourable press. It might at first seem strange that "such a cheerless view of life," as Freud has well described it, should have met with so ready a reception. Perhaps Adler's doctrines have a peculiar applicability in a land in which individual ambition to "make good" is regarded as of greater moral significance, and has at the same time (in many spheres) a greater chance of success, than in other longer-settled countries. Perhaps, however, Freud's further words in this connection point to an even more fundamental aspect of the Adlerian appeal; for "we must not forget," he says, "that, weighed down by the burden of its sexual desires, humanity is ready to accept anything when tempted with 'ascendancy over sexuality' as a bait."

Adler's departure from Freud takes the form of restriction and elimination, of much that in psycho-analysis was considered essential. Jung's revolt made use of the opposite method of extension. Thus, the "libido," which in the psycho-analytic sense meant the sum total of the "component instincts" entering into the sexual urge, means in Analytical Psychology the sum total of *all* impulses—the equivalent of Bergson's *élan vital*. The unconscious is extended so as to include a deeper layer, common to the whole race, the "Collective Unconscious," which contains the "archetypes" that express the primitive concepts, needs and aspirations of humanity, as well as the "Personal Unconscious," which contains repressed material from the individual's own experience. According to Jung, it is the business of analysis as a whole to envisage the future of the individual as well as to disentangle his past. Dreams and symbols have a "functional" as well as a "material" significance; by virtue of the former they refer to mental states and tendencies, whereas by virtue of the latter (which alone was stressed by Freud) they refer, of course, to material objects or persons. A good many of what are held to be direct (i.e. non-symbolic) expressions by the Freudians are regarded as functionally symbolic by Jung. Thus a dream-image of the father might stand for the primitive ideas of power, authority, tradition; the mythological story of castrating the father would stand for an overcoming of older or more conservative ways of life by newer ones; while numerous other ideas (including many of a sexual nature) may be symbols of the "libido." It is with regard to this "functional" symbolism that the rift between Freud and Jung first became clearly apparent. There is no serious dispute as to the existence of functional symbols (which were a discovery, not of Jung himself, but of Herbert Silberer); there is, however, much difference of opinion as to their relative importance. To Jung they are of great significance as indicating the general movements and orientation of the whole libido (in his wide sense); by the Freudians they are looked upon suspiciously as an endeavour (perhaps both on the part of the patient and on that of the analyst!) to escape from the unwelcome tendencies revealed by a study of "material" symbols. It must be admitted that much of Jung's psychology has a somewhat mystic air which makes it distinctly difficult both to grasp and to criticize. There is no doubt that, like Adler's, it has made some useful additions to the body of knowledge acquired by psycho-analysis itself. The question is whether these additions have not been paid for very dearly by the neglect of other, even more valuable, concepts, laboriously achieved in the course of analytic work.

Two other aspects of Jung's work must be mentioned here. In his earlier days he carried out a series of important researches on the associative word reaction. This method, invented by Galton and developed by Wundt, had been exploited by the latter for the investigation of the more cognitive aspects of the association process. To Jung belongs the great credit of showing how this process is also influenced by orectic factors—not the voluntarily induced determining tendencies of Watt and Ach, but more permanent (sometimes even unconscious) affective attitudes. If the subject is given a list of words and asked to react to each as quickly as possible with the first word that occurs to him, certain words in the list will very likely be connected with emotional tendencies or themes, and the reactions to these words display as a rule some special characteristic. The reaction may be long delayed; as though the subject were endeavouring to reject unpleasant associations; in extreme cases he may even be unable to respond at all (in the same way that an unpleasant situation tends to produce a temporary paralysis of action). The stimulus word may be repeated before the response is given (just as in ordinary life an astonishing, unusually significant, or unwelcome, phrase, that we have heard may be repeated). Or the subject may be unable to respond with the same reaction word, when the whole experiment is repeated after a short interval (as though he were in this case unwilling to remember, or were seeking, as it were, a new way of escape). The word association experiment thus provides us with a sort of psycho-analysis in miniature, and has indeed often been used as a preliminary orientation for a deeper study of unconscious complexes. Or again it may be employed as a means of detecting more recent and temporary emotional disturbances, such as the guilt connected with a real or fictitious crime. In the last-named form it has become a favourite classroom demonstration.

The other aspect of Jung's work to which we referred consists in an elaborate contribution to the theory of individual types. As soon as the interest of psychologists began to be directed to individual differences, there arose a very natural desire to classify individuals according to the type to which they belonged. Galton had made a beginning in the case of images, and many others have attempted to follow up his work by an endeavour to classify persons as "audiles," "visiles," "tactiles," etc., according to the kind of imagery that predominated with them. Unfortunately, here as elsewhere, it nearly always turned out that the great majority of people did not belong to any of the more obviously striking types, but, having no pronounced preponderance in any one direction, could only be described as belonging to an "intermediate" type. Ideally, if we are to distinguish individuals as belonging to types, there should be no overlap between the types. It should be as easy (after proper examination) to say to which of two (or more) types an individual belongs, as it is to say whether he is anatomically male or female (where cases of doubt, corresponding to an hermaphroditic "intermediate" type, are negligibly few). Actually, in matters of the mind, we find that there is practically always more or less of any characteristic, a continuous gradation from one "type" to another, and not a sharp division into groups. Nevertheless, both our practical needs and our intellectual comfort often demand that we should make some kind of classification, and in setting out on such a task we are apt to be struck by exceptional cases which present certain characteristics with unusual clearness. We search for others like them, and, in so far as we succeed, we group them together as a type. There is no harm in doing so, as long as we remember that there is almost sure to be a continuous transition from one type to its opposite, and that our types (just because they are exceptional and therefore striking) are likely to include only a minority of any fair sample of the total population. Anyhow, the limitations that have been shown to attach to the use of types have not discouraged psychologists from proposing ever new varieties.

Jung's list of psychological types is one of the most ambitious that has been proposed. He employs a twofold basis of classification into attitude types and function types. There are two general attitude types—introvert and extravert respectively. The introvert directs his libido inwards and orients himself towards the environment from the subjective point of view, adapting reality to his own subjective needs as far as may be. The extravert on the other hand is interested in reality for its own sake and adjusts himself to it. If a person is consciously extravert, he tends to be unconsciously introvert, and *vice versa*. There are four function types, the thinking, feeling, sensation, and intuition types respectively. Of these the thinking and feeling types (together called the rational types) bear the same relation to one another as the two attitude types; and similarly in the case of the sensation and intuition type (together called the irrational types). Kant would be an example of the thinking type, when introvert; Darwin of the same type, when extravert. A person of the feeling type is swayed more by his emotions than by his reason; when introvert, his feeling is intensive and strong, when extravert he (or more usually, in this case, she) is governed by the "logic of feeling," as in the case of a lady who protested "I can't think what I don't feel." An example of the introvert sensation type would be the artist who is interested in the outer visible world for what it suggests to him, whereas the country squire, who has a blunt crude interest in outer things for what they are, would represent the extravert sensation type. Finally Blake, the mystic, might stand for the introvert intuition type, Lloyd George, the politician with an amazing adaptability to the particular audience or situation with which he is confronted, for the extravert intuition type. Jung's *Psychological Types* (1923), in which he expounds and illustrates this doctrine, is a fascinating work, and very high claims have been made for it, as when Baynes, its English translator, says that "for practical psychologists it must assuredly be regarded as the foundation of the science, for in no other work do we find basic psychological principles whose validity is commensurate with the undeniable facts of man's historic development and the realities of individual experience." Few psychologists would be prepared to dispute the truth of the latter portion of this statement; but whether Jung has, in his type doctrine, really given us the "foundation" required, only time and much further work will show. Some statistical researches directed to this problem have been undertaken, but there is yet some doubt among investigators as to whether introversion and extraversion can be looked upon as unitary traits, as Jung's treatment suggests, or whether they are not rather a conglomeration of factors that must be further analysed. Nevertheless, if this doctrine stimulates research sufficiently to provide its own proof, confutation or correction, it will have proved as useful as we can reasonably expect at the present stage of knowledge.

Two other samples of type theory in recent psychology may be briefly touched on here. On the basis chiefly of a study of the physique of psychiatric patients, Kretschmer distinguishes four main types: the athletic type (with strong skeleton, broad chest and powerful musculature suggestive of the gorilla), the asthenic type (tall and thin, reminiscent of the chimpanzee), the pyknic type (short and broad, showing some resemblance to the orangoutang) and the dysplastic type (the inevitable intermediate category). On the mental side he finds that members of the pyknic type are liable to manic-depressive insanity, while the other types are more likely to succumb to dementia praecox, paraphrenia or paranoia, all of them diseases which involve some degree of dissociation or disintegration of the personality. Arguing from the abnormal to the normal, Kretschmer would make all persons fall into one or other of two large types, the cycloids, distinguished by their sociability, good nature and tendency to alternating moods, and the schizoids, with a greater tendency to be unsociable, reserved, timid, sensitive, silent or eccentric. These types have, since the publication of Kretschmer's book on

Körperbau und Charakter in 1921, been the object of consider-able thought and observation. Van de Velde, the author of a very popular book on marriage, has even made them the basis of his advice on the choice of a life partner. There seems little doubt that there is a real correspondence between bodily form and liability to particular types of mental disease in the sense indi-cated by Kretschmer, but the existence of any similar correla-tion between physique and certain mental characteristics within the range of normal variation is still a matter of dispute.

E. R. Jaensch's types are the result of following up an interest-ing psychological discovery. In 1907 Urbantschitsch drew atten-tion to the fact that there exist in some persons images of a per-ception-like clearness (so-called "eidetic" images), differing markedly in many respects from the images previously described in psychological literature. Ten years later Kroh started systematic work upon these images, and since that time they have been the principal object of interest in Jaensch's laboratory at Marburg. These images, it now appears, are found in a large proportion of children but tend to disappear in later life, though they are pre-served in the case of a minority of individuals. The images, when present, exhibit differences both in degree and kind. It is the latter or qualitative difference that serves as a basis for the pro-posed types. In some persons the eidetic image can be relatively well controlled, behaving in this respect like the "memory-image." In others it has more the intrusive character of the ordin-ary "after-image"; its form and colour cannot be changed, nor can it be banished by an effort of will. The first class of individuals constitute the B (or Basedowoid) Type and there is some evi-dence that they include an unusual number of persons of artistic ability, that they are distinguished by a somewhat enlarged thyroid gland and a liability to powerful reactions of the sym-pathetic nervous system. The second or T (tetanoid) Type seems to correspond somewhat to Jung's Extravert Type, reacting rather to external than to internal stimuli; still other characteris-tics, it is suggested, may be found in the various classes of "mixed" imagery. It is as yet too early to say what may be the ultimate value of these distinctions; here again, however, the distinction of types is giving rise to much useful work, which, if persevered in, can scarcely fail to produce results of value, though not necessarily of the kind originally anticipated.

It seems clear that the eventual significance of the "types" that we considered in the last chapter and of the many others that have been proposed must depend upon their treatment by statistical methods. Such statistical methods are now available, having entered psychology by another channel, that of mental tests. We have seen how both the mental test and the corresponding statistical procedures originated with Galton and were developed by Cattell. We have called attention also to two important adumbrations of mental testing, as it was later to be practised, the "combination method" of Ebbinghaus and the various experiments which Binet carried out on his daughters.

As in so many other cases, the stimulus to further progress in this field came largely from problems connected with the abnormal. In 1904, the year after the appearance of his *Étude Expérimentale*, Binet was asked by the French Minister of Public Instruction to serve on a committee appointed to study methods of dealing with the "backward" child. One of the most important problems encountered by this committee was to find some means of distinguishing between lack of ability on the one hand, and laziness or lack of interest on the other. Together with Simon, Binet devised a series of tests arranged in order of increasing difficulty. First published in 1905, these tests underwent a number of revisions, reappearing with modifications and additions in 1908 and again in 1911. In their later form the tests aimed at measuring intelligence in terms of "mental age," i.e. at establishing norms for each year of growth, and with their help, diagnosing quantitatively any given child's ability as normal, above normal, or below normal. In the two latter cases the child could, by means of the scale, be said to have a mental age that was just so many years or months in advance of or behind his chronological age.

The Binet tests proved a great success, were presently translated and adapted for use in various countries, notably by Goddard, Yerkes, and Terman in America, by Burt in England, by Treves and Saffiotti in Italy. Meanwhile other investigators, chiefly in America, had been devising further tests. Indeed, as already indicated, apart from Galton, Binet and Ebbinghaus, America was the true home of mental testing, which was a natural outcome of the predominant interest in individual differences that distinguished American psychology. The term "mental test" itself was due to Cattell, who, as we have mentioned earlier, tested students entering Columbia even in 1896; and during the nineties attempts at testing were made by at least some half-dozen investigators of repute. Early in the new century further important pioneer attempts were made by Kirkpatrick, Kelly, Norsworthy and others, the two last named comparing groups of normal and defective children, and showing that the defective were not a separate "species," but that there was a continuous transition from the most intelligent of the normal group to the most dull of the defectives.

What chiefly distinguished these earlier American tests from those of Binet was that, following the laboratory tradition, they were largely confined to the simpler sensory, perceptual and motor processes, in which laboratory measurements had hitherto been most successful, whereas Binet boldly took his test situations from ordinary life, and thus from the start found himself dealing with the "higher" mental processes. Binet's procedure (which was also to some extent that of Ebbinghaus) proved itself to be the more fruitful, for reasons that have since become apparent. In fact it is remarkable that "tests" have achieved their greatest success in just this field, into which laboratory methods, aiming principally at a determination of the "laws" of the mind, only penetrated slowly and with difficulty. Encouraged by the ease with which the Binet scale could be applied, and by the interest of the results obtained, there were soon a host of workers devising new tests and applying old ones. In fact, during the greater part of our last period, mental testing has been one of the most popular of all branches of psychology, and the importance of the new departure into the study of individual differences—which we owe to the insight of Galton and Cattell and what we may perhaps call the intuition of American psychologists generally—has become more and more apparent. Apart from the elaboration of

I

new tests of ever greater convenience and diagnostic value, the chief further developments achieved by all this work may perhaps be summarized as follows:

(1) The realization of the desirability of distinguishing in these tests between results due to innate ability on the one hand and to experience and education on the other.

(2) The distinction between "linguistic" tests (such as Binet's, in which facility in the use of language plays a part) and "performance" tests (of which the form-board—a simplified puzzle of the jig-saw kind—and the maze, are perhaps the best-known examples).

(3) The distinction between "individual tests," in which each subject is tested singly, and "group tests," in which a large number can be tested simultaneously. The former enjoy some of the advantages of laboratory conditions, in that the objective measurements obtained can be supplemented by observation of the subject's behaviour. They lend themselves, therefore, to the intensive study of important individual cases; whereas group tests have the advantage that they allow of a more extensive and statistical study of the distribution of abilities among certain *classes* of individual. The most magnificent of all the achievements of psychology on the quantitative side was the application of a set of linguistic and performance tests (the celebrated Army Alpha and Beta tests) to nearly two million recruits of the American Army upon the entry of the United States into the Great War in 1917—the data from which vast experiment have been, and still are being, used to throw light on many problems concerning differences in ability between persons of different races, social classes, occupations, etc.

(4) The comparison of test scores with estimates by qualified persons (teachers, fellow scholars, etc.), so that the tests might themselves be tested as to what they measured. In the early days of so-called "intelligence" tests, it was very desirable to see how far the individual's "intelligence," as measured by a test, corresponded to his intelligence, as estimated by those who had good opportunities of judging his capacity. It has since been found that good tests of intelligence generally correspond so highly with conscientious estimates made under favourable conditions, that these latter can now usually be dispensed with. Indeed there is every reason to suppose that a good set of tests gives a better

measure of ability than any estimates that can be obtained under ordinary conditions.

(5) The application of tests to problems of group differences. The original stimulus to the work of Ebbinghaus and Binet arose from the practical need of distinguishing between "normal" and mentally defective children for purposes of education. It was soon found that tests were equally suitable for dealing with other interesting group differences, such as those mentioned above under (3), differences of sex, of heredity, of age, etc. (these latter coming into prominence very early owing to the work of Binet himself and of Stern).

(6) The devising of tests for mental qualities or characteristics other than those of general ability or "intelligence," for the measurement of which they were first created. In the beginning there was a tendency to assume that this ability, as measured, was independent of what had been learnt by experience. It was soon found that, though this assumption was not entirely justified, it was at least possible to construct tests that depended very little on experience, but that on the other hand, an alteration of the tests in the opposite direction enabled them to measure the subject's degree of educational *achievement*, as distinct from his capacity. Thus there grew up a series of educational tests designed to measure progress in the ordinary subjects of the school curriculum—tests which to a considerable extent are capable of replacing the more usual forms of examination; they are in fact both easier and more reliable to mark and more convenient to apply, eliciting a much greater amount of information in a given time. Other tests were devised to deal with what appear to be the more "specific" abilities involved in school work, in ordinary life and in various careers. Still others aimed at measuring the orectic features of an individual, at throwing light upon his temperament and character, his tendency to neurosis, his moral development, and so on. Here, very considerable difficulties have been met with, and, in spite of a good deal of work during the last ten years, progress has been slow; although the situation is far from hopeless, it must be admitted that there exists today scarcely a single well-tried-out, convenient and reliable test in the sphere of character, the practical and theoretical significance of which is really understood. The complex conditions of the orectic life appear to make both the application of tests and the interpretation

of the results obtained more troublesome than in the sphere of cognition. Nevertheless the really determined attack made quite recently by Hartshorne and May (whose reports were published in three volumes dealing respectively with "Deceit," "Service and Self-Control" and the "Organization of Character") has achieved results of a definitely more promising kind, and many psychologists are now beginning to look forward to the time when some, at any rate, of the more important orectic qualities of the individual will be within range of the routine methods of the tester.

(7) The application of tests to wider practical problems. Thus the American Army tests aimed both at the elimination of those who were too stupid to be of use in military service, and at the discovery of those who might be expected to deserve rapid promotion, or who could be selected for special types of work calling for particular ability. In recent years tests have been applied to immigrants to the United States and the results obtained have played a part in fixing the relative size of the "quotas" assigned to various countries; they have thus become a factor in determining no less important a matter than the racial constitution of the population of America. Further applications of tests (both those of general ability and those of specific abilities) have been concerned with what has come to be known as vocational psychology, itself a twofold undertaking, embracing in the first place "vocational selection" of individuals suitable for any given kind of work, and in the second place "vocational guidance" of the individual with a view to discovering the most suitable work for his particular abilities.

(8) The development of statistical procedures for dealing with the data resulting from the use of tests—more especially of various methods of calculating "coefficients of correlation," i.e. single numbers expressing the degree of relationship between tests. According to all the principal methods in use these numbers become unity when there is a perfect correspondence between the two abilities intercorrelated, i.e. when the persons getting the first, second and third best scores in the one test occupy similar positions in the other test, and so on throughout; any lesser correspondence being expressed as a fraction. Thus 0·80 would indicate a high correlation and 0·20 a low one, 0·00 the complete absence of correlation and −0·65 a moderately high

inverse or "negative" correlation (where those who are good in one test tend to be bad in the other). The need for some such method of correlation had been realized by Galton, and the mathematical foundations of the method had been laid by Karl Pearson, who himself built upon the much earlier work of the French mathematician Bravais. But it was C. E. Spearman who first realized the full importance of correlation for psychology, who devised new and simpler methods of calculation, who elaborated methods for correction of the errors inherent in the "crude" correlation coefficient, and who by much further work, both mathematical and experimental, showed how mental tests could be used to attack an all-important problem of general psychology—no less a problem indeed than that involved in the ancient doctrine of faculties. He thus united the psychology of individual differences with the psychology of laws or principles, the apparently divergent schools of Galton and of Wundt, and proved that the former could frucitfy the latter. It is to Spearman, far more than to anyone else, that we owe our present knowledge, as to the structure or "make-up" of the human mind, together with the necessary methods for increasing this knowledge by further research. His achievement, which is one of the most remarkable in the whole history of psychology, has given an entirely new significance to mental tests and indeed to the study of individual differences generally. In what follows we must deal briefly with some of the main features of his work.

XI. SPEARMAN AND THE "FACTOR" SCHOOL

SPEARMAN entered psychology relatively late in life, studying with Wundt and Müller after resigning a commission in the British Army—an unusual approach to the problems of the mind. In 1907 he was put in charge of a small and new psychological department at University College, London, in succession to McDougall; his laboratory being equipped for the most part with apparatus brought from the Freiburg laboratory vacated by Münsterberg, when the latter left for America. Here he remained till he, in his turn, left for America in 1931, and in his twenty-four years' work in London he founded one of the most important modern schools (the "Factor School," as it has been appropriately called in *Psychologies of 1930*), attracted numerous students from various parts of the British Empire and elsewhere, and, together with them, produced a very large quantity of work, much of which was embodied in his two important books, *The Nature of Intelligence and the Principles of Cognition* and *The Abilities of Man*, published in 1923 and 1927 respectively.

Already in 1904, however, he had published an article in the *American Journal of Psychology*, which adumbrated the most important portion of his doctrine. This doctrine implies the existence, on the one hand, of a general factor of ability (subsequently called g), varying in power from one individual to another, but operative to some extent in all performances; and, on the other hand, of a large number of highly specific abilities (collectively called s), some one of which at least is also operative in each performance, though the relative importance of g and s may vary greatly from one performance to another. Spearman's view of the "abilities of man" may thus be designated a two-factor theory—a theory which, as he himself points out at length in his later works, differs from any of the theories of "intelligence" previously held. Such theories were of three kinds—the "monarchic" view, according to which there is one unitary

262

faculty or ability, strong in those who are intelligent, weak in those who are dull or stupid; the "oligarchic" view, according to which there are a few big faculties, "judgment," "memory," "imagination," etc.; and the "anarchic" view, according to which all abilities are independent of one another (so that any series or "battery" of tests can only measure an average, general level or sample of the whole). Now, if we apply a number of tests to a group of people and draw up a table of correlations between the tests, the result should vary according to which of these theories is true. The monarchic doctrine demands very high correlations throughout (since *ex hypothesi* the same general ability is involved in all the tests); the oligarchic doctrine demands that there should be very high correlations between some of the tests (those that measure the same faculty), and very low correlations in other cases (when the particular tests correlated measure different faculties); while the anarchic doctrine demands very low or zero correlations throughout (for *ex hypothesi* each test measures an independent ability). Actually the results obtained from the enormous mass of data now available are in accordance with none of these theories. Correlations tend to be positive, but on the whole are neither very high nor very low. Further inspection, however, shows that there is some sort of order or principle governing the size of the correlations; and by the application of various mathematical criteria (the latest and most convenient being known as the method of "tetrad differences") Spearman shows that the nature of this order is such as to imply the existence of *g* and *s*, as above described, the *s's*, moreover, being shown to be for the most part astonishingly specific, so that two tests have to be *extremely* similar before *s* is common to the two. We are left, therefore, with one quite general factor, corresponding roughly to the "intelligence" of common speech, which is supplemented by a great number of specific factors.

The next problems obviously lie in the direction of defining further the nature of both *g* and *s*. Spearman himself is inclined to think that in the last resort *g* corresponds to a general fund of cerebral *energy*, that *s* corresponds to particular *engines* and that (pursuing the same analogy) conation represents the *engineer*, who determines when and to what purpose the energy and engines shall be used. Others are inclined to consider *g* as corresponding to some general structural *quality* of the cortex or nervous system; still others look upon it as the total effect of a very large number of elements. It is generally admitted that at present we have no evidence which can enable us to decide conclusively in favour of one or other of these views. Our uncertainty as to the ultimate nature of *g*, however, in no way invalidates the concept of *g* itself, nor interferes with the measurement of *g* either for practical or for theoretical purposes. The pure or applied psychologist is indeed no worse off here than the physicist or the electrical engineer, who make their electrical measurements and use electricity for the satisfaction of human needs undeterred by their uncertainty as to the ultimate nature of electricity itself.

Nor are we debarred by this ignorance from carrying out further investigation into the particular ways in which *g* and *s* manifest themselves. Indeed, Spearman and his pupils have already gone far in this direction. It will be remembered that, in dealing with *Gestalt* (p. 209), we had occasion to mention Spearman's three "noegenetic laws," the laws according to which the mind *creates* new mental content: the laws of "apprehension of experience," of "eduction of relations" and "eduction of correlates" respectively. Reviewing the evidence available (mostly the result of his own "factor" school), Spearman concludes that *g* manifests itself in all operations involving noegenesis according to the second and third laws, just in proportion to the extent that these operations themselves are noegenetic. (Suitable data are not yet available for making any similar statement with regard to the first law, since adequate "tests" involving this law have not yet been devised.) Furthermore, if we study different *kinds* of noegenetic operations, we find that the presence and extent of *g* is unaffected by any change, either in the nature of the operation itself (as when we educe different kinds or relation, those of space, time, causality, attribution, etc.), or in the materials—in Spearman's terminology the "fundaments" —upon which the operations are carried out (sensations, perceptions, images, thoughts, feelings, etc.). If we wish to measure *g*, therefore, we must take care that our tests involve noegenesis in a high degree, but, apart from this, it matters little what the actual operations are—hence the justifiability of Binet's "hotchpotch" procedure.

On the other hand, it has been possible also to define the conditions of s, which seems to play a part in any performance just in so far as influences from one or other of three sources are involved, i.e. from the sense organs, from the motor organs or from retentivity. The last mentioned is perhaps the most interesting and novel of all these important discoveries. It was pretty well known, for instance, that (to take extreme cases) deafness, blindness or muscular weakness did not necessarily imply stupidity; it was not so clearly recognized that memory had no connection with intelligence—a fact assuredly of the greatest importance to general psychology and one of the many triumphs of the factor school. Spearman even goes further, and in a recent paper suggests that, in a sense, memory is responsible for all *error*, inasmuch as the proximate cause of all mistakes is to be found in the carrying over through retention of some character from one item of experience to another to which it does not properly belong, this displacement of the character being accompanied by a corresponding belief. The more remote cause of mistakes may, of course, lie in conation (as Freud in particular had shown), but the immediate mechanism through which the mistake is committed lies in the false trick of memory. Often in such cases we make use of a retentive process when a process of eduction is really called for; as in many mistakes committed in the performance of mental tests.

In addition to the three qualitative laws already mentioned Spearman enunciates five quantitative laws which indicate the conditions under which the noegenetic processes occur. These are:

(1) The law of span, according to which "every mind tends to keep its simultaneous output constant in quantity, however varying in quality." Quantity here seems at first to have two aspects, clearness and speed. Clearness itself, however, can be subdivided, since, within certain limits, we can focus our attention very narrowly, or "spread" it over a greater field (though at a proportionate sacrifice of the clearness with which we envisage any part). More correctly then, the law of span has really three aspects: intensity, extensity and speed; and it has been found that g manifests itself in all three.

(2) The law of retentivity. This also has three aspects: (a) the law of inertia, according to which "cognitive processes begin and end more gradually than their (apparent) causes"; (b) the law of

dispositions, according to which "cognitive events by occurring establish dispositions which facilitate their recurrence"; and (c) the law of associations, according to which "cognitive events by occurring in company tend to do so with greater ease." As already indicated, g plays little or no part in these; from a person's retentivity we can infer nothing as to the extent of his g.

(3) The law of fatigue, which is in a sense the opposite of the law of retentivity, and according to which "the occurrence of any cognitive process produces a tendency opposed to its occurrence afterwards." So far as the present evidence goes, there appears to be but little if any relation between an individual's g and his liability to fatigue.

(4) The law of conative control, according to which "the intensity of cognition can be controlled by conation." This law touches on a matter which has been supposed by some (by certain psycho-pathologists, for instance) to limit greatly the usefulness and reliability of mental tests aiming at a pure measure of cognitive ability independent of conative factors. It is evident, of course, that all tests of this kind imply a willingness to co-operate on the part of the subject. The necessary degree of willingness does appear, however, to be actually forthcoming from the vast majority of subjects under the usual circumstances in which tests are carried out. Even the more subtle influences which might come from more or less unconscious inhibitions or contra-suggestibility seem to be circumvented in most instances, though both conscious and unconscious opposition does undoubtedly occur *sometimes*, especially in pathological cases, and there is still need for research upon this most important point. Nevertheless, on the whole, it would appear that the very artificiality of the test situation, which thus to a large extent eliminates everyday habits, ambitions and anxieties, is of advantage here, the test being in this respect superior to the ordinary form of examination. Extremely high degrees of conation, moreover, appear to have much more effect on speed than on "intensity" or "extensity" of span; tests that depend primarily on clearness demand only a degree of conation that is readily put forth by everyone without any extraordinary incentives. Under the usual test conditions, therefore, and with the employment of reasonable precautions, it may be said that the measures of g obtained from mental tests are comparatively little influenced by conative factors.

(5) Finally there is the law of "primordial potencies," which "in a sense lies deeper than all the others." It states that "every manifestation of the preceding four quantitative laws is superposed upon, as its ultimate basis, certain purely physiological influences"—such influences as age, health, heredity, the effect of drugs, and so on. Considerable work has been done in this field, both inside and outside the "factor" school, though more still remains to be accomplished. As regards age, the rather surprising discovery has been made that g does not appreciably increase after the age of fifteen or thereabouts; the improvement in so many performances in ordinary life after this age being due to increased knowledge, experience and practice. There is even some possibility that g declines as soon as adolescence has been passed, though the evidence on this point is as yet by no means conclusive. What is certain, however, is that, in later life, memory declines much more rapidly than g—a fact for which casual everyday observation had fully prepared us, a fact, too, which again emphasizes the mutual independence of g and retentivity.

Much work has also been done on heredity, with the result that the general tendency of offspring to resemble parents in amount of g seems very well established—a matter that is, of course, of prime importance from the eugenic point of view. Of particular significance in this connection is the continuation of the work on twins—originally started by Galton. Thorndike, in 1905, and Merriman, in 1924, showed that twins resemble one another in intelligence more closely than do other brothers and sisters. Indeed, according to Merriman, the correlation in the intelligence measures of like-sex twins approaches even to unity! An extensive study of feeble-mindedness by Goddard, published in 1917, seemed to show that well-marked cases of mental deficiency depend on a Mendelian "recessive" trait, normal intelligence being "dominant." His results are difficult to bring into harmony with the fact that (as already mentioned) other researches have shown that feeble-mindedness is not a "species" but that there is a continuous transition from genius to imbecile. This last fact suggests dependence of g not upon one but upon many unit factors. An analogous case however is to be found on the physical side. We know that human stature depends on many factors, and has a similar statistical distribution; nevertheless one particular type of dwarfism is a Mendelian trait. In view, however, of the complexity of the problems of heredity, some discrepancies at this stage of our knowledge are hardly to be wondered at.

With regard to race, the present evidence points rather strongly to the existence on the average of somewhat greater g in persons of Germanic stock than among the inhabitants of Southern Europe; while in America the white race as a whole seems superior to the coloured (in mixed populations it has even been found that g increases with the proportion of white blood). But in all such work it is far from easy to obtain quite comparable samples of the respective populations, and the possibility of errors arising from this source cannot as yet be said to have been entirely eliminated. In any case, moreover, it must be born in mind that the individual differences within each group are vastly greater than the differences between the groups as such.

As regards health and bodily fitness, there is evidence to show that, on the whole, more intelligent persons enjoy bodily as well as mental superiority. In childhood, at any rate, greater g goes with greater height. Terman, who made a special study of a selected group of "gifted" children, found them to be more than usually immune from physical ailments (while at the other end of the scale the mentally defective are "notoriously susceptible to illness of every sort"). The same thing has been found with students. There is, however, urgent need of studies of g in the same individuals in various states of physical health; nor is it clear as to what is cause and what effect in the various positive relationships between intelligence and bodily condition that have been found.

As regards mental disease, Spearman and Hart found that g was impaired to some extent in a great variety of disorders—this, rather than any specific loss, being the most prominent feature in the majority of cases. Abilities were impaired also just in the proportion that they involve g. Needless to say results of this kind fit in admirably with the findings of Franz and Lashley in their studies of experimental injury to the brain. Even in the sphere of aphasia in which the great triumph of the localization theory of cerebral functions had been won, some of the later work, for instance, that of Head, published in 1926, shows that finer analysis of the functions involved has produced evidence which is definitely against the doctrine of "centres" for reading, writing, speaking, etc., of the kind that was formerly supposed. In these disorders also, it would now appear, the whole brain is to some extent involved.

We have little precise information at present concerning the influence of drugs on *g*. What does seem to emerge pretty clearly from the study of drug action is that in a great number of cases the influence of drugs (even of so-called stimulants like alcohol) is in reality always inhibitory, the apparently "stimulating" effect in many instances being due to the reduction of higher level control, so that the lower centres function more freely than under normal conditions. Under these circumstances it seems unlikely that a person's *g* would ever be improved by drugs except perhaps in cases where a quite unusual degree of inhibition is present; whereas in ordinary life, of course, a person's *performance* can be temporarily improved in some cases by the removal of normally excessive inhibitions. Such improvement, however, seems due rather to a release of conation than to any increase of cognitive ability.

Finally as regards sex, it would appear that differences between the two sexes are negligible, so far as average amount of *g* is concerned. At one time, on the basis of the data then available, Thorndike made much of a supposed greater variability of men, in virtue of which, he thought, a larger proportion of men is found both among extremely gifted and extremely stupid individuals. This would account well for the fact that in the world's past history we have records of a far greater number of male than of female geniuses, while at the opposite end of the scale there appear to be more males than females among idiots and imbeciles. More recent researches, however, have not in all respects confirmed this view, and the matter must be regarded as still not definitely established. As regards *s*, however, there do appear to be certain appreciable differences, sometimes in favour of one sex, sometimes in favour of the other. Men have notoriously greater muscular strength than women. On the other hand women seem to have a clear superiority in discrimination of colour, in discrimination of two points on the skin (Weber's famous experiment) and in certain forms of memory; while men again are superior in mathematics. It seems likely, moreover, that we may discover important differences on the conative side, if and when these become measurable with sufficient accuracy;[1] and such differences, together with social convention (which to a large extent determines the *expression* of ability), rather than greater male variability in *g*, may account for the apparent much greater frequency of male genius.

Owing to the extreme specificity of *s*, its investigation is likely to prove a very laborious matter, and comparatively little progress has been made in this direction. It is true that a few of the (perhaps many thousand) specific factors, are relatively easy to measure. This is the case, for instance, with certain kinds of sensory acuity and muscular power. But we are still in complete ignorance of the majority of these factors, and it is clear that they open up an almost endless vista for research. Naturally, however, before embarking on such research, we are inclined to ask, a little bewildered and incredulous: "Is there, then, *nothing* of a more general nature corresponding to the 'faculties' which have figured so largely in the sayings and writings of psychologists— not to speak of ordinary people—for so many centuries? Must we resign ourselves to the view that Imagination, Memory, Perception, Discrimination and the rest are nothing more than convenient names for groups of mental processes that appear to have some feature in common, but are in no sense general 'powers' or 'capacities' of such a kind as to allow us to infer from a person's performance in one manifestation of any one of them to his performance in another manifestation of the same 'capacity'?" It certainly appears as though we must—at least in the great majority of cases. And this implies also that we must abandon the hope of measuring a person's ability in "memory" or "imagination" by means of a single test or even a small battery of tests; all we can do is to measure one particular manifestation and refrain from making unjustifiable inferences as to his ability in other performances involving mental processes that we call by the same name. As regards *s*, we are, in fact, for the most part in the position in which we should have been if the "anarchic" theory held good of all capacities whatever. That we are actually as a whole in a much more favourable position is due to the fact that *g* exists and *can* be measured.

Though the methods of correlation introduced by the "factor"

---

[1] Though Valentine has endeavoured to show that the supposed superior intuition and psychological insight of women have no basis in fact.

school have thus failed to corroborate the existence of most of the classical "faculties," they have nevertheless produced evidence in favour of the existence of a few "broad factors" of a different kind; though this evidence is as yet far inferior to that which we possess concerning the existence and nature of g. Several of these broad factors concern general characteristics of cognitive functioning rather than actual abilities. One of the most remarkable concerns a factor known as p ("perseveration"), manifesting itself as a general inertia, which, when present in a high degree, makes it difficult for the subject to pass rapidly from one kind of mental operation to another. This is a factor, the existence of which had been suspected by a number of modern psychologists, notably by Otto Gross (who called it "secondary function"), and by Heymanns and Wiersma, who in 1906 carried out in Holland one of the most remarkable investigations ever attempted by the questionnaire method. They induced 450 family doctors to send in detailed reports on over 2,500 individuals well known to them. One of the results of this great piece of work was the indication that inertia was a general characteristic of an individual, affecting both his cognitive operations and his character. Subsequent work by two members of the factor school, Lankes and Webb respectively, showed that there was no simple correlation between these two aspects of "perseveration," as it was originally conceived. Simple inertia might account for p proper, which was confined to the cognitive field, while on the side of character there was an apparently independent factor, provisionally labelled w, which seemed to depend upon organization of character in such a way that those who possessed w in a high degree tended, quite generally, to act more upon principle and less on impulse than those who possessed it in a low degree. Very recent work by Pinard suggests that p and w may, after all, be related—in the sense that those with high w tend to have a moderate degree of p, whereas those who have little control over their impulses tend to have either a markedly high or low degree of p. Be this as it may, the discovery of p and w open up further problems of the greatest interest concerning the ultimate nature, extent and influence of these factors. Evidence for still other factors has been found, though our knowledge of them is as yet extremely incomplete. One is, like p, in the nature of a general characteristic. It concerns o ("oscillation")

a factor which appears to manifest itself in variation of output
from one moment to another; some people tend to vary more than
others, and such individual characteristics seem to manifest
themselves over a wide field. Turning to the abilities proper, the
work of J. W. Cox has brought some evidence for the existence
of a moderately broad factor concerned with mechanical ability—
the understanding of the working of apparatus; while there are
also indications of other factors connected with verbal ability,
motor ability, mathematics and music. The work with regard to
the last named has come chiefly from the laboratory of C. E.
Seashore, at the University of Iowa, where for many years a
remarkable series of researches on all branches of musical psychology has been carried on. Seashore has in fact become the true
successor of Stumpf, though more definitely an experimentalist
and less of a philosopher.

The "broad factors" thus discovered bear little resemblance
to any of the faculties previously assumed. Indeed, in the field
of sensation, discrimination, imagination, and above all, memory,
which had perhaps more often than any other been regarded as
a unitary power, only very narrow factors have so far been
demonstrated. The factor school has thus been destructive of
many cherished assumptions, though on the other side it is
beginning to build up a new knowledge of mental "make-up"
on novel and, for the most part, hitherto quite unexpected lines.
The correlation method is unusually laborious; every one of the
results we have mentioned above has been obtained as the outcome of a vast quantity of experimental work and calculation. But
there seems no doubt that it is proving itself one of the most
important weapons in the whole armoury of the psychologist.
As the ultimate outcome of much further work it may be
possible to map out the whole human mind into "factors" of
greater or lesser breadth (perhaps even into Mendelian units!).
The phrenologists' dream of a complete "faculty" psychology
will then eventually come true, at any rate so far as the purely
psychological side is concerned; and the striking parallelism
between the conclusions of Spearman in psychology and Lashley
in brain physiology suggests that by that time the corresponding
physiological and anatomical knowledge may also not be wanting.
Both for practice and for theory the promise of the "factor"
psychology is very bright indeed, though it will need long years

of work by many hands before the ground is adequately covered. It is interesting to note, however, that in this very year (1933) a research in this direction is being launched in America on a very wide scale. After consultation with psychologists all over the world, a group of workers, under the direction of an organizing committee, appointed by the American Council of Education, with Thorndike as Chairman, and Spearman and Lashley among its members, are setting out to measure very numerous functions and abilities in a relatively large population. A somewhat similar research, though on a much smaller scale, has actually been started in England, with special reference to mental disease, and it may be hoped that the exaggeration of certain normal features so often found in insanity will, here as elsewhere, prove a great help towards the discovery and understanding of such factors. Preliminary reports by W. Stephenson, who is now continuing the work on factors imaugurated by Spearman in London, have corroborated some earlier results obtained by Wiersma, showing that p is apt to be greatly in excess of the normal in cases of melancholia and depression and greatly below normal in cases of mania. The full results of carefully planned, large-scale, systematic investigations such as these, when they are available, should bring in a rich harvest of fresh knowledge on many of the most vexed questions concerned with "types" and "faculties." In fact, it is not easy to see limits to the usefulness of the methods of analysis introduced by the factor school.

It is true that it is in a sense only a "static" method; it exhibits the powers of the mind but does not reveal their actual working. It would appear, however, to be a relatively easy matter to supplement the statics of the correlation method by the dynamics of a more functional method of approach. It is clear, for instance, from the work already done, that the discoveries of the factor school have great significance for the practical questions involved in education and in industry. Thus it would seem that g cannot be improved by practice, whereas s can—at least in certain cases. Furthermore, owing to the specificity of s and the absence of real basis for the conventional faculties, the "formal training" doctrine, on which so much of education has been—explicitly or implicitly—founded, must inevitably lead to disappointment. Careful experiment in this field has corroborated the findings of correlation, inasmuch as it has shown that the "transfer of training" from one task to another is very much narrower indeed than had been popularly supposed. Here again, we have been deluded by words. Just as, on the one hand, it had been thought that it might be possible to measure "memory" as a whole, so also it was supposed that it might be possible to train memory as a whole; whether by learning poetry, Greek irregular verbs, or the multiplication table was a matter of indifference. Actually it now appears that transfer only occurs in so far as there is some common element involved—such as the acquirement of rhythm, the use of imagery, or the ability to resist the distractions always present in the schoolroom. Similar arguments probably apply to the exercise of any other faculty. In fact, many of the discoveries on the "static" side by means of correlation imply the possibility of further corresponding experiments on the side of transfer. Only when these also have been carried through, shall we have a complete knowledge of factors, not only as "energies" or "engines," but as functions. A long programme, but a fascinating one, which may well keep psychologists busy for several generations!

XII. SENSATION

We have now concluded our review of the principal schools which have played such a great part in twentieth-century psychology. It will have been noticed that *sensation*, which figures so largely in the earlier days of experimentalism, receives as a rule but little attention in the special lines of research that distinguish the different schools and in the matters in dispute between them. And, indeed, with the devising of fresh methods, able to cope with the "higher processes" in an accurate and systematic way, it was inevitable that interest should largely be deflected from the "gateways of knowledge" to knowledge itself, and to the other aspects of the mind that show, at best, but an indirect dependence on the senses. Nevertheless, a very considerable amount of work continued to be done in the psychology and physiology of sensation, though relatively to the whole, this amount is vastly less than in our second period. In direction, too, it is somewhat changed; for, as was perhaps to be expected, the most important discoveries have been made in those sense departments as regards which comparatively little progress had been made before. We may briefly indicate a very few of these developments.

We have seen how, in the field of cutaneous sensation, a new era began with the discovery of "spots" in 1884. Another period may be said to have begun in 1911, following an experiment which Head performed upon himself, in the hope of throwing light upon some anomalies of sensation that he had observed among his patients. The radial and external cutaneous nerves of one of his arms were divided at the elbow, and the effects of the slow process of recovery carefully noted. As a result of their observations, Head and his collaborators maintained that there are three separate systems of sensibility involved in skin sensation. These systems they called the deep, the protopathic and the epicritic respectively. Deep sensibility continued to be present

275

over the affected area immediately after the operation. It involved the response to the pressure of blunt objects on the skin, together with deep-seated pain, and must, they thought, be due to the excitation of sensory fibres contained in the nerves supplying the tendons and muscles. After about seven weeks, the second or protopathic system began to return. This involves the functions of the heat, cold and pain spots. But it was found that this system functions on the "all or nothing" principle; it is qualitative only, and the response is not graded according to the intensity of the stimulus. Furthermore, thermal sensations were produced only by stimuli of a temperature above 38° or below 24° C. Pain sensations radiated widely, and indeed sensibility as a whole was of a strongly affective character, similar in general nature to the "over-reactions" found by Head in certain cases of thalamic lesions (p. 225). Indeed, if Head's views with regard to the cause of these latter over-reactions is correct, the evidence strongly suggests that these sensations have their essential seat in the thalamus rather than the cortex. Finally, after an interval of more than a year, the third or epicritic system of sensibility returned. This involves the function of the touch spots, together with a diffused and graduated sensibility to warmth and coolness in the region between the temperatures mentioned above. Only with the recovery of this epicritic sensibility was it possible to distinguish as separate two neighbouring stimulated points upon the skin. During the period when deep and protopathic sensibility alone were present over the greater part of the area concerned, it was found that there were small regions sensitive only to the epicritic system, heat and cold (as distinct from graduated warmth and coolness) being absent, and the prick of a pin being felt only as a sensation of pointedness without pain. This seemed to corroborate the separateness of the two systems, and at the same time showed that protopathic and epicritic sensibility for a given area is not necessarily conveyed in the same nerves.

Head's interesting experiment has been repeated by Trotter and Davies (working in collaboration) in England and by Boring in America, the results being somewhat discrepant in all three cases. Both Trotter and Davies and Boring, however, failed to find evidence of a sharp division between protopathic and epicritic sensibility; they experienced continuous recovery throughout, without any well-marked stages. Boring, however, to some extent corroborated Head's affective hyperaesthesia for a certain period during recovery, whereas Trotter and Davies did not. The latter found continuous recovery as regards the two-point threshold, just as in the other functions that were investigated; but Boring found the same threshold unimpaired throughout! It is clear that these somewhat heroic experiments in human nerve division will have to continue, with more careful standardization of procedure, before we can be clear as to the meaning of the differences or the precise nature of any distinction that we may legitimately draw between the protopathic and the epicritic systems.

Further discoveries made during our present period relate to the obscure sensations from the interior of the body. Both Cannon and Carlson, about 1915, found that the experience of hunger is connected with muscular contractions of the stomach. The latter investigator considers that appetite has a sensory foundation which is distinct from that of hunger, and quite recently, basing her considerations on a correlation of physiological and psychological findings, Hilda Weber has endeavoured to show that appetite involves a higher psycho-physical level than does hunger, the latter depending probably on the thalamus, the former on the cortex. The difference between appetite and hunger is also shown in the fact that hunger ceases almost as soon as food begins to be taken, whereas, as everyone knows, "*l'appétit vient en mangeant.*" All these experiences, however, are complex in nature, and one result of modern research has been the demonstration of the important rôle of conation in a great many states which arise from internal conditions and which at first sight might appear to be purely sensory in nature. Thus, according to an elaborate introspective study carried out by Boring, the whole experience that we ordinarily designate as hunger involves: (a) pain and pressure sensations from the stomach, throat and mouth; (b) the desire for food (perhaps with appropriate images), and (c) a more or less unconscious "drive" or determining tendency, urging us to get it. Very similar analyses have been made of such complex experiences as thirst, defaecation, urination, the "call to defaecation," the "call to urination," and so on. Indeed, the conative element in such cases may often dominate the situation. Summarizing his evidence withregard to one such complex state—nausea—Boring gives an almost painfully realistic description of the factors that enter into it: "dizziness, or swimming sensations from the head, the sensations aroused by too-free perspiration, aches and pressure pain complexes in the head, in the eyes, in the jaws, in the arms; general bodily shivers and chills, general weakness. Besides these factors, which sometimes constitute the most prominent part of nausea, there are sensations which are referred to the alimentary tract proper. Pressure complexes referred to the stomach or pressure waves localized in the oesophagus, indicating incipient vomiting, are often present." Here again, experimental psychologists have shown themselves heroic in their tolerance both of the disagreeable and of the ridiculous!

Considerable work has been done also on the sensations from the region of the joints, muscles and tendons, and our detailed knowledge concerning the ability to judge weights and movements has been greatly extended. This is true also of the sensations coming from the organ of equilibrium in the inner ear, investigation in this case being stimulated by the practical needs of aviation. One very general outcome of all these researches on organic and kinaesthetic sensibility has been to show that there are throughout this field only the same four ultimate qualities of sensation as are found upon the skin. Pressure, heat, cold and pain, in various combinations, seem to form the ultimate basis of all the experience we get of our inner bodily selves. Furthermore, as a result of this work, the ambiguous meaning of the word "pain" in the English language, has at last been made apparent (especially by Wohlgemuth). Pain, in the strict sense, refers to a sensory quality, which is usually, but not invariably, unpleasant. The feeling quality opposite to that of pleasure is quite a different thing and should obviously be distinguished by a different word. "Unpleasure" (corresponding to the German *Unlust*) is now becoming adopted for this purpose.

Comparatively little work has been done on taste, but Henning's researches have considerably increased our detailed knowledge concerning smell, and he has produced a new sixfold classification of smells (flowery, fruity, spicy, resinous, foul and burnt) which—because it permits of being expressed in a geometrical figure, indicating the relationship between the classes in much the same way as is done by the famous "colour pyramid" (to be found in most textbooks) in the case of vision—bids fair to oust the older one of Zwaardemaker.

In the case of both visual and auditory sensation, we have much detailed work and a fairly rich crop of speculation, but the great fundamental questions raised by the classical theories put forward in our second period still remain without a definite answer. The English translation of Helmholtz's *Handbuch der physiologischen Optik* in 1924 (already referred to) and a new (and posthumous) edition of Hering's *Lehre vom Lichtsinn* in 1920, together with some other special treatises and several more or less encyclopaedic sections on sense physiology in the larger handbooks of physiology, have, however, served to bring together and to systematize the later additions to our knowledge in this field.

In spite of much progress, the study of sensation has undoubtedly suffered from the diversion of psychological interest to new fields, without any compensatory awakening of interest on the part of physiologists. Sensation constitutes a natural borderland between psychology and physiology, and its adequate investigation would now seem to demand a specialist whose training and interests lie in both departments. Perhaps the ideal arrangement, for the present time, would be for a Reader in Psychophysics to serve as liaison officer between the Professors of Psychology and Physiology, with a laboratory of his own so situated that he can freely dispose of the resources, human and material, available to both his colleagues. It may well be that only in this way will this important branch of knowledge receive all the attention it deserves.

WE may complete this review of the modern period by a brief
reference to some of the main fields to which psychology has been
applied. We have already had occasion to mention, here and
there, some of the ways in which other disciplines or the needs
of practical life have stimulated psychology, and how this latter,
in return, has begun to contribute to the solution of urgent and
important problems in science and in life. What we can attempt
here is, no exhaustive exposition of the applications already
hinted at or of others not yet mentioned, but merely an indication
of the manner and extent of psychology's contribution to the
work of those whose main interests and endeavours lie outside
the study of mind for its own sake.

We may conveniently distinguish three main fields of application: (a) anthropology and sociology; (b) education and paedo-
logy; (c) industry. With regard to the first of these fields, we
have seen how, quite early in his career as a psychologist, Wundt
had expressed his belief that experimental psychology would
require supplementation by *Völkerpsychologie*, and how he himself endeavoured, in a long series of volumes in the last twenty
years of his life, to do for this branch of his subject what he had
already done for experimentation. This great work definitely
brought modern psychology into relation with cultural anthropology, to the advantage of both sciences; not that there is as yet
the intimate *rapprochement* between them that will be necessary
in order that they may derive the fullest possible benefit from
one another. But it is greatly to the credit of psychology that,
through two at least among its foremost workers, Wundt and
Freud, it has seen the necessity of mutual help and the great
possibilities of mutual profit.

Though perhaps less explicitly and directly, help towards a
rapprochement has also been forthcoming from the other side.
We have already referred to the general psychological orienta-

tion of Tylor's work, especially his *Primitive Culture*, in the nineteenth century. Tylor paved the way for Sir James Frazer, who, in a series of great treatises, *Totemism and Exogamy*, *The Golden Bough*, *The Folklore of the Old Testament*, *The Belief in Immortality*, etc., each of them in several volumes (no less than twelve in the last edition of *The Golden Bough*), gave to the world a vast wealth of material presented in a most attractive form. Frazer had the patience and enthusiasm of the collector, combined with an astonishing power of marshalling his facts and a rare literary charm. His weakness lay, perhaps, in a lack of theoretical insight wherewith to interpret his results, and a want of critical discrimination with regard to the relative value of the innumerable sources from which his data were collected. Criticism was soon forthcoming in plenty from the "diffusionist" school (whose chief spokesman has been W. J. Perry). This school, as already noted (p. 115), was enthusiastic about the origins and movements of culture rather than about its psychological basis or significance. It rightly insisted on the importance of history, tradition, culture-contact and migration, and has been pitiless in its attack on the somewhat uncritical assumption of the more "evolutionary" and psychologically minded anthropologists that similarities in belief or practice tend to spring from similarities in underlying mental function. In their concentration on historical factors, the diffusionists are, for the moment, inclined to see no value at all in the psychological approach, so that, as things stand, there is little community of thought between them and psychologists.

Meantime, while the diffusionists were making up for Frazer's want of critical caution in certain directions, a few psychological writers were beginning to make good use for their own purpose of the material collected by Tylor, Frazer and like-minded anthropologists. In 1920 Carveth Read (who, after retiring from the chair formerly held by Sully at University College, London, stayed on for some years there as Lecturer in Comparative Psychology), published a charming and insightful work on *The Origin of Man and his Superstitions* in which he dealt psychologically with the general conditions of belief in primitive minds, magic, animism, the mind of the wizard and other kindred subjects. Previous to this, King in his *Development of Religion* and Ames in his *Psychology of Religious Experience* (both books published in

1910) had given the psychological study of religion a new turn by emphasizing the social nature of religious phenomena, the latter author dealing particularly with the early phases of religion, a matter which was taken up also about the same time by Durkheim in his *Formes Élémentaires de la Vie Réligieuse* and Leuba in his *Psychological Basis of Religion.* All these works differ rather markedly from the psychological studies of religion in our second period, which were concerned chiefly with individual religious experience in our present-day societies. As regards primitive mind in general, Lévy-Bruhl was an influential writer, who, in his *Mentalité primitive,* argued in dualistic fashion for the existence of a "pre-logical" and mystical form of thought among primitive peoples.

The most stimulating of all applications of psychology to anthropology, however, has undoubtedly been Freud's *Totem and Taboo,* first published in article form in *Imago* in 1912. This work was essentially a comparison of neurotic mechanisms, as revealed by psycho-analysis, with certain savage institutions, such as exogamy, "avoidance," taboo, totemism and magic. Taboo, in general, he endeavoured to show, exhibits the double attitude of fear and desire, of hate and love, that is found in obsessions and phobias. A strong prohibition, whether imposed from outside by society, or from inside by the moral factors of the individual's own mentality, always implies a correlative desire to do what is forbidden. Kings, for instance, are taboo, because they are the objects of an intensely "ambivalent" attitude. They are loved and reverenced on the one hand, feared and hated on the other; and the taboos affecting kings and rulers, which among many societies are so embarrassingly numerous, aim ultimately, either at diminishing the king's power and thus reducing the fears aroused by him (fears that are themselves often the result of a "projection" of his subject's hate) or else at frustrating the hostile wishes of his subjects. Ceremonial, which surrounds the life of kings and plays a large part in religious practices, similarly corresponds to the compulsive acts of the obsessional neurotic. The magical beliefs implied in many aspects of taboo and other savage institutions correspond to the "omnipotence of thought" that distinguishes unconscious tendencies that are immune from testing by "real" standards—the phrase being one that Freud borrowed from an early patient, and the characteristic itself being a feature of all primitive thought both in the individual and the race. Applying these notions to totemism, Freud endeavours to explain the two great taboos of totemic society—those against eating the totem animal and those against endogamy—as corresponding to the two aspects of the Œdipus complex, the desire to kill the father and marry the mother. The totem feast itself (which involves a ceremonial slaying and eating of the totem animal) together with its countless derivatives in later forms of religion—including the communion service of the Christian Church—would thus appear to be rooted in the primitive ambivalent attitude of men towards their fathers.

The main contentions of *Totem and Taboo* have given rise to much discussion. Considered phantastic by many, they have by others (mostly themselves belonging to the psycho-analytic school) been made the starting-point of further anthropological and sociological interpretations, the work of Reik, Ernest Jones and Róheim deserving special mention here. The last-named is as much anthropologist as psycho-analyst, and after producing several large works distinguished alike by their erudition and their ingenuity (but also, alas, by their lack of clarity in exposition), was enabled to carry out "field work" in Somaliland, Australia, New Guinea and North America. A preliminary account of his work appeared in 1932 and seems to afford ample justification for his own plea for a psychological training of the field worker. Meanwhile the psycho-analytic standpoint has been adopted in some measure by other anthropologists, of eminence. Notably among these are Seligman, who, in an important series of papers has approached ever nearer to the outlook of psycho-analysis, and who recently, on the significant occasion of a Huxley Memorial Lecture, took the opportunity of urging the great importance of psychology to the anthropologist; and also Malinowski, who, in a remarkable series of books dealing with the Trobriand Islanders, has given a more consistently psychological treatment than any previous field worker, and who, in his *Sex and Repression in Primitive Society*, endeavoured to amend Freud's explanation of totemism so as to make it apply to peoples who trace descent through the mother. One of the most striking differences between patrilineal and matrilineal society from this point of view is that, in the latter, the ambivalent attitude towards the father, as described by Freud, tends often to be split up into two elements

—love being directed to the real father (who, in the society described by Malinowski, is apt to play the rôle of an indulgent older playmate, helper and companion), fear, hate and respect to the maternal uncle (in whom is vested the chief authority and responsibility for the child's upbringing). Compared both with the primitive totemic attitude and the father-regarding attitude found in present-day society, we have here a case of "decomposition," similar to that which (as Ernest Jones has shown in a very remarkable book *On the Nightmare*, published in 1931) occurred in theology when the all-powerful Jehovah, who combined in one person the supreme elements of good and evil, was eventually split up into *Le bon Dieu* on the one hand and the Devil on the other; or (as Eder has pointed out) to the parts played by the king and his ministers respectively in modern British politics— for, whereas the former is always right, the latter are held responsible for all evil that has happened during their term of office, and are, each in turn, deposed to make room for the "new blood" of a younger generation. In his *Sexual Life of Savages* (1929) Malinowski studied the effects of the freer infantile sexuality of the Trobrianders, a matter which was taken up from the more sociological point of view by Money-Kyrle in a little volume entitled *Aspasia*, in which he sought to find an escape from the pessimistic outlook adopted by Freud in one of his latest works, *Civilization and its Discontents*, a book in which much stress is laid on the repression of hate required in modern, and to some extent in all, society. For Freud, hate is here something primordial and irreducible. In rebellion against this view, Money-Kyrle (in other respects a follower of Freud) takes up the position more usually adopted by psychologists in affirming that hate is only aroused by the frustration of desires. Diminish frustration, therefore, and, according to this view, we shall diminish hate; and where can we diminish frustration more effectively than in the sphere of sex, particularly the early manifestations of sex, as regards which we are at present so intolerant?

This plea for a more "enlightened" and less repressive attitude to sex is only one of the latest examples of a long series of protests which have been made throughout the twentieth century. It represents a movement in which psychologists have played a leading part—not so much, of course, by propaganda, as by their claim to investigate the sexual life of man impartially and without reference to existing taboos. Pre-eminent among those who have exerted this influence are Freud himself, and Havelock Ellis, who in the seven volumes of his *Studies in the Psychology of Sex*—published between 1897 and 1928 and based on a vast collection of original material, together with an almost encyclopaedic knowledge of the relevant literature—broke up the "conspiracy of silence" that had so largely stifled discussion of this subject in the nineteenth century, and, together with Magnus Hirschfeld and other investigators, at last accorded it its rightful place in psychology and sociology. Meanwhile, Freud's treatment of totemism, combined with an increasing knowledge of this obscure stage of evolution from the anthropological side, drew attention also to the psychological significance of eating and nutrition—a matter which has been much illuminated by psychoanalytic observations on the "oral" stage of the libido, a stage at which both love and hate are expressed by activities connected with the mouth. The full sociological and anthropological application of these psycho-analytic findings has yet to be made, but a few preliminary studies have been attempted, both by psychoanalysts themselves, and quite recently by Audrey Richards, a pupil of Malinowski, who, in her *Hunger and Work in a Savage Tribe*, has endeavoured to deal systematically with nutrition as a factor in family and social life. Perhaps the most astonishing of all the discoveries of psycho-analysis, however, were those concerned with the rôle of sublimated "anal" interests in character formation and social institutions (e.g. money), discoveries which have been extended, brought together and evaluated in a classic paper by Ernest Jones. The ultimate possibilities of the application of all this new knowledge to sociology are difficult to foresee, but we can scarcely doubt that the result will be important.

We have already, in dealing with psycho-analysis, dwelt upon the sociological importance of the concept of the super-ego, and we need not return to the matter here. Suffice it to say that a realization of the primitive nature of the cruder forms of morality still dominant in many of our social attitudes and institutions is beginning to manifest itself in a number of spheres; notably, perhaps, in religion, where it is leading men to understand the elements of hate and fear which, owing to the human sense of guilt and "need for punishment," tend to be constantly brought back into religious beliefs after having been temporarily reduced by the efforts of some religious leader of finer sensibility; as regards Christianity, in particular, there is a growing amazement among cultured persons at the almost unfathomable abyss that separates the official attitude and doctrine of the Churches from the actual teaching of Christ. Furthermore, the whole status of theological beliefs, as based upon an apparently delusional process of "projection," has been brought into prominence by Freud's book bearing the challenging title, *The Future of an Illusion*, which appeared in 1927.

Another field in which the new knowledge concerning the psychological basis of morality is proving effective is that of criminology and penology. Alexander and Staub's book *Der Verbrecher und seine Richter*, translated under the title of *The Criminal, the Judge and the Public*, is perhaps the most important here, while, even as we write, Pailthorpe's *What we put in Prison*, the result of personal investigation among prisoners, is creating some very considerable stir. For many years there has indeed been a growing realization of the futility of much of our punitive procedure. The recent advances of psycho-analysis have, however, for the first time revealed to us some of the more important motives underlying this procedure, and thus prepared the way for a true psychological approach to the whole problem of crime and punishment.

With regard to social psychology in general, following McDougall's *Group Mind*, there has been a whole series of books dealing with this subject, either quite broadly, or with special emphasis on some particular aspect or division of social phenomena. It is impossible for us to name them all. As one of the most recent examples of a general treatise, we may mention Kimball Young's *Social Psychology*, intended for use in conjunction with the same author's *Source Book for Social Psychology*. As an example of the treatment of a special field, we may mention Pear's *Voice and Personality*, a book which takes into consideration the increased importance that speech has acquired through broadcasting. The same author, in a recent communication, has drawn an interesting comparison between the two series of social phenomena presented respectively by speech and clothing, the latter being a subject that has also been treated by the present writer in his *Psychology of Clothes*.

A feature of many of these newer works on social psychology is the growing importance of quantitative treatment; and this shows us that, slowly but surely, experimental methods are proving themselves applicable to the study of the group, as well as of the individual. True, the experimental and quantitative studies yet available are obviously crude, unsystematic and exposed to many sources of error. Nevertheless, the fact that social attitudes such as those involved in religious and political beliefs, race prejudice, degree of agreement or disagreement with social standards, moral views, and even moral practice, are actually being measured, and with some degree of success, shows that experimental psychology is likely to give birth before long to an experimental sociology. An exact science of human society, in which our changing standards in religion, ethics, politics, fashions and etiquette will be duly recorded in graphs for the instruction of ourselves and the edification of posterity, would seem to be assured in the not too distant future.

Furthermore, it seems likely that sociology will become increasingly linked to biology. Hitherto, animal psychology, especially in so far as it has dealt with the higher animals, has been principally occupied with the study of the individual animal —just as human psychology was at first concerned almost entirely with the individual man. There is obviously room for a social psychology and sociology of animals, which shall study animals, not as isolated units, but in relation to one another. One of the first steps in this direction has been taken quite recently by Zuckerman, who, in his *Social Life of Monkeys and Apes*, has observed the behaviour of primates from a new angle. Day by day for a long period he studied the inhabitants of Monkey Hill in the London Zoo and his results are of immense interest both to the psychologist and the anthropologist. They have shown, for instance, the existence of a patriarchal form of society among baboons, with a number of "overlords," each dominating his own family of females, children and "bachelor" males, in a way that is irresistibly suggestive of Freud's reconstruction of primitive society based upon his study of totemism and the Œdipus complex—a reconstruction that is itself founded on earlier specutions of Darwin and Atkinson. They have shown also the immense importance of sexual factors in infra-human primates, above all the existence of auto-erotism and homosexuality, the close connection between sexuality and aggression, and the exploitation of sexual attraction in a way that Zuckerman compares to prostitution. There is, further, the purely psychological question of the qualities underlying the dominance of the overlord, qualities which do not, it appears, by any means depend entirely upon mere physical strength. The answers to this and other similar problems may eventually carry us a long way towards a better understanding of the most fundamental urges operative in the foundation of groups in men and animals.

THE contacts of psychology with education during the twentieth century have been of two main kinds; in the first place along the lines of mental testing and experiment; in the second place along those of psycho-pathology, and especially of psycho-analysis—though these two branches of psychology have very profitably interacted and supported one another at certain points. We have already seen how mental tests arose out of the practical needs of education. As they grew more perfect and more varied, they have been applied to children on an ever-larger scale, so that in some places in America children are beginning to know their own "intelligence quotients" almost as a matter of routine. Apart from the measurement of whole school populations, itself of great general interest to both psychology and education, perhaps the greatest practical value of intelligence tests has been found to lie in the diagnosis of cases where a child appears unable to profit from the ordinary school curriculum. The application of a battery of tests in capable hands will, as a rule, show clearly how far the trouble lies in inadequate g, or how far it must be sought for rather in physical defect or functional disturbance. Much the same applies to the case of "difficult" or delinquent children who have given rise to anxiety on account of their general behaviour rather than merely on account of their educational backwardness.

Organized attempts to deal with all cases of these kinds have given rise to two developments of great importance: the appointment by educational authorities of official "psychologists," whose duty it is to investigate the children referred to them and to make appropriate recommendations; and the establishment of "child guidance clinics," where more protracted investigation and treatment can be given. England, a country that, so far as official attitude was concerned, had for many years been backward and unenterprising in psychological matters, has the credit of being the first to adopt the former method, when in 1913 Cyril Burt was

K   289

appointed Psychologist to the London County Council. The choice was an exceptionally happy one, and London's example was, after a time, followed by a number of other large cities in various countries.

Witmer had founded the first child clinic in Philadelphia as early as 1896, and it was long before other similar institutions were established on any considerable scale. In quite recent years, however, they have grown rapidly in number, and are usually run (those at least on the American model) with three co-ordinated departments, staffed by psychiatrists, psychologists and social workers respectively. It has become increasingly recognized that the most satisfactory way of approaching the problems of crime and of asocial behaviour generally is to deal with the potential criminal in the early stages of his development and to treat him, not by the old methods of vindictive punishment, but by the new methods of psychological understanding and the provision of alternative and socially more desirable outlets for his energies. The two most important workers in this field of juvenile delinquency have been Cyril Burt, whom we have already mentioned, and whose book on *The Young Delinquent* appeared in 1925, and William Healy, the Director of a Psychopathic Institute attached to the Juvenile Court of Chicago, who produced a series of books on crime, beginning with *The Individual Delinquent* in 1915. Through the labours of these and others in the same field, the psychological method of approach is rapidly displacing the older attitude of reliance upon legal codes or moral principles, so far as youthful crime is concerned—to the great advantage of both the offender and society. In correspondence with this change, special re-educative institutions are taking the place of the older prisons, penitentiaries and reformatories. By far the most interesting of such institutions have been the juvenile colonies, such as the George Junior Republic, near New York, and the Little Commonwealth, founded by Homer Lane, in Dorsetshire, England. The principles on which these latter are run are self-government and an entire absence of adult constraint. Something of the general nature of such colonies, the difficulties which they encounter, and the results which under favourable circumstances they can achieve, has become known to the public quite recently through the medium of the Russian film, "The Road to Life."

What applies to the delinquent holds good also of the "normal" child, and for these, too, there have grown up a number of "free schools" distinguished by a more or less complete abolition of the old principles of discipline and compulsion, and by the substitution of a régime of toleration for the old insistence upon morals and taboos.

The founders and directors of these schools have realized the existence of large elements of hate and sadism in the conventional scholastic traditions (which have in many cases, as it were, institutionalized the more savage aspects of the super-ego), and they have put into practice what seem to be the practical corollaries of recent psycho-analytic doctrine. The abandonment of discipline and compulsion (even to the extent of making attendance at all classes optional, as is done in the more advanced "free schools") implies a compensatory emphasis on interest. The older education, relying on coercion and the doctrine of formal training, and insisting on the performance of unpleasant tasks in order to cultivate the "will," usually held—implicitly, if not explicitly—that it does not matter what a child is taught, so long as he hates it. The newer education would rather take the view that only what arouses a child's interest can be satisfactorily and profitably taught—and that there cannot be much wrong so long as a child loves what he is learning. Modern education aims, therefore, at training *through* life rather than *for* life, and in so far as the educator may consider it necessary for the child to learn some things to which it does not appear spontaneously attracted, it is his business to make these things attractive to the child by linking them on to existing interests; and provided the linking process is successful, it does not matter perhaps, for our immediate purposes, whether we call it a "conditioned reflex" or a "sublimation." We must, however, according to the new doctrine at all costs avoid "conditioning" by fear—except perhaps in the few things in modern life as regards which fear is really justified and is not merely a reaction to the menace of authority. To the inevitable objection that children brought up in this way will be so unused to making efforts that they will be unable to endure the rigours of "the battle of life," the upholders of the new régime reply that those who are encouraged to develop their real interests will be, and as a matter of fact have shown themselves to be, quite capable of taking pains to overcome difficulties in the way of attaining ends that seem to them genuinely desirable—even if these difficulties take the form of human institutions or traditions that are in themselves admittedly unpleasant, e.g. examinations. It is rather, they maintain, insistence on the performance of uninteresting tasks which dries up the springs of intellectual energy and begets a sort of dull resentment that extends even to subjects which might otherwise prove quite attractive. As was only to be expected, the "free schools" have met with very considerable difficulties, both external and internal; external, because of the suspicion inevitably aroused by their complete departure from tradition and also because of an equally inevitable opposition on the part of the archaic moral conscience of the community, the conscience which demands punishment and repression as a normal part of education; internal, because under present conditions at any rate, they demand exceptional qualities in their directors and their staff. In England the leaders of the movement at the present moment are A. S. Neill and Bertrand and Dora Russell, all of them outstanding personalities. The experiments which they are carrying on are of the very greatest interest, not only to the educationist, but also to the psychologist and sociologist. If we were right in saying that the understanding of human morality that psycho-analysis has brought is, from the point of view of practical importance to culture, perhaps the most significant of all the achievements of psychology, then these attempts to experiment on the lines that this new knowledge has suggested are surely among the most interesting of all the applications of psychology that have so far been made.

Such free schools (the principles of which, as applied to very young children, are largely those of the growing number of "nursery schools") naturally afford the best opportunities for observing the spontaneous behaviour of young children. Such observation is playing an increasing part in child psychology, one of the most notable contributions to this subject being that of Susan Isaacs, who, in her *Intellectual Growth in Young Children*, has produced the first of a series of three volumes to be devoted to observations made at the Malting House School, Cambridge. Her results, so far as they are published, are full of value both on the educational side in the narrow sense (particular care was taken in this school to provide opportunities for the sublimation of primitive tendencies towards an interest in "scientific" directions) and as regards the natural development of modes of thought and conduct. In this latter field her results challenge comparison with those of Jean Piaget, who, in a series of books, beginning with *The Language and Thought of the Child*, published in 1923, reported experiments he had been making at the Institut J. J. Rousseau, founded at Geneva in 1912 for the purpose of scientific child study and the training of teachers. These experiments for the most part took the form of conversations with the child, so conducted as to bring out as far as possible the child's thoughts, beliefs, attitudes and imagination upon the particular matter under investigation. Following the first book mentioned above, successive volumes have dealt with the child's methods of judgment and reasoning, his notions of causality, his ideas of the external world, and (1932) his moral judgments. This work of Piaget's is perhaps the most important single line of research that has been carried out at Geneva, where, throughout the twentieth century, under the very able guidance, first of T. Flournoy and then of E. Claparède (who has himself made many notable contributions both to psychology and education), there has been cultivated a tradition of broad tolerance in psychological doctrine, with ready acceptance of new truths in all departments from whatever school or quarter they might come. As the result of his now very extensive experiments, Piaget believes that we can distinguish various stages in the development of the child's mind. The infant's thinking is "autistic" (a phrase borrowed from the psychiatrist, Bleuler), immersed in phantasy, having little or no contact with reality, and being entirely at the service of immediate desire. Then follows a long phase of "ego-centrism," during which the child has an implicit belief in his own ideas and experiences little or no need of proof. At this stage, his ideas of causality are predominantly animistic, especially with regard to moving objects or forces (the sun, the moon, the clouds, the wind, etc.), while his language serves the purpose of self-expression rather than communication, so that children's conversation takes the form of "collective monologues," in which they pay little attention to each other, and enjoy no real exchange of ideas. This stage lasts till about the age of seven or eight, only after which does real social behaviour begin. Piaget's methods and conclusions have both been severely criticized by Susan Isaacs and others, and from the evidence available it now appears pretty certain that his stages cannot be taken as indicating the way in which the child's mind at a certain age invariably works. At all ages we get phantasy and realism, animism, magic and physical causality, monologues and communicative speech, intermingled in such a way that it requires close observation and analysis to detect the transitions from one form to another— transitions which are both rapid and frequent, and which may, of course, be in either direction. Nevertheless, Piaget has very materially advanced our knowledge of child mentality by drawing attention to certain general tendencies which may predominate at certain ages. From the point of view of comparative psychology, moreover, his formulations have the advantage that they bring into prominence certain general features of primitive mentality, as manifested in the immature mind, the deranged mind and the mind of the savage.

In dealing with mental tests, we have already indicated how the "statics" of the correlation method need to be supplemented by the corresponding "dynamics" of functional experiments. These dynamics are of especial importance in education (as also to some extent in industry). We have seen how experiments on the "transfer of training" have shattered one great educational delusion—a delusion that was itself a consequence of the false doctrine of faculties. By way of compensation, however, educational psychology has provided much that is of use to the teacher, not only as regards general knowledge of the child mind and general principles of method, but also matters dealing with detailed testing and instruction in the ordinary subjects of school study. We have already mentioned the "educational tests" that were developed on the pattern of "mental tests." With the aid of such tests it is now possible for the teacher in many countries to compare his pupils' attainments with those of large samples of the child population of similar age in such subjects as reading, writing, spelling, drawing and arithmetic. Further, there has been a good deal of valuable experimental work on the best methods of learning and teaching different subjects. Some of this we have referred to in dealing with experiments on memory and on *Gestalt*. In general it would seem that the doctrine of associationism, with its emphasis on unit "ideas," has led to an exaggeratedly "atomistic" approach to many problems of learning, and the general tendency in modern education has been to attack these problems in ever-larger wholes. Experimental studies of reading in which the eye movements of the reader were recorded photographically have, for instance, shown that in learning to read it is advantageous in many ways to use even from the start larger units consisting of words and sentences, rather than the elementary units corresponding to the letters of the alphabet. Similarly, in writing, it has been possible to arrange a series of exercises which develop proper habits of *fluent* movement from the very beginning. In these and other ways psychology has, throughout our last period, been making invaluable contributions to the detailed routine of the classroom.

THE problems of *work*, including those of *practice* and *fatigue*, are to some extent common to education and industry. From the pioneer researches of Kraepelin onwards, there has been a long series of studies dealing with work in all its aspects—with various kinds of *tasks* carried out under various *conditions* by different kinds of *subjects*. Some of these researches have been on a heroic scale, such as that of Arai, who, for days in succession, multiplied mentally one four-place number by another four-place number for twelve hours on end. Others, such as those of Phillips, Entwistle and the present writer have involved a relatively short experiment carried out by fairly numerous subjects for many days in succession. Still others have aimed at determining the influence of rest pauses, of the effect of varying the total length of the working day, and similar problems of importance to industry. In general, it has been shown that, as regards the effect of practice, the "curve of learning" rises sharply to begin with, and thereafter grows gradually flatter until the "limit of practice" has been attained. It is very clear, however, that the strength of the incentives in operation has an immense influence, both upon the steepness with which the curve rises, and upon the ultimate height attained—at any rate with simple kinds of work in which speed is an important factor (cp. p. 178). With relatively dull tasks, such as simple arithmetic, quite astonishingly good performances have been recorded by whole classes of school-children, when sufficiently powerful incentives have been offered. Rest pauses are nearly always beneficial, though their "spacing" and length in relation to the nature of the work and the duration of the work periods are matters that must be carefully studied if the full advantage from them is to be obtained. The question whether fatiguability is a general factor is one that has proved very difficult to answer. So far as the present evidence goes, a change of task usually involves some, but by no means a complete, "transfer" of fatigue-effect, so that it seems likely that fatigue is both "general" and "specific." Subjective fatigue appears to be for the most part a matter of failing interest, i.e., of conation, rather than a diminution of ability, and it is certain that in an emergency we can usually call upon very great reserves of energy, though at the cost of requiring a relatively long subsequent period of recuperation. With regard to the "curve of fatigue" itself, it would seem that, when other factors are kept constant, there is a rapid initial drop in output during the first minute or so, and that thereafter output declines very slowly in the form of a straight line, with an eventual sudden breakdown if work is continued long enough (which as a rule only occurs in experiments of the "heroic" kind). To use an analogy of Spearman's, human output thus resembles the output from an electric battery, when this is continuously and slowly discharged. The human curve, however, is complicated in any given instance by minor fluctuations—the result of o—which may have something in common with the "fluctuations of attention" studied by the early investigators in Wundt's laboratory. A recent very detailed study of the work curve by Philpott seems to show, however, that these fluctuations follow a geometrical rather than, as had previously been assumed, an arithmetical progression. As regards hours of work, it has been found that a very long working day tends to defeat its object—even from the limited point of view of immediate output. During the Great War, for instance, in which there were in many cases exceptional incentives to hard work, a ten-hour day often produced a higher daily output than a twelve-hour one.

It was indeed the war, with its demand for an unusually high output, that brought these problems into prominence, and thereby gave birth to the new applied science of Industrial Psychology, though the possibilities of such a science had already been foreseen, notably by Münsterberg in his *Psychology and Industrial Efficiency*, published in 1913. In spite of much inevitable opposition from the conservatism of both employers and employed, this new branch of psychology has made considerable headway in several countries, including the United States, Australia, Germany and England. In England, indeed, it is more systematically organized than elsewhere, for in this country there exist at the present moment two well-established institutions for the undertaking and co-ordination of research, i.e. the Industrial Health Research Board (formerly the Industrial Fatigue Research Board), a government body, and the National Institute of Industrial Psychology, a privately supported organization, founded in 1920 by C. S. Myers, formerly director of the psychological laboratory at Cambridge.

As now developed, industrial psychology comprises two great groups of problems, dealing respectively with the work itself and with the workers—though the two naturally have the closest relations to one another. Problems connected with the work arose partly, as we have just indicated, out of the industrial situation created by the war, partly out of certain researches carried out by Taylor and Gilbreth in America, who studied the movements involved in certain "repetitive" industrial operations. Comparing skilled with unskilled workers in these operations, these investigators showed that the former carried out the work with much greater economy of movement than the latter, who always indulged in unnecessary and ill-adapted movements, which hindered the efficiency and speed of their performance.

From this beginning, the investigations spread to the general arrangement and lay-out of the work, with a view to economy of effort in the running of the factory as a whole.

Although many of these pioneer studies enjoyed some real success, the earlier investigators, as is now pretty generally admitted, took a too crudely mechanistic view of their problems, stressed the factor of output too exclusively, and thus antagonized many of the workers, who looked upon the new methods merely as devices of their employers to get more work done at less cost to themselves. With the advent to this field of more capable all-round psychologists, who were able to envisage each individual problem as part of a larger whole, including the individual peculiarities of all the persons involved, the more "human aspects" of the industrial processes began to receive due attention. It was recognized that the earlier workers were perfectly right in stressing the superiority of some methods over others—there are many definitely inefficient and tiring ways of doing any given task— but that, on the other hand, it is rash to say that there is any one "best" way of doing this task; it is here that individual idiosyncrasies have to be allowed for, since equally skilled workers will, within limits, carry out the necessary movements in different ways, just as there is a characteristic stroke production in the case of every good golfer or cricketer, though all will avoid the more obvious faults of the beginner. With this very necessary allowance for individuality, and with the extension of research to deal with questions of heating, lighting, ventilation, seating, and other matters which have a very obvious bearing on the workers' comfort, the suspicions of the latter (which in some countries had never been very serious) were overcome, while at the same time the more efficient and economical working of the whole factory brought satisfaction to the employers.

The second group of problems, those concerning the workers rather than the work, falls into two chief sub-groups, which have come to be called vocational guidance and vocational selection respectively. Of these we have already spoken, and little need be added here. In this field, too, some serious mistakes were committed in the early stages, this time due (once again) to the influence of faculty psychology, which made it appear possible to measure a person's memory, dexterity, etc., by means of tests which had little in common with the actual processes involving "memory" or "dexterity" that the person would be called upon to do in the actual work for which his suitability was being tested. It is now becoming recognized that (owing to the high specificity of s and the absence of "faculties" of memory, dexterity, etc.) a vocational test, if it is to be of any high diagnostic value, must resemble very closely the actual conditions of the work—indeed, in many cases, the only modifications that can be permissibly introduced are such as may be absolutely necessary for obtaining a quantitative measure of the person's ability in a short time. The devising of reliable, and at the same time reasonably convenient tests, is therefore by no means an easy matter. Records of the person's past life and achievements (scholastic or otherwise) may, of course, be of great use in the absence of suitable tests, or to supplement them. The relation of a person's g to his proposed occupation is also of importance. To undertake work for which one is unfitted by reason of inadequate g is to court failure and disappointment, while for a person of superior intellect to devote himself to work of a mechanical order is not only economically wasteful, but is liable to produce boredom and discontent in the person himself. Qualities of temperament and character have naturally also to be taken into account. In particular it has been shown, especially through the work of Millais, Culpin and May Smith, that certain forms of work (e.g. telegraphy and coal-mining) are particularly trying to those inclined to suffer from neurosis, and indeed some "occupational diseases" (such as tele-graphist's cramp and miner's nystagmus) have been proved to have a neurotic basis. Ultimately, perhaps, with a greater under-standing of the processes of "sublimation" as revealed by psycho-analysis, and the development of more convenient methods of diagnosing the principal lines of sublimation, it may be possible to fit work and worker together with much greater assurance and accuracy than is possible at present. Meanwhile the field over which existing methods of investigation can be applied is con-stantly extending. As illustrating some of the outlying quarters of this field we may refer to the psychological studies carried out by Slocombe and others in America on the causation and pre-vention of accidents with tramcars and other motor vehicles, and also to the fact that in 1932 there was formed in England a Theatre Research Committee for the study of the many psycho-logical problems involved in the practice of dramatic art.

In recent years particular importance has been attached on the vocational selection side to the choice of leaders, superin-tendents and overseers. Persons in a position of authority must, of course, have a good knowledge of the processes that they are to supervise. But that is not enough; they must also have the ability to deal with men, so as to get the work done efficiently but with the minimum of discontent or friction; they must, therefore, have good "psychological" abilities, combined with sympathy, humanity and justice. Above all they must avoid nagging and anything in the nature of obsessive insistence upon unessential details. It seems likely that this new interest in the qualities of leadership in industry may ultimately prove of great value, both in the diagnosis of these qualities in other spheres (thus making an important contribution to social psychology), and in forcing psychologists to face the problems of "psychological" ability itself—a problem which, perhaps because it concerned themselves too nearly, they have, strange as it may appear, very much neglected.

XVI. THE POSITION OF PSYCHOLOGY IN 1933

THE history of our last period is now completed—and with it our whole story. It is clear that, though it is still only at the beginning of its labours, psychology has now, at the end of the first third of the twentieth century—very definitely arrived. It has made for itself a place, though still a humble one, in the hierarchy of sciences. It has a few really oustanding achievements to its credit and, apart from these, it has made some degree of progress over a wide front. Most important of all perhaps, it has succeeded in introducing the psychological point of view into the consideration of many questions—both practical and theoretical—which had never been contemplated from this point of view before. We have seen in our last chapters some of the consequences that followed the adoption of the new standpoint in sociology, in education and in industry—consequences that are obviously of the greatest importance for human efficiency and happiness. The political, theological, ethical or economic points of view have for too long enjoyed exclusive rights in these fields; it is becoming more and more evident that they are in urgent need of supplementation by psychology. If psychology is the science of human behaviour, then it must surely be consulted in all problems in which human behaviour is an important factor of the total situation. And when it is consulted, we usually find that it has valuable advice to give —advice which in the last resort may well be essential to the progress or (as we may perhaps add in view of the present crisis) even the continuance of our present civilization. Physical science has played its part in giving men a new and hitherto undreamed-of power over their environment. It is now the part of psychological science to see that they use this power for mutually beneficient, rather than for mutually destructive, ends. Intolerance, fear, hatred, cruelty, misunderstanding, the results of which have so disfigured human history in the past, are likely to have even more terrible consequences in the future, now that science has

301

put extremely dangerous weapons in man's hands, without at the same time teaching him how best to use them. Only psychology can perform this latter task. If it is true, as the old adage says, that *tout comprendre, c'est tout pardonner*, then we may reasonably hope that an increased general understanding of the workings of the human mind will really produce some increased measure of human kindness, toleration and co-operation, which may prevent that collapse of civilization with which, according to many authorities, we are genuinely threatened.

But such considerations, while they show the great importance of the task that psychology seems called on to perform, reveal all the more effectually the present inadequacy of psychology in the face of this task. Psychology has made great progress during the hundred years of our review, and particularly during the last thirty; but, as we said at the beginning, it is still infantile, still relatively unco-ordinated. To a pessimistic observer it might even seem that psychology is still utterly uncertain of its own true nature, mission and foundation. Of the various schools into which so much of psychology is now divided, each talks a language of its own; and most of them have relatively little interest in, or understanding of, the work of other schools; they are inclined to be sceptical of the value of any approach other than their own, and, therefore, but little disposed to seek a way of linking up their own terminology, viewpoint or discoveries with those of sister schools. Substituting schools for nations, it might appear that the state of our science mirrors the present political condition of the world, where a multitude of independent states are endeavouring—without much success—to solve their own problems by themselves, when all the time it is plain that these problems can only be solved by means of inter-state co-operation. Similarly, it may be that the problems of psychology can in many cases only be dealt with satisfactorily by means of a pooling of resources and a greater measure of co-operation between schools. There is room for planning in science, as well as in industry, and it may be that the history of the next "period" of thirty or forty years, when it comes to be written, will be largely occupied with efforts at consolidating the positions already won and at attempts at further systematic advance on a united front. Clearly enough, much valuable information has been won by the labours of the modern schools. But it is equally clear that the full advantage of their achievements can only be enjoyed when their detailed discoveries have been linked up in some more comprehensive system. There can be little doubt that each school has developed certain important aspects of psychological truth; but, if this is so, it follows that no one school possesses the sole key to truth. Each is justified, in so far as its outlook and method prove of value, but none is justified in assuming that its own approach is the only profitable one, and that only its own results have any considerable importance.

Now it is quite probable that schools are essential to real progress in psychology at the present stage of its development. The existing schools have shown conclusively that the phenomena that are commonly held to be the subject-matter of psychology can be approached by various roads, and there is good reason why we should endeavour to explore every road to the full. Indeed, we should be amply grateful to the pioneers who have opened up these roads. But we should regard these pioneers and their immediate followers as specialists engaged on trying out new weapons, which, if successful, will become part of the permanent armoury and equipment of the science. The great body of workers should be prepared to avail themselves of any of these weapons which seem to be appropriate for attack on the particular problems on which they are engaged. There should be many of them, too, whose chief business it is to link up the achievements of the different schools by a co-operative research on the same problems by the various methods distinctive of these schools, so that we may discover how far the ground conquered by them is in reality the same (and only appears different because looked at from another angle), and what is the nature of the intervening territory when it proves to be distinct. In this way there may come into being one "psychology" with many methods, in place of the several "psychologies" that exist today.

Some few attempts in this direction are already being made; for instance, in the research now being started by the American Council of Education to which we have already referred (p. 273), psychologists of many different schools were consulted as to possible "factors" that could profitably be studied by the method of tests, estimates and correlations; but so unused were many of these psychologists to thinking in terms of the "unit factors" that it was proposed to investigate, that in many cases the suggestions sent in were not so very helpful. Here the want of common thought and vocabulary has shown itself a barrier to full co-operation. There are, however, taking place a few systematic attempts to see how far the discoveries made by one school and usually described in the terminology of that school can be looked at from the point of view and described in the terminology of another school. Thus, of all the schools, those of psycho-analysis and behaviourism are perhaps in many respects the farthest apart; and yet, in a very original recent book, *The Development of the Sexual Impulses*, Money-Kyrle (himself a follower of the former school) has, with some very considerable degree of success, described the most essential discoveries of psycho-analysis in a way that seems to fit in well with the behaviouristic outlook and in a terminology to which no behaviourist could reasonably object.

Large international congresses serve also as a means whereby psychologists working along different lines can make sympathetic contact. Of such congresses there have been ten in all, the first in Paris in 1889, the last in Copenhagen in 1932; and Claparède, with his broad views and interests (and with his own laboratory very suitably located in Geneva!), is admirably qualified for the post of permanent secretary of these congresses, which he occupies. There have been frequent smaller reunions also, such as those of the *Gesellschaft für experimentelle Psychologie* in Germany and the American Psychological Association in the United States. These congresses have established various committees for co-ordination or standardization on certain special points. But it looks as though the time were rapidly approaching when a much bigger effort in this direction may be needed.

On the literary side America has realized the need for summaries and indices which will help the individual worker to discover the publications on his own special subject that are appearing in the now very large and scattered literature (there are, apart from books, about one hundred current serial or periodical publications devoted to psychology). The *Psychological Index* of current literature has appeared in connection with the *Psychological Review* since 1895 (while the *Zeitschrift für Psychologie* has published a somewhat similar index). The *Psychological Bulletin*, first published in 1904, has provided useful summaries, reviews and abstracts. Most valuable of all at present are the

Psychological Abstracts, published by the American Psychological Association (since 1927), which provide systematic summarized accounts of all the literature of importance—an achievement of which American psychologists may well be proud. This same press has also in the last few years incurred the debt of psychologists by issuing (under the able editorship of C. Murchison) a whole series of volumes, each presenting under one cover an extremely useful conspectus of the work and standpoint of different schools, the present status of our knowledge on certain given subjects, or the study of such subjects by a variety of methods. Among such volumes have been *Psychologies of 1925, Psychologies of 1930, Feelings and Emotions* (a symposium on this subject by a large number of eminent psychologists who were invited to attend a gathering to commemorate the opening of a new laboratory at Wittenberg), *Foundations of Experimental Psychology, Foundations of Child Psychology.* Most impressive of all, perhaps, is the *Psychological Register,* which is ultimately intended to provide an account of all important psychologists from Socrates onwards, and the most recently issued volume of which contains the names of about 2,400 living or quite recently living writers, all of whom have been "passed" by some specially appointed representatives for their own country as of sufficient importance to be included in this list of those who are seriously engaged in building up the science at the present day. A rough calculation shows that these psychologists between them have (including translations) contributed over 40,000 separate books and articles. Psychology may be inadequate when compared to the demands that we should like to make upon it, it may still be uncertain about its own nature and the proper lines of its development, but there can no longer be any doubt as to its existence as an important branch of knowledge that is growing rapidly and that (granted the continuance of our present civilization) is in all likelihood destined to exert a profound influence on the future of our race.

PART V

DEVELOPMENTS, 1933–1963

THE last three decades have seen a bewildering proliferation of psychological studies. The sheer quantity of published work makes it impossible to treat recent developments in the same detail as those of the preceding hundred years. That invaluable periodical, *Psychological Abstracts* (published by the American Psychological Association) now includes some ten thousand items annually, taken from over five hundred different periodicals, and grouped into sections as varied as psychosomatics, cultural relations and mental deficiency. Within the compass of this supplementary section, one can do no more than list some outstanding trends and refer to a few researches chosen almost haphazard according to one's particular interests, prejudices and limitations.

In some respects, such as the application of Freudian ideas to the practice of child guidance and social work, research has continued along traditional lines and progress has come through the broadening of established concepts. In other areas, notably in physiological psychology, developments in related sciences, such as cybernetics, electro-encephalography and psycho-pharmacology, have led to entirely new fields of research, each with their own methods, theories and technical language. At the same time the use of the psychological approach has spread to almost every field of human endeavour so that the modern psychologist may find himself concerned with matters as diverse as racial prejudice, the effects of sensory deprivation on astronauts, the unconscious associations of advertising material, the allocation of criminals to different penal establishments, or the respective merits of teaching reading with letters or whole words.

No single individual can keep abreast of all this. Inevitably, specialists in a particular area have difficulty in following psychological researches concerned with matters far removed from their own experience. A clinical psychologist, expert in exploring patients' emotional problems by means of projection tests, will often remain unaware of the latest discoveries in cerebral physiology or animal ethology. Those trained in methods of social or clinical research often find the mathematical and engineering approach of cybernetics beyond their comprehension, and equally those at home in the physiology laboratory may find the languages of psycho-pathology or factor analysis utterly foreign. Nevertheless, research in all these fields utilises the same standards of objective observation and pursues the same goal of systematic, scientific elucidation, so that despite the unavoidable fragmentation of work one hopes that some unifying theoretical syntheses will emerge. Those who manage to preserve contacts with more than one field of research can already point to some successes in this direction. To give but one example, the zoologist W. H. Thorpe (1961) and the psychiatrist Russell Davis (1957) have pointed out the relevance of concepts of "imprinting" and critical periods of learning in animals to questions of education and personality development in humans.

The period at present under review includes the years of turmoil associated with the Second World War, when the activities of many scientists in the chief belligerent nations became concerned with war effort, and psychologists began to apply their skills to the resolution of urgent practical problems created by the upheaval. The mobilization of the civilian population into a highly mechanized fighting force involved tasks of personnel selection and allocation of unprecedented magnitude. Psychologists were required to test the aptitudes and determine the suitability of potential recruits for all classes of duty, from fighter pilots to cooks. The urgency of the situation demanded selection methods of maximum objectivity and efficiency, regardless of tradition, sentiment and social prejudice. In this crisis the pragmatic, experimental approach of American and British psychologists proved more successful than the subjective interview methods employed by the Germans.

From the experiences gained in wartime the techniques of vocational guidance made great strides forward. The testing process applied to officers and men involved not only tests of intelligence (often of a non-verbal kind) but also attempts to measure a very considerable variety of special aptitudes and skills, some of which proved of great importance for particular jobs in a war demanding greater specialization and training than ever before. In general it was found that tests involving processes as nearly as possible resembling those of the actual work required were preferable to tests based on the measurement of any elementary processes that appeared (*a priori* or on superficial analysis) to be involved in the job. The procedure thus tended to become at once more holistic and more realistic—as for instance when air pilots were tested in an apparatus that reproduced all the chief characteristics of a cockpit in a moving aeroplane. Recent engineering developments, for instance the advent of space travel, and of new methods of deep sea exploration, require tests of reactions to gravity changes, sensory isolation and other unfamiliar stresses in which the duplication of realistic conditions become evermore essential. As regards the psychology of work and work curves, interest has centred more on factories and workshops than on the laboratory, but some studies of a more theoretical kind have been made, some of which have great interest. Studies connected with "levels of aspiration," which differ according to personality, and studies of the relative effects of immediate and remote incentives, deserve special note (Mace, 1935; Himmelweit, 1947). Study of work groups, of the phenomena of leadership (especially as applied to the organization of management and the supervision of workers), and of the influence of social structure in industry represent fields of research in which sociological and psychological concepts come together (Klein, 1956; Burns, 1960). Concern with the limits within which the individual can function efficiently, and the range of his particular skills, has given rise to a branch of applied psychology sometimes colourfully referred to as human engineering (McCormick, 1957). Industrial and military tasks are subjected to detailed analysis in terms of the human reactions required, such as the speed and degree of co-ordination of movement needed to control a new machine, or the accuracy of sensory discrimination called for in some checking operation, or the length of time a given task may be carried on before fatigue renders performance inadequate. On the basis of this kind of knowledge, mechanical adjustments will often bring tasks within the capacity of a larger number of operatives.

Work on the assessment and analysis of individual abilities and characteristics, on the lines inaugurated by Spearman, has been vigorously carried on both during and since the war, but the view that all abilities can be accounted for in terms of a unitary and constant general intelligence "g," and a few specific factors "s," has had to be increasingly modified. While general intelligence retains its supreme usefulness as a practical measure for educational and other purposes, broad or "group" factors of the kind indicated on page 271 have been shown to be of great significance. It is now well recognized that tests measure the level of individual functioning in a variety of respects at a given time, so that persons may vary considerably in their abilities in verbal, arithmetical or manipulative tasks and still—by doing badly on different items—produce the same I.Q. score on a standard battery of tests. Furthermore, studies in which the same persons have been re-rested after long intervals reveal a surprising inconstancy of results. Thus, Honzig and others (1948) showed that a prediction of adult I.Q. based on tests given at six years of age would be wrong to the extent of 20 I.Q. points for one in three children by the age of eighteen.

Developments in this field have taken two main directions. The first is methodological—the discussion and application of various statistical procedures for discovering factors and for dealing generally with the interrelations between measurable human powers. This branch of study, now generally known as factor analysis, has produced an extensive literature, among which the works of Burt (1940) in England and Thurstone (1944) in America are worthy of special mention. The study has proved a highly complicated and controversial one, owing to the very real technical difficulties involved, but the problem of the nature and interrelationships of abilities (corresponding as it does to the age-old and ever-recurrent question of "faculties") cannot be shelved merely because it is difficult. Although the progress made by the factor analysts has sometimes seemed slow the methods they have developed (out of techniques first applied to agricultural research) have already proved of value in other sciences, especially in sociology, so that in this connection psychology, becomes a giver rather than a borrower, as has usually been the case.

The second direction of development, referred to above, lies in the attempt to devise tests of the orectic qualities of man (the affective and conative tendencies that enter into his character and temperament, as distinct from his cognitive abilities.

Inspection of the *Mental Measurements Yearbook*, or the 1961 edition of Anastasi's *Psychological Testing*, shows how remarkably techniques of mental testing have multiplied since the war. In addition to a greatly increased choice of tests of ability, aptitude and achievement, the most noteworthy development has been the extension of testing methods, including the factor analysis approach, to the identification and measurement of personality traits and social attitudes (Cattell, 1957). One of the boldest exponents of this approach, H. J. Eysenck (1953), who lays great stress on the importance of replacing intuitive assessments by objective measures, claims to have isolated three fundamental dimensions along which human personalities vary. Mapping an individual's position on each dimension, using relatively simple tests, serves to predict his likely reactions to all kinds of situations. One of Eysenck's dimensions, extraversion–introversion, corresponds closely to Jung's typology of that name, and might be regarded as some vindication of Jung's intuitions, although Eysenck himself would regard the correspondence as largely fortuitous.

Eysenck's earlier explorations of personality took the form of questionnaires devised to explore feelings of anxiety, inferiority, and so forth which clinical observation had suggested as being of special importance. Factor analysis of the responses of large numbers of subjects revealed unexpected constellations of correlated replies whereby one group of persons might be distinguished from another independently of any other considerations. The questionnaires thus began to assume a life of their own so that traits and types came to be defined exclusively in terms of test results. A cluster of responses collectively suggesting a cautious, reflective, sensitive, somewhat inhibited person whose phantasy life seemed richer than his overt behaviour, defined the trait of introversion. Conversely, another cluster of responses, defining a different group of individuals and suggesting a cheerful, matter-of-fact character, adapting himself instinctively without need for thought, represented the trait of extraversion. Eysenck's system differs from the older typological classifications in that it describes a continuous dimension, the classic examples of extravert and introvert appearing at the opposite poles of

variation, but with the majority of individuals ranged in intermediate positions.

Evidence produced by Eysenck and his school shows not only
that individuals vary in temperament along the well-recognized
continuum of extraversion–introversion, but that this variable
correlates with an unexpectedly large number of other qualities.
For example, borrowing a term of William James, extraverts are
prone to tough-mindedness, and tend to hold their opinions
staunchly and to advocate action. Thus, if conservatively inclined, they are likely to support flogging and the death penalty,
to agree with race and class barriers, and to be enthusiastic pat-
riots and nationalists. Tender-minded characters on the other
hand are less aggressive and generally more thoughtful and
restrained by moral and community considerations. Thus, if
they have left-wing affiliations, they are likely to support demo-
cratically regulated reforms, to believe in world government,
pacifism and similar idealistic policies (Eysenck, 1954). If the
introvert has a neurotic breakdown he more often becomes over-
anxious or phobic, whereas the extravert more often develops
hysteria (pseudo-physical symptoms) or disordered behaviour
(psychopathy) accompanied by attitudes of emotional unconcern.
Introversion also correlates to some extent with asthenic
physique as well as with measures of a semi-physiological kind,
such as biochemical stress reactions, sedation threshold, respon-
siveness to Pavlovian conditioning, speed/accuracy ratio in performance tests, and perceptual habits. In addition to opening up new
approaches to the study of the bodily correlates of mental phenomena, these relationships provide methods of exploring personality
that do not depend upon subjects answering questions truthfully.

Over the years, questionnaire methods have become increasingly sophisticated, incorporating items to which the "correct"
response is far from obvious, as well as items intended to test
truthfulness and consistency and items aimed at matters beyond
the ostensible verbal content of the question. Psychologists emphasize that it is the pattern of responses and not what the subject
says which furnishes the test result. To give a crude example, one
American questionnaire purporting to deal with medical matters
asks about all sorts of symptoms. A high percentage of affirma-
tions tells nothing about the subject's physical condition but does
provide an index of neurotic tendency.

In spite of refinements in the questionnaire methods, non-verbal tests have obvious advantages. Projection tests of personality make use of productions over which the subject exerts less deliberate control than speech, such as expressive movements, handwriting and drawing styles, the composition of a fictional story, or Jung's word associations. In the most famous of these methods, Rorschach's ink blot test, first devised in 1921, the subject is shown a standard sequence of cards bearing irregular blots and is asked to say what he "sees" in them, rather as one might play at seeing pictures in glowing coals. Rorschach found by experience that different personality types, and patients suffering from different forms of psychological disorder, gave characteristically distinct associations. Such measures as productivity (number of associations volunteered), location (whether associations based on the whole shape or on small segments), popularity (whether associations common place or unusual) and determinants of response (i.e. whether the subject reacts most to the shapes, colours or textures) are supposed to correlate with personality variables like introversion and neurotic tendency. Unfortunately in the course of time Rorschach technique has acquired a somewhat unhealthy mystique. with a large and conflicting literature of over 2,000 published articles, and various rival systems of expert interpretation. A number of investigators claim to have demonstrated that when Rorschach responses are interpreted blindly, without knowledge of the subject's personal history, the results show no valid relationship to clinical diagnosis or to other methods of personality assessment.

Simpler projective techniques, with responses less liable to influence from the tester and susceptible to more objective methods of scoring, have been derived from recent work on perception (Gibson, 1950; Vernon, 1962). Experiments have revealed a relation between perceptual responses and motivations and emotions. One of the earliest observations in this connection concerned the tendency of hungry subjects to interpret blurred pictures as representing items of food. Later workers have sought to identify certain relatively fixed perceptual peculiarities and to relate these to personality traits (Thurstone, 1944). For instance, in some investigations extraverted individuals showed greater size constancy, that is, they compensated better for the diminishing effects of distance, than did introverts. In other investigations, neurotic individuals showed a relative intolerance of perceptual ambiguity, and had difficulty in perceiving the shifting appearance of drawings which might be interpreted in more than one form of Gestalt. In experiments in which they were allowed momentary glimpses of a word exposed in a tachistoscope, neurotics showed a tendency to adhere to their inaccurate initial perceptions when subsequent exposures should have enabled them to correct themselves. Examples of tests based on these perceptual phenomena include tests of flicker fusion level (the speed required for a flickering light to appear constant) and speed of closure (time taken to perceive the total figure in an incomplete picture).

Particularly interesting from a theoretical viewpoint are the correlations discovered between physical measures and personality traits. An early example of the kind, the Porteus Maze Test, introduced in 1914, consisted of printed mazes of graded difficulty which the subject was required to trace through with a pencil. Although in the first instance this was intended as a test of intelligence, Porteus found that the way subjects tackled the task, the sort of movements they made (psychomotor style) provided clues to personality. Individuals who made bold, swift movements executed with a careless disregard of instructions not to touch edges or cut corners, were found with special frequency among groups of psychopaths and delinquents. In view of Kretchmer's work on correlations between physique and temperament, one might expect to find some connection between body build and psychomotor style, and indeed some evidence on the point has been reported. Since Kretchmer's pioneer efforts more systematic and objective methods of somatotyping have been developed, notably by Sheldon (1942), who used standardized photography and rated each person on three dimensions of variation, endomorphy, mesomorphy and estomorphy corresponding roughly to the pyknic, athletic and leptosomatic tendencies respectively. Although mixtures of all three are common, many persons reveal a dominant trend, and Sheldon claimed to have demonstrated that such trends in physique correlated with differences in temperament. Thus mesomorphy (muscular, hyper-masculine) is said to correlate with adventurousness, aggressiveness, insensitivity to the feelings of others, and extraversion. Following up this clue the Gluecks (1956), in a study of monumental proportions, found that mesomorphy was one of the most conspicuous factors distinguishing a group of American delinquents from a control group of law-abiding persons. In England, T. C. N. Gibbens, in a study of Borstal youths (1963), found that the Porteus Maze "Q" Score, mesomorphy, and aggressive delinquency were all significantly correlated.

An example of a test based upon rather more subtle physiological measures is the method developed by Funkenstein (1957), who classifies individuals according to the reactivity of the autonomic nervous system as indicated by their response to standard doses of the drug mecholyl, which has the effect of neutralizing the action of adrenaline. He distinguishes two contrasting responses, the first, elicited from those whose autonomic system secretes a high level of adrenaline, includes a sharp and prolonged fall in blood pressure as the adrenaline becomes neutralized. The second type of reaction, in which blood-pressure changes are minimal, is given by those who secrete nor-adrenaline rather than adrenaline in response to stress. Temperamentally, the first type is prone to anxiety and their aggressions are inhibited or directed inwards against themselves, whereas the second type is more outwardly aggressive and anxiety-free.

As yet, research into all these variables is often of more theoretical than practical interest, the correlations involved being too slight or inconsistent to provide much practical guidance in an individual case. Indeed, the dogged persistence of effort in the field of personality testing and of factor analysis, in spite of the many difficulties encountered, reveals in an interesting way the faith of British and American psychologists in the experimental approach and their dissatisfaction with the more intuitive attitude towards problems of typology and individual differences favoured by certain German schools. In that country, under the leadership of Dilthey, Spranger and others, a movement arose which (in contrast to the attitude of the pioneer experimentalists) asserted that the methods appropriate to psychology were different from those of the natural sciences. Whereas these "sciences" it was maintained, legitimately sought to "explain," psychology should endeavour only to "understand" or "describe," through a sort of intuitive apprehension of "meaning" or of the relation of parts to a greater whole, often the whole that is provided by the cultural milieu—a view that has become associated with the names *Geisteswissenschaft* or *Kulturwissenschaft*.

It might seem that the difficulties and confusions encountered in the endeavour to apply quantitative treatment to personality and orectic qualities generally had provided some argument in favour of this school. The experimentalists on their part, while admitting the difficulties, have replied (as Spearman, for instance, did in his great historical review, *Psychology Down the Ages*): (a) that, while description is a necessary stage in psychology, as in every other science, they can see no reason for stopping there; (b) that the types and classifications arrived at by the use of "intuitive" understanding are at least as numerous and confusing as those provisionally formulated as the result of quantitative studies, and that the former method, unlike the latter, provides no tool with which we may hope eventually to attain more precise and generally agreed knowledge.

Nevertheless, in spite of this deep cleft between the *Geisteswissenschaftler* and the experimentalists, the former has not been without influence on the latter. The whole Gestalt school, in spite of its rich experimentation, based itself upon much the same revolt against atomism and associationism as was voiced by Spranger. In America G. W. Allport (1937), an experimental psychologist of note, in his insistence on the unique features of personality and his defence of the "idiographic" as supplementary to the "nomothetic" approach (i.e. the use of descriptions and case histories in all their essential individuality, as well as the endeavour to subsume particular cases under general laws or categories) is another striking example of the same kind. In a somewhat different context another prominent American psychologist, Gardner Murphy (1947), has emphasized that personality manifests largely in human interactions which may conform to laws which can never be deduced from isolated performance in perception, learning, etc. This emphasis, and particularly the the great interest taken recently in the influence of cultural patterns on the development of individual behaviour, is in fair harmony with Spranger's outlook. On the whole the intuitive typologies originating in Central Europe (Freud's oral-erotic and anal-sadistic types, Fromm's exploiting sadistic type, Adler's life styles) have proved useful in proportion to the degree to which they have stimulated and proved amenable to practical experiment. The example of the use by experimentalists of Jung's introversion–extraversion typology has already been mentioned.

Similarly, Spranger's view that personality becomes meaningful when it is related to the predominant "values" of the person concerned has been seized upon by experimentalists, notably Allport and Vernon (1960). Indeed the assessment of social opinions, interests and values has become one of the most important approaches to the study of personality, in spite of the difficulties inherent in the measurement of such intangibles. In Fechner's classic experiments in sensation (page 135) the results suggested that just noticeable differences in sensation corresponded to a constant proportional increase in the strength of the physical stimulus. Applying this principle to attitude testing, Thurstone (1959) has developed an ingenious system of scaling values by "equal appearing intervals." On each topic to be investigated he collected a large number of statements of opinion which he gave to a group of judges to rank along a scale varying from one point (most condemnatory) through six points (neutral) up to eleven points (most approving) all statements considered of approximately equal value being placed on the same scale point. Only those statements about which there was a good measure of agreement as to their position were selected. These were allocated scale values according to the median position assigned to them by the judges, a statement rated up to three by half the judges being given a scale value of three. For the final questionnaire a series of statements with scale values spaced at equal intervals along the continuum would be selected, and the subject would be asked to indicate those with which he agreed. His score would be given by the median scale value of the statements endorsed.

Despite the practical success of the objective, statistical approach, the traditional preference for intuitive assessments makes its appearance in recurrent controversies about the proper use of statistics in psychological research. Determination of the relative efficiency for prediction purposes of human judgments based upon interview material and biographical data, as opposed to simpler psychometric data statistically processed, has occupied a number of researchers (Kelly *et al.*, 1951). In general, it appears that where predictions are made by the two methods on the same set of information (e.g. a series of previous examination marks in the prediction of future academic progress) the statistical approach, by assigning correctly calculated weights to different features of the data, achieves a more accurate prediction than the average

individual's unaided judgment. On the other hand clinical observations and interview methods sometimes, although not so often
as one might expect, elicit information of closer relevance and so
produce a better prediction (Meehl, 1954).

As with any other scientific tool, the more effective mental tests
become the more ethical problems are raised by their application.
In England the practice of applying tests to children of eleven
attending state schools, in order to identify those to be given the
privilege of secondary or higher education, has attracted much
criticism. In such controveries disputes which are really about the
ethics of making a selection of any kind tend to spill over into
sometimes irrelevant criticism of the techniques employed. In
America, where some large industrial organizations have used
mental testing very extensively for personnel selection, it has
been found that the undiscriminating application of these tools
can lead to unexpected complications. In his well-known book on
The Organization Man W. H. Whyte (1956) argued that the
continual selection of well-adjusted persons of similar, conventional attitudes for executive posts was producing a conformist
élite lacking in the initiative to make the bold innovations required in a competitive world of rapidly advancing technology.
The temptation for subjects to cheat on questionnaires when promotion is thought to be at stake represents an obvious danger. In
a recent investigation using volunteer apprentices as controls for
comparison with a criminal group, the former also produced substantial lie scores when they mistakenly imagined the results
might affect their chances of promotion. The American Psychological Association (1959) has adopted a code of professional ethics
which seeks to restrict the sale of tests to those qualified to interpret them, asks psychologists working in situations in which
conflicts of interest occur (as for instance between labour and
management) to make public their loyalties and responsibilities,
and directs that subjects participating in tests should always be
informed of the use to which the results will be put. In similar
vein to Whyte, but in a slightly different context, the English
sociologist Michael Young, in a well-known satirical essay on
The Rise of the Meritocracy (1958), has indicated the potential
dangers of an educational system in which opportunity and promotion follow too slavishly the results of intelligence tests.

The social upheavals of the Second World War, and the

continued conflicts between nations and ideologies that have ever since dominated the scene and now threaten the extinction of mankind, have naturally fostered interest in social psychology, and have brought about a great expansion in this branch of study. The war stimulated many psychologists to a concern with their responsibilities as regards social tensions (Murphy, 1945). From questions of nationalism and politics interest has spread to a wide range of community issues including advertising and the economic system, group tensions in industrial relations, the effects on individuals of culture and social class origins, and of course the traditional problems of crime, divorce, suicide, drunkenness, sexual deviation and mental illness. Immediately after the war Kurt Lewin formed the Research Centre for Group Dynamics at Massachusetts Institute of Technology, while in Great Britain the Tavistock Institute of Human Relations was founded for the diagnosis and treatment of community problems. The United Nations World Health Organization and the World Federation for Mental Health have taken an active part in promoting studies of mental health and community affairs, and the rapid appearance of social psychiatry as a subject in itself, with its own professorships and journals, testifies to the increasing importance attributed by clinicians to social factors in the genesis of mental disturbance (Opler, 1960).

The increasing appreciation of psychological factors in war and politics has led to greatly increased sophistication in techniques of propaganda and advertising, which have of course been further facilitated by developments in mass communications, particularly television. Like St. Paul, the modern propagandist tends to become "all things to all men" in the sense that he tunes his appeal to the particular aspirations, fears, grievances and general susceptibilities of those he wishes to influence—a tendency the importance of which must be realized for the part it may play in hastening beneficial as well as harmful social change. Corresponding to propaganda at the transmitter end there has been at the receiver end a development of public opinion research which by questionnaires or interviews seeks to assess opinions on particular topics. A number of organizations have come into being (some of them under government sponsorship) devoted to such work, which to a considerable extent grew out of the efforts of advertisers to judge the effects of their campaigns or of news-

papers to forecast election results, but which are now recognized
as a potent instrument whereby politicians, government officials
and the directors of large organizations can "feel the pulse" of
their public. Elaborate procedures have been devised for building
up samples representative of the population under survey by
taking individuals from the main geographical regions, from
urban and rural areas, from different age groups and social classes,
and income levels, the sub-groups thus formed being weighted in
proportion to the numbers they contribute to the total population.
Relatively small samples carefully selected have been found to
provide surprisingly accurate information about public opinion as
a whole. Since the (American) Social Science Research Council
set up a committee to investigate the reasons for the incorrect
forecasts of the 1948 Presidential election by the Gallup and
similar organizations, investigators have gained a clearer appreciation of such complicating factors as the under-representation
of the less educated and vocal among the population, the re-
spondents' habit of declaring socially acceptable opinions rather
than their private views, and the markedly varying turnout at
the polls between different sectors of the population. These techniques have improved and it is likely that they will play an
increasingly important part in the political life of democracies, as
they afford a simple means (far less expensive and cumbersome
than the referendum) whereby elected rulers can determine
public opinion and discover how far their policies are approved or
understood and in what ways the people need enlightenment or
information.

Logically connected with public opinion research, but for the
most part actually carried out by different workers, have been
the numerous studies of social attitudes. Questionnaires have
been devised to ascertain the attitude of selected groups towards
religion, church, prohibition, communism, political reforms,
racial discrimination and similar topics. In an early but well-
known example of this type of research, Bogardus (1933) drew
up a "social distance" scale indicating the degree of social in-
timacy to which the respondent would willingly admit a member
of some other race or class. The scale ranged from "close kinship
by marriage" through various intermediate stages to "exclusion
from my country." Work of this kind has amply demonstrated
the existence of stereotypes, according to which we tend to judge

members of other groups in a fixed way, attributing qualities like cruelty, industriousness or cunning to various nationalities or races, even though we may possess practically no knowledge of these groups either from study or from personal acquaintance. The Nazi persecutions, and the consequent migration of large numbers of Jewish intellectuals to the New World, brought about a special concern with the origins of racial prejudice and unfavourable social stereotypes. In a famous research on this topic carried out in the United States by Adorno (1950), Frenkel-Brunswick and others, the investigators employed personality inventories and projection tests to identify what they called authoritarian personalities who were characterized on the one hand by a high degree of social prejudice and on the other by a rigid, defensive character with pronounced neurotic traits and feelings of insecurity and anxiety. Such persons try to relieve their feelings of frustration and inadequacy by projecting the blame on to some convenient scapegoat—Jews, coloured people, Catholics, immigrants, "Teddy boys"—chosen according to cultural tradition.

The next step was obviously to see how far these attitudes can be altered by exposure to suitable social or propagandist stimuli. It was shown, for instance (Smith, 1943), that the attitude of white Americans towards Negroes can be favourably influenced by week-ends spent with them in Harlem. On the other hand, a fair amount of work has shown that propaganda based on the dissemination of factual information is comparatively ineffective, since the possession of knowledge and intelligence has little to do with the strength of social prejudices. In general, the evidence would seem to point to the conclusion that actual contacts on equal terms with representatives of another group (as for instance during army service), and especially contact with individuals of higher social status, stand more chance of changing unfavourable attitudes—a fact which in turn points to the undesirability, from the point of view of peaceful understanding, of "iron curtains," whether these be imposed for political or any other reasons.

Directly connected with the topic of social attitudes are those investigations concerned with the real facts of racial and cultural differences and the determination of how far these may be due to hereditary or environmental influences. As often happens in difficult and controversial problems of this kind (compare what was said in an earlier chapter on the relative importance of generalized and localized function of the brain) most of the new evidence that has been forthcoming over a given period has favoured one side rather than the other. In this case—perhaps as a reaction against the totally unscientific exaggeration of hereditary influences with which the Nazis sought to justify their criminal policies—recent research seems to favour the preponderant importance of nurture over nature. Especially significant in this context has been the work of the culture pattern school of social anthropology of whom Ruth Benedict (1935) represents the pioneer exponent, ably followed by such workers as Margaret Mead (1935) and A. I. Hallowell (1955). On the basis of their field studies among primitive peoples, these workers maintain that each culture possesses a certain "pattern," in accordance with which certain of the potentialities of human nature are picked out, emphasized and knitted into a socially acceptable ideal, while others are neglected, underdeveloped or actively suppressed. The "modal personality" in any given culture may differ markedly from what in our own society is regarded as normal. Thus the Kwakiutl Indians are (to use Nietzsche's term) "Dionysian"; they exalt emotional experiences, especially emulousness, which they manifest particularly through conspicuous waste of property. On the other hand, among the "Apollonian" Zuni of New Mexico, emotions and individual differences are soft pedalled, while the dwellers of Dobu Island off the south of New Guinea are governed by a "dour suspiciousness." Among the inhabitants of New Guinea itself, related stocks show conspicuous differences in pattern. The Mundugumor are quarrelsome and aggressive to a degree that would be regarded as psychopathic in our own society, while the Arapesh adhere to the opposite extreme of gentleness and pacifism. Among the Tchambuli the rôles of the sexes as we know them are largely reversed, the men assuming a passive, almost ornamental function, devoting their time to art and ritual, while the women take the lead in the conduct of affairs and do most of the productive work.

The more psycho-analytic minded among cultural anthropologists have tried to trace the origin of these differences in the influence of child-rearing practices upon subsequent character development. Thus Róheim, on the basis of his own field work,

L

interpreted the thoroughly masculine outlook and power distribution in the tribes of Central Australia as to some extent a reaction to infantile traumata received from the mother, while the matrilineal society in Dobu in his view to some extent represented a similar reaction to suffering at the hands of the father. More specifically, he connected the rather happy-go-lucky economic attitude of the Central Australians and the anxious concern for the future of the Dobuans with the long period of breast-feeding and the early weaning practised in these two cultures respectively. A similar distinction between two contrasting "oral character" types had already been drawn by certain psychoanalysts, notably Glover, which they attributed to similar causes, but more research is necessary before we can assess the true value of these suggestions. Systematic surveys of the effects of different methods of infant feeding have not so far confirmed the direct relationships assumed in psycho-analytic theory, but in principal at least these hypotheses provide an ontogenetic method of approach which may eventually supplement and clarify the more generalized explanations in terms of culture patterns.

The work of the cultural anthropologists has helped to bring together psychologists and sociologists in new, united approaches to the study of contemporary society. Attention has been directed to the widely divergent attitude and behaviour characteristic of different segments of our society, to the conflict of outlook between classes, and to the stresses and individual maladjustments consequent upon the modern trend towards greater social mobility. Good examples of the combined socio-psychological approach are to be found in recent studies of delinquency (McCord, 1959). This topic has been given a good deal of official notice since the war, and in England the formation of a British Society of Criminology (1961), and of an Institute of Criminology at Cambridge University (1960), brings formal recognition to yet another branch of behavioural studies. The fashionable theory of the "delinquent sub-culture" seeks to explain the close association between social class and incidence of crime by showing that the problem arises primarily among social groups in which the prevalent and approved attitudes are at variance with the standards of the socially dominant group of middle-class law makers. According to one sociological interpretation, derived from such well-known studies as Cohen's investigation of gang culture (1955), these aberrant sub-cultures arise from the frustrations experienced by members of socially under-privileged groups (made up of uncouth, unskilled, uneducated persons) who find themselves handicapped in the race to achieve socially approved goals (usually defined as property or status or keeping up with the Joneses) by legitimate means. More psychoanalytically orientated theorists, while agreeing on the importance of social groupings in the genesis of delinquency, emphasize that underprivileged parents, by careless, inconsistent and rejecting attitudes towards their unwanted infants, play a decisive part in fostering the development of characters defective in social and moral sense (Friedlander, 1947). A recent spate of psychological studies of prisoners of different ages (Andry, Gibbens, West, 1963) has called attention to the complex connections between personal, social and medical problems in the causation of criminal conduct, and has emphasized the relative normality from a psychological standpoint of juvenile offenders in contrast with older recidivists. In this area psychological research and theory have had very apparent effects in the succession of enactments passed in recent years in England (e.g. the Criminal Justice Acts of 1948 and 1961, and the Mental Health Act of 1959), which have diversified the methods of dealing with offenders of different ages and psychological characteristics and by means of hospital and probation orders greatly enlarged the categories of offenders treated by medical instead of penal authorities. Furthermore, within the penal establishments as well, an increasing number of psychologists are employed in interviewing and testing offenders, largely in connection with the task of allocation to one or other of the varied régimes available in approved schools, Borstals, and special prisons.

From time to time workers in cultural anthropology have tried to scrutinize modern nations in the same way as they are used to studying primitive tribes. The outcome is usually illuminating, although their interpretations cannot be other than speculative and controversial in view of the enormous complexity of contemporary civilizations and the many contradictory elements which they contain. Ruth Benedict (1947), for instance, made an analysis of Japanese culture, and although her conclusions about the Japanese mentality have since been challenged (Stoetzel, 1955), her observations proved very useful at the time of the

American occupation. Margaret Mead (1950), in a penetrating study of the contrasting social rôles of the sexes in present-day American society, pointed out that some individuals have difficulty in conforming to the expected stereotype, and thus become anxious about their adequacy as men or women. This could be a factor in causing some persons to take refuge in socially disapproved forms of adjustment, such as homosexuality, because these seem easier. Clearly the importance to be attached to cultural factors in the genesis of personal neurosis cannot be determined by general impressions, however inspired, but must await the outcome of painstaking comparative social surveys. In point of fact, a large amount of research effort is at present being expended on epidemiological surveys to determine the incidence and distribution of psychological disturbance in the community at large. The finding that a large proportion of the population falls short of conventional standards of mental health, and that disturbance tends to assume different forms in different social classes (Hollingshead *et al.*, 1958), has led to a clearer understanding of the intimate connections between modal personality, neurotic disposition, and cultural influences.

Medical interest in epidemiological studies has tended to concentrate on what is perhaps the biggest unsolved health problem, namely the cause of the two major "functional" mental diseases schizophrenia and manic-depressive psychosis. Although in both instances a strong hereditary factor has been demonstrated, it remains an open question to what extent psychological stresses and cultural pressures provoke these illnesses or shape their symptoms. Faris and Dunham's pioneer work in Chicago (1939) showed a relatively high incidence of schizophrenia in the poorer, central areas of the city where many individuals lived in lodging-houses in conditions of "social isolation." Since then, many studies have tried to determine whether certain races or social classes are especially predisposed to the disease, or whether the onset of symptoms brings about a "drift" downwards, both economically and socially. By comparing the social class and occupation of young adult schizophrenics with that of their fathers, Professor J. N. Morris has recently adduced some striking evidence in favour of the "downward drift" hypothesis (Gruneberg *et al.*, 1961). Inspired by psycho-analytic theory, other investigators have sought to show that certain psycho-dynamic constellations within the parental families of psychotic patients have an important influence. Thus, schizophrenic men are found frequently to have been only boys of dominating, over-protective, possessive mothers, and to have been reared in households in which father was disinterested or absent (Gerard and Siegel, 1950). Recent surveys of schizophrenic patients discharged from hospital have shown that those who go to friends or strangers fare better than those who return to wife or mother!

Epidemiological surveys, whether based on samples from the whole community (e.g. all persons born on a particular day) or from one locality (e.g. the clients of a given medical practice) regularly yield unexpectedly high figures for neurosis. In a study of working class couples in London (Pond *et al.*, 1963) some degree of neurosis was found in half the husbands and in the majority of wives. The criteria were a substantial score on the Cornell Medical Index questionnaire, or a consultation with the local doctor for a neurotic complaint. Such findings cut across the sharp distinctions once thought to exist between healthy and pathological mental processes and suggest that neurosis is as much a product of the prevalent circumstances of living as it is a consequence of individual peculiarity. Nevertheless, surveys also reveal differences in susceptibility. Thus, the incidence of neurosis in either marital partner was strongly related to the individual's childhood experience of emotional disturbance in the parental home. The self-perpetuating effects of such misfortunes are further illustrated by the finding that neurotic disturbance in one partner is associated to a significant degree with disturbance in the other. The effect was not entirely due to neurotic husbands choosing neurotic wives, since there was no great tendency for persons from a bad parental background to marry persons from similar backgrounds. Moreover, the degree of concordance between husbands and wives increased with the number of years of marriage, strongly suggesting that neurotic disturbances may be provoked, in persons who would otherwise remain free from them, by constant association with an established neurotic.

On the topic of sexual adjustment it is curious that although Kraft Ebbing and other Germans long ago compiled meticulous catalogues of perversions, and although the psycho-analytic school has laid such emphasis upon attitudes to sex, factual in-

formation about the normal range of marital and sexual behaviour has been conspicuously lacking until the recent development of social survey methods. One of the first big surveys in
this field, carried out by Terman and others (1938), covered a
sample of over a thousand married couples, each member
answering a long series of questions independently, anonymously
and simultaneously. The main conclusion that emerged was
that freedom from neuroticism was by far the most important
factor in making for a happy marriage, all the other matters
often suggested in this connection being at most of relatively
minor importance. Directed specifically to sexual behaviour, the
two great surveys by Kinsey and his collaborators (1948, 1953)
drew attention to a number of points of outstanding interest to
psychologists: the wide range of sexual habits and attitudes
prevalent in American society, the striking differences in this
regard between social classes, the great individual variation in
strength of the sex drive, and the very high incidence among
otherwise normal persons of sexual behaviour generally considered
perverse.

Conflict between instinctive drives and socializing forces was
always a key point in psycho-analytic theory, but recognition of
the supreme importance of social setting in guiding behaviour
and determining the form such conflicts take has meant considerable re-thinking on the part of many psycho-analysts (Brown,
1961). In his later days Freud indulged in various speculations
about social forces and cultural influences, but his ideas on these
matters have never attained the same degree of acceptance as his
theories on the mental mechanisms of individuals. It has fallen to
the lot of his successors, notably his daughter Anna Freud (1935),
working in England, and the community minded neo-Freudians
like Karen Horney (1939), working in America, to apply the
psycho-analytic approach to the social determinants of personality structure and the social factors in neurotic breakdowns.
Horney found that socially induced stress (as for instance in the
contradiction between the high valuation put upon aggressively
competitive behaviour and getting ahead of the next man on the
one hand, and individual dependence upon security and affection
on the other) was at least as often responsible for precipitating
breakdowns among Americans as conflicts about forbidden instinctive drives. Like Alfred Adler, the neo-Freudians lay relatively

greater emphasis on ego analysis through examination of contemporary relationships and attitudes rather than on protracted
exploration of childhood conflicts. This trend has been favoured
by the great demand for shorter methods of psychotherapy and
for methods which can be applied without the therapist himself
undergoing a long training analysis. The trend is exemplified in
extreme form by the ever-increasing army of social workers concerned with such matters as industrial welfare, child guidance,
rehabilitation, problem families, and marriage counselling.
Nearly all of these, whether they realize it or not, by delving into
clients' conflicts, are applying in attenuated form principles
derived from psycho-analysis. Their popularity and success in
many fields bears witness to the usefulness of the psycho-
dynamic approach in human affairs, while their concentration
upon factors in the contemporary environment suggests that the
necessity for deeper analysis may have been somewhat exaggerated in the past. Thus, in a marital situation in which the
wife nags and the husband drinks, the wife may be encouraged
to think about the development of their squabbles, to recognize
more clearly the matters which arouse her resentment or irritation, and thereby to accept more constructive ways of dealing
with the problem. All of this may sometimes be successfully
accomplished on a predominantly rational, conscious level without reference to deeply repressed motives.

Inspired by similar considerations of practicability, the Rogers
technique of non-directive psychotherapy with limited goals
deliberately selects a circumscribed problem and requires the
therapist to limit his activity to steering the patient towards the
problem area and to repeating back insights or near insights
which the patient has himself produced. Another and related
development is the technique of group psychotherapy (Foulkes
and Anthony, 1957) in which a number of patients meet together
with a therapist to describe and discuss their difficulties in common session. Almost any kind of psychotherapy, with the exception of prolonged individual free association, can be applied in
groups, but the technique lends itself particularly well to the
analysis of social relationships. The discovery of "fellow feeling"
the reduction of the individual sense of guilt, and the possibility
for the less introspective types to achieve by interaction within
the group insights they could never attain by solitary free

association, combine to give this method indubitable advantages in selected cases. A further innovation deserves mention, namely, the special development of group treatment called psycho-drama, advocated especially by J. C. Moreno (1953), in which the patient is made to act the traumatic experiences which pre-occupy him, sometimes by taking his own part (a therapist taking the rôle of spouse, parent, etc.) and sometimes acting the part of a person with whom he has been in painful conflict, the whole per-formance being witnessed and discussed by the group. Experience gained by therapeutic rôle-playing may have a direct practical influence on subsequent behaviour in special situations, such as being interviewed for a new job.

Moreno was also a pioneer of sociometry, a method of investi-gating the psychology of groups by questioning members about their feelings of attraction, antipathy, etc., towards others in the group, and thereby obtaining measures of the relative dominance, popularity and so forth of each individual in the group. The emergent characteristics of groups, notably the leadership con-flicts and scapegoat phenomena, have provided a new hunting ground in which sociologists, psychologists and psychotherapists (Taylor, 1961) have an equal interest.

The more orthodox psycho-analysts, though they would not support the almost exclusive concentration on social issues advo-cated by some of the American neo-Freudians, have not remained impervious to the general trend (Fenichel, 1945). Anna Freud, taking up her father's hint that the ego was confronted with the difficult task of striking some sort of balance between the often conflicting demands of outer (social) reality, the id and the super-ego respectively, has dealt in an illuminating way with the various "defences" by which it seeks to preserve its integrity. Her findings, and those of other analysts, with reference to the super-ego (see Chapter VIII of Part IV) throw considerable light on the origins of community attitudes to morality—which on purely intellectual examinations so often appear primitive and vindictive—and several writers have attempted to expound these findings in relation to social and ethical problems (Odier, 1943: Flugel, 1945). Anna Freud herself, by specializing in child development, has remained more strictly in line with her father's tradition. In particular, she has tried to work out in greater detail the connections between parental attitudes and behaviour and the development of the child's individual ego. The findings of her school of thought, largely embodied in the journal *Psychoanalytical Study of the Child*, provide material which may well form a bridge between the impressionistic views of clinicians and the more systematized and quasi-experimental approach of the social psychologist. Indeed, the more factual the psycho-analysts become, in the way of making predictions verifiable by social observation, the greater the possibility of a *rapprochement* between the psycho-dynamic and the experimental schools of thought. Some of the mental mechanisms postulated by Freudian theory have been demonstrated up to a point in laboratory experiments, such as those designed to bring out the effect of repression upon retention and recall. In the field of personality testing, some interesting tests using photographs have demonstrated the tendency to "project" one's own mental characteristics upon other people, while other work has tended to confirm the theory of an inverse relation between attitudes of extra- and intrapunitiveness—that is aggression or blame turned outwards to others or inwards against the self respectively. In spite of great ingenuity in the design of such experiments (Sears, 1944), real-life situations and genuinely important conflicts cannot be reproduced to order, and the results of laboratory tests, although often in line with psycho-analytic findings, have sometimes (as in the work on recall) been found to be subject to many confusing influences. Perhaps observation of social phenomena in their natural setting offers a better chance of evaluating some psychoanalytic assumptions.

One example of a theory which can be tried out in social research is that of maternal deprivation, as expounded by the psycho-analyst John Bowlby (W.H.O. 1952, 1962), according to which there is a critical period in early life when an infant needs a close and continuous affectionate contact with his mother if his capacity for responding to others is not to remain permanently retarded so that he becomes one of those apathetic, purposeless, unsocialized characters who drift through life getting into every kind of trouble. Social psychologists have in fact made many systematic studies of the effects of separation of infants from their mother, in prolonged confinement in hospitals, in the wartime evacuation of children to places of safety, and in the placement of illegitimate or unwanted children in orphanages. Broadly speaking, critical analysis of these surveys confirms the infant's need for human contact, but is less certain in regard to the extent of the critical period, the supposed permanency of the damage sustained or the rôle of separation itself as opposed to other traumatic experiences which are usually concurrent (Lewis, 1954). Another interesting observation, with some relevance to psychoanalytic theories of pathological mourning, is the effect of bereavement in early life in producing a predisposition to suicide or depressive illness in later life (J. F. Brown, 1961). Evidence for this is rapidly accumulating at the present time. Indeed the whole question of traumatic experiences in childhood, and the subtle effect of parental handling upon character development, have been taken up in a big way by social psychologists (Glidewell, 1961; Sears, 1957), whose observations sometimes exceed in richness and complexity those of the psycho-analysts themselves.

Melanie Klein, another psycho-analyst who has affirmed the importance of studying early life, has been particularly influential in encouraging clinical interest in the interpretation of children's play, and in the use of a permissive nursery situation for the therapeutic release of emotion, especially through the expression of aggression against dolls representing in the child's phantasy his own parents or siblings. Klein's theories place great emphasis on the child's early aggression and his tendency to attribute similar aggressiveness to his parents, who are thus transformed into what might be called bogy figures and endowed with a sort of infantile ferociousness which is really the child's own but is not recognized as such. She also emphasizes the anxieties created by infantile ideas of the omnipotence of aggressive phantasies and the harm and retaliation they are supposed to produce. Susan Isaacs (1933) and other analysts working with children have found Klein's observations corroborate their own experience, but in so far as these doctrines have been made the basis of a separate Kleinian school of analysis they have had a somewhat disruptive effect on psycho-analytic theory and practice. A renewed interest in the behaviour of infants has also occupied the attention of academic psychologists bent on objective observation without commitments to interpretation along psycho-analytic lines (Gesell, 1934; Valentine, 1942). The unification of all these disparate observations by different schools to produce a coherent picture of child development remains a task for the future.

One more field in which the influence attributed to environment has increased in the light of recent findings is that of intelligence. Although hardly any psychologist would deny that, given the opportunity for normal development, the enormous individual variation in general intelligence is mainly due to inborn and relatively unalterable factors, there is less confidence now than there was some twenty years ago that our measures reflect only innate endowment. Even when tests are devised as carefully as possible to avoid questions dependent upon educational experience, it seems that those who have enjoyed a more favourable social environment obtain higher scores than others (including siblings) of originally equal ability who have lived in less fortunate circumstances. Evidence from the few investigated cases of identical twins reared apart agrees with this, for they show an average difference in I.Q. points about twice as large as when both twins are reared together. That improvement in a deprived child's environment may produce remarkable changes in I.Q. over a relatively short period was convincingly demonstrated by Clarke and Clarke (1953) who reported that adolescents admitted to an institution for the mentally subnormal showed a considerable rise of I.Q. (an average of 10 points in two years) whereas those from satisfactory homes showed no substantial change. Whether these improved performances are due to freedom from distracting anxieties, or increased knowledge and experience in the new environment, or to an actual change in intelligence potential, is still an unsettled question and one that partly depends on the theoretical justification for distinguishing between present functioning and a hypothetical, underlying intelligence.

As regards the supposed differences in inborn intelligence between the different races of mankind the pendulum has swung still further in the direction of environment. The older view that white races were superior to Negroes has been largely rebutted as later work has shown that, the greater the care taken to choose tests of equal familiarity to persons from different cultures, or to compare individuals who have enjoyed similar educational and social privileges, the smaller the difference becomes. Klineberg (1940), for instance, showed that Negro children reared in the

more liberal northern states in America were on the whole
superior in intelligence to white children in the south, presumably because the benefits of the northern culture were more
helpful than the privileged status of the southern whites. A
similar fate has befallen the time-honoured belief that imprisoned
criminals are intellectually inferior (Woodward, 1955). Today it
seems doubtful whether there exists any appreciable difference
in average potential intelligence associated with race or sex,
and in any case any difference that might be present would be
negligible compared with individual variations. This statement
refers to potential rather than actual performance, the jungle
dweller is of course much "brighter" than the civilized man
would be in coping with that habitat. Differences in average intelligence between occupational groups, and therefore to a lesser
extent between social classes, remain evident, doubtless because
professional occupations of status generally require and attract
persons of superior intelligence. In view of the relatively high
fertility of the labouring masses in many countries, and of the
general evidence in favour of the inheritability of intelligence,
misgivings have been expressed by some authorities (e.g. by
R. B. Cattell and Sir Cyril Burt) as regards the possibility of a
slow decline of the average intelligence of the population as a
whole, but as yet the evidence on this point remains inconclusive.

An emphasis on the importance of present stresses, as distinct
from explanations in terms of ontogenesis, has also been forthcoming from a very different quarter, namely the Gestalt school.
Following the appearance of Koffka's monumental *Principles of
Gestalt Psychology* in 1935, this school entered upon a new phase
in which interest passed increasingly from the sphere of perception to that of orexis, and Kurt Lewin (1935, 1936) became the
leading figure. The Gestalt school had always minimized the significance of past experience as manifested through association, and
tried to explain perception in terms of dynamic principles operating at the time of the perceptual state under consideration.
Lewin boldly extended this view to include orexis, and according
to his "principle of concreteness" maintained that "only existing facts can influence behaviour." Concurrently with this change
he substituted physical analogies for the more usual biological
outlook in dealing with orectic problems, endeavouring to reduce
the apparent differences between mechanical and teleological pro-

cesses by drawing attention to the fact that physical forces are often considered to be "directed quantities." "Direction," of course, was the chief characteristic of the goal seeking stressed by all hormic psychologists, including McDougall and the psycho-analysts. The energy systems depicted by Lewin were not completely closed, in fact he emphasized that the dynamic relations between the whole organism and its "field" were of great importance. Lewin's theoretical system has already passed out of fashion, but the practical experiments instituted by the Gestalt school remain fruitful, and some of them have become classics, as for example Zeigarnik's investigation showing that uncompleted tasks are better remembered than completed ones.

Perhaps the most spectacular change to have taken place in psychology in recent decades is the great extension of the behaviourist school of thought, with its emphasis on the study of objective, measurable responses in preference to the analysis of hypothetical thought processes. It was previously mentioned (p. 223) that in Watson's day this school was slow to take root outside of the United States, but at the present time, except perhaps for some small tradition-bound groups at universities on the European continent, behaviouristic experiment and theory constitutes the major preoccupation of academic psychologists everywhere, and nowhere more so than in the Soviet Union (Simon, 1957; O'Connor, 1961) where Pavlovian theory underlies even psychiatric diagnosis. This emphasis on the directly observable and the experimentally verifiable reflects the modern philosophical trend, set by Wittgenstein's school of logical positivism, according to which the only meaningful statements possible concern factual matters, metaphysical problems being the artificial creation of a wrong use of language. On this view the proper function of philosophy consists in clarification of the language of science, re-defining meaningless abstractions (like "mind" and "will") in "operational" terms according to the observable data from which they were originally derived. The great change that has come about in the philosophical approach to *The Mind and its Place in Nature* is shown in the contrast between C. D. Broad's famous thesis of that title (1925) and *The Concept of Mind* by G. Ryle (1949) which takes the logical positivist's standpoint.

Concomitant with this changed outlook, the psycho-dynamic

schools of thought, which rely heavily upon intuitive insights into patients' free associations, and postulate mental processes which are not susceptible to observation, have lost status in academic circles. In social psychology, as has just been described, concepts derived from psycho-dynamics still enjoy a favoured position, but laboratory psychologists prefer "learning theory" which utilizes almost exclusively theoretical models based upon the results of conditioning experiments. Learning theory, however, has become elaborated almost beyond recognition since the days of Watson's association principle, when mere contiguity of stimuli, as in Pavlov's bell and food association, was regarded as the means by which all conditioned linkages were established. Hull greatly improved this theoretical system by means of a few additional principles the expected consequences of which he worked out in precise, logical and even mathematical form (1943, 1952). Watson postulated a limited repertoire of innate responses to primary stimuli, such as the dog's salivation at the sight of food, and supposed that learning adaptive behaviour consisted in the transfer of these primary responses to appropriate secondary, conditioned stimuli. He neglected the fact that animals learn quicker when under pressure of hunger. Hull, however, extending the earlier work of Thorndike, stressed the factor of "drive" (in human terms, motivation). He assumed that an animal's level of activity depended upon the state of tension produced by basic instinctive needs, and from this he went on to formulate the celebrated Law of Effect (reinforcement by reward) according to which activities leading to the successful reduction of drive-tension (consummation of an instinctive need, as for instance in reaching and swallowing the prize of food) tend to be repeated (learned). Trial-and-error behaviour, of a rapidity governed by the strength of the drive, with learning taking place the moment a response achieved "drive reduction," was for a long time the orthodox interpretation of all learning processes.

But this was only the beginning: as experimental evidence accumulated learning was seen to be more complicated. For instance, a rat's preliminary (and unrewarded) exploratory meanderings through a maze involve an amount of latent learning which enables the animal to find its way swiftly when a food reward appears. E. C. Tolman (1949) advanced an alternative theory of learning according to which the problem is registered sensorially and solutions rehearsed "mentally" before action occurs. Such cognitive theories explain more readily "insightful" problem-solving behaviour such as that reported by the pioneers Köhler and Yerkes, as well as by innumerable observers since. The stricter behaviourists, however, explain these phenomena by "fractional anticipatory goal responses," that is, tiny, symbolic motor acts of a trial-and-error type, which have been learned previously in connection with approximately similar situations. One such "fractional" act triggers off another, and if the sequence finally arrives at an end-point corresponding to goal and reward, the whole series is then translated into action, even though that particular sequence may never have been performed before. With the introduction of such subtleties behaviouristic hypotheses sometimes come very close to the ideational theories they were meant to replace.

Controversy arose at one time over the interpretation of conditioned avoidance reactions (e.g. cringing, attempts to escape) which tend to occur without reward and in response to any stimulus (e.g. the sight of the experimental apparatus) that has been associated with painful experiences in the past. It is supposed that "anxiety," the state of tension induced by threat of punishment, acts as a (secondary) drive, and that any act serving to relieve this carries an automatic (consummatory) reward. It is further supposed by most behaviourists (e.g. Skinner, 1953; Mowrer, 1950) that "anxiety" may spread from one stimulus to another by simple contiguity, without need for reinforcement.

Learning theorists have often been criticized for their preoccupation with animals in artificially simplified situations, but their justification lies in the hope of establishing fundamental principles of learning which have some general validity for all circumstances and all species, including man. As an example of the application of learning theory to human affairs, one may mention Broadbent's (1961) succinct discussion of the merits of training by reward and punishment respectively. Punishment has the advantage that it has a lasting effect even though not frequently repeated, for once the conditioned avoidance of wrongdoing is firmly established this automatically delays the discovery by experience that wrong-doing may no longer be punished. On the other hand, for punishment to work effectively in experiments or in real life, the avoidance reaction must first be established firmly by a clear, repeated and immediate association between the undesired behaviour and the consequential punishment. Punishment which is a remote contingency has little effect. Reward, on the other hand, need not be invariable, for both animals and man will keep on trying, or may even try harder, where rewards are irregular and only occasional. Speed of learning in simple tasks is generally proportional to the severity of punishment for failure, but where the task before the rat is difficult there is an optimal level of punishment beyond which learning speed deteriorates, and the more difficult the task the less the tolerance of punishment. This Yerkes-Dodson Law, as it is called, harmonizes easily with the common human experience that over-anxiety spoils a delicate performance. Another consequence of too severe punishment, apparent in rats and man, is the tendency towards over-inclusive avoidance reactions, the animal ignores the prize and gives up trying. In humans punishment may produce revulsion against right as well as wrong actions, as in the well-known association between sexual frigidity and puritanical upbringing. The greatest advantage of reward methods of training, however, is that they strengthen those stimulus-response linkages leading to desirable goals, whereas punishment may merely block detectable forms of misconduct, leaving the undesirable goal just as attractive and still attainable by stealth.

Analogies between the reactions of animals in the laboratory and spontaneous human behaviour can be pressed too far. Maladaptive behaviour in humans, especially of the type encountered in neurotic patients, such as irrational compulsions, phobic reactions, or the self-defeating ditherings of the over-anxious, have long been recognized as apparent exceptions to the simple rule that rewarding responses are reinforced and unrewarding ones are gradually extinguished. In recent years, however, experimentation has extended to the study of similar anomalous responses in animals. These were first recorded by Pavlov himself, who discovered that if he gave his dogs learning tasks of steadily increasing difficulty a point came when they "broke down" and produced all kinds of inappropriate and seemingly agitated behaviour which persisted after the experiment was over and hindered further learning. This phenomenon, now called "experimental neurosis," has been further investigated, notably by Masserman (1943), and it appears especially liable to occur in "conflict" situations in which the animal is confronted with a difficult choice with no chance of escape. N. R. F. Maier (1949) classified the anomalous responses as indiscriminately aggressive, regressive, fixated, and resigned—that is apathetic. The "fixations" consisted of stereotyped habits, such as always taking the left-hand path regardless of obvious changes in the situation and regardless of consequent punishments. In humans, contrived situations of a frustrating kind may produce analogous reactions. R. G. Barker (1943), in some classic experiments with children, demonstrated that mild frustrations, such as the sight of tempting toys placed out of reach, provoked regressive behaviour like whimpering, withdrawal, and non-constructive forms of play, which would normally be displayed by much younger subjects.

Basing themselves upon such experiments, the behaviourists have produced alternative theoretical models for phenomena which previously only the psycho-dynamic schools had attempted to explain. Whereas the psycho-analytic approach seeks always the hidden purpose of neurotic reactions in unconscious motivations, behaviourists have suggested that fixated frustration responses may be in themselves tension-relieving and therefore self-rewarding without reference to any external goal. Maier, for example, cited the example of some criminals, who go on repeating the same stupid act in the face of inevitable punishment, as instances of motiveless fixation. Freud, noting the same phenomenon, had suggested an unconscious need for punishment to assuage guilt feelings. In studies of aggression, experimental psychologists have advanced ideas equally divergent from psycho-analytic theory. Freud and McDougall both regarded aggression as a primary instinctive drive from which some tension-relieving outlet must be found. In his later writings Freud went still further, and assumed aggression to be part of a still more fundamental death instinct, an essentially destructive force, opposed to the life-promoting libidinal instincts, and aimed at avoidance of stimulation and ultimate extinction, but few analysts of note, with the exception of Karl Menninger (1942), have adopted this view. In contrast, the behaviourist Dollard (1944) and his colleagues of the Yale school have developed a theory according to which aggressive behaviour is a learned response which would not occur in the absence of frustration. A great deal of their experimental work has been devoted to the elucidation of certain general laws, for example that the strength of the aggressive response is proportional to the strength of the drive that has been frustrated and also to the number of occasions on which frustration has been experienced. As has happened in other connections, further research on animal and human reactions has shown the need for elaboration of the earlier theoretical model, so that with the introduction of evidence for such phenomena as "generalization" or "displacement" of aggression the behaviourist and the psychoanalytic descriptions seem less contradictory. An important practical conclusion, emphasized by J. P. Scott (1958), concerns the reinforcement of aggression by success, so that the tough animal (or boy) who gets his way by force more readily responds by force on subsequent occasions. One of the original propositions of the Yale school, that the degree of inhibition of aggression varies with the amount of punishment anticipated, has proved correct only in regard to the suppression of immediate reaction and not to the elimination of generalized aggressiveness. A wealth of social and experimental evidence (McCord, 1959; Sears, 1957; Bandura, 1959) favours the view that violence in child-rearing techniques in the long run encourages the development of an aggressive type of personality by inducing a tension state of chronic anger which finds a "displaced" outlet in hostility against weaker victims.

As will be gathered from what has just been said, psychoanalytic concepts have suggested fruitful lines of research to the animal experimentalists, who in turn have contributed valuable evidence on the general applicability and accuracy of such concepts as the origin of neurosis in conflict, regression after frustration, and substitute formation or displacement. The successful use of animals in this connection shows the deep biological significance of these mechanisms, and the fundamental nature of the issues raised by psycho-analytic findings. The heat of controversy engendered by the staunch adherence of the different schools to their own particular theoretical models too often obscures the common ground of important empirical observation shared by all. One development of the behaviourist school, however, seems altogether opposed to psycho-dynamic ideas, namely the use of behaviour therapy in cases of neurosis. According to the protagonists of this method (Wolpe, 1958; Eysenck, 1963), neurotic symptoms are special instances of conditioned responses, analogous to those induced in experimental animals, and the analysis of hypothetical repressed conflicts has no relevance to their causation or their cure, the latter being best accomplished by systematic de-conditioning. Thus a person suffering from a phobia of cats, presumably originating in the fortuitous association of a cat with some very painful experience in the past, by avoiding cats continually 'never gives [himself [the opportunity to learn a different response. De-conditioning [in such a case takes the form of forcing the patient to approach the object feared, first perhaps looking at a picture, then seeing the real thing at a distance, finally coming right up to it and handling it. As no further painful experiences ensue from these experiences, the conditioned association between cat and panic gradually becomes extinguished. Psycho-analysts challenge such procedures on the grounds that they are likely to be ineffective, since they take no account of the symbolic, unconscious meaning of the phobia, and even though sometimes one symptom is temporarily suppressed, others are likely to take its place. Time will show who comes nearer to the truth of this question, but at least it is one which should be answerable in the light of experience.

In recent years the behaviourists have become at once more sophisticated and more liberal in their interests, but for a long time research was retarded by the insistence on studying the relations between stimulus and response without regard to the mediation processes within the organism, although the introspective schools of psychology, and also the physiologists and neurologists, have amassed a great deal of highly relevant information. Even within their self-imposed limitation, the earlier behaviourists could ignore such matters as innate instinctive rituals, or the influence of different modes of perception, only by virtue of an exclusive concentration upon the confined laboratory rat. As regards sensation and perception, many more details of the neurological processing of sensory stimuli and of the pshyico-chemical processes of the receptor organs have come to light (Adrian, 1947). But perhaps the most significant change in ideas about perception is the one that has been brought about directly or indirectly by the Gestalt school. In the past, the orientation of research had been unduly biased towards analysis of the elements of sensation, and a whole set of distinctively psychological problems concerned with the integration and meaningfulness of sensations had been neglected. Perception is an active process, in which present stimuli are interpreted with reference to previous experience, so that our picture of the world corresponds more closely to reality than a literal reproduction of the data from individual receptors. For instance, we tend to see a round coin as round from whatever angle it is viewed, and whatever the shape of the image on the retina. Similarly, in looking up the street we see the familiar houses and lamp-posts as we know them to be, and not as in a photographic image, with a vast expanse of foreground, and tiny figures in the distance. Although the retina has a blind spot, and is not equally sensitive to colours at the centre and the periphery, we do not see any dark blank area in our field of view, and when the sky is of uniform colour we see it so. Provided a familiar background is visible, we can also compensate for variations in illumination, so that a white surface in shadow is easily distinguished from a brighter-lit grey one, though the two surfaces may be photometrically equal. As was mentioned earlier, the degree of approximation of perception to reality, which has been called "phenomenal regression," varies in degree between persons of different race, age and sex, and has been made the basis of tests of personality. The art of seeing, and more especially, the art of co-ordinating information from different sense modalities, is largely a matter of learning. The baby cannot at first correlate vision and hand grasp, and the congenitally blind person whose sight is suddenly restored cannot at first use it effectively or recognize objects he has known only by touch. Long experience of the sensory patterns aroused by familiar objects in familiar surroundings enable us to perceive them at a glance for what they are, but in different circumstances, as when catching moving objects spot-lighted in a dark room, perception of size, distance and movement becomes wildly inaccurate. The wearing of spectacles which invert the image on the retina for a time (until automatic compensation develops) disorganizes other senses as well. Normally, the integrative and interpretative functions of perception proceed without conscious intervention, and we do not always recognize originating sensations. Only after some accident has obscured the olfactory receptors does it appear how much of the flavour of what we think we taste actually derives from aroma. Only after the blind man is shut inside a soundproof room does it appear that his ability to avoid stumbling into objects has depended (like the bat's) on sensitivity to echoes. On the topic of obscure methods of perception some psychologists have ventured towards the problems of psychical research, that strange border-line of science and charlatanry associated with claims for the existence of powers of divination, telepathy, clairvoyance, or precognition, whereby certain persons appear to respond to stimuli beyond the range of the senses (Murphy, 1961). A new era in this field was inaugurated by J. B. Rhine (1934) who used on a large scale the method of "guessing" the order of cards concealed from the view, thereby obtaining data susceptible to strict experimental control and statistical analysis. Many such experiments are now on record, especially in the *Journal of Parapsychology* (Duke University) and the publications of the Society for Psychical Research (London), but the results remain largely unpredictable and unrepeatable and therefore a focus of much controversy but relatively little enlightenment. However, if the claims made by workers in this subject have any founda-tion, they raise such complex issues with regard to the relation of mind to time and to the physical universe as will keep philo-sophers and psychologists busy for generations.

A new method of research in perception was introduced in 1953 by D. O. Hebb, who noted the disruptive effects of mono-tonous stimulation, or the absence of stimulation, upon learning capacity. It had long been known that animals reared in the dark, or otherwise deprived of sensory stimulation, subsequently showed aberrant behaviour and inability to learn, as did "feral" children reared without human contacts. Hebb saw the theoreti-cal importance of these observations and was largely responsible for initiating experiments in which human volunteers were isolated in soundproof cubicles, their eyes covered with frosted goggles, their ears muffled with a persistent hum, their limbs gloved and cuffed, and their bodies recumbent on foam rubber. This reduction of sensory input proved seriously stressful, sub-jects complaining of confusion of thought, inability to concentrate, feelings of irritability and sometimes panic, disruption of percep-tion (e.g. loss of visuo-motor co-ordination, illusions of movement and change of size) and the occurrence of vivid imagery often difficult to distinguish from reality. Such findings strongly sug-gest that smooth brain-functioning requires a certain optimal level of external stimulation (Solomon *et al.*, 1961). Older theoretical formulations, such as Freud's death instinct, Köhler's "law of Präganz," and the various attempts by Raup, Rignano, Cannon and many others to explain behaviour in terms of reduction of tension or re-establishment of equilibrium (entropy, homeostasis), seem to imply that avoidance of stimulation and the attempt to revert to an inert state is the chief determinant of behaviour. Empirical observations of exploratory behaviour, both in animals and children, as well as the effects of sensory deprivation, suggest a contrary view, namely that the seeking of new experience fulfils a major instinctive need.

These considerations lead back once more to the still controversial question of the nature and number of human instincts and how far the concept of instinct can be profitably applied to human beings at all. Over the three decades with which we are concerned interest in this question has ebbed and flowed according to the availability of new lines of evidence. An original contribution was provided by Burt's factor-analytic approach (1939), as a result of which he postulated a general factor (sometimes called "e" or "general emotionality"—with a reference of course to McDougall's theory of the relation between instinct and emotion) standing to all instinctive emotional manifestations in much the same way as "g" stands to intellectual work and distinguishing individuals according to the intensity of their reactions to all kinds of emotional situations. In addition he found two bipolar factors corresponding to pleasant and unpleasant emotion respectively. Thus McDougall's views concerning qualitative specific emotions attached to specific instincts require considerable modification in the light of evidence as to the fluidity and interchangeability of emotions, fear giving way to anger, or assertiveness to submissiveness, in the space of a few seconds.

In McDougall's famous attempt to demonstrate Lamarckian inheritance of acquired characteristics (see page 234) he tried to show how specific instinctive reactions might be transmitted through generations of rats. His theory received yet another setback when successive repetitions of the experiment by later workers (Drew, 1939) consistently failed to confirm the results, which are now generally attributed to experimental errors.

On the other hand, physiological researches have from time to time produced fairly clear evidence that stimulation (or destruction) of particular areas of the brain may produce (or prevent) quite specific emotional and instinctive responses. For example, spayed female guinea-pigs will respond to sex hormones by the customary behaviour of an animal on heat, but small lesions of the anterior hypothalamus abolish this response. Stimulation of specific areas of an animal's brain, either with needle electrodes or by introducing traces of hormones, will induce definite sequences of behaviour, especially those associated with anger, sex, thirst or hunger. Such evidence strongly suggests the presence of separate neurological correlates for these particular instincts (F. V. Smith, 1960).

Another field of research closely concerned with the nature of instincts is ethology, the comparative study of behaviour in different species, a subject that in recent years has aroused increasingly the attention of psychologists, both on account of the relevance of the findings to an understanding of the neurological correlates of behaviour, and for the analogies with human reactions which are sometimes apparent. The subject has developed from the pioneer work of continental zoologists, notably Lorenz and Tinbergen (1951), who were among the first to try the effect of experimentally modified conditions upon unlearned activities like nest- and web-building, mating displays and care of the young. It was soon discovered that such behaviour includes highly rigid, stereotyped elements, as well as highly flexible elements. Some ritual behaviour is transmitted from one generation to the next as precisely as the anatomical features of the species. These elaborate sequences are performed only in response to quite complex patterns of stimulation. It is as if the animal has an inborn release mechanism awaiting appropriate arousal like a lock awaiting a key, much as McDougall had assumed. The specificity of the "releaser" ensures that instinctive reactions normally occur only in appropriate circumstances; thus only the forms, movements or sounds characteristic of the species will evoke mating behaviour. The sensory components which constitute an effective releaser can be identified by experiment, so that it is possible to construct models which will arouse the animal's instinctive reactions, although to human eyes the model may seem ridiculously unrealistic.

Work on these lines opens the door to a number of productive lines of inquiry. It is of great interest to determine which behaviours are fluid, and easily modifiable by conditioning, and which are stereotyped patterns. Of course such findings do not apply directly to man, but they sometimes have considerable relevance to the attempts to understand the instinctive elements in human reactions. In the matter of sexual behaviour, for example, studies of animals have revealed many interesting facts about the linkage between sexual responses and the objects (heterosexual or homosexual) which arouse them, and about the association between aggressive-submissive reactions and copulatory behaviour (Ford and Beach, 1952). The manner in which individual experience may cause instinctive reactions to become attached to unusual stimuli has great importance for the understanding of learning processes. Well known in this context is the "following" behaviour of young birds who can readily be made to attach themselves to an experimenter or to some other moving object in place of the natural mother. A striking part of this phenomenon is that the following response will only occur if the stimulus is presented at a very precise stage of development (13 to 16 hours in the case of ducklings). Observations of this sort have led to a renewed interest in sensitive periods of learning, both in animals and man. In infants, the learning of speech by imitation occurs most readily at 12 to 18 months, and Russell Davis (1957) has reported cases of functional speech disorder attributable to trauma occurring during this critical phase. A considerable body of evidence has been collected tending to show that, as the nervous system matures, so receptivity to different types of learning changes. Conditioned responses, for instance, are both difficult to establish and poorly retained in babies. On the other hand, six weeks old babies, like baby birds, are very ready to respond to anything resembling a mother, so that at this age smiling responses can be evoked by crude masks (Ahrens, 1954). Learning appropriate social responses may well consist in large measure of the early attachment of instinctual patterns to social stimuli. It has been shown that animals kept in isolation during a critical period of development remain permanently retarded in their social reactions when normal contacts are resumed. Guide dogs, for instance, are difficult to train unless they have been reared consistently in the house in close contact with humans. In this connection the deleterious effect of depriving an infant of maternal or other contacts, which was mentioned earlier, becomes easier to understand.

Another aspect of recent developments in ethology is the

opportunity afforded for studying the modifications of animal behaviour consequent upon experiments in the extirpation of selected areas of the cerebrum (Thorpe and Zangwill, 1961). Beach has shown that maternal behaviour in the female rat, and copulatory behaviour in the male, both deteriorate progressively according to the amount of cerebral cortex removed, the actual position of the lesion having little relevance. This resilience to injury recalls Lashley's classic researches from which he concluded that the limiting condition for efficiency was the amount of intact cortex and not the anatomical relations of the parts that had been removed. This still holds true to a large extent in primates and in men. Although more or less the whole brain seems to participate in the integrative aspects of perception, and in memory, substantial positions of the "association areas" may be removed or destroyed without serious impairment of intelligence. All the same, injury to particular regions will cause a disproportionate loss of function, injury to the dominant hemisphere (that is the left in right-handed persons) causing more disturbance than a corresponding lesion on the opposite side. Without the specialized receptor areas sensory input is blocked, so that any substantial injury to the occipital pole (striatal cortex) in man causes total blindness. Nevertheless, modern evidence will not fit the once fashionable view that the brain consists of a system of fixed connections, like wires in a telephone exchange.

Hebb (1949) put forward a more plausible theory commencing with the assumption that the brain at birth is virtually a clean slate. In support of this assumption one may mention the fact that extensive injury to one hemisphere at birth, followed by its subsequent removal surgically, does not necessarily prevent normal mental development or produce intellectual defect (Krynauw, 1950). On Hebb's theory, sensory experiences produce recurrent patterns of stimulation, so that certain groups of cells habitually receive impulses simultaneously or in quick succession and tend to fire off responses together, as a unit or "cell assembly." The responses may occur just the same even though, on any particular occasion, the sensory stimulus pattern is incomplete. These "assemblies" may include cells from widely separated areas of cortex, corresponding to different sense modalities, which have become linked by experience. Hebb's theory goes a little way towards accounting for the way the brain seems to fill in gaps in the sensory input, perceiving the whole "Gestalt" rather than the sum of the parts.

In recent years, new insights into brain functions have been attained by means of analogies with "feed back" mechanisms and computers. Sherrington long ago described how motor reflexes are "guided" by a continuous barrage of regulating impulses derived from the senses, and others have worked out in great detail the systems by which sensory impressions become coded and transmitted through the nerve fibres as a sequence of impulses of varying frequency, rather like a morse signal. The essential new feature of cybernetics and information theory—as the study of these processes is now called—is the application of engineering principles and mathematical equations to neurological processes (Cherry, 1957). The relationships between (for instance) the maximum frequency of impulses and the amount of information that can be carried in a given time are the same whether the system under consideration is a telephone cable, a computing machine, or the auditory nerve. By close study of the limits of neurological performance, as given by thresholds of discrimination, transmission times, reactions times, etc., deductions can be made as to which physical principles are being utilized in brain processes. One has, for instance, the curious fact that men can make millions of delicate discriminations in perception, and yet if more than seven objects are seen momentarily he cannot count them. Anatomically, there are some 3×10^6 input fibres entering the brain, but less than 10^{10} cells in the cortex, far too few to analyse all the possible combinations of activity in these fibres unless they are somehow reduced or simplified by what information theorists call "redundancy-reducing" codes. An example of coding economy is the property most sense receptors have to respond to changes in stimulation with bursts of impulses, but to represent a constantly applied stimulus (like a steady tactile pressure) by increasingly slow discharges. Some information is definitely lost rather than condensed. The maximum rate at which sensory impulses influence motor responses has been estimated at 25 bits per second, although it is known that the senses collect information much faster than this. Mixtures of light of different wave-length will cause the same sensation as pure light of a single wave-length, although each could be distinguished if presented individually.

The search for the engineering principles underlying neurological function brings out the significance of phenomena that might otherwise be neglected. The detailed study of tremors, long since recognized clinically as a means of distinguishing different areas of cerebral damage, has now assumed a new importance in the analysis of cerebral servo mechanisms. A particularly interesting line of exploration is the construction of mechanical models which operate on physical principles similar to those believed to be utilized by the brain. The behaviour of such man-made brains may give further clues what to look for in the human counterpart. The distinctive attribute of all such machines is ability to react according to circumstances, which implies ability to sort out incoming signals on the basis of regularities of sequence, or coincidences in timing between different signals. In other words the machine must include a counting device or statistical analyser which will rank the incoming signals into "meaningful" ones which always cluster together at one end, and background "noise," consisting of purely random signals, at the other. The step-by-step development of one such machine, and the functions it could perform, are vividly described by Grey Walter in *The Living Brain* (1953).

Some important developments in recent decades have come out of collaboration between psychologists and medical men, for instance in the investigation of stress diseases and psychosomatic disorders, in the diagnosis of mental illness (both emotional and neurological), and in the correlation of mental and physiological phenomena by means of encephalographic and psycho-pharmacological studies.

In the rapidly expanding field of psychosomatic medicine, which now has special journals devoted to it on both sides of the Atlantic, a host of bodily disturbances have been identified in which mental factors play an important part. Of these, eczema, migraine, peptic ulcer, asthma, colitis and rheumatoid arthritis are among the most obvious examples. Much of the earlier work in this connection was concerned with digestive functions, which the psycho-analysts had long believed to be involved with emotional development (Dunbar, 1938). Research has taken two main directions, the first being to establish links between physical syndromes and emotional reactions in general. As is now well known, the redness or pallor of complexion accompanying strong emotion corresponds with still more marked changes in blood supply and secretion of the stomach wall which may be watched and even photographed through appropriate instruments. Some individuals are especially prone to react to psychological threats in ways more appropriate to noxious physical stimuli (for instance by engorgement of the bowel and movements of ejection), or by excessive secretion of mucus in the air passages) so that the timing of attacks of colitis or asthma in relation to frustrating experiences becomes understandable. The second line of research seeks to associate particular physical syndromes with particular emotional conflicts. Franz Alexander led the way in this by suggesting unconscious desire for love, symbolized by food, as the emotional factor in gastric over-activity, in which the system behaves as though food were about to be taken and consequently produces symptoms of nausea, heartburn and epigastric pain which are the precursors of ulceration. This interpretation is interestingly supported by Silbermann's experiments on the sham feeding of dogs with an artificial oesophageal fistula, through which food fell to the floor instead of entering the stomach—the dogs in this case tending to develop ulcers as a result of long-continued gastric stimulation.

On a more strictly physiological level Selye (1957) has pioneered research into the bodily reactions to "stress," which are found to have much in common whether the attack takes the form of violence, infectious disease or psychological trauma. The initial "alarm reaction" includes increased activity of the adrenal glands with release of additional quantities of hormones into the bloodstream (notably ACTH) which has the effect of increasing the excitability of the whole organism and mobilizing its powers of resistance to deal with the emergency. If this process occurs too often, or becomes too protracted, the excessive hormone changes so produced may cause ulcers or tissue degenerations by a self-poisoning effect. Seyle has suggested that some fatal heart diseases may be the result of prolonged stress reactions. Work on these lines is of great interest in showing something of the nature of the links between psychological troubles and their possible physical consequences, a connection which has often been thought of as peculiarly mysterious. Discovery of these relationships has opened the door to some fascinating studies on the interrelated incidence of mental and physical illness. H. G. Wolff (1960) takes the view that the majority of illnesses, whether medical, surgical or psychiatric, are remarkably influenced by environmental circumstances. In the life histories of individuals one finds periods, when they perceived their circumstances as threatening or frustrating, associated with clusters of illnesses, both mental and physical. Personal misfortunes, even though they may involve but little actual physical damage, sometimes lower resistance and increase mortality remarkably. Rats introduced by an experimenter into an alien colony where they are attacked and excluded as outsiders die quickly, although under natural circumstances they would easily survive the wounds received. American survivors of the prison camps of the Korean war, investigated six years later, showed a surprising degree of accident proneness and vulnerability to disease, more than twice the expected number having died, twice the expected number from cancer, heart disease and suicide, and three times the expected number from accidents.

The use of psychological tests in psychiatric practice, as an aid in the assessment of psychotic and neurotic tendency, and for the identification of topics of emotional conflict by means of projection techniques, has already received mention. In addition, tests for mental deterioration, like the Babcock Test, or the Goldstein-Scheerer Test for abstract and concrete thinking, have proved their worth in detecting early senility, or the effects of brain damage, before the disturbances reach a level when they are clinically obvious and readily distinguishable from the confusion of thought which accompanies over-anxiety. One useful indication of deterioration is discrepancy between the scores on verbal and on other scales of intelligence tests, verbal fluency being relatively well preserved in the early stages of senility. Traditional wisdom about the peculiarities of thought specific to schizophrenia has recently been made the basis for systematic tests designed to reveal such disturbances as tendency to "over inclusion" of associations and inability to handle abstract concepts. In time these may prove more reliable or more sensitive than clinical impressions.

On the physiological side one of the most important developments has been the use of the electro-encephalograph, an instrument for amplifying and recording as a wave tracing the minute rhythmic changes of electrical potential which accompany brain activity. These waves, to which Berger had called attention in 1928, remained neglected until just before the war when Adrian at Cambridge produced more convincing methods of registering them, but after that their usefulness in diagnosis soon became apparent, especially in epilepsy and in the localization of cerebral tumours. Various systems of waves have been identified in the normal brain, which vary in sleeping and waking, in states of passivity and active attention, and in individuals whose thinking is predominantly visual and predominantly auditory respectively. In the exploration of emotional life the encephalograph is of potentially greater importance than the older "expression methods" like the psycho-galvanic reflex, which in turn had proved superior to the non-electrical measures used by Wundt and Lehmann. So far, however, the attempts to correlate orectic qualities with specific wave patterns are only just beginning to show their potential usefulness. Recent work by Grey Walter and others at the Burden Neurological Institute, taking advantage of new refinements in the analysis of wave patterns (e.g. averaging out wave reactions obtained on separate occasions so as to eliminate random background variations) seems to provide means of identifying neurotically anxious or phobic individuals by their peculiar brain responses to sensory stimulation. Earlier work had already shown that slow, "theta" rhythms, originating deep in the thalamic region of the brain, which are normal for children but less so for adults, are apt to appear when subjects are annoyed or frustrated, and have been shown by Hill to occur with particular frequency in aggressive psychopaths who are prone to uncontrolled rages at slight provocation. The artificial induction of such rhythms by stroboscopic stimulation (rhythmic flashing) has been shown to provoke irritability, while the ability to suppress theta rhythms quickly would seem to be the mark of a robust brain and a mature personality in full control of his emotional reactions.

Soon after the war the operation of prefrontal leucotomy came into fashion for the treatment of severe mental illness, or painful and incurable physical disease. The procedure consists of severing nerve tracts connecting the frontal lobes of the brain with the deeper thalamic areas which are believed to mediate emotional reactions. The effect, which varies greatly with the individual, is usually to produce a more placid and less anxious person, so that even though the patient remains deluded, hallucinated or in pain, his misery and his preoccupation with his symptoms lessens. The improvement is produced at the cost of some loss of judgment, initiative and creativity, although on formal testing significant intellectual deterioration may not be evident. Fortunately, relief from tortures of guilt, anxiety, doubt, over-scrupulousness or depression, and a swing in the direction of happy-go-lucky extraversion and increased self-satisfaction, can be attained in most cases in less drastic fashion by using drugs, which have the advantage of being easily withdrawn or changed if their effects on a particular patient prove undesirable. Self-dosing with alcohol for this purpose receives some cultural sanction, although the side effects are often unfortunate. In clinical practice, the use of tension-relieving drugs for the treatment of neurotic anxiety, either as a substitute for or in combination with psychotherapy, represents an uneasy balance between radically different approaches which have not as yet become fully integrated. For the alleviation of schizophrenic symptoms the newer "tranquillizing" drugs, such as chlorpromazine, have largely replaced surgery. Another group of drugs which act by virtue of their influence on the metabolism of serotonin—a substance which helps regulate the excitability of cerebral neurones—have a specific beneficial effect upon melancholics who suffer from irrational and paralysing depressive states. The synthesis of more and more drugs with a selective or preferential action upon particular areas of the brain provides a fruitful method of exploring mental life. As with many of the more important scientific developments, the practical applications of psychopharmacology suggest some alarming possibilities for social manipulation which leave Aldous Huxley's *Brave New World* far behind. The hallucinogenic drugs, like mescaline and LSD, which distort perception of reality, and may provoke intense emotional reactions or the vivid recollection of long-forgotten experiences, have aroused the imagination of doctors and laymen alike. The fact that these drugs, which are chemically related to human hormones, induce in normal subjects a temporary state resembling schizophrenia has led to a renewed search for the biochemical origin of this disease. In spite of these developments a renewed interest in the surgical approach is to be expected as a consequence of recent experiments in which multiple electrodes, in the form of gold filaments, are inserted into the living brain and electric currents passed along them sufficient to cause minute lesions at the terminals. The advantages of the method are that it enables electro-encephalographic changes following stimulation of particular areas to be studied with great precision, that it can be used to produce lesions smaller and more accurately placed than is possible with conventional surgery, and that by first passing very small currents temporary, reversible effects are obtained from which the clinician may decide whether the operation is desirable (Crow *et al.*, 1961).

Another field in which medical men and psychologists have collaborated with success is that of hypnosis, a subject which, as was noted earlier in this book, had for long suffered from unwarranted neglect. C. L. Hull, whose notable contributions to the development of the behaviourist school have already received mention, also produced a classical work on *Hypnosis and Suggestibility* (1933) which established hypnotism for the first time as a proper subject to which to apply the methods of experimental psychology. He put to the test of objective experiment, using non-hypnotized subjects as controls, many of the old beliefs about the virtues of hypnosis in increasing powers of memory, sensory discrimination, muscular power and so forth. He found, as many other experimenters have since confirmed, that hypnosis does not help in the recall of recent experiences (though it does often improve the ability to recall events of childhood and the remote past), that it does not *as such* produce improved voluntary motor or sensory capacity (though suggestion may perhaps produce some real improvement in motor tests of endurance and will produce belief in the subject that he has increased motor and sensory powers). It is doubtful whether there is any improvement in the capacity to carry on two tasks simultaneously (such as might be expected on the theory that hypnosis is a functional dissociation) while as regards sensitivity to pain it was found that suggested analgesia would abolish almost completely manifestations of pain that are under voluntary control, such as cries, withdrawal movements and grimaces, while producing only partial reduction of involuntary autonomic responses such as are revealed by pulse changes and the psycho-galvanic reflex. Other workers have claimed more startling changes as a result of hypnosis, such as alterations in pupillary and other reflexes, the reduction of bleeding during dentistry, and the improvement of muscular control as well as the abolition of pain during childbirth. The literature on hypnosis contains a profusion of contradictory evidence on these matters (Weitzenhoffer, 1953), so much so that one school of thought denies that any such entity exists and maintains that hypnosis is just a name for a miscellaneous collection of largely unrelated psychological phenomena.

One of Hull's most important findings was that susceptibility to hypnosis was highly correlated with tests of suggestibility. Eysenck (1947) and his collaborators have taken this further and shown that suggestibility may be divided into the ideo-motor type (as shown for example by the amount of body sway in response to suggestions of falling) and another type depending on "indirection" or deception produced verbally or otherwise. Hypnotizability is strongly correlated with ideo-motor suggestibility, and both are in turn related in a rather complex way to Eysenck's personality dimensions, stable extraverts being the most easily hypnotized among normal volunteers (Furneaux and Gibson, 1961). While these results have robbed hypnotism of at least some of its mystery, it cannot be said that they have as yet led to a satisfactory and agreed theory of the ultimate nature of hypnotic phenomena. On the assumption that the hypnotic state possesses special virtues with regard to facilitating recollections of childhood and overcoming emotional resistances to communication, it has been considerably used, especially in America, as an adjunct to psycho-analytic treatment. Apart from the use of direct suggestion to overcome reluctance to confide, indirect methods for promoting insight may be applied, such as suggesting situations or acts which the hypnotist knows are liable to provoke the patient's symptoms, thereby demonstrating associations which the patient would otherwise be slow to recognize. The psychotherapeutic use of hypnosis has much in common with the use of intravenous injections of barbiturates or other drugs to produce a similar state of increased emotionality in which a violent release of deeper feelings (abreaction) may sometimes occur (Sargent and Slater, 1944). Abreaction by either hypnosis or drugs has been found particularly efficacious in restoring memory-loss or other functional disabilities resulting from severe shock or exhaustion such as occur very often in wartime. Some of the most startling of recent claims for the effects of hypnosis have been made in connection with "age regression," that is, causing subjects to

M

think themselves back into infancy so that their speech, memories and even reflexes alter accordingly (Yates, 1961). Unfortunately, as with so much else in connection with hypnosis, the phenomena appear variable and controversial.

Although this supplementary chapter is already over-long, a host of other matters no less interesting than those already cited clamour for attention. In conclusion one can do no more than mention almost at haphazard, a few other important topics that have so far been omitted. Up to now very little has been said about memory—a subject that since the days of Ebbinghaus has had a fascination for the experimental psychologist, but about which the last word is still far from being said. The older work, dominated by the nineteenth-century associationist tradition, undoubtedly took too mechanical a view of memory. The psycho-analysts, the Gestaltists and such writers as F. C. Bartlett (1932) have all in their different ways stressed the fact that retention and recall depend upon dynamic factors. Bartlett has recorded experiments on the changes that the past undergoes in retro-spect—a matter that deserves taking up in greater detail, for its bearings on testimony and rumour have important social and legal implications. There have been interesting experiments on retroactive inhibition, the wiping out effect of new mental events, while other work has been concerned with the ways in which powers of learning and retention are affected by increasing age (Welford, 1958). Some of the experimental findings on memorizing, for example, the advantage of actual performance over passive recall, the facilitating effect upon re-learning of apparently forgotten previous attempts, the use of mediational associations as in mnemonics, and the importance of attention directing activity during learning, have some application to the question of desirable habits of study for examinations (Mace, 1932).

Educational psychology has expanded greatly in England especially so since the Education Act of 1944 which envisaged the employment of psychologists by every local authority. Further recommendations along the same lines appeared in the Report of the Committee on Maladjusted Children in 1955, and by 1958 a survey of 102 local education authorities in England showed that 86 had set up school psychological services. In practice the psycho-logist's skills may not be put to full use in every locality, not at least as regards research into new methods of teaching, but the potentiality for great changes in education is certainly present (Cronbach, 1957). In England, the National Foundation for Educational Research performs a valuable function in organizing surveys, devising and standardizing tests of scholastic ability and attainment, comparing the performance of school children in different countries, and arranging systematic trials of new teaching methods. Techniques for teaching reading (such as the "phonic" techniques, or the "look and say" methods of Schonell) have received particular attention (Morris, 1959), and psychologists have made considerable contributions in determining the nature of specific learning handicaps—such as word blindness—and to devising appropriate remedial methods. As with new methods in other spheres, the effects of novelty and enthusiasm may produce remarkable temporary improvements in performance at schools where they are being tried out, although the methods used may possess no intrinsic superiority. In general, variety of methods seems to work best, especially if they enlist the child's active participation and stimulate his curiosity. The elimination of anxiety from the learning situation, and the fostering of adequate motivations, are factors of cardinal importance, especially in the retarded child who feels defeated and discouraged by repeated failure. In this connection, the use of "latent learning," by contriving situations in which the child does not realize he is being taught, will sometimes overcome the blockage. Another approach employs "teaching machines" and has been applied both to school children and industrial workers (Lumsdaine, 1960). The pupil is given a sequence of questions or other stimuli to which he must make an appropriate response. The machine checks the response and indicates whether it is correct. In the more elaborate versions, incorrect responses lead to the presentation of supplementary items designed to show where the mistake occurred. With these machines the pupil can learn at his own pace, with as many repetitions as he likes, and free of the distractions and miseries of public failures.

The application to educational tasks of the findings from studies of memorizing has taken a new direction with recent work on the nature of concepts and meanings and their relevance to learning (Osgood, 1957: Underwood, 1960). In building up vocabulary in a foreign language, for instance, various methods may be adopted to associate new words with material already learned, i.e. by similarities of sound, by linkage with other words, by incorporation in a sentence. Children may be more impressed by clang associations, students by syntactic meaning. Studies of language and communication have special relevance to classroom situations. Bernstein (1960) has studied the verbal habits of different social classes and called attention to the predominance in working-class speech of ejaculations and stereotyped phrases carrying emotional implications (e.g. disapproval or solidarity) rather than a factual message. The use of grammatical sequences suited to the transmission of information and reasoned argument is more typical of middle-class language. The fact that language serves different purposes among different classes may create a barrier between teacher and pupil, and by emphasizing the distinction between those who learn by "feeling" and those who are guided by "reason," may contribute to the differences in outlook and modes of thought prevalent among the various social classes.

A recent research trend of particular interest to educationists is the study of higher cognitive processes, particularly as revealed in difficult problem-solving activities (Bartlett, 1958). Faced with similar problems, methods of approach are found to vary with personality, age and experience, as well as with level of intelligence. Thus, some people will not make decisions or hazard a solution except on the basis of a lengthy sequence of evidence. Some people are relatively more inclined to experiment, to try a variety of hypotheses or approaches, while others show greater "method fixity," that is they prefer to stick to a tactic which has proved successful in similar situations in the past (Rokeach, 1960). According to their experience, people learn to categorize problems and to select their tactic according to the class to which the problem appears to belong. Polya (1957) has suggested means for educating students to make more efficient use of their experience in solving problems.

At the other end of the scale very encouraging progress has occurred in the methods of educating the mentally subnormal (Pritchard, 1963). Intelligence tests applied to the inmates of institutions for the feeble-minded have shown that about a fifth of the patients give scores in the average range or above, and many more are no worse on testing than the dullest five per cent of the ordinary working population (O'Connor and Tizard, 1956). In the moderately subnormal problems of personality, employment and social setting are largely intermingled with that of intellectual handicap, but given the necessary social support and occupational training a substantial proportion can learn to live in the community. The provision of special schools for the educationally subnormal (which in England was one of the major concerns of the 1944 Education Act) has kept many children from unnecessary admissions to institutions, However, by admitting to these schools a proportion of backward, troublesome and maladjusted children—especially naughty boys—whose difficulties are only partly cognitive, the authorities have shown that in practice there is an inevitable overlap between social and intellectual handicap. Indeed there is much to be said for the view that subnormality is divided into two broad categories, the severe forms, which are often accompanied by physical defects and congenital abnormalities, being chiefly medical and pathological, whereas the moderate forms are mostly of cultural origin, occurring predominantly in poorer homes as a result of neglect, ignorance and lack of opportunity (Clarke, 1958). The outlook for treatment therefore seems more promising than it did when all subnormality was assumed to be the outcome of inborn and unmodifiable defects. Intensive training programmes have shown that with carefully graded instruction, stimulation of motivation, and most important of all sympathetic individual attention, many feeble-minded persons can learn elementary reading and other basic social skills. Luria and his colleagues in the Soviet Union have given special attention to the nature of the learning defects in the mentally subnormal, and in particular to the difficulties experienced in establishing connections between verbal instructions and motor manipulations (O'Connor, 1961). In normal children speech plays an important part in the development of perceptual discriminations, as well as in learning generally. The analysis of speech defects (including both disorders of articulation arising from malformations of the mouth or throat or from cerebral palsy and disorders of symbolization or aphasias arising from cortical damage) and the development of teaching techniques to overcome them, represents a particularly happy example of applied psychological research.

In the space of this brief review many developments remain

unmentioned, particularly those that have taken place outside of the English-speaking countries, and there are whole new fields of study represented by the barest catalogue heading. Nevertheless, one must somehow call a halt. The impression remaining may well be of a somewhat disorderly advance along a wide front, and in some places it may seem that the winning of new ground has done little more than present vistas of further difficulties ahead. But advance there has undoubtedly been, and in some places recent years have seen the coming together of psychologists from various directions and various schools to talk over their common problems and occasionally to join forces and consolidate their positions. As examples of this encouraging development the attempts to trace parallels between experimental studies with animals and clinical studies of humans, and between the findings of personality research and those of cerebral physiology, have been singled out for mention, although others might equally well have been chosen. The increasing number of international conferences, and the increasing acceptance of psychologists as legitimate contributors to conferences in related disciplines, should ensure a continuation of this integrative process, but the day is still far off when all may speak the same language and comprehend each other's work. Nevertheless, the advances of the last thirty years have been more than substantial, and the practical contributions psychologists can make in every field of human endeavour is now beyond question. In 1933 Flugel commented (p. 302) that the advice of psychologists might be essential to the progress and even the continuation of our present civilization. The humanizing influence of the psychological approach in education, social welfare and group conduct is already making itself felt, but in the field of international relations Flugel's comment carries an even greater sense of urgency in this nuclear age.

In a summary of this kind so much has to be left out or merely alluded to in passing that the best advice one can give the disappointed reader is to turn to the bibliography, where some of the most important works of the period are listed. Perusal of these should provide a fuller and more just appreciation of what has been accomplished.

BIBLIOGRAPHY

PARTS I–IV

(The dates indicate the first appearance of a work or any part thereof.)

Abraham, K.: *Selected Papers*, 1927.
Ach, N.: *Über die Willenstätigkeit und das Denken*, 1905.
Über den Willensakt und das Temperament, 1910.
Adler, A.: *Studie über Minderwertigkeit der Organe und die Seelische Kompensation*, 1907.
Über den nervösen Charakter: Grundzüge einer vergleichenden Individualpsychologie und Psychotherapie, 1912.
Praxis und Theorie der Individualpsychologie, 1924.
Alexander, F.: *Psychoanalyse der Gesamtpersönlichkeit*, 1927.
Alexander, F., and Staub, H.: *The Criminal, the Judge and the Public*, 1931.
Alrutz, S.: *Skandinav. Archiv für Physiologie*, 1897, VII, p. 321.
Ames, E. S.: *The Psychology of Religious Experience*. 1910.
Angell, D. R., and Moore, A. W.; "Reaction Time: A Study in Attention and Habit," *Psychol. Rev.*, 1896, III, p. 245.
Angell, J. R.: *Psychology*, 1904.
Arai, T.: "Mental Fatigue," *Columbia Contributions to Education*, 1912, No. 54.
Aveling, F.: "The Psychology of Conation and Volition," *British Journal Psychology*, 1926, XVI, p. 339.
"Emotion, Conation and Will," in *Feelings and Emotions*, ed. Murchison, 1928.
Personality and Will, 1931.
Bain, A.: *The Senses and the Intellect*, 1855.
The Emotions and the Will, 1859.
Baldwin, J. M.: *Mental Development in the Child and the Race*, 1895.
"Types of Reaction," *Psychol. Rev.*, 1895, II, p. 259.
History of Psychology. A Sketch and Interpretation, 1913.
Bechterev, V. M.: *La Psychologie Objective*, 1907 (Russian original). *General Principles of Human Reflexology* (English translation).
Bell, C.: *Idea of a New Anatomy of the Brain*, 1811.
The Nervous System of the Human Body, 1830.
Beneke, F. E.: *Physik der Sitten*, 1820.
Lehrbuch der Psychologie als Naturwissenschaft, 1832.
Bernard, L. L.: *Instinct. A Study in Social Psychology*, 1924.
Berry, C. S.: "The Classification by Tests of Intelligence of ten thousand first-grade Pupils," *J. Educational Research*, 1922, VI, p. 185.
Bethe, A.: "Dürfen wir den Bienen und Ameisen psychische Qualitäten zuschreiben?" *Pflüger's Archiv*, 1898, LXX, p. 15.
Binet, A.: *La Psychologie du Raisonnement*, 1886.
Les Altérations de la Personnalité, 1891.
La Suggestibilité, 1900.
L'Étude Expérimentale de l'Intelligence, 1903.
Numerous articles in *Année Psychologique* from 1905 onwards.
Biran, Maine de.: *Essai sur les Fondements de la Psychologie*, 1812.

Bon, G. le: *The Crowd*, 1895.
Boring, E. G.: "Processes referred to the Alimentary Tract," *Psychol. Rev.*, 1915, XXII, p. 306.
"Cutaneous Sensation after Nerve Division," *Quarterly J. Exp. Physiol.*, 1916, X, p. 1.
A History of Experimental Psychology, 1929.
Braid, J.: *Neurypnology*, 1843.
Brentano, F.: *Psychologie vom empirischen Standpunkte*, 1874.
Brett, G. S.: *A History of Psychology*, 1921.
Breuer, J.: *Pflüger's Archiv*, 1891, XXXXVIII, p. 195.
Breuer, J., and Freud, S.: *Studien über Hysterie*, 1895.
Brill, A. A.: *Psychoanalysis. Its Theories and Practical Application*, 1912.
Broca, P.: *Bulletin de la Société anatomique*, 2me ser., 1861, VI, p. 350.
Brown, Thomas: *Lectures on the Philosophy of the Human Mind*, 1820.
Bryan, W. L., and Harter, N.: "Studies in the Physiology and Psychology of the Telegraphic Language," *Psychol. Rev.*, 1899, IV, p. 27.
Bühler, K.: "Tatsachen und Probleme zu einer Psychologie der Denkvorgänge," *Archiv f. d. ges. Psychol.*, 1907, IX, p. 297.
Burt, C.: "Experimental Tests of General Intelligence," *Brit. J. Psychol.*, 1909, III, p. 94.
Mental and Scholastic Tests, 1921.
The Young Delinquent, 1925.
Burt, C., and Moore, R. C.: "The Mental Differences between the Sexes," *J. Experimental Pedagogy*, 1912, I, p. 273.
Cannon, W. B.: *Bodily Changes in Pain, Hunger, Fear and Rage*, 1915.
Carlson, A. J.: *The Control of Hunger in Health and Disease*, 1916.
Cattell, J. McK.: "Über die Zeit der Erkennung und Benennung von Schriftzeichen, Bildern und Farben," *Phil. Stud.*, 1885, II, p. 635.
"Über die Trägheit der Netzhaut und des Sehcentrums," *Phil. Stud.*, 1885, III, p. 94.
"Psychometrische Untersuchungen," *Phil. Stud.*, 1886, III, p. 30.
"A Statistical Study of Eminent Men," *Popular Science Monthly*, 1903, p. 359.
"Statistical Study of American Men of Science," *Science N.S.*, 1906, XXIV, p. 658.
Cattell, J. McK., and Fullerton, G. S.: *On the Perception of Small Differences*, 1892.
Cattell, J. McK., and Farrand, L.: "Physical and Mental Measurements of the Students of Columbia University," *Psychol. Rev.*, 1896, III, p. 618.
Charcot, J. M.: *Leçons sur les Maladies du Système Nerveux*, 1873.
Claparède, E.: *L'Association des Idées*, 1903.
Psychologie de l Enfant et Pédagogie expérimentale, 1905.
Comment diagnostiquer les Aptitudes des Écoliers, 1924.
L'Éducation Fonctionelle, 1931.
Codrington, R. H.: *The Melanesians*, 1891.
Cohn, J.: "Experimentalle Untersuchungen über die Gefühlsbetonung der Farben, Helligkeiten und ihre Combinationen," *Phil. Stud.*, 1894, X, p. 562.
Coover, J. E.: *Experiments in Psychical Research*, 1917.
Cornelius, H.: *Psychologie als Erfahrungswissenschaft*, 1897.
Cox, J. W.: *Mechanical Aptitude*, 1928.
Culpin, Millais, with Smith, May, and Farmer, E.: "A Study of Telegraphists' Cramp," Industrial Fatigue Research Board, *Report* No. 43, 1927.
"Nervous Disease in Industry," *J. Indust. Hygiene*, 1929, XI, p. 114.

Darwin, C.: *Origin of Species*, 1859.
  Descent of Man, 1871.
  Expression of the Emotions in Man and Animals, 1872.
  "Biographical Sketch of an Infant," *Mind*, 1877, II.
Delboeuf, J. R. L.: *Étude Psychophysique*, 1873.
Dessoir, Max: *Abriss einer Geschichte der Psychologie*, 1911.
Dewey, J.: *Psychology*, 1886.
  "The Reflex Arc Concept in Psychology," *Psychological Review*, 1896, III, p. 357.
Dietze, G.: "Untersuchungen über den Umfang des Beweusstseins bei regelmässig aufeinander folgenden Schalleindrücken," *Phil. Stud.*, 1885, II, p. 362.
Dodge, R.: "Habituation to Rotation," *J. Exper. Psychol.*, 1923, VI, p. 1.
Donaldson, H.: "On the Temperature Sense," *Mind*, 1885, X, p. 399.
Donders, F. C., and Jaager, J. J. de: *Over den physiologischen tijd der psychische processen*, 1865.
Drever, J.: *Instinct in Man*, 1917.
Durkheim, E.: *Formes Élémentaires de la Vie Religieuse*, 1912.
Ebbinghaus, H.: *Über das Gedächtnis*, 1885.
  Grundzüge der Psychologie, 1897 (1st part).
  "Über eine neue Methode zur Prüfung geistiger Fähigkeiten bei Schulkindern," *Zsch. f. Psychol.*, 1897, XIII, p. 401.
  Abriss der Psychologie, 1908.
Ehrenfels, C. v.: *Über Gestaltqualitäten. Vierteljahresschrift für wissenschaftliche Philosophie*, 1890, XVI, p. 249.
Ellis, H. Havelock: *Studies in the Psychology of Sex*, 1897.
Elliotson, J.: *Numerous Cases of Surgical Operations without Pain*, 1843.
  Harveian Oration, 1846.
Esdaile, J.: *Mesmerism in India*, 1846.
Fabre, J. H.: *Souvenirs Entomologiques*, 1879.
Fechner, G. T.: *Beweis dass der Mond aus Jodine besteht*, 1821.
  Vergleichende Anatomie der Engel, 1825.
  Nanna, 1848.
  Zend-Avesta, 1851.
  Elemente der Psychophysik, 1860.
  Vorschule der Aesthetik, 1876.
  In Sachen der Psychophysik, 1877.
Ferenczi, S.: *Contributions to the Theory and Technique of Psycho-analysis*, 1915.
  Further Contributions to the Theory and Technique of Psycho-analysis, 1926.
Ferrier, D.: *The Functions of the Brain*, 1876.
Flourens, M. J. P.: *Recherches expérimentales sur les Propriétés et les Fonctions du Système Nerveux*, 1824 and 1842.
Flugel, J. C.: "Practice, Fatigue and Oscillation. A Study of Work at High Pressure," *Brit. J. Psychol. Mon. Sup.*, 1928, No. 13.
  The Psychology of Clothes, 1930.
Franz, S. I.: "The After Image Threshold," *Psychol. Rev.*, 1895, II, p. 130.
  "On the Functions of the Cerebrum," *Am. J. Physiol.*, 1902, VIII, p. 1.
  "On the Functions of the Cerebrum. The Frontal Lobes," *Archives of Psychology*, 1907, I, No. 2.
  How the Brain Works, 1929.
Franz, S. I., and Lafora, G. R.: "On the Functions of the Cerebrum. The Occipital Lobes," *Psych. Monog.*, 1911, XIII, No. 56.

Franz, S. I., and Lashley, K. S.: "The Effects of Cerebral Destruction upon Habit Formation and Retention in the Albino Rat," *Psychobiology*, 1917, I, p. 71.

Frazer, J. G.: *The Golden Bough*, 1890.
Totemism and Exogamy, 1910.
The Belief in Immortality, 1913.
Folklore of the Old Testament, 1918.

Frey, M. v.: *Abhandl. d. Sächs. Ges. der Wiss.*, 1896, XXIII, p. 175.
"Studien über den Kraftsinn," *Zsch. f. Biologie*, 1913, LXIII, p. 129.

Freud, A.: *Einführung in die Psychoanalyse für Pädagogen*, 1930.

Freud, S.: *Die Traumdeutung*, 1900.
Zur Psychopathologie des Alltagslebens, 1904.
Der Witz und seine Beziehung zum Unbewussten, 1905.
Drei Abhandlungen zur Sexualtheorie, 1905.
"Zur Einführung des Narzissmus," *Jahrbuch für Psychoanalytische and Psychopathologische Forschungen*, 1914, VI, p. 1.
Totem und Tabu, 1913.
Vorlesungen zur Einführung in die Psychoanalyse, 1917.
Massenpsychologie und Ichanalyse, 1921.
Das Ich und das Es, 1923.
Collected Papers, 1925.
Die Zukunft einer Illusion, 1927.
Das Unbehagen in der Kultur, 1930.

Fritsch, G., and Hitzig, E.: "Über die elektrische Erregbarkeit des Grosshirns," *Archiv. f. Anat. u. Physiol.*, 1870, p. 300.

Gall, F. J., and Spurzheim, G.: *Recherches sur le Système Nerveux*, 1809.

Galton, F.,: *Hereditary Genius*, 1869.
English Men of Science, 1874.
Inquiries into Human Faculty, 1883.
Natural Inheritance, 1889.

Glover, E.: "Notes on Oral Character Formation," *Int. J. Psycho-analysis*, 1925, VI, p. 131.

Goddard, H. H.: "A Measuring Scale for Intelligence," *The Training School*, 1910, VI, p. 146.
Feeble-mindedness: Its causes and consequences. 1914.

Goethe, J. W.: *Farbenlehre*, 1810.

Goldscheider, A.: *Gesammelte Abhandlungen*, 1898.

Golgi, C.: *Untersuchungen über den feineren Bau des centralen und peripheren Nervensystems*, 1885.

Gopalaswami, M.: " 'Intelligence' in Motor Learning," *Brit. J. Psychol.*, 1924, XIV, p. 274.

Groos, Karl: *The Play of Animals*, 1896.
The Play of Man, 1899.

Hall, G. Stanley: *Adolescence*, 1904.
Jesus the Christ in the Light of Psychology, 1917.
Senescence, 1922.

Hall, Marshall: *Philosophical Transactions*, 1833, p. 635.

Hammond, M.: "Gestalttheorie: its Significance for Teaching " *Brit. J. Educ. Psychol.*, 1932, II, p. 159.

Head, H., and May, M. A.: *Studies in Deceit*, 1928.
Studies in Service and Self Control, 1929.
Studies in the Organization of Character, 1930.
Aphasia and Kindred Disorders of Speech, 1926.

Head, H., and Rivers, W. H. R.: "A Human Experiment in Nerve Division," *Brain*, 1908, XXXI, p. 323.
Head, H., and Holmes, G.: "Sensory Disturbances from Cerebral Lesions," *Brain*, 1911, XXXIV, p. 102.
Head, H., and others: *Studies in Neurology*, 1920.
Healy, W.: *The Individual Delinquent*, 1915.
 Mental Conflicts and Misconduct, 1919.
Helmholtz, H. v.: *Handbuch der physiologischen Optik*, 1856.
 Die Lehre von den Tonempfindungen, 1863.
Henning, H.: *Der Geruch*, 1924.
Herbart, J. F.: *Lehrbuch zur Psychologie*, 1816.
 Psychologie als Wissenschaft, 1825.
Hering, E.: *Zur Lehre vom Lichtsinne*, 1872.
 "Der Temperatursinn," in *Hermann's Handuch der Physiologie*, 1880.
Hermann, I.: "Gustav Theodor Fechner," *Imago*, 1925, XI, p. 371.
Hermann, L.: *Handbuch der Physiologie*, 1879.
Heymans, G., and Wiersma, E. D.: "Beiträge zur speciellen Psychologie auf Grund einer Massenuntersuchung," *Zsch. f. Psychol.*, 1906, XLII, p. 81 and following volumes.
Hirschfeld, M.: *Geschlechtskunde*, 1926.
Höffding, H.: *Outline of Psychology*, 1886.
Hobhouse, L. T.: *Mind in Evolution*, 1901.
Hunter, W. S.: "The Problem of Consciousness," *Psych. Rev.*, 1924, XXXI, p. 1.
 Human Behavior, 1928.
 "The Delayed Reaction in Animals and Children," *Behavior Monographs*, 1913, II, No. 1.
Isaacs, S.: *Intellectual Growth in Young Children*, 1930.
 Social Development in Young Children, 1933.
Jackson, Hughlings: *The Factors of Insanities*, 1894.
Jaensch, E. R.: "Zur Analyse der Gesichtswahrnehmungen," *Zsch. f. Psychol. Ergänzungsband*, 1909, IV, p. 1.
 Die Eidetik und die typologische Forschungsmethode, 1925.
Jaensch, E. R., and others: *Über den Aufbau der Wahrnemungswelt*, 1923.
James, W.: *Principles of Psychology*, 1890.
Janet, P.: *Automatisme Psychologique*, 1889.
 L'État mental des Hystériques, 1892.
 The Major Symptoms of Hysteria, 1907.
Jones, E.: *Papers on Psycho-analysis* (1st ed.), 1913.
 Essays in Applied Psycho-analysis, 1923.
 On the Nightmare, 1931.
 "Psycho-analysis and Anthropology," *J. Roy Anthrop. Institute*, 1924, LIV, p. 47.
Jones, J. H.: *Equilibrium and Stability*, 1918.
Josey, C. C.: *The Social Philosophy of Instinct*, 1922.
Jung, C. G.: *Über die Psychologie der Dementia Praecox*, 1907.
 "Wandlungen und Symbole der Libido," *Jahrbuch f. Psychoanalytische und Psychopathologische Forschungen*, 1912, II and III.
 Collected Papers on Analytical Psychology, 1916.
 Studies in Word Association, 1919.
 Psychological Types, 1930.
Kant, I.: *Kritik der reinen Vernunft*, 1781.
 Kritik der praktischen Vernunft, 1788.

Kantor, J. K.: "The Problems of Instincts and its Relation to Social Psychology," *J. Abn. and Soc. Psychol.* 1932, XVIII, p. 56.

Kelly, R. L.: "Psychophysical Tests of Normal and Abnormal Children," *Psychol. Rev.*, 1903, X, p. 345.

King, I.: *Development of Religion*, 1910.

Kirkpatrick, C.: *Intelligence and Immigration*, 1926.

Kirkpatrick, E. A.: "Individual Tests of School Children," *Psychol. Rev.*, 1900, VII, p. 274.

Klein, M.: *The Psycho-analysis of Children*, 1932.

Koffka, K.: *Beiträge zur Psychologie der Gestalt*, 1919.
The Growth of the Mind, 1930.

Köhler, W.: *The Mentality of Apes*, 1927.
Gestalt Psychology, 1930.

König, A.: *Sitz. d. Akad. d. Wiss.*, Berlin, 1894.

Köttgen, E., and Abelsdorff, G.: "Absorption und Zersetzung des Sehpurpurs bei den Wirbeltieren," *Zsch. f. Psychologie*, 1896, XII, p. 161.

Kraepelin, E.: *Psychiatrie*, 1883.

Krasnogorski, N. I.: *Über die Bildung der künstlichen Bedingungsreflexe bei Säuglingen*, 1907.

Kretschmer, E.: *Körperbau und Charakter*, 1921.

Kroh, O.: *Subjektive Anschauungsbilder bei Jugendlichen. Eine psychologisch-pädagogische Untersuchung*, 1922.

Krüger, F.: *Über Entwicklungspsychologie, ihre sachliche und geschichtliche Notwendigkeit*, 1915.

Külpe, O.: *Grundriss der Psychologie*, 1893.

Kuo, Z. Y.: "Give up Instincts in Psychology?" *J. Phil.*, 1921, XVIII, p. 645.

Ladd, G. T.: *Elements of Physiological Psychology*, 1887.

Lange, C. G.: *Om Sindsbevoegelser*, 1885.

Lange, L.: "Ein Chronograph nebst Controllapparat für sehr genaue Zeitmessungen." *Phil. Stud.*, 1888, IV, p. 457.

Lange, N.: "Beiträge zur Theorie der sinnlichen Aufmerksamkeit und der aktiven Apperception," *Phil. Stud.*, 1888, IV, p. 390.

Lashley, K. S.: *Brain Mechanisms and Intelligence*, 1929.

Lehmann, A.: *Grundzüge der Psychophysiologie*, 1912.

Leuba, J. H.: *A Psychological Study of Religion*, 1912.

Levy-Bruhl, L.: *Mentalité Primitive*, 1922.

Liébault, A. A.: *Du Sommeil et des États analogues*, 1866.

Lipps, T.: *Grundtatsachen des Seelenlebens*, 1883.
Raumaesthetik, 1897.
Aesthetik, 1903.

Lloyd Morgan, C.: *Animal Life and Intelligence*, 1890.
Introduction to Comparative Psychology, 1894.
Habit and Instinct, 1896.
Animal Behaviour, 1900.

Loeb, J.: *Der Heliotropismus der Thiere*, 1890.
Einteilung in die vergleichende Gehirnphysiologie, 1899.

Lotze, H.: *Medicinische Psychologie*, 1852.

Lubbock, J.: *Ants, Bees and Wasps*, 1882.

McDougall, W.: "Observations in Support of Young's Theory of Light and Colour Vision," *Mind*, N.S., 1901, X, p. 52.
"The Psychological Factors of the Attention Process, 1903," *Mind*, N.S., XII, p. 316.

"The Nature of the Inhibitory Process within the Nervous System," *Brain*, 1903, XXVI, p. 153.
Physiological Psychology, 1905.
Introduction to Social Psychology, 1908.
Psychology, the Study of Behaviour, 1912.
The Group Mind, 1920.
National Welfare and National Decay, 1921.
"The Use and Abuse of Instinct in Social Psychology," *J. of Abn. and Soc. Psychol.*, 1922, XVI, p. 285.
Outline of Psychology, 1923.
"Men or Robots," in *Psychologies of 1925*.
Outline of Abnormal Psychology, 1926.
"An Experiment for the Testing of the Hypothesis of Lamarck," *Brit. J. Psychol.*, 1927, XVII, p. 267.
Mach, E.: *Grundlinien des Lehre der Bewegungsempfindungen*, 1875.
Zur Analyse der Empfindungen, 1885.
Magendie, F.: *Journal de Physiologie expérimentale et pathologique*, 1822, II, pp. 276, 366.
Leçons sur les Fonctions et les Maladies du Système Nerveux, 1839.
Malinowski, B.: "Mutterrechtliche Familie und Œdipuskomplex," *Imago*, 1924, X, p. 228.
Crime and Custom in Primitive Society, 1926.
The Father in Primitive Psychology, 1926.
Sex and Repression in Savage Society, 1926.
The Sexual Life of Savages in North Western Melanesia, 1929.
Marbe, K.: *Experimentell-psychologische Untersuchungen über das Urteil*, 1901.
Mateer, F.: *Child Behaviour*, 1918.
Mayer, A., and Orth, J.: "Zur qualitativen Untersuchung der Associationen," *Ztsch. f. Psychologie*, 1901, XXVI, p. 1.
Merriman, C.: "The Intellectual Resemblance of Twins," *Psychol. Mon.*, 1924, XXXIII, No. 152.
Mesmer, F. A.: *Mémoire sur la Découverte du Magnetisme animal*, 1781.
Mesmerismus, 1814.
Messer, A.: "Experimentell-psychologische Untersuchungen über das Denken," *Archiv f. d. ges. Psychol.*, 1906, VIII, p. 2.
Meumann, E.: *Ökonomie und Technik des Lernens*, 1903.
Michotte, A., and Prüm, E.: *Étude expérimentale sur le choix volontaire et ses antécedents immediats*, 1910.
Mill, James: *Analysis of the Phenomena of the Human Mind*, 1829.
Mill, J. S.: *Logic*, 1843.
Examination of Sir William Hamilton's Philosophy, 1865.
Mitchell, T. W.: *The Psychology of Medicine*, 1921.
Money-Kyrle, R.: *The Development of the Sexual Impulses*, 1932.
Aspasia, or the Future of A-Morality, 1932.
Moore, T. V.: "A Study in Reaction Time and Movement," *Psychol. Mon.*, 1904, VI, No. 24.
"Temporal Relations of Meaning and Imagery," *Psychol. Rev.*, 1915, XXII, p. 177.
Müller, Joh.: *Textbook of Physiology*, 1838.
Müller, G. E.: *Zur Theorie der sinnlichen Aufmerksamkeit*, 1873.
Zur Grundlegung der Psychophysik, 1878.
Revision der Hauptpunkte der Psychophysik, 1882.
Zur Psychophysick der Gesichtsempfindungen, 1893.

Gesichtspunkte und Tatsachen in der Psychophysik, 1903.
Zur Analyse der Gedächtnistätigkeit und des Vorstellungsverlaufes, 1917.
Komplextheorie und Gestalttheorie, 1923.
Abriss der Psychologie, 1924.
Müller, G. E., and Martin, L. J.: *Zur Analyse der Unterschiedsempfindlichkeit,* 1899.
Münsterberg, H.: *Beiträge zur experimentellen Psychologie,* 1889.
Psychology and Industrial Efficiency, 1913.
Murchison, C. (edited by): *Psychologies of 1925,* 1926.
(edited by) *The Foundations of Experimental Psychology,* 1929.
(edited by) *Psychologies of 1930.*
(edited by) *Foundations of Child Psychology,* 1931.
(edited by) *Psychological Register,* 1929 and 1932.
Murphy, Gardner: *An Historical Introduction to Modern Psychology,* 1930.
Myers, C. S.: *A Text Book of Experimental Psychology,* 1909.
Industrial Psychology in Great Britain, 1925.
Neill, A. S.: *The Problem Child,* 1925.
Norsworthy, N.: "The Psychology of Mentally Deficient Children," *Archives of Psychol.,* No. 1, 1906.
Orth, J.: *Gefühl und Bewusstseinlage,* 1903.
Pailthorpe, G. W.: *What we put in Prison,* 1932.
Pavlov, I. P.: *Conditioned Reflexes,* 1927.
Pear, T. H.: *Voice and Personality,* 1931.
Peckham, G. W. and E. G., *Wasps, Social and Solitary,* 1905.
Perry, J.: *The Origin of Magic and Religion,* 1923.
Pfungst, O.: *Der kluge Hans,* 1911.
Phillips, G. E.: *Mental Fatigue,* 1920.
Philpott, S. J. F.: "Fluctuations in Human Output," *Brit. J. Psychol. Mon. Sup.,* 1932, No. 17.
Piaget, J.: *Le Langage et la Pensée chez l'Enfant,* 1923.
Le Jugement et le Raisonnement chez l'Enfant, 1924.
Le Représentation du Monde chez l'Enfant, 1926.
La Causalité physique chez l'Enfant, 1927.
Le Jugement moral chez l'Enfant, 1932.
Pillsbury, W. B.: *Essentials of Psychology,* 1911.
The History of Psychology, 1929.
Pinard, J. W.: "Tests of Perseveration," *Brit. J. Psychol.,* 1932, XXIII, p. 5.
Preyer, W.: *Die Seele des Kindes,* 1881.
Ramon y Cajal, S.: *Riv. trimestr. micrograph,* 1889, p. 2.
Rank, O.: *Das Inzest-Motiv in Dichtung und Sage,* 1912.
Psychoanalytische Beiträge zur Mythenforschung, 1917.
Das Trauma der Geburt, 1924.
Read, Carveth: *The Origin of Man and his Superstitions,* 1920.
Reik, T.: *Probleme der Religionspsychologie,* 1920.
Geständniszwang und Strafbedürfnis, 1925.
Reports of the Cambridge Anthropological Expedition to Torres Straits, 1903.
Ribot, T. A.: *La psychologie anglaise contemporaine,* 1870.
La psychologie allemande contemporaine, 1879.
Les Maladies de la Mémoire, 1881.
Les Maladies de la Volonté, 1883.
Les Maladies de la Personnalité, 1885.
Richards, A. I.: *Hunger and Work in a Savage Tribe,* 1932.
Rignano, E.: *Problemi della Psiche,* 1928.
Róheim, C.: *Australian Totemism,* 1925.

"Psycho-analysis of Primitive Cultural Types," *Int. J. Psycho-analysis*, 1932, XIII, p. 1.
Rolando, L.: *Saggio sopra la vera Struttura del Cervello*, 1908.
Romanes, G. J.: *Animal Intelligence*, 1882.
Mental Evolution in Animals, 1883.
Mental Evolution in Man, 1888.
Rubin, E.: *Synsoplevede Figurer*, 1915.
Russell, B.: *On Education, especially in early Childhood*, 1926.
Russell, Dora: *In Defence of Children*, 1932.
Saffiotti, V.: *La Misura dell' Intelligenza*, 1916.
Sandford, E. C.: *Course in Experimental Psychology*, 1898.
Schneider, G. H.: "Die Orientierung der Brieftauben," *Zsch. f. Psychol.*, 1905, XL, p. 252.
Schumann, F.: "Beiträge zur Analyse der Gesichtswahrnehmungen," *Zsch. f. Psychol.*, 1900, XXIII, p. 1.
Scripture, E. W.: *Thinking, Feeling, Doing*, 1895.
The New Psychology, 1897.
Seashore, C. E.: *The Psychology of Musical Talent*, 1919.
"The present Status of Research in the Psychology of Music at the University of Iowa," *University of Iowa Studies*, 1928, II, No. 157.
Seligman, C. G.: "Anthropology and Psychology. A Study of Some Points of Contact," *J. Roy. Anthrop. Instit.*, 1924, LIV, p. 13.
"Anthropological, Perspective and Psychological Theory" *J. Roy. Anthrop. Instit.*, 1932, LXII, p. 193.
Sherrington, C. S.: *The Integrative Action of the Nervous System*, 1906.
Shinn, M. W.: "Notes on the Development of a Child," *University of California Studies*, 1893.
Slight, W. G.: *Educational Values and Methods based on the Principles of the Training Process*, 1915.
Slocombe, C. S., and Brakeman, E. E.: "Psychological Tests and Accident Proneness," *Brit. J. Psychol.*, 1930, XXI, p. 30.
Small, W. S.: "An Experimental Study of the Mental Processes of the Rat," *Am. J. Psychol.*,1899, XI, p. 133.
Smith, E. M.: "Colour Vision in Dogs," *Brit. J. Psychol.*, 1912, V, p. 119.
Smith, May: "The Nervous Temperament: Its Definition and History; its Expression in Industry and Importance from the Point of View of Health and Efficiency," *Brit. J. Med. Psychol.*, 1930, X, p. 101.
Spalding, D. A.: "Instinct," *Macmillan's Magazine*, 1873, XXVII, p. 282.
Spearman, C.: "General Intelligence objectively Measured and Determined," *Amer. J. Psychol.*, 1904, XV, p. 201.
The Nature of Intelligence and the Principles of Cognition, 1923.
"The new Psychology of 'Shape'," *Brit. J. Psychol.*, 1925, XV, p. 211.
"The Origin of Error," *J. Gen. Psychol.*, 1928, I, p. 29.
"Formalism or Associationism," *Brit. J. Psychol.*, 1929, XIX, p. 238.
Creative Mind, 1930.
"*G* and After," in *Psychologies of 1930*, p. 339.
Spearman, C., and Hart, B.: "Mental Tests of Dementia," *J. Abn. Psychol.*, 1914, IX, p. 217.
Spencer, H.: *Principles of Psychology*, 1855.
First Principles, 1862.
Principles of Biology, 1864.
Principles of Sociology, 1876.
(edited by) *Descriptive Sociology*, 1873.

Starbuck, E. D.: *Psychology of Religion*, 1899.

Stephenson, W.: "Some Contact of *p* Factor with Psychiatry," *J. Mental Science*, 1932.

Stout, G. F.: *Analytic Psychology*, 1896.

Manual of Psychology, 1899.

Stumpf, C.: *Tonpsychologie*, 1883.

Sully, J.: *Illusions*, 1881.

Teacher's Handbook of Psychology, 1886.

Human Mind, 1892.

Studies of Childhood, 1895.

Taine, H. A.: *De l'Intelligence*, 1870.

Tarde, G.: *Les Lois de l'Imitation*, 1890.

Terman, L. M., and Childs, H. G.: "A Tentative Revision and Extension of the Binet-Simon Measuring State of Intelligence," *J. Educ. Psych.*, 1912, III, p. 61.

The Measurement of Intelligence, 1916.

Genetic Studies of Genius, 1925.

Thorndike, E. L.: *Animal Intelligence*, 1898.

Measurement of Twins, 1905.

Educational Psychology, 1910.

Human Learning, 1931.

Titchener, E. B.: "The Type Theory of the Simple Reaction," *Mind*, N.S., 1895, IV, p. 506.

Outline of Psychology, 1896.

"Postulates of a Structural Psychology," *Philos. Rev.*, 1898, VII, p. 449.

"Structural and Functional Psychology," *Philos. Rev.*, 1899, VIII, p. 290.

"Experimental Psychology," *A Manual of Laboratory Practice*, 1901.

Experimental Psychology of the Thought Processes, 1909.

Trautscholt, M.: "Experimentelle Untersuchungen über die Association der Vorstellungen," *Phil. Stud.*, 1883, I, p. 213.

Trotter, W., and Davies, H. M.: "Experimental Studies in the Innervation of the Skin," *J. Physiol.*, 1909, XXXVIII, p. 134.

Tylor, E. B.: *Primitive Culture*, 1871.

Urbantschitsch, V.: *Über subjektive optische Anschauungsbilder*, 1907.

Valentine, C. W.: "The Relative Reliability of Men and Women in Intuitive Judgments of Character," *Brit. J. Psychol.*, 1929, XIX, p. 213.

Volkmann, W. F.: *Lehrbuch der Psychologie*, 1876.

Waldeyer, W.: *Über einige neuere Forschungen im Gebiete der Anatomie des Centralnervensystems*, 1891.

Waller, A. D.: *Philosophical Transactions*, 1850, p. 423.

Ward, J.: Article "Psychology," in *Encyclopaedia Britannica*, 9th ed., 1886.

Psychological Principles, 1918.

Warren, H. C.: *A History of the Association Psychology*, 1921.

Washburn, M. F.: *Animal Mind*, 1908.

Watson, J. B.: "Kinaesthetic and Organic Sensations: Their Role in the Reactions of the White Rat to the Maze," *Psychol. Rev. Mon. Suppl.*, 1907, VIII.

"Psychology as the Behaviorist views it," *Psychol. Rev.*, 1913, XX, p. 158.

Behavior. An Introduction to Comparative Psychology, 1914.

Psychology from the Standpoint of a Behaviorist, 1919.

Behaviorism, 1924.

Webb, E.: "Character and Intelligence," *Brit. J. Psychol. Mon. Suppl.*, 1915, I, No. 3.

Weber, E. H.: *De Tactu*, 1834.
  Der Tastsinn und das Gemeingefühl, 1846.
Weber, H.: "Hunger and Appetite: A Suggested Correlation between Physiological and Psychological Processes," *J. Mental Science*, 1930.
Welch, H. C., and Myers, C. S.: *Ten Years of Industrial Psychology. An Account of the first decade of the National Institute of Industrial Psychology*, 1932.
Wernicke, C.: *Der aphasische Symptomencomplex*, 1874.
Wertheimer, M.: "Experimentelle Studien über das Sehen von Bewegungen," *Zsch. f. Psychol.*, 1912, LXI, p. 161.
  Drei Abhandlungen zur Gestalttheorie, 1925.
Whipple, G. M.: *Manual of Mental and Physical Tests*, 1910.
Wohlgemuth, A.: "On Memory and the Direction of Associations," *Brit. J. Psychol.*, 1913, V, p. 447.
  "On the Feelings and their Neural Correlate, with an Examination of the Nature of Pain," *Brit. J. Psychol.*, 1917, VIII, p. 423.
Wolff, C.: *Rational Psychology*, 1734.
Woodworth, R. S.: *Psychology, A Study of Mental Life*, 1921.
  Contemporary Schools of Psychology, 1931.
Wundt, W.: *Beiträge zur Theorie der Sinneswahrnehmung*, 1858.
  Vorlesungen über die Menschen- und Thierseele, 1863.
  Grundzüge der physiologischen Psychologie, 1873.
  Grundriss der Psychologie, 1896.
  Völkerpsychologie, 1900.
  Einleitung in die Psychologie, 1911.
  Elemente der Völkerpsychologie, 1912.
Yerkes, R. M.: "Reactions of Entomostraca to Stimulation by Light," *Am. J. Physiol.*, 1900, III, p. 157.
  "Space Perception of Tortoises," *J. Comp. Neur. and Psych.*, 1904, XIV, p. 17.
  "Inhibition and Reinforcement of Reactions in the Frog," *J. Comp. Neur. and Psych.*, 1904, XIV, p. 124.
  The Dancing Mouse, 1907.
Yerkes, R. M., and Watson, J. B.: *Behavior Monographs*, 1911, I, No. 2.
Yerkes, R. M., with Bridges and Hardwick, R. S.: *A Point Scale for Measuring Mental Ability*, 1915.
  Almost Human, 1925.
Yoakum, C. S., and Yerkes, R. M.: *Mental Tests in the American Army*, 1920.
Young, Kimball: *Source Book for Social Psychology*, 1927.
  Social Psychology: an Analysis of Social Behavior, 1930.
Young, Thomas: *Course of Lectures on Natural Philosophy and the Mechanical Arts*, 1807.
Zuckermann, S.: *The Social Life of Monkeys and Apes*, 1932.
Zwaardemaker, H.: *Physiologie des Geruchs*, 1895.

BIBLIOGRAPHY

TO PART V

(As in the main bibliography, this list does not aim at indicating all the important works in the period under review but only those referred to in the text, together with a few others bearing on the topics treated.)

Adorno, T. W., et al.: *The Authoritarian Personality*, 1950.

Adrian, E. D.: *The Physical Background of Perception*, 1947.

Ahrens, R.: "Beiträge zur Entwicklung des Physiognomie- und Mimikerkennes," *Z. Exp. Angew, Psychol.*, 1954, 2, 412–54, 599, 633.

Allport, G. W.: *Personality*, 1937.

Allport, G. W., Vernon, P. E., and Lindyey, G.: *Study of Values*, 3rd ed., 1960.

American Psychological Association: "Ethical Standards of Psychologists," *American Psychologist*, 1959, 14, 279–82

Anastasi, A.: *Psychological Testing*, 2nd ed., 1961.

Andry, R. G.: *The Short Term Prisoner*, 1963.

Ansbacher, H. L., and R. R. (eds.): *The Individual Psychology of Alfred Adler*, 1956.

Bandura, A., and Walters, R. H.: *Adolescent Aggression*, 1959.

Bannister, D.: "The Nature and Measurement of Schizophrenic Thought Disorder," *Journal Mental Science*, 1962, 108, 825–42.

Barker, R. G., et al. (eds.): *Child Behaviour and Development*, 1943.

Bartlett, F. C.: *Remembering*, 1932.
 Thinking, 1958.

Bass, B. M., and Berg, I. A. (eds.): *Objective Approaches to Personality Assessment*, 1959.

Benedict, R.: *Patterns of Culture*, 1935.
 Race and Racism, 1942.
 The Chrysanthemum and the Sword, 1947.

Berkowitz, L.: *Aggression*, 1962.

Bernstein, B.: "Language and Social Class," *Brit. Journal Sociology*, 1960, 11, 271–6.

Bogardus, E. S.: "A Social Distance Scale," *Social and Soc. Res.*, 1933, 17, 265.

Boring, E. G.: *A History of Experimental Psychology*, 2nd ed., 1950.

Bowlby, J.: *Maternal Care and Mental Health*, 1952.

Brayier, M. A. B. (ed.): *Brain and Behaviour*, 1961.

Broadbent, D. E.: *Behaviour*, 1961.

Brown, J. F.: "Depression and Childhood Bereavement," *Journal Mental Science*, 1961, 107, 754–77.

Brown, J. A. C.: *Freud and the Post-Freudians*, 1961.

Buckle, D. and Leborici, S.: *Child Guidance Centres*, 1961.

Bühler, C.: *From Birth to Maturity*, 1935.

Burlingham, D., and Freud, A.: *Young Children in Wartime*, 1942.
 Infants without Families, 1943.

Burns, T.: *The Management of Innovation*, 1960.

Burt, C.: *Factors of the Mind*, 1940.
 "Intelligence and Fertility," *Occasional Papers on Eugenics*, No. 2, Eugenics Society, 1946.

"The Factorial Analysis of Emotional Traits," *Character and Personality*, 1939, 7, 238–54, 285–9.

Cantril, Hadley: *Gauging Public Opinion*, 1944.

Cattell, R. B.: *Description and Measurement of Personality*, 1946.
Motivation Structure and Measurement, 1957.

Cherry, C.: *On Human Communication*, 1957.

Clarke, A. D. B., *et al.*: "How Constant is the I.Q.?" *Lancet*, 1953, 2, 877—80.

Clarke, A. M., and A. D. B.: *Mental Deficiency*, 1958.

Cohen, A. K.: *Delinquent Boys, The Culture of the Gang*, 1955.

Cronbach, L. J.: *Educational Psychology*, 1958.

Crow, J. H., *et al.*: "Controlled Multifocal Frontal Leucotomy," *Journal Neurol. Neurosurg. and Psychiat.*, 1961, 24, 353–60.

Dearborn, W. P., and Rothney, J. W. N.: *Predicting the Child's Development*, 1941.

Dollard, J., *et al.*: *Frustration and Aggression*, 1944.

Drew, G. C.: "McDougall's Experiments on the Inheritance of Acquired Characteristics," *Nature*, 1939, 143, 188—91.

Dunbar, F.: *Emotions and Bodily Changes*, 1938.

Eccles, J. C.: *The Neurophysiological Basis of Mind*, 1953.

Eysenck, H. J.: *Dimensions of Personality*, 1947.
The Structure of Human Personality, 1953.
The Psychology of Politics, 1954.
Experiments in Behaviour Therapy, 1963.

Faris, R. E. L., and Dunham, H. W.: *Mental Disorders in Urban Areas*, 1939.

Feinstein, A.: *Foundations of Information Theory*, 1958.

Fenichel, O.: *The Psychoanalytic Theory of the Neuroses*, 1945.

Flugel, J. C.: *Man, Morals and Society*, 1945.
Studies in feeling and Desire, 1955.

Foulkes, S. H., and Anthony, E. J.: *Group Psychotherapy*, 1957.

Freud, A.: *The Ego and Mechanisms of Defence*, 1935.

Freud, S.: *New Introductory Lectures*, 1933.
Civilisation and its Discontents, 1930.

Friendlander, K.: *The Psycho-analytical Approach to Juvenile Delinquency*, 1947.

Fromme, E.: *The Fear of Freedom*, 1942.

Funkenstein, D. H., *et al.*: *Mastery of Stress*, 1957.

Furneaux, W. D., and Gibson, H. B.: "The MPI as a Predictor of Susceptibility to Hypnosis," *Internat. Journal Clinical and Exptl. Hypnosis*, 1961, 9, 167–77.

Gallup, G., and Rae, S. F.: *The Pulse of Democracy: The Public Opinion Poll and How it Works*, 1940.

Gerard, D. L., and Siegel, J.: "Family Background of Schizophrenia," *Psychiatric Quarterly*, 1950, 24, 47–73.

Gesell, A.: *Atlas of Infant Behaviour*, 1934, 2 vols.

Gesell, A., and Ilg, P. L.: *The Child from Five to Ten*, 1948.

Gibbens, T. C. N.: *Psychiatric Studies of Borstal Lads*, 1963.

Gibson, J. J.: *The Perception of the Visual World*, 1950.

Glidewell, J. C. (ed.): *Parental Attitudes and Child Behaviour*, 1961.

Glueck, S. and E.: *Physique and Delinquency*, 1956.

Grey Walter, W.: *The Living Brain*, 1953.

Gruneberg, E. M., *et al.*: *Causes of Mental Disorders*, 1961.

Healy, W., and Bronner, A.: *New Light on Delinquency and its Treatment*, 1936.

Hebb, D. O.: *The Organization of Behaviour*, 1949.

Hertz, M. R.: "Rorshach Twenty Years After," *Psychological Bulletin*, 1942, 529.

Hilgard, E. R., and Marquis, D. G. (eds.): *Conditioning and Learning*, 1961.

Hallowell, A. I.: *Culture and Experience*, 1955.

Himmelweit, H. T.: "A Comparative Study of the Level of Aspiration in Normal and Neurotic Persons," *Brit. J. Psychol.*, 1947, 37, 41.

Hollingshead, A. B., and Redlich, F. C.: *Social Class and Mental Illness*, 1958.

Honigmann, J. J.: *Culture and Personality*, 1954.

Honyig, M. P., *et al.*: "The Stability of Mental Test Performance," *Journal Exptl. Education*, 1948, 17, 309–24.

Horney, K.: *New Ways in Psychoanalysis*, 1939.

Hull, C. L.: *Hypnosis and Suggestibility*, 1933.
  A Behaviour System, 1953.
  Principles of Behaviour, 1943.

Hunt, J. McV. (ed.): *Personality and the Behaviour Disorders*, 1944, 2 vols.

Hunt, J. McV.: "Experimental Psychoanalysis," *Ency. of Psych.* (ed. P. L. Harriman), 1946.

Isaacs, S. S.: *Social Development in Young Children*, 1933.
  The Cambridge Evacuation Survey, 1941.

Jones, E.: *Sigmund Freud, Life and Works*, 1957, 3 vols.

Kardiner, A., and Linton, R.: *The Individual and his Society*, 1939.

Katz, D.: *The World of Colour* (revised edition), 1935.
  Animals and Men, 1937.

Kelly, T. L.: *The Essential Traits of Mental Life*, 1935.

Kelly, E. L., and Fiske, D. W.: *The Prediction of Performance in Clinical Psychology*, 1951.

Kinsey, A. C., *et al.*: *The Sexual Behaviour of the Human Male*, 1948.
  The Sexual Behaviour of the Human Female, 1953.

Klapman, J. W.: *Group Psychotherapy, Theory and Practice*, 1946.

Klein, J.: *The Study of Groups*, 1956.

Klein, M.: *Psycho-analysis of Children*, 1932.

Klineberg, O.: *Social Psychology*, 1940.

Klopfer, B., and Kelly, D.: *The Rorschach Technique*, 1942.

Koffka, K.: *Principles of Gestalt Psychology*, 1935.

Krynauw, R. A.: "Infantile Hemiplegia treated by removing one Cerebral Hemisphere," *J. Neurol. Neurosurg. Psychiat.*, 1950, 13, 243–67.

Lewin, K.: *A Dynamic Theory of Personality*, 1935.
  Principles of Topological Psychology, 1936.
  Field Theory in Field Science, 1951.

Lewis, Hilda: *Deprived Children*, 1954.

Lumsdaine, A. A., and Glader, R.: *Teaching Machines and Programmed Learning*, 1960.

MacCoby, E. E., *et al.* (eds.): *Readings in Social Psychology*, 3rd ed., 1958.

Mace, C. A.: "Incentives: Some Experimental Studies," *Industrial Health Board Report*, No. 72, 1935.
  The Psychology of Study, 1932.

McCormick, E. J.: *Human Engineering*, 1957.

McDougall, W.: "Dynamic Principles of Gestalt Psychology," reprinted from *Character and Personality* (date not given).

McKeller, P.: *Imagination and Thinking*, 1956.

Maier, N. R. F.: *Frustration: The Study of Behaviour without a Goal*, 1949.

Maier, N. R. F.: "Frustration Theory: Restatement and Extension," *Psychological Review*, 1956, 63, 370–88.

Masserman, J. H.: *Behaviour and Neurosis*, 1943.

Mead, M.: *Male and Female*, 1950.
  Sex and Temperament in Three Primitive Societies, 1935.
Meehl, P. E.: *Clinical versus Statistical Prediction*, 1954.
Meuninger, K.: *Love against Hate*, 1942.
Money-Kyrle, R.: *Superstition and Society*, 1939.
  Psychoanalysis and Politics, 1951.
  Man's Picture of his World, 1962.
Moreno, J. L.: *Who shall Survive?* 1934.
  "Foundations of Sociometry," *Group Psychotherapy and Sociodrama*, 2nd ed., 1953.
Morgan, C. T., and Stellar, E.: *Physiological Psychology*, 2nd ed., 1950.
Mowrer, O. H.: *Learning Theory and Personality Dynamics*, 1950.
Morris, J. M.: *Reading in the Primary School*, 1959.
Munroe, R. L.: *Schools of Psychoanalytic Thought*, 1955.
Murphy, G., Murphy, L. B., and Newcomb, T. M.: *Experimental Social Psychology* (revised ed.), 1937.
Murphy, G. (ed.): *Human Nature and Enduring Peace*, 1945.
Murray, H. A., et al.: *Explorations in Personality*, 1938.
O'Connor, N. (ed.): *Recent Soviet Psychology*, 1961.
O'Connor, N., and Tizard, J.: *The Social Problem of Mental Deficiency*, 1956.
Odier, C.: *Les Deux Sources de la Moralité, Consciente et Inconsciente*, 1943.
Ohler, M. K.: *Culture and Mental Health*, 1960.
Osgood, C. E.: *Method and Theory in Experimental Psychology*, 1953.
Osgood, C. E., et al.: *The Measurement of Meaning*, 1957.
Polya, G.: *How to Solve It*, 1957.
Pressey, S. L., Janney, J. E., and Kuhlen, R. C.: *Life: A Psychological Survey*, 1939.
Pritchard, D. G.: *Education and the Handicapped*, 1963.
Rhine, R. B.: *Extra-sensory Perception*, 1934.
Rogers, C. R., and Dymond, R. F. (eds.): *Psychotherapy and Personality Change*, 1954.
Róheim, G.: *The Riddle of the Sphinx*, 1934.
Rokeach, M.: *The Open and Closed Mind*, 1960.
Ryle, G.: *The Concept of Mind*, 1949.
Sargant, W., and Slater, E. A.: *Introduction to Physical Methods of Treatment in Psychiatry*, 1944, 3rd ed., 1954.
Scott, J. P.: *Aggression*, 1958.
Scottish Council for Research in Education: *The Intelligence of Scottish Children*, 1933.
Sears, R. R.: *Experimental Analysis of Psychoanalytic Phenomena in Personality and the Behaviour Disorders* (ed. J. McV. Hunt), 1944.
Sears, R. R., et al.: *Patterns of Child Rearing*, 1957.
Selye, H.: *The Stress of Life*, 1957.
Sheldon, W. H., Stevens, S. S., and Tucker, W. B.: *The Varieties of Human Physique*, 1940.
Sheldon, W. H.: *The Varieties of Temperament*, 1942.
Simon, B. (ed.): *Psychology in the Soviet Union*, 1957.
Skinner, B. F.: *Science and Human Behaviour*, 1953.
Smith, F. T.: *An Experiment in Modifying Attitudes towards the Negro*, 1943.
Smith, F. V.: "Social Theory and the Basic Motives," *Bull. Brit. Psychol. Soc.*, 1960, 42, 1–22.
Solomon, P., et al. (eds.): *Sensory Deprivation*, 1961.
Spearman, C.: *Psychology down the Ages*, 1937.
Spranger, E.: *Types of Men*, 1928.

374   BIBLIOGRAPHY

Stoetzel, J.: *Without the Chrysanthemum and the Sword*, 1955.
Suttie, I. D.: *The Origins of Love and Hate*, 1935.
Taylor, F. Krauple: *The Analysis of Therapeutic Groups*, 1961.
Terman, L. M., et al.: *Psychological Factors in Marital Happiness*, 1938.
Thomson, G. H.: *The Factorial Analysis of Human Ability*, 1939.
Thorne, W. H. and Zangwill, O. L. (eds.): *Current Problems in Animal Behaviour*,
    1961.
Thurstone, L. L.: *The Vectors of the Mind*, 1944.
    A Factorial Study of Perception, 1944.
    The Measurement of Values, 1959.
Tinbergen, N.: *The Study of Instinct*, 1951.
Tolman, E. C.: "There is more than one King of Learning," *Psychological
    Review*, 1949, 56, 144–55.
Tyrrell, G. N. M.: *The Personality of Man*, 1947.
    Apparitions, new ed., 1953.
Underwood, B. J., and Schulz, R. W.: *Meaningfulness and Verbal Learning*,
    1960.
Valentine, C. W.: *The Psychology of Early Childhood*, 1942.
Vernon, M. D.: *The Psychology of Perception*, 1962.
Vernon, P. E.: "The Assessment of Psychological Qualities by Verbal
    Methods," Industrial Health Research Board, *Report* No. 83, 1938.
Weiss, E., and English, O. S.: *Psychosomatic Medicine*, 1945.
Weitzenhoffer, A. M.: *Hypnotism*, 1953.
Welford, A. T.: *Ageing and Human Skill*, 1958.
West, D. J.: *The Habitual Prisoner*, 1963.
Whyte, W. H.: *The Organization Man*, 1956.
Wiener, N.: *Cybernetics*, 1948.
Wolff, H. G.: "Stressors as a Cause of Disease in Man," in Tanner, J. M. (ed.):
    Stress and Psychiatric Disorder, 1960.
Wolff, W.: *The Expression of Personality*, 1943.
Wolpe, J.: *Psychotherapy by Reciprocal Inhibition*, 1958.
Woodward, M.: *Low Intelligence and Delinquency*, 1955.
Woodworth, R. S.: *Experimental Psychology*, 1938.
World Health: "Deprivation of Maternal Care," *Public Health Papers*, 1962,
    No. 14.
World Health Organization: "Epidemiology of Mental Disorders," *Technical
    Report Series*, No. 185, 1960.
World Health Organization: *WHO and Mental Health*, 1962.
Yates, A. J.: "Hypnotic Age Repression," *Psychological Bulletin*, 1961, 58,
    429–40.
    Frustration and Conflict, 1962.
Young, K.: *Handbook of Social Psychology*, 1946.
Young, M.: *The Rise of the Meritocracy*, 1958.
Zeigarnik, B.: "Ueber das Behalten von erledigten und unerledigten Hand-
    lungen," *Psychol. Forsch.*, 1927, 9, 1.

CHRONOLOGICAL TABLE

1807 Young's wave theory of light.
1808 Gall's *Physiologie du cerveau.*
1810 Goethe's *Farbenlehre.*
1811 Bell's differentiation of sensory and motor nerves.
1812 Maine de Biran's *Essai sur les Fondements de la Psychologie.*
1816 Herbart's *Lehrbuch zur Psychologie.*
1810 Thomas Brown's *Lectures on the Philosophy of the Human Mind.* Second Committee on Mesmerism.
1823 Bessel's first published observations on the "personal equation."
1824 Flourens's experiments on brains of pigeons.
1829 Weber's muscle sense work begins. James Mill's *Analysis of the Phenomena of the Human Mind.*
1832 Beneke's *Lehrbuch der Psychologie.* Marshall Hall discovers reflex action. Birth of Wundt.
1833 J. Müller first professor of physiology (Berlin) and begins his Textbook of physiology. Discovery of difference in structure between grey and white matter of the brain. Wheatstone invents stereoscope.
1834 Weber's *De Tactu.*
1836 Fechner's *Little Book of Life after Death.*
1838 Elliotson's experiments on hypnotism.
1840 Dorothea Dix's work begins.
1843 J. S. Mill's *Logic.* Braid's *Neurypnology.*
1844 Lotze becomes professor at Göttingen.
1846 Weber's *Tastsinn und Gemeingefühl.*
1850 Fechner's psycho-physical work begins. Helmholtz measures rate of nervous impulse.
1852 Lotze's *Medicinische Psychologie.* Waller explains "secondary degeneration."
1855 Bain's *Senses and Intellect.* Spencer's *Principles* (1st edition).
1856 Helmholtz's *Physiologische Optik* (to 1866).
1858 Wundt's *Beiträge zur Theorie der Sinneswahrnehmung* (to 1862).
1859 Darwin's *Origin of Species.* Hamilton's *Lectures on Metaphysics* published posthumously. Bain's *Emotions and Will.*
1860 Fechner's *Elemente der Psychophysik.*
1861 Broca's discovery of speech area in brain.
1862 Helmholtz's *Tonempfindungen.* Charcot begins work at Salpêtrière.
1863 J. S. Mill's *Examination of Sir William Hamilton's Philosophy.* Donders elaborates reaction experiment. Wundt's *Vorlesungen über Menschen- und Thierseele.*
1866 Liébault's *Sommeil et États Analogues* (Nancy school). Schultze's duplicity theory of vision.
1867 Maudsley's *Physiology and Pathology of Mind.*
1869 Galton's *Hereditary Genius.* New and revised edition of James Mill's *Analysis.*

375

1870 Work of Fritsch and Hitzig on brain localization. Second edition of Spencer's *Principles*.
1871 Darwin's *Descent of Man*. Tylor's *Primitive Culture*.
1872 Darwin's *Expression of the Emotions*.
1873 Wundt's *Physiologische Psychologie* (1st edition). Hering's *Lehre vom Lichtsinne*. Delboeuf's *Étude Psychophysique*.
1874 Brentano's *Psychologie vom empirischen Standpunkte*. Wernicke's work on aphasia.
1875 Wundt becomes professor at Leipzig. Mach's *Bewegungsempfindungen* and the Mach-Breuer theory of the ampullar sense.
1876 Fechner's *Vorschule der Aesthetik*. Ferrier's *Functions of the Brain*. Bain founds *Mind*.
1877 Darwin's *Biographical Sketch of an Infant*.
1878 G. E. Müller's *Zur Grundlegung der Psychophysik*.
1879 Wundt founds first psychological laboratory at Leipzig. Hering's *Temperatursinn*. Ebbinghaus begins his experiments on memory. Galton's questionnaire on imagery.
1881 Preyer's *Mind of the Child*. G. E. Müller becomes professor at Göttingen.
1882 Stanley Hall establishes first American laboratory at Johns Hopkins University.
1883 Galton's *Inquiries into Human Faculty*. Stumpf's *Tonpsychologie*. Wundt founds *Philosophische Studien*. Lipps's *Grundtatsachen*.
1884 Blix discovers "spots." James's theory of emotions. Sully's *Outlines*.
1885 Ebbinghaus's *Gedächtnis*. Lange's theory of emotions. Goldscheider's discovery of "spots." Mach's *Analyse der Empfindungen*.
1886 Ward's *Encyclopaedia Britannica* article. Sully's *Teacher's Handbook of Psychology*. Dewey's *Psychology*.
1887 Stanley Hall founds *American Journal of Psychology*. Höffding's *Outline*. Ladd's *Physiological Psychology*.
1888 Cattell professor at University of Pennsylvania.
1889 Ribot made director at first French laboratory at Collège de France. Münsterberg's *Beiträge zur experimentellen Psychologie* (to 1892). First International Congress of Psychology (in Paris).
1890 James's *Principles*. Ehrenfels on "form quality." Tarde's *Lois de l'Imitation*. Ebbinghaus and König found *Zeitschrift für Psychologie*.
1891 Stanley Hall founds *Pedagogical Seminary*. Waldeyer's neurone theory.
1892 American Psychological Association founded. Münsterberg at Harvard. Titchener at Cornell. Sully's *Human Mind*. Second International Congress (London). Fifteen laboratories in U.S.A.
1893 Külpe's *Grundriss*.
1894 *Psychological Review* founded. Müller's experiments on memory begun. Shinn's *Notes on the Development of a Child*. Benussi founds first Austrian laboratory at Graz. von Kriess's duplicity theory.
1895 *Psychological Index* and *Année Psychologique* founded. Le Bon's *Crowd*. Janet begins teaching at Sorbonne. Breuer's and Freud's *Studien über Hysterie*.
1896 Stout's *Analytic Psychology*. Witmer founds first child clinic in Philadelphia. Titchener's *Outline*. Third International Congress (Munich).
1897 Lipps's *Raumaesthetik*. First beginnings of laboratories in Cambridge and London. Bryan's and Harter's first experimental study of skill. Havelock Ellis's *Studies in the Psychology of Sex* (to 1928). Thorndike begins his animal experiments.

1898 Sanford's *Course in Experimental Psychology*.
1899 Stout's *Manual*.
1900 Wundt's *Völkerpsychologie* (Vol. I). Münsterberg's action theory. Freud's *Traumdeutung*. Yerkes starts work on animal psychology. Fourth International Congress (Paris). Twenty-six laboratories in U.S.A.
1901 Külpe's Würzburg school begins work. Titchener's *Experimental Psychology* (to 1905).
1902 James's *Varieties of Religious Experience*. Franz begins his work on the brain. British Psychological Society founded.
1903 Binet's *Étude Expérimentale de l'Intelligence*. Pavlov's first report on salivary reflex. Lipps's *Aesthetik* (to 1906) Müller's *Gesichtspunkte und Tatsachen der psychophysischen Methodik*.
1904 Binet begins work on tests. Stanley Hall's *Adolescence*. First German Congress for Experimental Psychology. Spearman first states Two-Factor theory.
1905 Ebbinghaus's *Grundzüge*. Watt's and Ach's work on will and determining tendencies. McDougall's *Physiological Psychology*. Fifth International Congress (Rome).
1906 Sherrington's *Integrative Action of the Nervous System*. Heymans's and Wiersma's questionnaire. Messer's and Bühler's work on thought (to 1908).
1907 Spearman starts work in London. Bechterev describes "associated reflex." Seashore begins work on psychology of music at Iowa.
1908 McDougall's *Social Psychology*. Washburn's *Animal Mind*.
1909 Sixth International Congress (Geneva). Myer's *Textbook*.
1910 International Psycho-analytical Association founded. Whipple's *Manual of Mental and Physical Tests* (1st edition).
1911 Head's and Holmes's work on sensation and on the thalamus.
1912 Wertheimer's first work on Gestalt. Forty laboratories in U.S.A. Adler and Jung break with Freud.
1913 Watson outlines behaviouristic programme. Freud's *Totem and Taboo*. Burt appointed psychologist to London County Council.
1915 Cannon's *Bodily Changes*. Healy's *Individual Delinquent*.
1917 U.S.A. Army tests. Kroh starts work on eidetic imagery.
1918 Foundation of National Institute of Industrial Psychology in England.
1919 Watson's *Psychology from the Standpoint of a Behaviorist*.
1920 Death of Wundt. Lashley starts work on destruction of cortical centres. McDougall's *Group Psychology*.
1921 Rorschach's *Psychodiagnostik*, which later arouses great interest in "projection" tests of personality.
1924 Berger records electrical potentials of human brain—subsequently leading to electroencephalography.
1925 Terman's first report on *Genetic Studies of Genius* (with intention for follow-up studies to 1970).
1926 May's and Hartshorne's character studies begun. Eighth International Congress (Groningen).
1927 Spearman's *Abilities of Man*. Pavlov's *Conditioned Reflexes*. *Psychological Abstracts* founded.
1928 Merriman's work on twins.
1929 Lashley's *Brain Mechanisms*. Ninth International Congress (New Haven, U.S.A.).
1930 Isaac's *Intellectual Growth in Young Children*.
1932 Melanie Klein's *Psycho-Analysis of Children*. Bartlett's *Remembering*.

Social Life of Monkeys and Apes. Tenth International Congress (Copenhagen).

1933 Hull's *Hypnosis and Suggestibility* marks revival of study of hypnotism on experimental basis. Isaac's *Social Development of Young Children*. Nation-wide survey of intelligence of Scottish children. Bogardus Social Distance Scale marks attempt to study race prejudice. Nazi régime leads to large-scale departure of central European psychologists to other countries (to 1939).

1934 Gesell's *Atlas of Infant Behaviour*. Rhine's *Extra-sensory Perception* starts large-scale experimental work on physical research.

1935 A. Freud's *Ego and Mechanisms of Defence*. Benedict's and Mead's work starts psychological interest in "patterns of culture." Klineberg's *Race Differences*. Lewin's *Dynamic Theory of Personality* and later studies extend experimental Gestalt approach to orectic sphere. Koffka's *Principles of Gestalt Psychology*. Charlotte Bühler's *From Birth to Maturity*. Katz's *World of Colour* (revised edition).

1936 Healy and Bronner's *New Light on Delinquency and its Treatment*. Egas Moniz (Lisbon) reports first prefrontal leucotomy.

1937 Allport's *Personality*. Eleventh International Congress of Psychology (Paris).

1938 Woodworth's *Experimental Psychology*. Terman *et al.*: *Psychological Factors in Marital Happiness*. Murray's *Explorations in Personality* marks rapprochement between experimental and psycho-analytic approaches. First appearance of the *Mental Measurements Year Book* (ed. O. K. Buros).

1939 Wide-scale participation of psychologists in war activities, military, social, medical, industrial, etc. (to 1945). Studies of wartime evacuation of children in Great Britain. Thomson's *Factorial Analysis of Human Abilities*.

1940 Burt's *Factors of the Mind*. Widespread arousal of interest in measurement of public opinion.

1941 Dearborn's and Rothney's *Predicting the Child's Development* reports on "longitudinal" studies of children over long periods.

1942 Sheldon's *Varieties of Temperament*. Valentine's *Psychology of Early Childhood*.

1943 W. Wolf's *Expression of Personality*. Arousal of wide interest in group psycho-therapy.

1944. Thurstone's *Vectors of the Mind*.

1945 Rapaport's *Diagnostic Psychological Testing* marks wider use of experimental methods in clinical work.

1946 R. B. Cattell's *Description and Measurement of Personality*.

1947 Eysenck's *Dimensions of Personality*.

1948 Terman's fourth report on Genetic Studies of Genius (*The Gifted Child Grows Up*). Kinsey *et al.*: *Sexual Behaviour of the Human Male* makes first report on a nation-wide survey of sexual life in the U.S.A. Twelfth International Congress of Psychology (Edinburgh). International Congress on Mental Health (London) and foundation of World Federation for Mental Health.

1949 Interest in cybernetics beginning. D. O. Hebb's *The Organization of Behaviour: A Neuropsychological Theory*. Ryle's *Concept of Mind*. Foundation of the Ergonomics Research Society. N. R. F. Maier's frustration theory of animal neurosis.

1950 Widespread interest in social problems. Adorno's *The Authoritarian Personality*. M. Mead applies cultural anthropology to sex rôles in America.

Mowrer applies learning theory to human affairs. Slavson publishes an extensive bibliography of group psychotherapy. Concern about physiological effects of stress. Seyle starts annual reports entitled *Stress*. First London conference on Information Theory. First International Congress of Psychiatry.

1951 Kurt Lewin's *Field Theory in Social Science*. Interview assessments doubted, Kelly and Fiske's study.

1952 Osgood reports on his studies in nature and measurement of meaning. Osmond and Smythies introduce a chemical theory of schizophrenia. Early reports on the tranquillizing drug chlorpromazine. M. D. Vernon's *Further Study of Visual Perception*. Bowlby's infant deprivation theory published by W.H.O.

1953 Hull's *A Behaviour System*, the final statement of his theory. Eysenck's *Structure of Human Personality*. Kinsey's *Sexual Behaviour in the Human Female*. Start of the *Journal of Clinical and Experimental Hypnosis*. W. Grey Walter's *The Living Brain*.

1954 Rogers and Dymond attempt to demonstrate objectively the effects of psychotherapy. Criticized by Eysenck. Aldous Huxley arouses public interest in hallucinogenic drugs with his *The Doors of Perception*.

1955 U.S. National Institute of Mental Health hold a conference on the socio-environmental aspects of treatment in mental hospitals. Start of the *International Journal of Social Psychiatry*.

1956 Renewed interest in animal behaviour. International Union of Biologists forms an Animal Psychology Section, W. H. Thorpe's *Learning and Instinct in Animals*. Start of the journal *Sociometry*. K. W. Spence develops Hull's behaviour theory.

1957 Fifteenth International Congress of Psychology at Brussels, includes symposia on biochemical processes and behaviour, psycho-social aspects of automation, and early childhood experiences and personality development. Intensive studies of child rearing by Sears. Cherry's *On Human Communication*, a text for information theory.

1958 Havard symposium on Sensory Deprivation. Start of journals *Educational Research* and *Language and Speech*. First International Congress for Neuro-psychopharmacology at Rome. Wolpe's *Psychotherapy and Reciprocal Inhibition*, a standard text for behaviour therapy. D. E. Broadbent's *Perception and Communication* connecting learning theory and information theory. Feinstein's *Foundations of Information Theory*.

1959 The first International Directory of Psychologists lists 7,000 psychologists outside the United States. *Behavioural Science* introduces a newsletter devoted to the use and programming of computer machines. Commencement of *Psychopharmacologia*.

1960 World Mental Health Year and arousal of interest in the epidemiology of psychological disorders. W.H.O. monograph on the topic. Sixteenth International Congress of Psychology at Bonn: includes symposia on language and comprehension, personality and perception, instinct behaviour, national stereotypes and infant deprivation. Lumsdaine and Glaser's *Machines and Programmed Learning*. Appearance of *Journal of Child Psychology and Psychiatry*. First congress of the International Ergonomics Association.

1961 Fourteenth International Congress of Applied Psychology produces five volumes, the first on *Psychology and International Affairs*. First conference on psychogenetics, held at Stanford Center for Advanced Studies in the Behavioural Sciences. Widespread interest in the Russian psychophysiological approach as represented by Luria and others. Foundation of British Society of Criminology. Start of the *Journal of Psychiatric Research*.

1962 I. Oswald's *Sleeping and Waking*. Aubrey Yates reviews the state of experimental research on frustration and conflict. Interest in childhood bereavements in relation to depression and suicide. W.H.O. publishes further survey on deprivation of maternal care. Announcement of new journal *Behaviour Research and Therapy* under editorship of H. J. Eysenck. Several longitudinal surveys of child and adolescent development in progress in England.

INDEX OF SUBJECTS

N*

INDEX OF NAMES